"This book provides expert insights and thoughtful perspectives that are immensely useful for policymakers and stakeholders in understanding innovation and digital opportunities for Africa–Europe cooperation. This is a must for your reading list".

Rob Floyd, *Director for Innovation and Digital Policy at the African Center for Economic Transformation (ACET), Ghana*

"It is encouraging to see that the authors of this book have made an important contribution to guide the discourse on digital development and North–South collaboration towards a much-needed holistic awareness of digital challenges and opportunities, while addressing many of the SDGs".

Dimo Calovski, *Economic Affairs Officer at the UNCTAD, Switzerland*

AFRICA–EUROPE COOPERATION AND DIGITAL TRANSFORMATION

Africa–Europe Cooperation and Digital Transformation explores the opportunities and challenges for cooperation between Africa and Europe in the digital sphere.

Digitalisation and digital technologies are not only essential for building competitive and dynamic economies; they transform societies, pose immense challenges for policymakers, and increasingly play a pivotal role in global power relations. Digital transformations have had catalytic effects on African and European governance, economies, and societies, and will continue to do so. The COVID-19 pandemic has already accelerated the penetration of digital tools all over the globe and is likely to be perceived as a critical juncture in how and to what purpose the world accepts and uses new and emerging technologies. This book offers a holistic analysis of how Africa and Europe can manage and harness digital transformation as partners in a globalised world. The authors shed light on issues ranging from economic growth, youth employment, and gender, to regulatory frameworks, business environments, entrepreneurship, and interest-driven power politics. They add much-needed perspectives to the debates that shape the two continents' digital transformation and innovation environments.

This book will interest practitioners working in the areas of innovation, digital technologies, and digital entrepreneurship, as well as students and scholars of international relations. It will also be relevant for policymakers, regulators, decision-makers, and leaders in Africa and Europe.

Chux Daniels is Research Fellow at the Science Policy Research Unit (SPRU) and Director of the Transformative Innovation Policy Consortium (TIPC) Africa Hub, both at the University of Sussex Business School, UK. He is also a Senior Fellow at the African Centre for Economic Transformation (ACET), Ghana, and visiting faculty at the Universities of Pretoria and Johannesburg, South Africa.

Benedikt Erforth is Senior Researcher in the Programme Transnational- and International Cooperation at the German Institute of Development and Sustainability (IDOS), where he co-leads the "Megatrends Afrika" project.

Chloe Teevan is Head of Digital Economy and Governance at the European Centre for Development Policy Management (ECDPM), the Netherlands. She is also a non-resident scholar with the North Africa and Sahel programme at the Middle East Institute in Washington DC, USA.

Innovations in International Affairs
Series Editor: Raffaele Marchetti, *LUISS Guido Carli, Italy*

Innovations in International Affairs aims to provide cutting-edge analyses of controversial trends in international affairs with the intent to innovate our understanding of global politics. Hosting mainstream as well as alternative stances, the series promotes both the re-assessment of traditional topics and the exploration of new aspects.

The series invites both engaged scholars and reflective practitioners, and is committed to bringing non-western voices into current debates.

Innovations in International Affairs is keen to consider new book proposals in the following key areas:

- **Innovative topics**: related to aspects that have remained marginal in scholarly and public debates
- **International crises**: related to the most urgent contemporary phenomena and how to interpret and tackle them
- **World perspectives**: related mostly to non-western points of view

For more information about this series, please visit: https://www.routledge.com/Innovations-in-International-Affairs/book-series/IIA

AFRICA–EUROPE COOPERATION AND DIGITAL TRANSFORMATION

Edited by Chux Daniels, Benedikt Erforth and Chloe Teevan

Routledge
Taylor & Francis Group
LONDON AND NEW YORK

Designed cover image: © Getty Images

First published 2023
by Routledge
4 Park Square, Milton Park, Abingdon, Oxon OX14 4RN

and by Routledge
605 Third Avenue, New York, NY 10158

Routledge is an imprint of the Taylor & Francis Group, an informa business

Funding for making this publication Open Access was provided by the
German Institute of Development and Sustainability (IDOS) and the
European Centre for Development Policy Management.

British Library Cataloguing-in-Publication Data
A catalogue record for this book is available from the British Library

Library of Congress Cataloging-in-Publication Data
Names: Daniels, Chux, editor, author. | Erforth, Benedikt, editor, author. |
Teevan, Chloe, editor, author.
Title: Africa-Europe cooperation and digital transformation / edited by
Chux Daniels, Benedikt Erforth and Chloe Teevan.
Other titles: Innovations in international affairs.
Description: New York : Routledge, 2022. |
Series: Innovations in international affairs | Includes bibliographical
references and index.
Identifiers: LCCN 2022033831 (print) | LCCN 2022033832 (ebook) |
ISBN 9781032228129 (hardback) | ISBN 9781032228235 (paperback) |
ISBN 9781003274322 (ebook)
Subjects: LCSH: Digital communications–Political aspects–Africa. |
Digital communications–Social aspects–Africa. | Information
technology–Political aspects–Africa. | Information technology–Social
aspects–Africa. | Technological innovations–Political aspects–Africa.|
Technological innovations–Social aspects–Africa. |
Africa–Relations–Europe. | Europe–Relations–Africa.
Classification: LCC HM851 .A33 2022 (print) | LCC HM851 (ebook) |
DDC 303.483096–dc23/eng/20220714
LC record available at https://lccn.loc.gov/2022033831
LC ebook record available at https://lccn.loc.gov/2022033832

ISBN: 978-1-032-22812-9 (hbk)
ISBN: 978-1-032-22823-5 (pbk)
ISBN: 978-1-003-27432-2 (ebk)

DOI: 10.4324/9781003274322

Typeset in Bembo
by Deanta Global Publishing Services, Chennai, India

CONTENTS

ACKNOWLEDGEMENTS

This book benefitted from the support of a great number of people and institutions. As editors, we wish to express our gratitude to all contributors. Over the course of two years, they remained committed to this exciting project, and with their professionalism and tireless efforts in developing the individual chapters, helped transform an initial idea into a substantive academic project with no lesser ambition than to improve our understanding of cooperation patterns between Europe and Africa in the digital realm.

We are deeply grateful for the institutional and financial support provided by the German Institute of Development and Sustainability (IDOS) and the European Centre for Development Policy Management (ECDPM). Thanks to their support, we are able to present our findings as an open access collection.

We are immensely grateful to Raffaele Marchetti at LUISS Guido Carli University, for considering our book for his Routledge series on "Innovation in International Affairs". We are equally grateful to Hannah Rich and Emily Ross at Routledge for their excellent editorial support throughout.

At the African Centre for Economic Transformation (ACET), we wish to thank Rob Floyd for his valuable advice along the way.

The European Think Tanks Group (ETTG) in cooperation with ACET deserves an additional mention for facilitating together with IDOS and ECDPM the production of an early policy brief on the topic "Strengthening the Digital Partnership between Africa and Europe". The briefing paper, which was published with the financial support from the Deutsche Gesellschaft für Internationale Zusammenarbeit (GIZ) GmbH on behalf of the German Federal Ministry for Economic Cooperation and Development (BMZ), informed initial ideas behind this book project.

Our gratitude further extends to all colleagues who reviewed and commented on the different chapters as well as the anonymous reviewers whose valuable comments allowed us to further sharpen the book's core messages and arguments. We wish to thank Lennart Diepmans, Anna Hörter, Laureen Migacz, and Alma Wisskirchen at IDOS for their outstanding research assistance at various stages of the project.

NOTES ON CONTRIBUTORS

Joe Abah is Nigeria Country Director for DAI, an international development company that works on the frontlines of global development in more than 100 countries. He is a governance and institutions expert with a PhD in Governance and Public Policy Analysis.

Rachel Adams is Principal Researcher at Research ICT Africa, South Africa, where she leads the AI4D Africa Just AI Centre, the African Observatory on Responsible AI(AI4D), and the Global Index on Responsible AI. She has published widely in areas such as AI and society, gender and AI, transparency, open data, and data protection.

Andrew Agyei-Holmes is Research Fellow at the Institute of Statistical, Social and Economic Research at the University of Ghana. His research interests are in property rights, productivity, household welfare, and gender outcomes in developing country contexts.

Eike Albrecht is Head of the Department of Public Law, and Co-director of the Centre for Law and Administration, at Brandenburg University of Technology Cottbus-Senftenberg, Germany, specialising in environmental and planning law. His core research interest is in environmental law, governance, and decision-making.

Felix Ankomah Asante is Professor of Development Economics and Pro Vice-Chancellor for Research, Innovation and Development (ORID) at the University of Ghana. His research interests include development economics relating to poverty and household food security, decentralisation, provision of public goods and services, and health-related dynamics.

Tamanna Ashraf is Adjunct Instructor in the Department of Politics and International Relations at Florida International University, USA. Her research interests include South Asian politics, water security, hydro-politics, and security studies. Her current research project scrutinises terrorist attacks on South Asian dams to explore the connections between water nationalism, development, and security.

Karishma Banga is an economist with a focus on international trade, digitalisation, and development. She works as Research Fellow in the Digital and Technology Cluster at the Institute of Development Studies, UK. She holds a PhD in global value chains and upgrading in the Indian economy from the Global Development Institute at the University of Manchester, UK.

Krista Baptista is Head of DAI's Center for Digital Acceleration, where she is responsible for leading the team, advancing the Center's strategy, and delivering high-quality digital work. She holds frequent speaking engagements on the future of technology and digital jobs, digital principles, and women and digital.

Sajitha Bashir is former adviser to the Global Director of the Education Practice at the World Bank and former education manager for over 20 countries in Africa. She led the work on digital skills as part of regional Digital Economy initiatives of the World Bank in different regions. She holds a PhD in economics from the London School of Economics, UK.

Sumbal Bashir is a gender and policy expert, and has worked extensively on social inclusion, innovation, and data and evidence. She is a recipient of the Fulbright scholarship (U.S. Department of State) and Policy Leader Fellowship (School of Transnational Governance at the European University Institute, Italy). She is also a member of the Internet Society, and an active advocate for meaningful connectivity for all.

Francine Beleyi is an award-winning digital and change strategist specialised in personal and business branding. She is the founder of Nucleus of Change, a boutique consultancy that specialises in helping individuals and organisations to thrive in the digital age and become the leading voice in their industry, an international speaker, and an author.

Dumisani Chirambo obtained his PhD from Brandenburg University of Technology Cottbus-Senftenberg, Germany. His current interests and research areas include South–South climate finance and promoting climate change entrepreneurship.

Chux Daniels is Research Fellow at the Science Policy Research Unit (SPRU) and Director of the Transformative Innovation Policy Consortium (TIPC) Africa Hub, both at the University of Sussex Business School, UK. He is also Senior Fellow at the African Centre for Economic Transformation (ACET), Ghana, and visiting faculty at the Universities of Pretoria and Johannesburg, South Africa.

Sarah Durr graduated from Rhodes University, South Africa, in 2019. Her thesis focused on the development and introduction of a mobile application, "Food For Us", into small-scale farming communities within the Eastern Cape, South Africa. She continued her research work within the online learning space for the Environmental Learning and Research Centre at Rhodes University.

Karim El Aynaoui is Executive President of the Policy Center for the New South, Morocco, and the Executive Vice-President, and the Dean of the Faculty of Governance, Economics and Social Sciences, of the Mohammed VI Polytechnic University, Morocco. He has wide research experience in labour market dynamics and trade policies in Morocco and North Africa.

Benedikt Erforth is Senior Researcher in the Programme Transnational- and International Cooperation at the German Institute of Development and Sustainability (IDOS), where he co-leads the "Megatrends Afrika" project. His current research focuses on Europe-Africa relations, digitalisation, and EU development finance.

Tunde Fafunwa is an advisor to the UNECA and Managing Partner at Kitskoo Inc. He leads teams that create continental policies, digital initiatives, and services across Digital ID, ePayments, Digital Transformation, and eCommerce. With an MBA from MIT, USA, he has built and managed businesses with annual revenues between USD 5 million and USD 5 billion.

Kerstin Fritzsche is a political scientist with a special research interest in digital and sustainable transformations in the Global South and North. Until October 2021, she headed the Digitalisation Research Department at the Institute for Futures Studies and Technology Assessment (IZT) in Berlin, Germany. She now works in the public sector on digital policy issues.

Michael Gastrow is Director of the Science in Society unit at the Human Sciences Research Council, and Professor of Practice at the DST/NRF/Newton Fund Trilateral Research Chair in Transformative Innovation, the 4th Industrial Revolution and Sustainable Development at the University of Johannesburg, South Africa. His research focuses on innovation systems, the public understanding of science, and science communication.

Larabi Jaïdi is Senior Fellow at the Policy Center for the New South, Morocco, and Professor at Mohammed VI Polytechnic University, Morocco. He is also a member of the board of Bank al-Maghrib, Morocco's Central Bank. His areas of focus are international economy, social development, international relations, and Mediterranean studies.

Bulelani Jili is Meta Research PhD Fellow at Harvard University, USA. He is also Visiting Fellow at Yale Law School, USA; Cybersecurity Fellow at the Harvard Kennedy School, USA; Fellow at the Atlantic Council, USA; Scholar-in-residence at the Electronic Privacy Information Center, USA; Futures Fellow at Mercator Institute for China Studies, Germany; and Research Associate at the University of Oxford, UK.

Heila Lotz-Sisitka is Distinguished Professor at Rhodes University, South Africa, and holds a Tier 1 South African National Research Foundation Chair in Transformative Social Learning and Green Skills Learning Pathways. Her research interests include critical research methodologies, transformative environmental learning, agency, and education system transformation.

Connor MacKenzie is Associate Digital Specialist on the Digital Advisory team within DAI's Center for Digital Acceleration. He provides research and expertise on various topics at the intersection of international development and digital technology, including digital policy-making, the digital economy, and e-governance.

Charles Martin-Shields is Senior Researcher at the German Institute of Development and Sustainability (IDOS). His research focuses on technology and innovation in development aid and humanitarian response. Outside academia, he has served as a consultant for UNHCR, the U.S. Institute of Peace, and the World Bank.

Dirk Marx MBL is Transdisciplinary Researcher for Sustainable Development in the Department of Public Law, in particular environmental and planning law, at Brandenburg University of Technology Cottbus-Senftenberg, Germany.

Luke Metelerkamp works on TMG's Urban Food Futures Programme based in Berlin, Germany. He is a transdisciplinary researcher with a background in food systems, education, and youth. He obtained his PhD from Stellenbosch University, South Africa, and has experience developing inclusive collaborations in civil society organisations, learning networks, and research institutions.

Fola Odufuwa is a trusted advisor and recognised ICT expert with over 25 years of experience in ICT, telecoms, and business consulting, serving numerous private and public organisations on four continents. Based in Nigeria, his expertise is multidisciplinary, and he brings a broad perspective and deep analytical thinking to each assignment.

Eleonore Pauwels is an international expert in the security and governance implications generated by the convergence of artificial intelligence with dual-use technologies, including cybersecurity, genomics, and neurotechnology. She provides expertise to public and private sector actors, the World Bank, the United Nations, and the Global Center on Cooperative Security in New York, USA.

Bernardin Senadza is Associate Professor of Economics at the University of Ghana. His research interests include the impact of livelihood strategies on the well-being of rural households, spatial and gender inequality in education and health, and sustainable consumption of the middle classes in developing countries.

Niyanta Shetye is an academic employee with the chair of Public Law, Environmental and Planning Law at the Brandenburg Technical University of Cottbus-Senftenberg, Germany. His current interest is in the applications of ICTs in environmental governance, public participation, education, and awareness.

Zuzana Sladkova is a development policy expert with a passion for digital transformation. She has worked in policy and advocacy at national and EU levels for more than ten years. She holds a PhD from the University of Economics in Bratislava, Slovakia, and is a recipient of the Policy Leader Fellowship from the European University Institute, Italy.

Daniel Spoiala is currently advising GIZ, Germany, on data economy aspects. Previously, he worked for eight years in the European Commission leading the design of the EU Digital for Development policy as well as tackling Internet Governance issues. He started his career as the Romanian representative to the International Telecommunication Union (UN) and was engaged in high-level negotiations regarding the future of the Internet.

Chloe Teevan is Head of Digital Economy and Governance at the European Centre for Development Policy Management (ECDPM), the Netherlands. She is also a non-resident scholar with the North Africa and Sahel programme at the Middle East Institute in Washington DC, USA. Her research interests focus on the geopolitics of EU foreign and development policy, digital regional integration in Africa, and EU D4D policy.

Klaus Tilmes is Senior Policy Advisor and former World Bank Director for Trade and Competitiveness. He provides policy advice to international organisations, governments, and private sector companies on economic risks, technology strategies, data policies, and human development. His affiliations include the African Center for Economic Transformation, Ghana, and the National Academies of Science, Engineering, and Medicine, USA.

Verena van Zyl-Bulitta works in the areas of Systems Engineering, Quantitative Finance, and socio-technical and social-ecological applications of Common Pool Resource approaches across the Global North–South divide.

Anand Varghese is Associate Director of Digital Advisory within DAI's Center for Digital Acceleration. He works with international donors to develop digital strategies, design and implement digital-focused activities, and train others on digital tools. He is also an Adjunct Faculty Member at the Johns Hopkins School for Advanced International Studies, USA.

Akram Zaoui is the manager of the Public Policy Lab at the Policy Center for the New South, Morocco. His recent areas of research have been territorial and industrial policies in Morocco. His interests also include political developments in the Maghreb and the geopolitics of the MENA Region.

FOREWORD

This book is extraordinarily timely given the multiplicity of challenges and opportunities facing the African continent as it deepens its transition to a digital society and economy. As Executive Secretary of the United Nations Economic Commission for Africa (UNECA) I am in constant dialogue with African policymakers on the importance of leveraging innovation and digital technologies to create prosperity, accelerate job growth, ensure access to finance, and position their countries to benefit from the Fourth Industrial Revolution. The book's authors have brought together an important array of voices and perspectives on new frontiers for digital transformation – and particularly for the Africa–Europe collaboration.

The book usefully organises around politics, policies, and people. These are, of course, building blocks for our economies and society. But politics, policies, and people are complex. Navigating politics in the global political economy can be a difficult terrain to navigate, especially in the current context of global polarisation. Africa must stake its unique claim. Policies and regulatory frameworks are challenging to implement, while citizens need to see the benefits of digitalisation before they will embrace new technologies. This trust building element of the social contract is critical.

Ultimately, politics and policies should serve the people to help improve livelihoods, ensure sustainable development, and create equitable opportunities, but as the book points out in numerous chapters, that is easier said than done. I appreciate that Chux Daniels from the University of Sussex, Benedikt Erforth from the German Institute of Development and Sustainability (IDOS) and Chloe Teevan from the European Centre for Development Policy Management (ECDPM) have drawn upon authors from Africa, Asia, North America, and Europe to inform an agenda that is critical to Africa's future.

The UNECA, along with the African Union, the African Development Bank, the Regional Economic Communities (RECs), and other development partners, is seeking to address many of the issues raised in the book. For example, Chapter 4 looks at artificial intelligence (AI) and how Europe is well placed to support a growing bio-economy potential in Africa. Last year the UNECA supported the establishment of the continent's first AI centre in Congo. AI will contribute more than USD 15 trillion to the global economy by 2030 and is expected to double the incomes of smallholder farmers; hence, its importance cannot be underestimated.

Much of the book is focused on policies and regulatory issues. While these topics may not always be the most exciting, they are hugely important to the future of a digital single market (DSM) for Africa, as well as creating robust frameworks that will incentivise investment on the continent. Authors in the book, particularly from Africa, address the trade-offs that policymakers face, as well as opportunities that can be created from well-informed policy decisions. For example, Chapter 5 addresses potential benefits to micro, small, and medium-sized enterprises (MSMEs) from the African Continental Free Trade Area (AfCFTA) agreement and particularly the importance for companies of this size to digitise their businesses, and for governments to support them. Chapter 6 looks at the linkages between digital policy and industrialisation, particularly deepening value chains and increasing competitiveness.

Likewise, Chapter 7 addresses how countries are seeking to expand manufacturing sectors and deepen regional value chains. Leveraging the positive impact of digitalisation is ever more important in this era of strained global value chains. Conversations of on-shoring and friend-shoring, which mask the emergence of a new era of uncompetitive behaviour, mean Africa must contend with and use technology to compete and dominate. Chapter 12 addresses the many risks that can emerge from digitalisation, including threats to privacy, data protection, and cybercrimes. The chapter looks at how policymakers engage with key stakeholders on technology policy to ensure better informed laws and regulations.

The final chapters of the book are highly recommended for anyone interested in the future of international development. They touch upon feminist digital development, the importance of digital skills development, green digital transitions, and entrepreneurship. Interestingly the book notes that in many cases these are areas where there is, in principle, strong alignment between Europe and Africa, but yet there is not always consensus on approaches and how collaboration can lead to the greatest outcomes. A common future on this must build on shared interests and objectives.

It is clear that innovation and digital policy, if well designed and implemented, can support Africa's economic transformation. Cooperation between Africa and Europe can help accelerate that transformation. There are many examples of engagement such as the AU–EU Digital for Development (D4D) Hub, the Africa–EU summits, and private sector investment by European companies, but more must be done.

The book points to the need for deeper AU–EU digital cooperation, including a stronger collective voice from African leaders. At the same time it highlights prospects for mutual benefits, ranging from shorter-term improvements in learning or commerce, to long-term structural change in economies. For Africa to benefit fully, this collaboration must also include innovations happening in other geographies that are leading on aspects of the digital agenda.

And the book highlights frontiers where cooperation can lead to greater competitiveness and economic growth for both continents. These will, in many cases, also lead to greater development outcomes for Africa and address socio-economic hurdles as well as the demographic transition.

I commend the authors for expanding our understanding of key challenges and opportunities for digital cooperation between Africa and Europe, but I believe the book actually provides an insight into the global digital agenda more broadly. Africa must ensure its digital cooperation spans the globe, learning from best practices and avoiding pitfalls. For those interested in the future of development, which will be based on a digital transformation, I highly recommend they read this book. Upon completion, they will have a greater appreciation for the possible.

Vera Songwe
Executive Secretary, United Nations Economic Commission for Africa (UNECA),
Addis Ababa, Ethiopia

FOREWORD

This book will be an important resource. It provides a timely and focused contribution around the nexus of digitalisation and international partnerships, specifically capturing the challenges and opportunities of digital cooperation between Africa and Europe.

Digitalisation is a huge societal transformation shaping our future, in parallel with the green transition stemming from the challenge of climate change and biodiversity loss. The digital space has proven to be one of strategic competition. It has brought the need for more multilateral governance and ambitious global standards into sharper focus. The COVID-19 pandemic has also played a part in accelerating the global digital transition by several years. It exposed the digital divide, as societies with stronger digital infrastructure, skills, and services coped consistently better with challenges brought on by the pandemic.

We can capitalise on the digital transition and promote accessible, inclusive, and secure digital connectivity that puts people first, in coherence with our declaration of digital principles adopted by the European Commission on May 2022. In Africa, digital technologies have enormous potential for economic growth, improved governance and service delivery, as well as human development. Digitalisation has already been driving the continent's post-pandemic recovery, and digital trade is growing rapidly. However, challenges, such as internet affordability and access, cybersecurity, and lack of e-IDs or access to e-Governance services, remain.

Under the Global Gateway strategy, the EU is actively seeking to build strong international digital partnerships and promote a human-centred digital agenda around the world. The strategy, launched in December 2021, is the EU's bid to narrow the global infrastructure investment gap, boost post-pandemic recovery, and make the green and digital transitions a reality.

With Global Gateway, we aim to mobilise investments worth up to €300 billion in physical infrastructure in the areas of digital, climate, energy, and transport but also promote enabling environments, including regulatory frameworks and investments in areas such as education, research, and health. Global Gateway is a positive, values-driven offer to our partners worldwide, including in Africa. Its key objective is to replace unsustainable dependencies with sustainable links between continents, regions, and people.

Our vision for the digital economy and society is human-centric and upholds fundamental values. We champion an open, secure, and global internet and foster global cooperation and multi-stakeholder alliances on research and innovation. We envision a cyberspace where citizens can navigate with trust and security, where young entrepreneurs can access pools of open data for driving innovation, and where governments can ensure sovereignty over their country's data.

In fair and inclusive digital economy, digital technologies can be great enablers of sustainable development in Africa. Digitalisation can lower greenhouse gas emissions by boosting efficiency across sectors, virtualising services, and moving to more circular economies. Digital and earth observation services can be leveraged for climate action and disaster risk management.

Digital businesses can create new business models and employment opportunities driven by the power of data, while the digital transformation of traditional businesses promises to increase productivity across African economies.

The digital transformation promises to enhance human development in Africa, for example, by offering improved education opportunities, also for people living in remote and rural areas. It opens up a plethora of opportunities and can empower women and girls – economically, socially, politically, and culturally. However, to do so, we will have to close the digital gender gap, which is wider in Africa than anywhere else in the world. We are working to that end by mainstreaming digital transformation in key areas of regional and national programming for sub-Saharan Africa, including gender, the green transition, transport, education, and employment.

At the EU–AU Summit in February 2022, leaders from both continents confirmed great ambitions to boost digital connectivity on the African continent, and between different continents, to help create open digital societies and economies. We affirmed our support to our African partners in advancing their vision of an African digital single market. The AU–EU Digital for Development (D4D) Hub supports African institutions to lay grounds for an inclusive and sustainable digital transformation that benefits everyone.

Under our Global Gateway Africa-Europe Investment Package, we are rolling out substantial digital infrastructure projects, with the aim of speeding up universal access to reliable, safe, and secure internet networks for all in Africa by 2030. We will invest in an international submarine fibre cable connecting the EU with Africa along the Atlantic Ocean coast, in constructing networks of fibre-optic cables across sub-Saharan Africa, and in space technologies both for Secure Satellite Communications and for Earth Observation. We will invest in African data infrastructure and increase regulatory convergence to foster a more enabling and inclusive data economy. The EU has also set up an African European Digital Innovation Bridge to promote cooperation on digital innovation, particularly in small and medium-sized enterprises and start-ups. Needless to say, this support will go hand-in-hand with support to the development of digital skills and literacy.

Global Gateway will cement a strong digital partnership between Africa and Europe and help build a digitally connected world that upholds European values and leaves no one behind. Together, Africa and Europe can walk the path of digital transformation that puts people first, grows economies, and improves governance and services.

Jutta Urpilainen
Commissioner for International Partnerships, European Commission,
Brussels, Belgium

1

DIGITALISATION FOR TRANSFORMATION

New Frontiers for Africa–Europe Cooperation

Chux Daniels, Benedikt Erforth, and Chloe Teevan

1.1 Digitalisation, Transformation, and Cooperation

Digital technologies are transforming the lives of *people* in societies across the world, shaping and reshaping *policies* at continental, regional, and national levels, and impacting *politics* in ways that were not imagined in the past. Digital technologies, viewed as a public good, are key to fostering economic and human development globally. As a cross-cutting theme, digitalisation, if appropriately directed by public policies, can help achieve the United Nations Agenda 2030 and the Sustainable Development Goals (SDGs) (UN, 2015). By "transformation" we mean three-dimensional change in relation to (a) economic, (b) social, and (c) environmental challenges, as articulated in the SDGs. Such transformations are not linear, nor are their outcomes guaranteed. In Africa, for example, we know that at the firm level the adoption of technology does not necessarily lead to increased productivity (economic gains), and therefore may not be transformational, in that sense (ACET, 2021). Despite fundamental technological changes, economies have not become more diverse, nor has total factor productivity increased. In this context, therefore, achieving economic gains without exacerbating inequality, exclusion, and gender gaps (social challenges) or increasing biodiversity loss and climate change (environmental challenges) requires additional policy guidance – that is, frameworks – that help establish standards whilst reflecting local contexts and needs.

However, the perspectives and narratives on digital technologies and the motives behind the quest for high rates of digitalisation differ across the globe and between stakeholders. In some cases, state actors adopt digital technologies as surveillance tools to exercise control over people, maintain power structures, or quash opposition (see, for example, Jili, this volume). At the same time, a small number of private sector actors have gained outsized influence through

DOI: 10.4324/9781003274322-1

their control of vast amounts of personal data, which is used to predict and influence individual and societal behaviour with potentially grave implications for personal choice and political outcomes (The Great Hack, 2019; Zuboff, 2019). These trends have serious implications for citizens' digital rights and on efforts to achieve inclusive development. If not accompanied by corrective policy measures, digital technologies can increase economic exploitation and inequalities, or deepen digital divides globally and within societies.

The transformations across societies, and the envisaged potential of such transformations, coupled with the introduction of new policies and regulations on digital technologies, have led to new geopolitical tensions and rivalries on the one hand, and partnerships and cooperation on the other hand. For many African actors, China's ever-growing presence in Africa's digital infrastructure is a welcome diversification of their international partnerships, but for the European Union (EU) this growing presence is considered a geopolitical threat. The EU fears China's growing influence on Africa's development and governance models. Recent efforts, notably the announcement of the EU's Global Gateway,[1] are testimony to the EU's concerns and efforts to engage with this new form of power politics (see Fritzsche and Spoiala, and Erforth and Shields, this volume). However, these policies and their potential to succeed need to be juxtaposed with the political realism of African leaders, who contrast proposals from the EU with Chinese technologies and interventions that are often considered to be more "lucrative", cheaper, and, in some cases, better quality. The digital realm is no different from other policy realms insofar as we are in the middle of an era that can be best described with reference to the rise of a multipolar disorder, which in turn challenges long-established principles of cooperation and the functioning of the international system. These tendencies bring the status quo and emerging powers directly into opposition with one another. For Africa, global shifts have brought more options in terms of partners and more negotiating space and leverage vis-à-vis external actors, thereby potentially enhancing African agency, meaning the ability of African actors "to negotiate and bargain with external actors in a manner that benefits Africans themselves" (Chipaike and Knowledge, 2018). Yet, global shifts have also caused competition between democratic and autocratic systems that fuel distrust and open conflict.

The geopolitical tensions and rivalries, in turn, have implications on the ways that governance, structural arrangements, narratives, ideas, and interests held by actors (as agents) and institutions influence and shape digital technologies at regional and national levels (Chataway et al., 2019; Daniels et al., 2020a, 2021a). Russia's invasion of Ukraine is an example of the fragility of the current global order. Partnerships, once taken for granted, are put into question and are ended altogether. The transatlantic alliance is experiencing new momentum that is likely to also affect future choices on digital partnerships, and by extension the global digital ecosystem. It is too early to tell what the outcome of these rapidly unfolding events will be.

To do justice to the different narratives, ideas, and interests held by actors, we discuss digital transformation as a so-called megatrend shaping large-scale developments in the world and in Africa in particular (Erforth and Gutheil, 2022) to which actors react and adapt. Futurologist John Naisbitt (1982), observing the change from an industrial to a knowledge society, characterised megatrends as "large social, economic, political, and technological changes [that are] slow to form, and once in place, influence us for some time". Subsequently, further attributes were added to the definition leading to a list of characteristics that include longevity, ubiquity, global relevance, complexity, and irreversibility. While longevity is relative to the reference frame one assumes, it is fair to assume that digitalisation's ubiquity and irreversibility will make it a lasting social structure. Structures, according to Anthony Giddens (1984), are not only the basis for but also the result of human practices. Building on the mutually constituting nature of structure and agency, as identified by Giddens, we understand digitalisation as a social force that reproduces our world order whilst simultaneously being shaped by human action (Erforth and Gutheil, 2022).

Put differently, digitalisation constitutes an enabling frame (in both the positive and the negative sense) that reproduces social action and is equally influenced by it. To fathom the complexity of this interaction, we advance a multi-level analytical approach, using people, policies, and politics as different layers and guiding threads to orient the reader on this agency-structure spectrum. The book covers discussions that cut across various sectors bringing human (individual and societal) development into conversation with macro-level policy discussion at the national, regional, continental, and bi-continental levels. The ongoing geopolitical rivalries around digital technologies coupled with debates on digital governance, privacy and protections, and citizens' rights continue to influence international cooperation and, therefore, need to be brought into conversation with the literature on digital for development.

The conversation we propose here extends beyond academia and involves practitioners in the discussion – both as contributors and as readers we seek to reach. Contributions are thus arranged in a way that they allow for reflexivity and simultaneously offer concrete recommendations. The insights in the book are expected to help build an academic community around the nexus of digitalisation and international cooperation. By unpacking potential areas for digital cooperation between Africa and Europe, and covering academic and practitioners' views, the book improves the prospects of a multidisciplinary conversation between communities that hitherto rarely speak to one another.

1.2 Two Regions, One Megatrend, Different Priorities

Digital transformation is causing major changes in both Africa and Europe, leading to new challenges. The two continents certainly share some of the challenges and opportunities, but their distinct levels of development mean that they each have different priorities. For example, in the EU and the Global North, "corrective policies" may be what is needed to address digital rights or strengthen data and consumer protection. In Africa, however, it might not be primarily correction that matters most, but rather establishing minimum standards, policies, and regulatory frameworks that reflect local conditions and that are implementable. Therefore, understanding and responding to the distinct levels of developments, contexts, and local conditions is vital to realising the aspirations of digital transformation in the AU–EU digital cooperation.

In Africa, digitalisation is transforming productive sectors, creating solutions to social problems, and driving political mobilisation, for example, by influencing political participation in novel ways. In 2019, 25% of the African population had internet access. This figure is expected to rise (ITU, 2020; World Bank, 2019). Even at today's much lower penetration rate, mobile technologies alone "have already generated 1.7 million jobs and contribute $144 billion to the continent's economy, or roughly 8.5% of GDP" (Allen, 2021; GSMA, 2021). African countries have also become host to many innovation hubs, demonstrating the continent's entrepreneurial potential, and funding to start-ups is on the rise (Azzioui and Sandri, 2021; Daniels et al., 2021b; Dosso et al., 2021; Martins et al., 2021). In a comprehensive mapping exercise, Afrilabs and Briter Bridges identified 643 tech hubs in Africa in 2019. The underlying trend becomes visible when comparing this number to the 442 tech hubs identified in 2018 and 324 in 2016 (Giuliani et al., 2019; see also AfricArena, 2021). Technologies such as mobile money have shown the potential for Africa to "leapfrog" (that is, skip technological steps in development processes), while COVID-19 demonstrated the essential role that electronic payments, e-commerce, and e-services (such as online banking and telemedicine) could play.

Despite the progress and the expectations regarding the positive impacts of digital technologies on Africa's economic and social development, major investments in data, infrastructure, capabilities, and skills are needed for Africa to harness the benefits offered by the Fourth Industrial Revolution (4IR) – characterised by its scale, speed, and complexity and the fusion of a group of technologies that include Artificial Intelligence (AI), gene editing, and advanced robotics (UK Government, 2019).

The African Union's (AU) Digital Transformation Strategy (DTS) for Africa (2020–2030) articulates Africa's vision, objectives, and priority areas of digital policy (African Union Commission (AUC), 2020). The DTS points to the ways that digitalisation can contribute to the achievement of the AU's Agenda 2063, while emphasising alignment with the Science, Technology and Innovation Strategy for Africa 2024 (STISA-2024) (AUC, 2014). The approach adopted by the AU emphasises the vital linkage between digital technologies, science, and innovation, and their potential to play a role in the continent's industrialisation and in the roll-out of the African Continental Free Trade Area (AfCFTA). In addition, the AU approach recognises the potential for digital technologies, if effectively deployed, to contribute to addressing pressing development challenges such as poverty and unemployment, reducing inequality, enhancing inclusion, and boosting the production of goods and services (AUC, 2020).

Inadequate governance of digital technologies and lack of harmonised regulatory regimes across borders pose barriers to businesses and leave citizens' data open to exploitation and abuse by a variety of actors. Further, there is the risk of Africa becoming a battleground in the growing US–China rivalry. Adding to this is the fear of so-called "algorithmic colonialism" or "digital colonialism", signifying that Africa might become dependent on Western-developed AI, unsuited to the needs of local markets, while local tech ecosystems are impoverished (Birhane, 2020). Similar fears persist around algorithms embedded in Chinese digital infrastructure and systems installed in Africa, for example, along the digital Silk Road (see Chapter 2, this book). Schelenz and Schopp (2018) describe such parallel trends as the duality of digitalisation, where technological innovation constitutes both an opportunity and a challenge – a line of reasoning that this book subscribes to as well.

The European Union (EU) is engaged in a race to catch up with the leaders of the digital revolution – namely, China and the United States – and hopes to strengthen its own digital economy with an increasingly active industrial policy, including a growing number of planned projects and investments focused on digital technologies. Several nascent EU projects and programmes aim to advance the EU's digital economy and improve its competitiveness by pooling resources and investments, in areas such as cloud computing (Gaia-X) and semiconductor manufacturing (Gaia-X, n.d., EC, 2022a). The EU also hopes to become a global leader in digital governance by fiat of developing the world's most advanced regulatory frameworks, with a model centred on data protection and democratic values. The recent adoption of the Digital Markets Act by the European Parliament and the Council is the latest example of the EU's twofold strategy that consists of strengthening the consumer's choice and focussing on individual rights whilst ensuring more competition (European Commission (EC), 2022b). Given that the EU regulation mainly targets the Big Five (Google, Amazon, Meta, Apple, and Microsoft), it not only improves consumers' choice and safeguards competition but also constitutes by extension a means of tackling US digital hegemony. The new post-Ukraine invasion realignment and the strengthening of the transatlantic alliance might shift this discourse again and put a stronger emphasis on shared interests in the area of technology, data, and governance.

Just like the AU, the EU too is aware of, and wishes to harness, the huge transformative potential that digital technology offers. To this end, the EU's Digital Strategy lays out four goals: a digitally skilled population and highly skilled digital professionals; secure and sustainable digital infrastructures; digital transformation of businesses; digitisation of public services (EC, 2021a). The European Commission has put a strong focus on digital rights also, proposing a Declaration on Digital Rights in January 2022 (EC, 2022c). The EU's goal is to ensure that digital transformation works for European society at large, balancing the needs of citizens (*people*), businesses, and governments.

In line with the above vision, in its foreign and development policy the EU hopes to promote a European model of digital governance, to support sustainable development and to develop new markets outside of the EU for what is hoped will be a growing European digital sector. The EU seeks to establish itself as a major player in the digital economy in Africa, taking advantage of the pace and scope of Africa's digital transformation. As Africa works towards creating its own Digital Single Market (DSM), the EU hopes to proactively share its experiences and expertise in building a DSM and to influence Africa's digital governance model in the process (Daniels et al., 2020b, Teevan, 2021). The EU seeks to secure its commercial interests – including easy access for its own companies to the African market, to further its development agenda, and to promote values such as freedom of expression and data protection. These aspirations are reflected in the EU Digital For Development (D4D) Hub, which was launched by the European Commission and five EU member states (Belgium, Estonia, France, Germany, and Luxembourg) in December 2020. The majority of the D4D Hub's initial flagship projects focus on Africa (AU–EU D4D Hub) and seek to build on the work of the AU–EU Digital Economy Task Force (DETF) (DETF, 2020). These goals also fed into the EU's Global Gateway, a strategy focused on developing a global vision for infrastructure development, which has been framed as a counteroffer to China's Belt and Road Initiative (EC, 2021b). Much of the success or failure of the EU's new digital global policy will depend on how well the Union can translate strategic promises into tangible policies producing visible results. Coherence across policy areas is at least as important as thorough impact monitoring, both of which should be at the heart of European efforts during the current budget cycle (2021-2027).

In Africa and Europe, countries and continental institutions seek to harness the potential of digital transformation whilst dealing with its challenges. For Africa, digitalisation and its transformative potential offer huge opportunities as the continent seeks to achieve its development agenda as laid out in Agenda 2063. Yet, the continent is also uniquely vulnerable to the growing inequalities of the digital age, and the exploitative practices, such as digital and data extraction, and commercialisation, that have accompanied digital technologies (Iyer et al., 2021). The EU, despite its much stronger economy and industrial fabric, has ultimately fallen behind other global powers in some aspects of digital development. And as mentioned in the previous section, the EU is making efforts to catch up in the development of key digital technologies, cloud computing, for example whilst also protecting and promoting its vision of digital governance and regulatory frameworks that is human- and citizen-centric. It sees cooperation with Africa as a development imperative, but also as an economic opportunity and an avenue to greater global influence through the promotion of its human-centric governance model.

On both continents, we see a strong emphasis being put on advancing the potential of digital technologies to achieve development goals and foster strategic interests. For closer cooperation between Africa and Europe to become fruitful and add mutual value in a highly competitive field, both complementary goals and diverging objectives need to be identified and addressed. In this book, we examine the potential for cooperation on three levels: politics, policies, and people.

1.3 AU–EU Digital Cooperation: A New Frontier

In official declarations and public statements, the AU and EU have identified digital cooperation as a new priority area between both continents. In the joint statement following the AU–EU Summit in February 2022, digital transformation was highlighted as a priority to "[support] trusted connectivity through investments in infrastructures and an affordable and enhanced access to the digital and data economy while boosting digital entrepreneurship and skills" (AU–EU, 2022). Although this joint statement remains a vague list of priorities, it encompasses and reinforces different focus areas of the digital partnership laid out in the 2019 AU–EU DETF Report, which highlighted four priority areas: broadband connectivity, skills, support to improving the business environment and e-services. The DETF brought together multiple actors from Africa and Europe, including private sector actors, international organisations, donors, and civil society organisations (CSOs), and provided an avenue for the development of a shared vision based on mutually agreed principles. This growing interest from the AU and EU in working together to advance digital development also makes us examine cooperation between the AU, EU, and their Member States in this book.

There is undoubtedly ample room for digital cooperation between the AU, the EU, and their Member States, but there remain key differences in the ways that they approach the *politics* of the current geopolitical climate. It has become increasingly clear that the choice of digital governance models and even of partners for digital infrastructure investments has wider political connotations that are not entirely neutral (see Fritzsche & Spoiala, Chapter 2, this book). While the EU takes a less hard line than the United States vis-à-vis Huawei and Chinese technologies more widely, it is still focused on building a stronger and more sovereign digital economy at home and offering an alternative to Chinese (and American) technologies abroad that strongly caters to individual rights and the right to privacy. This is evident in the focus on trusted connectivity in the EU's announcements to date related to the digital element of the Global Gateway Initiative (EC, 2022d).

On their part, African countries have tried to steer clear of these geopolitical struggles or even to leverage them where possible to support their own development agendas. Gagliardone (2019) examines how Chinese digital actors have gained ground in this sector by working closely with governments to roll out major expansions in internet and mobile phone access. He contrasts this with what he considers a Western model that continues to struggle with the dilemma of providing basic services, whilst wishing to guarantee human rights and freedom of expression. It is unclear how long it may be possible for African governments to adopt a "neutral" position in the face of growing divergences around the governance of digital and bilateral cooperation (see Jili, this volume).

Success in this new frontier of AU–EU digital cooperation demands that these key differences are resolved in ways that foster mutual benefits and transformative change for both partners. Both Africa and Europe are keen to harness digitalisation and innovation in addressing their strategic and development targets and achieving the Sustainable Development Goals (SDGs). Doing so will require the right *policies*. Given the EU's own experience of building a Digital Single Market (DSM), there are clear opportunities for deepened cooperation around the roll-out of the AfCFTA and a future African DSM. These developments have the potential to transform Africa's economy and speed up industrialisation, particularly if they fully integrate the transformative potential of digital technologies in line with the ambitions of the African Digital Transformation Strategy (see Fafunwa and Odufuwa, Banga, and El Aynaoui et al., this volume). Yet attaining these goals will require huge steps forward in terms of regulatory harmonisation across Africa, together with associated investments. The EU, with its long-standing expertise on regulatory harmonisation and its own evolving approach to digital governance, has potentially important experiences to share with African partners. Beyond offering new forms of cooperation, the EU also follows an interest-driven strategy in digital governance. By this we mean that in fashioning out its digital partnerships in Africa (and elsewhere), the EU primarily seeks to advance its interests.

Studies that examine the EU's regulatory power highlight digital regulation as one of the areas where the EU has shown leadership, and this is an area where EU actors express the hope of having an influence on African partners. In "The Brussels Effect", Bradford (2020) notes the important global implications of the EU's 2016 General Data Protection Regulation (GDPR), and that legislation in South Africa and Senegal was influenced by (earlier) European data protection standards. Bradford encourages future research to include Africa, a hitherto under-researched region. However, this body of literature is still sparse and requires more research to understand the scope for regulatory alignment between Africa and Europe, but also the challenges. The question of regulatory alignment, norms externalisation, and the impact of new data protection frameworks are examined in this book drawing on case studies from Kenya and South Africa (see Erforth and Shields, and Gastrow and Adams, this volume). The undeniable linkage between digital technologies and the norms and values that are inherent to their algorithmic design brings to the fore a long-standing debate on the EU as a normative power (Manners, 2002). We engage with this debate in this book.

Ultimately, the main goal of digital development should be to lead to real improvements in the lives of *people*, acting as a lever allowing greater access to education, training, employment, and health. The AU's Digital Transformation Strategy outlines a clear vision for the roles that digital technologies can play in human development in Africa. COVID-19 led to important technological innovations in e-healthcare, e-learning, and social protection using digital payments in Africa, but huge gaps remain in terms of the ability of citizens across countries and even within counties to access these technologies. Achieving the full potential of digital transformation will require major investments in digital skills to allow all citizens to access digital technologies and make use of the emerging services, but even doing this will require a shared understanding of digital skills (see Bashir & Daniels, this volume). Similarly, ensuring that women and girls are not left behind will require that the specific needs of women and girls are integrated into the design and roll-out of digital technologies and digital for development projects (see Sladkova & Bashir, this volume).

1.4 Organisation of the Book

To do justice to the complexity and multiple layers of the digital transformation and its impact on societies and economies in Africa and Europe, the book adopts multiple perspectives on the topic of digital cooperation. Chapters 2–4 in the first part of the book deal with power *politics* in the broader sense with a consideration of the geopolitics of digital cooperation. They elaborate on what politics and geopolitics may mean for different models of digital development and governance. Following an introduction to the topic, we engage with one dominant actor and one new frontier in the digital field in order to showcase the underlying power dynamics.

In Chapter 2, Kerstin Fritzsche and Daniel Spoiala examine digital development cooperation between the EU and the AU and argue that the EU employs both its Digital4Development policy and its recent infrastructure strategy, Global Gateway, to strengthen the bloc's strategic autonomy. The authors continue to assess the impact of such an interest-driven approach on Africa's digital sovereignty and advance a set of conditions that are necessary for the partnership to become beneficial to both the EU and the AU. The discussion is particularly relevant considering the EU's Global Gateway strategy, which was published in late 2021, at least in part as a response to the Chinese Belt and Road Initiative.

The latter is also the subject of Chapter 3. In his contribution, Bulelani Jili examines the introduction of Chinese surveillance technologies in Kenya and Ethiopia. Unlike most studies that focus on supply factors, the chapter explores the quality of local and global features in the spread of Chinese surveillance tools. It analyses surveillance technologies as a dynamic social process. Drawing attention to the often-neglected Chinese operations in Kenya and Ethiopia helps to deepen our understanding of how China's growing geopolitical footprint in Africa is mediated by local conditions and actors. The discussion also reveals the potential of an alternative form of cooperation that takes a human- and citizen-centric approach with potentials for enhancing local ownership.

One potential area of forward-looking EU-Africa cooperation is discussed in Chapter 4. Eleonore Pauwels and Klaus Tilmes examine the nexus between

AI, bioinformatics, and genomics as a field of increased geopolitical competition. In the authors' view, the main point is the need to align long-term support (financial, knowledge) in key strategic areas with the gradual build-up of an Africa-wide strategy and network that can now stand on its own and is open for partnering on equal terms. According to the authors, Africa's vibrant bio-ecosystem can provide new impulses for innovation that Europe would be well advised to support and draw on. With normative leadership, strategic funding commitments, and capacity-building partnerships with the private sector, the EU is well positioned to connect its genomic strategy with the growing bio-economy potential across Africa.

Following the classification of the digital realm as a part of global geopolitics and the assessment of the implications, the book then moves on to consider the potential for Africa–Europe digital cooperation in different *policy* areas – Chapters 5–12. The first of these areas focusses on economic development and explores the potential of digital technologies to transform African economies. In Chapter 5 Tunde Fafunwa and Fola Odufuwa examine the potential benefits African micro, small, and medium-sized enterprises (MSMEs) can expect from the AfCFTA. The chapter explores why digitalising their businesses is necessary for MSMEs to participate and benefit from the reduced trade barriers that the AfCFTA will offer.

Looking beyond MSMEs as an aggregate, it is useful to consider specific sectors individually. In Chapter 6, Karishma Banga examines the scope of AU–EU digital cooperation for productive job creation in agriculture, manufacturing, and the service sector. The author argues that although digital agricultural platforms can boost productivity and access to formal work, the uptake is low in African countries with large-scale employment gains limited. As for manufacturing and the service sector, the chapter's findings suggest that increasing cross-sector productivity is possible by shifting labour towards more productive sectors of manufacturing and services. One way to address the diverse challenges, according to Banga, is for the AU–EU digital cooperation to focus on facilitating digital infrastructure development in rural areas, coordinate and scale up capacity and awareness building programmes, and foster women's access to technology.

The sector-related focus is further narrowed down in Chapter 7. Karim El Aynaoui, Larabi Jaïdi, and Akram Zaoui focus on how Egypt, Morocco, and Tunisia are trying to safeguard and expand their manufacturing sectors. The authors observe how decision-makers in the three countries seek to strengthen their country's respective position in global and regional value chains. The three case studies also provide evidence for a net positive impact of digitalisation on manufacturing and highlight the financial and technological benefits of closer cooperation with the EU.

With Chapters 6 and 7 unveiling sector-specific challenges and opportunities of digitalisation and digital cooperation, the next chapter turns to the topic of Water that is sometimes referred to either as a common good, a human right, or a commodity. In Chapter 8, Tamanna Ashraf takes a closer look at water and the infrastructure and policies that govern it. *Digital water* – or the digitalisation of water – is considered a means to improve climate resilience and human development in the world's most water stressed regions. Making the case for the effectiveness of digital water, the author then discusses how the European Union Water Initiative (EUWI) is aiming to coordinate EU and member states' funding in the field of water development to elaborate on the benefits of additional EU support to deploy digital technologies that help improve water quality.

EU cooperation and support is needed beyond sectors such as water. Digitalisation, similar to the related fields of science and innovation, requires finance, which is often scarce in the African context as governments strive to address competing development priorities with available and sometimes meagre resources. Andrew Agyei-Holmes, Bernardin Senadza, and Felix Ankomah Asante, in Chapter 9, focus on tax and resource mobilisation. The authors show how the introduction of digital tools in tax collection systems is driving improvements in revenue collection, helping to address existing challenges, and the importance of stakeholder engagement. These and other challenges that remain in the finance, tax and resource mobilisation systems provide opportunities for AU–EU digital cooperation.

Addressing development challenges, by harnessing opportunities that digitalisation presents, requires attention to rights and local ownership. Human-centric regulatory frameworks and trust in existing digital ecosystems are quintessential to this objective. In Chapter 10, Benedikt Erforth and Charles-Martin Shields analyse the EU's promotion of interests through the so-called "human centric" model of digital governance. Using Kenya as an illustrative case study, the authors argue that the EU's desire to use regulatory externalisation to achieve the concept of human-centric digitalisation assumes that African partners' social and political notions of privacy align with the EU's. The authors conclude that the EU's externalisation of regulatory frameworks on digital transformation creates new opportunities for commercial cooperation with Africa. However, these prospects must be balanced with the political and social aspects of regulation to achieve the wider governance and human rights goals of EU cooperation.

The EU's regulatory cooperation, influence, and power in Africa goes beyond Kenya; it includes countries such as Senegal, Nigeria, and South Africa. In Chapter 11, Michael Gastrow and Rachel Adams, deepen the discussions on this theme. Central to the discussions in this chapter is an investigation of how South Africa has engaged with the EU in its pursuit of strengthened local capabilities, and alignment with international changes in the regulation of data and digital technologies. In this context, Michael Gastrow and Rachel Adams juxtapose the emergence of data privacy and data protection regulation in both jurisdictions. A clear lesson from the discussion in this chapter is that the regulation of the digital environment needs to be rapid and responsive – or risks falling behind changes in the technological and political spheres.

In continuing the discussions on privacy, policy, and people, Joe Abah, Krista Baptista, Connor MacKenzie, and Anand Varghese, in Chapter 12, examine the development process for national-level digital policies, regulations, and bills that seek to maximise the benefits of digital technology and mitigate its risks, such as threats to privacy. With Nigeria as the focus, they present a detailed analysis of how policymakers engage with key stakeholders on technology-related policies, regulations, and bills. Their insights help deepen the readers' understanding of how actors and institutions, including the recently formed AU–EU D4D Hub, can assist African countries in developing citizen-centric and inclusive digital policymaking processes.

As the entirety of this book has argued, digital transformations have a significant impact on human development. To this end, Chapters 13–16 examine the impact of digital governance on *people* by assessing its implications for economic development and social progress.

In Chapter 13, Sajitha Bashir and Chux Daniels analyse the EU's Comprehensive Strategy with Africa, which prioritises digital skills in three of its five thematic areas. Despite the existence of such formal declarations, the analysis indicate that the conditions do not yet exist for a meaningful cooperation between the AU and EU in the area of digital skills due to lack of conceptual clarity and agreed consensus on what is meant by digital skills. Further, the authors stress the need to develop the entire ecosystem for digital skills training, including infrastructure, connectivity, training of teachers, and local digital content, in the education and training sectors. Progressive AU–EU collaboration in building digital skills must focus on these areas.

Learning is an essential aspect of capacity building and inclusion, as Niyanta Shetye et al., discuss in Chapter 14. By focusing on new and emerging trends in the cooperation between the AU and the EU, this chapter highlights low-cost and effective digital learning solutions and argues that in addition to digital technology transfer, innovation and investments are needed in building a learning-centred support for green transitioning and digital cooperation. In response to ICTs becoming a catalyst for transformative learning, the authors provide insights on how constructive AU–EU cooperation and co-learning can pave ways for societal transformations, particularly in rural communities.

Despite many efforts, education systems, especially in STEM, continue to leave some segments of the society behind – especially women and marginalised communities. In Chapter 15, Zuzana Sladkova and Sumbal Bashir explore ideas around *Feminist Digital Development*. The authors echo the point made in various chapters of this book that Africa and Europe are embracing a new era of development cooperation that is digital. However, questions remain about the ability of the EU to effectively deliver on the promise of a value-based digital partnership, as well as the willingness of African partners to overcome the trust deficit from the past and to work with the EU towards a common vision for digital transformation. Still on the concept of female inclusion, Francine Beleyi, in Chapter 16, focusses on the importance of African female entrepreneurs, showing that dedicated digital networks are vital for supporting thriving businesses and job creation. According to the author, digital networks can facilitate access to peer support, mentorship, and business training, which help to boost women's confidence and capabilities to run more successful businesses.

In summary, the book opens with ideas on global politics and the implications on digital transformation, shifts to policies and regulations on digitalisation as they relate to economic development, and ends with discussion on the important roles that digitalisation plays in human development, that is, the impact of digital revolution on people. Overall, the rich insights presented in the book point to three key messages: (1) the necessity for a deeper AU–EU digital cooperation, (2) the prospects for mutual benefits that could result from the strategic partnership between the two regions, and (3) new frontiers for AU–EU cooperation in digitalisation that can open further opportunities for increased competitiveness and development outcomes for both continents. Increased digital cooperation between the AU and EU can lead to transformative change in Africa and Europe – jobs, better health and wellbeing, reduced inequality and environmental degradation, greater inclusion, and social progress.

Note

1 Global Gateway is an EU initiative that seeks to foster a sustainable connectivity, with the aim to invest EUR 300 billion between 2021 and 2027 in both physical and digital infrastructure.

References

ACET (African Center for Economic Transformation) (2021) *African Transformation Report 2021, Integrating to Transform, ACET.* Available at: https://acetforafrica.org/acet/wp -content/uploads/publications/2021/07/ACET_ATR3_report_web.pdf   (Accessed: 3 May 2022).

AfricArena (2021) *The State of Tech in Africa 2021.* Available at: https://f1d0651a-c40a- 4877-b5d5 (Accessed: 6 May 2022).

Allen, N. (2021) *The Promises and Perils of Africa's Digital Revolution.* Brookings Institute. Available at: https://www.brookings.edu/techstream/the-promises-and-perils-of -africas-digital-revolution/ (Accessed: 26 April 2022).

AU-EU (2022) 6th European Union African Union Summit: a Joint Vision for 2030. Available at: https://www.consilium.europa.eu/media/54412/final_declaration-en .pdf (Accessed: 17 March 2022).

African Union Commission (AUC) (2014) *AU Strategy for Science, Technology and Innovation for Africa 2024, STISA-2024.* African Union, Addis Ababa.

AUC (2020) *The Digital Transformation Strategy for Africa (2020–2030).* Available at: https://au.int/en/documents/20200518/digital-transformation-strategy-africa-2020 -2030 (Accessed: 27 April 2022).

Azzioui, I. and Sandri, S. (2021) What Do We Know About Nascent and Young Innovative Entrepreneurship in Africa? Insights and Perspectives from Morocco. In: Daniels, C., Dosso, M., Amadi-Echendu, J. (eds) *Entrepreneurship, Technology Commercialisation, and*

Innovation Policy in Africa. Springer, Cham, pp. 99–134. https://doi.org/10.1007/978 -3-030-58240-1_5

Birhane, A. (2020) Algorithmic Colonization of Africa. *Scripted*. 17(2), pp. 389–409. August 2020. Doi: 10.2966/scrip.170220.389

Bradford, A. (2020) *The Brussels Effect*. New York: Oxford University Press.

Chataway, J., Dobson, C., Daniels, C., Byrne, R., Tigabu, A. and Hanlin, R. (2019) Science Granting Councils in Sub-Saharan Africa: Trends and Tensions. *Science and Public Policy*, 46(4), pp. 620 –631. https://doi.org/10.1093/scipol/scz007

Chipaike, R., Knowledge, M. H. (2018) The Question of African Agency in International Relations. *Cogent Social Sciences* 4(1). https://doi.org/10.1080/23311886.2018.1487257

Daniels, C., Byrne, R., Hanlin, R., Pointel, S. and Numi, A. (2020a) *Updating the Case Studies of the Political Economy of Science Granting Councils in Sub-Saharan Africa*. Available at: https://idl-bnc-idrc.dspacedirect.org/handle/10625/59313 (Accessed: 26 April 2022).

Daniels C., Erforth, B., Floyd, R. and Teevan C. (2020b) *Strengthening the Digital Partnership between Africa and Europe*. ETTG (DIE, ECDPM and ACET). Available at: https://ettg.eu/2020/10/26/strengthening-the-digital-partnership-between-africa -and-europe/ (Accessed: 26 April 2022).

Daniels, C., Byrne, R., Pointel, S. Hanlin, R., and Numi, A. (2021a) Political Economy Insights for Science System Transformations in Sub-Saharan Africa, *Policy@Sussex*. Available at: https://blogs.sussex.ac.uk/policy-engagement/files/2021/02/Political -economy-insights-for-science-system-transformations-in-sub-Saharan-Africa -Policy-Brief.pdf (Accessed: 26 April 2022).

Daniels, C., Dosso, M., and Amadi-Echendu J. (2021b) *Entrepreneurship, Technology Commercialisation, and Innovation Policy in Africa*. Cham: Springer Nature. https://doi .org/10.1007/978-3-030-58240-1

DETF ((AU-EU) Digital Economy Task Force) (2020) *New Africa-Europe Digital Economy Partnership: Accelerating Achievement of the Sustainable Development Goals*. Available at: https://ec.europa.eu/international-partnerships/system/files/new-africa-eu-digital -economy_en_0.pdf (Accessed: 26 April 2022).

Dosso, M., Braoulé Méïté, F., Ametepe, G., Gbogou, C., Guiella, G. and Oulaï, D. (2021) New Entrepreneurial Narratives in Urban West Africa: Case Studies of Five Innovation Hubs and Communities. In: Daniels, C., Dosso, M., Amadi-Echendu, J. (eds.) *Entrepreneurship, Technology Commercialisation, and Innovation Policy in Africa*. Cham: Springer, pp. 169–193. https://doi.org/10.1007/978-3-030-58240-1_8

European Commission (EC) (2021a) *Communication from the Commission to the European Parliament, the Council, the European Economic and Social Committee and the Committee of the Regions. 2030 Digital Compass: the European way for the Digital Decade*. Available at: https://eur-lex.europa.eu/legal-content/en/TXT/?uri=CELEX%3A52021DC0118 (Accessed: 26 April 2022).

EC (2021b) *Joint Communication to the European Parliament, the Council, the European Economic and Social Committee of the Regions and the European Investment Bank. The Global Gateway*. JOIN (2021) 30 final. Available at: https://ec.europa.eu/info/sites/ default/files/joint_communication_global_gateway.pdf (Accessed: 18 March 2022).

EC (2022a) *Digital Sovereignty: Commission proposes Chips Act to Confront Semiconductor Shortages and Strengthen Europe's Technological Leadership*. Available at: https://ec.europa .eu/commission/presscorner/detail/en/ip_22_729 (Accessed 28 April 2022).

EC (2022b) *Digital Markets Act: Commission Welcomes Political Agreement on Rules to Ensure Fair and Open Digital Markets*. Available at: Digital Markets Act: Commission welcomes political agreement (europa.eu) (Accessed 4 April 2022).

EC (2022c) *Declaration on European Digital Rights and Principles.* Available at: https://digital-strategy.ec.europa.eu/en/library/declaration-european-digital-rights-and-principles#Declaration (Accessed: 26 April 2022).

EC (2022d) *EU-Africa: Global Gateway Investment Package: Digital Transition.* Available at: https://ec.europa.eu/commission/presscorner/detail/en/fs_22_1117 (Accessed: 26 April 2022).

Erforth, B. and Gutheil L. (2022) Why We Should Talk About Megatrends in Africa. *Megatrends Afrika.* Available at: https://www.megatrends-afrika.de/publikation/why-we-should-talk-about-megatrends-in-africa (Accessed: 25 April 2022).

Gagliardone, I. (2019) *China, Africa, and the Future of the Internet.* London: Zed Books.

Gaia-X (n.d.) *What is Gaix-X?* Available at: https://www.data-infrastructure.eu/GAIAX/Navigation/EN/Home/home.html (Accessed: 28 April 2022).

Giddens, A. (1984) *The Constitution of Society.* Berkeley and Los Angeles: University of California Press.

Giuliani, D., With H.L., Ekeledo A. and Isedowo T. (2019) Building a Conducive Setting for Innovators to Thrive: A Qualitative and Quantitative Study of a Hundred Hubs across Africa. *Afrilabs and Briter Bridges.* Available at: https://briterbridges.com/s/40_AFRILABS_REPORT-FINAL-compressed-9yhj.pdf (Accessed: 18 March 2022).

GSMA (2021) *The Mobile Economy Sub-Saharan Africa 2021.* Available at: https://www.gsma.com/mobileeconomy/wp-content/uploads/2021/09/GSMA_ME_SSA_2021_English_Web_Singles.pdf (Accessed:26 April 2022).

ITU (International Telecommunication Union) (2020) *Measuring Digital Development Facts and Figures 2020.* Geneva, Switzerland. Available at: https://www.itu.int/en/ITU-D/Statistics/Documents/facts/FactsFigures2020.pdf (Accessed: 28 April 2022).

Iyer, N. Achieng, G., Borokini, F. and Ludger, U. (2021) *Automated Imperialism, Expansionist Dreams: Exploring Digital Extractivism in Africa.* Available at: https://archive.pollicy.org/digitalextractivism/ (Accessed: 26 April 2022).

Manners, I. (2002) Normative power Europe: A contradiction in terms? *Journal of Common Market Studies* 40(2), pp. 235–258. https://doi.org/10.1111/1468-5965.00353

Martins, R.M., Park, E., Hain, D.S. and Jurowetzki, R. (2021) Mapping Entrepreneurial Ecosystem for Technology Start-ups in Developing Economies: An Empirical Analysis of Twitter Networks Between Start-ups and Support Organizations of Nairobi's Digital Economy. In: Daniels, C., Dosso, M., Amadi-Echendu, J. (eds.) *Entrepreneurship, Technology Commercialisation, and Innovation Policy in Africa.* Cham: Springer, pp. 55–97. https://doi.org/10.1007/978-3-030-58240-1_4

Naisbitt, J. (1982) *Megatrends: Ten new Directions transforming our Lives.* London: Warner Books.

Schelenz, L. and Schopp, K. (2018) Digitalization in Africa: Interdisciplinary Perspectives on Technology, Development, and Justice. *International Journal of Digital Society (IJDS),* 9(4), pp. 1412–1420.

Teevan, C. (2021) Building Strategic European Digital Cooperation with Africa. *ECDPM,* Briefing Note No. 134, September 2021. Available at: https://ecdpm.org/publications/building-strategic-european-digital-cooperation-with-africa/ (Accessed 28 April 2022)

The Great Hack. Directed by K. Amer and J. Noujaim *[Documentary film].* Netflix.

UK Government (2019) *Regulation for the Fourth Industrial Revolution.* White Paper, June 2019. Available at: Regulation for the Fourth Industrial Revolution - GOV.UK (www.gov.uk) (Accessed 18 March 2022).

UN (2015) *Transforming our World: The 2030 Agenda for Sustainable Development.* Available at: https://sdgs.un.org/2030agenda (Accessed 27 April 2022).

World Bank (2019) *Individuals Using the Internet in percentage of population (sub-Saharan Africa).* Available at: Individuals using the Internet (% of population) - Sub-Saharan Africa | Data (worldbank.org) (Accessed 6 May 2022).

Zuboff, S. (2019) *The Age of Surveillance Capitalism: The Fight for a Human Future at the new Frontier of Power.* New York: Public Affairs.

2

THE EU–AU DIGITAL PARTNERSHIP

Between Digital Geopolitics and Digital Sovereignty

Kerstin Fritzsche and Daniel Spoiala

2.1 Introduction

Given the dominance of the United States and China in the global digital economy (UNCTAD 2019) and the rivalry between these two countries for global technological leadership, two dynamics can be observed.

First, countries in both the Global North and South are increasingly concerned about their dependence on foreign, especially US and Chinese, digital technologies and services, and are making greater efforts to take better control of their own digital development. This dynamic is often associated with the concept of digital sovereignty or related notions such as cyber sovereignty or technological sovereignty. The European Union's (EU) efforts to strengthen its digital sovereignty and India's quest for data sovereignty (Basu 2021) are just two examples of this dynamic.

Second, international partnerships and collaborations for digital connectivity and development are forged and become important instruments for digital geopolitics.[1] Digital geopolitics play a central role in the economic and technological rivalry between the United States and China (Bendiek et al. 2019). It is evident, for example, in the G7 infrastructure initiative Build Back Better World (B3W) announced by US president Joe Biden in June 2021, which aims to meet the infrastructure needs of developing countries, including digital technologies as one focal area (The White House 2021). The B3W is explicitly intended as a measure to counterbalance China's growing global influence through the Belt and Road Initiative (BRI), which was launched in 2013. With a similar motivation, and in an effort to strengthen its role as a geopolitical actor, the EU announced a global connectivity initiative called Global Gateway in September 2021 (Kuo 2021).

DOI: 10.4324/9781003274322-2

The African continent is an important focus area for these initiatives. Strong economic growth rates in the years leading up to the COVID-19-pandemic, young populations, a growing middle class as well as rising internet penetration rates and the need to further improve internet connectivity have attracted the interest of foreign investors and technology companies in many African countries, such as Ghana, Kenya, Nigeria, and Rwanda. African countries, being highly dependent on foreign, especially Chinese, digital technologies and services are bound to be affected by the geopolitical struggle over shaping the global digital transformation (Aggad 2021). This chapter, therefore, focuses on initiatives for connectivity and digital development cooperation, particularly from the perspective of digital sovereignty of African states. It takes a closer look at the EU's Digital for Development (D4D) approach and discusses its potentials as well as challenges regarding digital sovereignty of African countries and how it could be tailored to their digital development priorities.

The chapter is organised as follows: First, we provide an overview of the various meanings of the concept of digital sovereignty and related terms, including the notion of data colonialism. We conclude this section by outlining how digital sovereignty is understood for the analysis in this chapter. Second, we examine the digital policies and development priorities of the African Union (AU) and its member states and explore African agency in shaping the digital transformation. We argue that African countries should use their potential to act as a collective actor to shape the digital transformation according to their development priorities and needs. Third, we discuss the EU's approach to digital development cooperation with Africa and the opportunities and challenges of EU–AU digital development cooperation in relation to African digital sovereignty. Finally, we conclude with some reflections on how EU–AU digital development cooperation could be used to strengthen self-determined digital development paths of African countries.

2.2 Grasping the Notion of Digital Sovereignty

There is no universally accepted definition of the term "digital sovereignty", with sovereignty itself being a highly criticised concept (Couture and Toupin 2019, pp. 4–5). The meaning of digital sovereignty is manifold. It was reframed and shifted over time and depends highly on the context it is used in. Moreover, the meaning of digital sovereignty depends on who is formulating its claim for digital self-determination and which aspects are emphasised in this claim (Pohle 2020). Couture and Toupin identify five different perspectives on digital sovereignty, namely "Cyberspace Sovereignty", "Digital Sovereignty, Governments and States", "Indigenous Digital Sovereignty", "Social Movements and Digital Sovereignty", and "Personal Digital Sovereignty" (Couture and Toupin 2019, p. 6). Pohle and Thiel structure the meanings of digital sovereignty along the three levels of autonomy addressed in claims for digital sovereignty, namely state autonomy, economic autonomy, and the autonomy of the individual in the digital sphere (Pohle and Thiel 2020).

Digital sovereignty as state autonomy refers to "the idea that a nation or region should be able to take autonomous actions and decisions regarding its digital infrastructures and technology deployment" (Pohle and Thiel 2020, p. 8). With the global digital transformation that transcends borders and asymmetric power relations in the digital economy, the state's autonomy to shape its digital transformation in a self-determined way is increasingly challenged. State-centred notions of digital sovereignty stand for this challenge and for the quest to reconfigure the meaning of sovereignty of states in a networked world. Pohle and Thiel (2020) identify two strands of the debate: while authoritarian and semi-authoritarian states view the internet as a threat to their existing political systems, liberal countries underscore the need for independence and control over their digital infrastructures and policy issues (Pohle and Thiel 2020). Creemers (2020) argues that the different approaches to digital sovereignty of China, the United States, and Europe are due to differences in the underlying concepts of security. He explains that China views security through the lens of information security, therefore putting a particular focus on the control of flows of data – while the United States and Europe share more technical approaches to security, therefore emphasising the security and integrity of telecommunication infrastructures (Creemers 2020). Consequently, the policy choices and actions for digital sovereignty of China, the United States, and Europe differ. For example, while China favours strict data localisation rules (Liu 2020), the United States and Europe promote a more open flow of data.

This example also shows that state autonomy and economic autonomy as elements of digital sovereignty are closely interlinked (Pohle and Thiel 2020). Economic competition and the aspiration to reduce dependency from foreign technology imports are important drivers for digital sovereignty policies that target the development of domestic digital sectors and structural change. Increasing competitiveness in key digital sectors such as artificial intelligence (AI) and semi-conductors is, for example, a key element of the EU's striving for greater digital sovereignty (EC 2021a). The heavy dependence on leading platform companies, particularly from the United States, and the notion of surveillance capitalism (Zuboff 2019) have driven the discourse on data sovereignty. Data sovereignty can be understood as the "self-determination of individuals and organisations with regard to the use of their data" (Jarke et al. 2019, p. 550). Moreover, this concept can be understood in terms of data security and raises the issue of to what extent states can have sovereignty with regard to storing and making data available (Kaloudis 2021, pp. 6–7). It can therefore be understood as one specific facet of digital sovereignty.

The increasing penetration of societies by data-generating and data-using technologies, often referred to as datafication, has given rise to the notion of data colonialism (Couldry and Mejias 2019). First and foremost, Couldy and Mejias (2019) understand data colonialism as a new form of capitalism based on the "reconfiguration of human life around the maximisation of data collection for profit" (Couldry and Mejias 2019, p. 3). They argue that the struggle against data colonialism is bifold and includes "struggles over particular practices of technology and struggles over knowledge and rationality" (Couldry and Mejias 2021, p. 12), meaning the narratives and imaginaries that frame the use of technologies and data. The terms "data colonialism" or "digital colonialism" are also used to describe the use of citizens' data in the Global South by large-platform companies without a corresponding creation of value for developing countries (Ávila Pinto 2018). Data or digital colonialism therefore also stands for a new form of *extractivism* of resources from the Global South by (mainly) Western actors (Iyer et al. 2021).

Finally, the third dimension of digital sovereignty is that of individual autonomy. It highlights individuals as autonomous actors in the digital sphere, whether as consumers, employees, or users of digital services and technologies and is an element of the digital sovereignty discourse, especially in democratic countries (Pohle and Thiel 2020). For example, with its people-centric approach, the EU explicitly underpins its digital transformation policies with the aim of safeguarding individual rights and privacy (EC 2021a) and therefore gives special weight to individual digital sovereignty. The strand of the digital sovereignty discourse related to individual autonomy in the digital realm, again, is closely interlinked with the autonomy of the state and the economy.

In summary, digital sovereignty is a multifaceted and contested concept, given its vast range of meanings and its instrumental use for different – often contrasting policy agendas. Against this backdrop, we take a broad perspective on digital sovereignty, acknowledging the different, yet closely interrelated dimensions of state, economic, and individual autonomy as key elements of a holistic understanding of digital sovereignty. However, autonomy is not to be confused with autarky, in particular when considering states. Indeed, strategic dependencies can strengthen the sovereignty of states if they are deliberately chosen and are not without alternatives.

2.3 Digital Development and Digital Sovereignty in Africa

Since the early to mid-2000s, most African countries have recognised the increasing importance of the internet and modern information and communication technologies (ICTs) in achieving their development goals and have made efforts to harness digital technologies in their interest. Only a few countries have no digital policies or strategies in place; however, the form and depth of such documents vary considerably (Korovkin 2019; Abimbola et al. 2021). While some countries such as Gambia, Namibia, and Gabon for example, have integrated their digital agenda into their national development plans, others, such as Ethiopia, Botswana, Nigeria, and South Africa, have stand-alone digital policy documents, some of them dealing with specific issues such as data and privacy, cybersecurity or e-commerce (Abimbola et al. 2021). Nonetheless, most African states lack a comprehensive framework for regulating and shaping the digital transformation.

Many African countries heavily rely on Chinese tech companies throughout the whole digital technology stack (Bratton 2015), ranging from submarine cables, data centres, and mobile networks to mobile devices and apps (Adegoke 2021). This is not a new development, but rather the outcome of well-established economic relations between African countries and China (Agbebi and Virtanen 2017). The business activities of Chinese technology companies such as Huawei and ZTE in African countries have only subsequently been integrated into China's Digital Silk Road in Africa (Adegoke 2021). The role of African countries themselves in global ICT production remains marginal (UNCTAD 2019). One of the few exceptions is Rwanda, which has built its own capacities for the production of a smartphone, called the Mara Phone (Mwai 2019).

As for digital platforms, the African platform economy is on the rise, but still faces many constraints such as lack of sufficient infrastructure, lack of financial inclusion and mobile payment systems, inadequate digital content, and low internet penetration as well as consumer distrust and lack of funding (David-West and Evans 2015). Eighty-two per cent of platforms operating in Africa are home-grown. However, research suggests that foreign platform companies have a significantly larger user base, which could be due to a first-mover advantage since foreign platforms launched on average five years earlier (Johnson et al. 2020). Moreover, less than 1% of the total available global data centre capacity is located in Africa, despite approximately 17% of the world's population living on the continent according to data by Xalam Analytics (Kimeu 2021). The development of data centres has experienced a surge in recent years. For example, in June 2021 the Diamniadio National Datacenter was launched. Senegal's government plans to migrate all government data and digital platforms from servers located outside the country to the new data centre, aiming to strengthen the country's digital sovereignty (Reuters 2021). However, commentators point to the fact that the data centre was financed with a loan from China and built by Huawei, highlighting China's dominance over Senegal's digital infrastructure (Tanchum 2022). Besides, in academia, it is a controversial issue whether data localisation contributes to greater data sovereignty or does more harm than good to countries with a high dependence on foreign digital technologies and services that fear losing control over their citizens' data (Wu 2021).

In summary, African countries are highly dependent on digital infrastructures, digital services, and devices from non-African actors. Moreover, African governments take very different normative positions towards the digital transformation, ranging from approaches that heavily restrict digital innovations and social media up to internet shutdowns to the active creation of more enabling environments for digital developers and businesses (Ndemo 2021). Finally, African states compete with each other in order to attract foreign investments (Okeke 2021).

Against this backdrop, African agency in digital geopolitics mirrors the current debate on African agency in international relations: it is multifaceted and involves multiple actors, ranging from the AU and sub-national intergovernmental bodies to nations states and their leaders and representatives as well as sub- and non-state actors (Brown 2012). Some authors argue that collective action such as implementing joint strategies and pooling resources on key digital issues is important to strengthen the role of African states in digital geopolitics and to cope with asymmetries in the current political economy geography of digital transformation (Kathure 2021). As Chipaike and Knowledge (2018) show, Africa has acted as a collective actor in international relations on several occasions stemming from a sense of solidarity and sense of unity, which is deeply embedded in the principles guiding the African Union. Currently, however, the development of more suitable framework conditions for a digital economy and society in Africa is driven by a few front-runner countries and initiatives.

For example, in 2013, the Smart Africa Manifesto was launched by seven African heads of state and endorsed by all heads of state and government of the African Union in 2014 (Smart Africa 2020). The Smart Africa Manifesto declares a "bold and innovative commitment to accelerate sustainable socio-economic development on the continent and usher Africa into the knowledge economy through affordable access to Broadband and usage of Information and Communications Technologies" (Smart Africa 2013). Today, the Smart Africa Alliance also comprises a long list of multinational tech companies, such as Facebook, Microsoft, Intel, Orange, and Huawei, and is partnering with a broad range of international organisations such as the African Union (co-chair), the International Telecommunication Union (ITU), the World Bank, the African Development Bank (AfDB), the Deutsche Gesellschaft für Internationale Zusammenarbeit (GIZ), the Agence Française de Dévelopement (AFD), and others. Guided by its vision to transform Africa into a digital single market, Smart Africa has become one of the cornerstones of regional digital development efforts in Africa.

The African Union has also recognised the need to step up joint efforts to develop the digital economy in Africa and has presented a Digital Transformation Strategy for Africa (AU 2020). It highlights the digital transformation as an opportunity for socio-economic development on the African content and underscores the strategic aim of building a digital single market in Africa by 2030, in particular in the context of the African Continental Free Trade Area (AfCFTA). The strategy stresses the relevance of a digital development process, "[l]ed and owned by Africa's Institutions (…) embedded in Africa's realities and unleashing the African spirit of enterprise and creativity, to generate home-grown digital content and solutions, while embracing what is good and relevant" (AU 2020, p. 6). Moreover, the strategy explicitly mentions the need to develop data centres on African soil to enable the development of a local digital industry and to ensure the data sovereignty, arguing that "soon it will be necessary to ensure localization of all personal data of Africa's citizens" (AU 2020, p. 11).

The debate on digital sovereignty is still nascent in African countries, and despite gaining momentum, it remains fragmented and rarely reaches the regional level (Teevan 2021). Still, there is increasing awareness that the continent can no longer ignore the issue and needs to develop appropriate regulations to ensure state autonomy over the digital space, in particular with regard to data (Monyae 2021). The AU Digital Strategy for Africa is one of the few official documents mentioning African data sovereignty. Another one is South Africa's Proposed National Data and Cloud Policy presented in April 2021, which, however, takes a national perspective. The policy "seeks to strengthen the capacity of the State to deliver services to its citizens, ensure informed policy development based on data analytics, as well as promote South Africa's data sovereignty and the security thereof" (Ministry of Communications and Digital Technologies 2021, p. 11). Similar references to data or digital sovereignty are neither found in Kenya's Data Protection Act (Republic of Kenya 2019) nor Rwanda's Law Relating to the Protection of Personal Data and Privacy (Ministry of Justice 2021). In general, data regulation schemes in many countries of the African Union are still in a developing stage (Adeniran and Osakwe 2021) and even if legislation is in place, it often lacks proper implementation (CSEA 2021). The AU Convention on Cyber Security and Personal Data Protection, in short "Malabo Convention", has so far only been signed by twelve and ratified by six countries – despite being adopted in 2014 (Velluet 2021).

Data regulation furthermore needs to find a balance between data protection and the commercial use of data to allow African countries to reap the benefits of the digital economy. There are hopes that the negotiations of an e-commerce chapter for the AfCFTA will promote a harmonisation of data regulation throughout the continent and also strengthen the African Groups' position regarding the negotiation of binding rules for digital trade at the level of the World Trade Organization (WTO) (Kathure 2021). In 2017, the African Group refused to open negotiations on e-commerce rules on the grounds that already "multilateral rules as they are, are constraining our domestic policy space and ability to industrialize" and that "new rules would entrench existing imbalances and further constrain the ability of [developing countries'] governments to implement industrial policy and catch-up" (African Group 2017, p. 2). However, meanwhile, several African states have expressed interest in the Joint Statement Initiative on e-commerce negotiations, showing cracks in the joint position of African countries (Kathure 2021). While this can be interpreted as a move by some countries to strengthen their national interests in the emerging data regulatory frameworks at the international level, the implications for Africa as a collective actor in digital geopolitics remain uncertain and may well weaken its position.

2.4 EU–AU Digital Development Cooperation

The EU–AU partnership on digital development needs to be considered against the backdrop of the EU's own quest for digital sovereignty. Digital or technology sovereignty has become a major concern of the EU in particular under the Commission Presidency of Ursula von der Leyen. Past years have seen increasing efforts to develop regulatory frameworks for AI, data governance, and the digital market in the EU and to strengthen key technology sectors such as the semiconductor industry. The overall objective of these efforts is to strengthen the EU's global competitiveness (EC 2020). The EU's notion of digital sovereignty is closely linked to the concept of "strategic autonomy", which the EEAS outlined in the "Global Strategy for the EU's Foreign and Security Policy" (EEAS 2016). The strategy already highlighted the role of international partnerships in the EU's security. With regard to digital sovereignty, the EU is aware that it can strengthen its position in digital geopolitics only if it succeeds in disseminating its standards and values for the digital transformation at the international level. Forging international partnerships is therefore an important element of the EU's strategy to shaping its Digital Decade (EC 2021b). The European Commission (EC) made clear that in order to "truly influence the way in which digital solutions are developed and used on a global scale, [the European Union] needs to be a strong, independent and purposeful digital player in its own right" (EC 2020, p. 3). It "strives to foster a human-centric vision for the digital economy and society across the globe" and "aims to build strategic international partnerships and lead international negotiations on digital" (EC 2021c).

With its human-centric, or sometimes also called regulatory, approach (Bastion and Mukku 2020), the EU offers its African partner countries an alternative to the liberal, market-oriented approach of the US- and the Chinese state–led model of digital transformation. In recent years, digital development cooperation with the countries of the Global South has become an important instrument for putting this offer into practice. In 2017, the EC Staff Working Paper on Digital4Development provided a first draft for a joint digital development approach of the EU and its member states aiming "to promote information and communication technologies in developing countries as powerful enablers of growth, and to better mainstream digital solutions in development" (EC 2017, p. 5). The document suggests four priority areas, namely improving connectivity in developing countries through the development of digital infrastructures and appropriate regulation, strengthening digital skills and competencies, leveraging digital technologies for entrepreneurship and job creation, and digital technologies as an enabler for socio-economic development (EC 2017). The EC Staff Working Document furthermore recommended to focus EU digital development cooperation on Africa arguing that a harmonisation of digital policies of the EU and the African countries would "contribute to developing business relationships in the fast-growing markets of the developing world, based on co-development and co-innovation" (EC 2017, p. 15).

In December 2018, the EU–AU Digital Economy Task Force (DETF) was launched and, in June 2019, presented a report outlining a shared vision and key principles for the digital transformation as well as priority areas for the cooperation on digital policy issues between the EU and the AU (AU-EU DETF 2019). These included, amongst others, the continuous development of telecommunication infrastructure in Africa, support of digital entrepreneurship, and easier access to funding for digital businesses. The task force also encouraged the development of e-government services and intra-African digital trade. In the light of the EU's aspirations to strengthen its position as a geopolitical actor, the digital development cooperation with Africa was further developed. In December 2020, the D4D Hub was launched, which focuses particularly on the cooperation with African countries and the African Union (D4D Hub 2021).

The D4D Hub hosts three main projects. Aside from the African European Digital Innovation Bridge (AEDIB) and the Innovation Dialogue Europe Africa (IDEA), the EU–AU Data Flagship plays a key role in building common grounds between EU and African data policy frameworks. The EU–AU Data Flagship supports the "development of an EU/AU joint and non-binding data framework based on shared values and principles and with the objectives of protecting citizens' rights, assuring data sovereignty and supporting the creation of the African Single Digital Market" (D4D Hub 2021). Under the Flagship, the German development cooperation and the EC have started a project to develop a pan-African data governance model and to develop two national data governance strategies, the first one in Senegal. Keeping Senegal's cooperation with China on data centres in mind, it shows that African countries can choose between different partners for different purposes and digital development projects.

Furthermore, the AU and EU foreign ministers concluded at their meeting in October 2021 to support "further EU-AU cooperation on data to foster the development and implementation of harmonised data regulations on the African continent" (Council of the EU and European Council 2021, p. 8). Moreover, the German development cooperation supported the AU Commission (AUC) in developing the Continental Data Policy Framework (DataCipation) that is creating the guidelines for harmonised data regulations across the continent. This provides evidence that cooperation on data regulation has become a central element of the EU's D4D approach with African countries.

Besides, the EU is stepping up its efforts to strengthen connectivity in countries of the Global South. As discussed earlier, one of the latest moves to advance digital international partnerships is the Global Gateway, a connectivity initiative announced by the president of the EC at her State of the Union Address in September 2021. Just like the B3W initiative it is intended to counterbalance China's engagement in infrastructure and digital development in countries around the world (Farand 2021; Lau and Cokelaere 2021). The Global Gateway aims to build infrastructure and connectivity partnerships which will "create links and not dependencies" (EC 2021d) and plans to mobilise €300 billion between 2021 and 2027 for that purpose (EC 2021e). However, criticism has been raised that the Global Gateway merely repackages existing programmes (Kliem 2021). At the Sixth EU–AU Summit in February 2022, a €150 billion Global Gateway Investment package was announced for Africa tackling, amongst others, a "digital transformation that supports trusted connectivity through investments in infrastructures and an affordable and enhanced access to the digital and data economy while boosting digital entrepreneurship and skills" (EU and AU 2022, pp. 3-4).

These examples show that, while strengthening its own digital sovereignty, the EU has also expanded its international digital development cooperation in recent years. In this context, the EU relies on its experience and competence as a regulatory power and offers itself to African countries as a partner for the design of data regimes and markets. More and more, however, the perspective is gaining ground on the European side that this cannot be enough to counter China's strong influence in the African countries. Increasingly, large-scale infrastructure investments are being sought – although it is doubtful whether the EU can compete with China or the United States in terms of both the scope and the conditions for such investments. Where quantity cannot win, qualitative aspects could be the deciding factor. So far, however, it remains to be seen how the EU will implement its human-centred approach for the benefit of African countries in its investments in digital infrastructure.

2.5 Conclusion: Joint Action for Digital Sovereignty

Digital development in African countries is not independent of the general dynamics of digital geopolitics and the competition between the United States, China, and the EU to shape the global digital transformation. Developing and maintaining a strong digital sovereignty will therefore be critical for African countries to safeguard their development interests. In this endeavour, African countries are not passive pawns of the more powerful players – state and non-state – but can use their agency to develop things to their advantage. African countries, especially those with advanced digital ecosystems, can leverage bilateral and multilateral digital partnerships to contribute to their national economic and development priorities. However, Africa's capacity to act as a collective actor will be critical in shaping digital transformation at the regional level, as well as key digital policy issues, such as e-commerce regulation, at the global level. For Africa as a region, digital sovereignty is therefore not just the sum of individual countries' digital sovereignty. Rather, it results from collective action and the deliberate choice of policies and partnerships that strengthen collective interests. For this to succeed, African countries must find common ground on key digital policy issues – even if this requires significant delegation of power and concessions for the good of the region – and do so quickly, as the scope for shaping digital development is rapidly narrowing. Front-runner countries and initiatives can pave the way for stronger collective approaches.

Connectivity and digital partnership initiatives must be interpreted in light of digital geopolitics and the sovereignty interests of donor countries and investors. In the case of the EU and its digital development cooperation with African countries, it is in the EU's interest not only to promote the digital development of African countries, but also to support an alignment of European and African digital – and in particular data – policies. Strengthening the digital sovereignty of African countries – for example, by contributing to the development of digital skills and competencies, developing digital infrastructure, and promoting enabling regulatory environments – is therefore not a stand-alone objective. To ensure that these measures do not only serve the interests of the donor, the interests and development priorities of the African partners must be given a more central role in digital cooperation, and the dialogue on this must be intensified.

Note

1 The concept of digital geopolitics lacks a generally accepted definition. In this chapter it is understood as the "power politics of states to pursue their interests (…) and extend their influence in a (…) world networked by digital infrastructures, technologies, platforms and data streams" (Fritzsche and Spoiala 2021, 5).

References

Abimbola, Olumide, Aggad, Faten and Ndzendze, Bhaso (2021). What is Africa's digital agenda? Berlin. Available at: https://afripoli.org/uploads/publications/Africas_Digital_Agenda_final.pdf (Accessed: 04 October 2021).

Adegoke, Yinka (2021). The real reason China is pushing "digital sovereignty" in Africa. Available at: https://restofworld.org/2021/the-real-reason-china-is-pushing-digital-sovereignty-in-africa/ (Accessed: 12 January 2022).

Adeniran, Adedeji and Osakwe, Sone (2021). Why digitalization and digital governance are key to regional integration in Africa. Center for Global Development. Available at: https://www.cgdev.org/blog/why-digitalization-and-digital-governance-are-key-regional-integration-africa (Accessed: 5 April 2022).

African Group (2017). *The Work Programme on Electronic Commerce. Statement by the African Group.* World Trade Organization. Available at: https://www.tralac.org/images/Resources/MC11/mc11-work-programme-on-electronic-commerce-statement-by-the-african-group-6-december-2017.pdf (Accessed: 14 January 2022).

Agbebi, Motolani and Virtanen, Petri (2017). Dependency theory: A conceptual lens to understand China's presence in Africa? *Forum for Development Studies* 44(3), pp. 429–451. https://doi.org/10.1080/08039410.2017.1281161.

Aggad, Faten (2021). Africa's digital transformation risks becoming trapped in geopolitical competition. Available at: https://mg.co.za/africa/2021-02-08-africas-digital-transformation-risks-becoming-trapped-in-geopolitical-competition/ (Accessed: 15 January 2022).

AU (2020). The digital transformation strategy for Africa 2020–2030. Addis Ababa. Available at: https://au.int/sites/default/files/documents/38507-doc-dts-english.pdf (Accessed: 4 October 2021).

AU-EU DETF (2019). New Africa-Europe digital economy partnership. Accelerating the achievement of the sustainable development goals. European Commission. Brussels. Available at: https://digital-strategy.ec.europa.eu/en/library/new-africa-europe-digital-economy-partnership-report-eu-au-digital-economy-task-force (Accessed: 7 October 2021).

Ávila Pinto, Renata (2018). Digital sovereignty or digital colonialism? New tensions of privacy, security and national policies. *SUR* 27, pp. 15–27. Available at https://

sur.conectas.org/wp-content/uploads/2018/07/sur-27-ingles-renata-avila-pinto.pdf (Accessed: 10 January 2022).

Bastion, Geraldine de and Mukku, Sreekanth (2020). Data and the Global South: Key issues for inclusive digital development. Available at: https://us.boell.org/sites/default /files/2021-01/20201216-HB-broschure-data%20and%20global%20south-A4-01 .pdf (Accessed: 22 March 2022).

Basu, Arindrajit (2021). Sovereignty in a 'Datafied' world. *Observer Research Foundation. ORF Issue Brief 501.* Available at: https://www.orfonline.org/research/sovereignty-in -a-datafied-world/ (Accessed: 24 January 2022).

Bendiek, Annegret, Godehardt, Nadine and Schulze, David (2019). The age of digital geopolitics & proxy war between US and China. Available at: http://www.ipsnews .net/2019/07/age-digital-geopolitics-proxy-war-us-china/ (Accessed: 22 March 2022).

Bratton, Benjamin H. (2015). *The Stack. On Software and Sovereignty.* Cambridge, MA: MIT Press.

Brown, William (2012). A question of agency: Africa in international politics. *Third World Quarterly* 33(10), 1889–1908. https://doi.org/10.1080/01436597.2012.728322.

Chipaike, Ronald and Knowledge, Matarutse H. (2018). The question of African agency in international relations. *Cogent Social Sciences* 4(1), pp. 1–16. https://doi.org/10.1080 /23311886.2018.1487257.

Couldry, Nick and Mejias, Ulises A. (2019). Making data colonialism liveable: How might data's social order be regulated? *Internet Policy Review* 8(2). https://doi.org/10 .14763/2019.2.1411.

Couldry, Nick and Mejias, Ulises Ali (2021). The decolonial turn in data and technology research: What is at stake and where is it heading? *Information, Communication & Society*, 1–17. https://doi.org/10.1080/1369118X.2021.1986102.

Council of the EU and European Council (2021). The Second African Union – European Union Foreign Affairs Ministerial Meeting. Kigali, Rwanda, 25–26 October 2021. Joint Communiqué. Available at: https://www.consilium.europa.eu/media /52671/20211026-au-eu-fam-meeting_joint-communiqu%C3%A9.pdf (Accessed: 24 January 2022).

Couture, Stephane and Toupin, Sophie (2019). What does the notion of "sovereignty" mean when referring to the digital? *New Media & Society* 21(10), pp. 1–18. https://doi .org/10.1177/1461444819865984.

Creemers, Rogier (2020). China's conception of cyber sovereignty: Rhetoric and realization. In: Dennis Broeders and Bibi den van Berg (Eds.). *Governing Cyberspace. Behavior, Power, and Diplomacy.* Lanham/Boulder/New York/London: Rowman & Littlefield, pp. 107–142.

CSEA (2021). Strengthening data governance in Africa. *Project Inception Report.* Abuja. Available at: https://cseaafrica.org/wp-content/uploads/2021/08/Strengthening -Regional-Data-Governance-in-Africa-1.pdf (Accessed: 14 January 2022).

D4D Hub (2021). Eight innovative projects. Available at: https://d4dhub.eu/projects (Accessed: 5 October 2021).

EC (2017). Digital4Development: Mainstreaming digital technologies and services into EU Development Policy. Commission staff working paper. European Commission. Brussels. Available at: ec.europa.eu/newsroom/document.cfm?doc_id=44806 (Accessed: 7 July 2021).

EC (2020). *Shaping Europe's Digital Future. Communication from the Commission to the European Parliament, the Council, the European Economic and Social Committee and the Committee of the Regions.* Brussels: European Commission. Available at: https://eur-lex

.europa.eu/legal-content/EN/TXT/PDF/?uri=CELEX:52020DC0067&from=EN (Accessed: 29 September 2021).

EC (2021a). *2030 Digital Compass: The European way for the Digital Decade*. Brussels: European Commission. Available at: https://eur-lex.europa.eu/resource.html?uri =cellar:12e835e2-81af-11eb-9ac9-01aa75ed71a1.0001.02/DOC_1&format=PDF (Accessed: 24 October 2021).

EC (2021b). Europe's digital decade: Digital targets for 2030. Brussels. Available at: https://ec.europa.eu/info/strategy/priorities-2019-2024/europe-fit-digital-age/ europes-digital-decade-digital-targets-2030_en (Accessed: 30 June 2021).

EC (2021c). Global digital partnerships. European Commission. Brussels. Available at: https://ec.europa.eu/international-partnerships/topics/digital-partnerships_en (Accessed: 5 April 2022).

EC (2021d). State of the Union address. Strengthening the soul of our union. European Commission. Strasbourg. Available at: https://ec.europa.eu/commission/presscorner/ detail/en/SPEECH_21_4701 (Accessed 28. October 2021).

EC (2021e). Global Gateway: Up to €300 billion for the European Union's strategy to boost sustainable links around the world. Available at: https://ec.europa.eu/ commission/presscorner/detail/en/ip_21_6433 (Accessed: 14 January 2022).

EEAS (2016). Shared vision, common action: A stronger Europe. A global strategy for the European union's foreign and security policy. European External Action Service. Available at: https://eeas.europa.eu/sites/default/files/eugs_review_web_0.pdf (Accessed: 10 January 2022).

EU/AU (2022). 6th European Union - African Union Summit: A Joint Vision for 2030. Available at: https://www.consilium.europa.eu/media/54412/final_declaration-en .pdf (Accessed: 19 February 2022).

Farand, Chloé (2021). As EU seeks to rival China's infrastructure offer, Africans are sceptical. Available at: https://www.euractiv.com/section/energy-environment/news /as-eu-seeks-to-rival-chinas-infrastructure-offer-africans-are-sceptical/ (Accessed: 10 January 2022).

Fritzsche, Kerstin and Spoiala, Daniel (2021). Digital for development: An analysis from a geopolitical perspective. Berlin. Available at: https://www.izt.de/fileadmin /downloads/pdf/2021_IZT_Digital_for_Development_Analysis_from_geopolitical _perspective_final.pdf (Accessed: 1 December 2021).

Iyer, Neema and Achieng, Garnett/Borokini, Favour/Ludger, Uri (2021). Automated imperialism, Expansionist dreams: Exploring digital extractivism in Africa. Available at https://archive.pollicy.org/wp-content/uploads/2021/06/Automated-Imperialism -Expansionist-Dreams-Exploring-Digital-Extractivism-in-Africa.pdf (Accessed 14. January 2022).

Jarke, Matthias and Otto, Boris/Ram, Sudha (2019). Data sovereignty and data space ecosystems. *Business & Information Systems Engineering* 61 (5), 549–550. https://doi.org /10.1007/s12599-019-00614-2.

Johnson, Chernay and Bester, Hennie/van Vuuren, Pieter Janse/Dunn, Matthew (2020). Africa's digital platforms. Overview of emerging trends in the market. Available at: https://cenfri.org/wp-content/uploads/Africas-digital-platforms-trends-report.pdf (Accessed: 12 Janurary 2022).

Kaloudis, Martin (2021). Digital sovereignty: European Union's action plan needs a common understanding to succeed. *History Compass* 19(12). https://doi.org/10.1111 /hic3.12698.

Kathure, Megan (2021). Africa's digital sovereignty: Elusive or a stark possibility through the AfCFTA? Available at: https://www.afronomicslaw.org/category/analysis/

africas-digital-sovereignty-elusive-or-stark-possibility-through-afcfta   (Accessed: 12 January 2022).

Kimeu, Jackson (2021). The growth and demand for data centres in Africa. Available at   https://www.cioafrica.co/the-growth-and-demand-for-data-centres-in-africa/ (Accessed: 13. January 2022).

Kliem, Frederick (2021). Europe's global gateway: Complementing or competing with BRI? Available at https://thediplomat.com/2021/12/europes-global-gateway -complementing-or-competing-with-bri/ (Accessed: 14 January 2022).

Korovkin, Vladimir (2019). National digital economy strategies: A survey of Africa. ORF issue brief. Available at: https://www.orfonline.org/research/national-digital -economy-strategies-a-survey-of-africa-53468/ (Accessed: 5 April 2022).

Kuo, Mercy A. (2021). Global gateway: The EU alternative to China's BRI. Insights from Benjamin Barton. *The Diplomat*. Available at https://thediplomat.com/2021 /09/global-gateway-the-eu-alternative-to-chinas-bri/ (Accessed: 24   October 2021).

Lau, Stuart and Cokelaere, Hanne (2021). EU launches 'Global Gateway' to counter China's Belt and Road. POLITICO of 15.09.2021. Available at: https://www .politico.eu/article/eu-launches-global-gateway-to-counter-chinas-belt-and-road/ (Accessed: 28 October 2021).

Liu, Jinhe (2020). China's data localization. *Chinese Journal of Communication* 13(1), pp. 84–103. https://doi.org/10.1080/17544750.2019.1649289.

Ministry of Communications and Digital Technologies (2021). Invitation to submit written submissions on the proposed national data and cloud policy. Available at: https://www.gov.za/sites/default/files/gcis_document/202104/44389gon206.pdf (Accessed: 13 January 2022).

Ministry of Justice (2021). Law relating to the protection of personal data and privacy. Kigali, Rwanda. Available at https://cyber.gov.rw/fileadmin/user_upload/NCSA /Documents/Laws/OG_Special_of_15.10.2021_Amakuru_bwite.pdf   (Accessed: 13 January 2022).

Monyae, David (2021). Africa's digital sovereignty a timely and relevant debate. Available at   https://www.businesslive.co.za/bd/opinion/2021-09-27-david-monyae-africas -digital-sovereignty-a-timely-and-relevant-debate/ (Accessed: 13 January 2022).

Mwai, Collins (2019). Kagame: The Mara Phone is a milestone for Rwanda. Available at: https://www.newtimes.co.rw/news/kagame-mara-phone-milestone-rwanda (Accessed: 15 January 2022).

Ndemo, Bitange (2021). Digital transformation and cyberstability: Effects on economic development in Africa. In: Alexander Klimburg (Ed.). *New Conditions and Constellations in Cyber*. The Hague: The Hague Centre for Strategic Studies, pp. 123–133.

Okeke, Chinweizu (2021). Pan-Africanism in foreign policy. African Organizations as Pan-African agents in the 'New Scramble'. Available at: https://republic.com.ng/ february-march-2021/pan-africanism-in-foreign-policy/?mc_cid=abdc5ba651&mc _eid=34931a3a86 (Accessed: 13. January 2022).

Olayinka, David-West and Peter Evans (2015). *The Rise of African Platforms: A Regional Survey*. https://doi.org/10.13140/RG.2.2.23965.72165.

Pohle, Julia (2020). Digital sovereignty. A new key concept of digital policy in Germany and Europe. Berlin. Available at: https://www.kas.de/documents/252038/7995358 /Digital+sovereignty.pdf/a8d0cb4b-c777-3e72-1bc7-b5fda656329a?version=1.0&t =1608034389334 (Accessed: 15 August 2021).

Pohle, Julia and Thiel, Thorsten (2020). Digital sovereignty. *Internet Policy Review* 9(4). https://doi.org/10.14763/2020.4.1532.

Republic of Kenya (2019). *Data Protection Act*. Nairobi. Available at: http://kenyalaw.org
/kl/fileadmin/pdfdownloads/Acts/2019/TheDataProtectionAct__No24of2019.pdf
(Accessed: 13 January 2022).

Reuters (2021). Senegal aims for digital sovereignty with new China-backed data centre.
Available at: https://www.reuters.com/article/senegal-datacenter-idINL5N2O44D3
(Accessed: 14 January 2022).

Smart Africa (2013). *The Smart Africa Manifesto*. Endorsed by Heads of State and
Government in Kigali on 29th October 2013. Available at: https://smartafrica.org
/2019/IMG/pdf/smart_africa_manifesto_2013_-_english_version.pdf   (Accessed:
22 March 2022).

Smart Africa (2020). *Overview*. Available at: https://smartafrica.org/about/overview/
(Accessed: 22 March 2022).

Tanchum, Michaël (2022). Gateway to growth: How the European Green Deal can
strengthen Africa's and Europe's economies. Available at: https://ecfr.eu/publication
/gateway-to-growth-how-the-european-green-deal-can-strengthen-africas-and
-europes-economies/ (Accessed: 19 February 2022).

Teevan, Chloe (2021). Europe, Africa and digital sovereignty. Available at: https://ettg
.eu/blog-posts/europe-africa-and-digital-sovereignty/ (Accessed: 13 January 2022).

The White House (2021). *Fact sheet: President Biden and G7 Leaders Launch Build Back Better
World (B3W) Partnership*. Washington, DC. Available at: https://www.whitehouse.gov
/briefing-room/statements-releases/2021/06/12/fact-sheet-president-biden-and-g7
-leaders-launch-build-back-better-world-b3w-partnership (Accessed: 2 July 2021).

UNCTAD (2019). *Digital Economy Report 2019. Value Creation and Capture: Implications for
Developing Countries*. New York. Available at: https://unctad.org/system/files/official
-document/der2019_en.pdf (Accessed: 14 April 2021).

Velluet, Quentin (2021). Can Africa salvage its digital sovereignty? Available at: https://
www.theafricareport.com/80606/can-africa-salvage-its-digital-sovereignty/
(Accessed: 22 March 2022).

Wu, Emily (2021). *Sovereignty and Data Localization*. Cambridge, MA: Belfer Center for
Science and International Affairs, Harvard Kennedy School. Available at: https://
www.belfercenter.org/sites/default/files/2021-07/SovereigntyLocalization.pdf
(Accessed: 13 January 2022).

Zuboff, Shoshana (2019). *The Age of Surveillance Capitalism. The Fight for a Human Future
at the New Frontier of Power*. New York: PublicAffairs.

3

THE SPREAD OF CHINESE SURVEILLANCE TOOLS IN AFRICA

A Focus on Ethiopia and Kenya

Bulelani Jili

3.1 Introduction

To date, 16 African countries are using Chinese digital surveillance technology (Feldstein, 2020). The digital surveillance technologies arrive predominantly under Huawei's "smart city" banner, as a development infrastructure and supplementary technology to the Belt and Road project. Chinese officials began promoting the "Digital Silk Road" (DRS) initiative in 2015 (Kurlantzick, 2020), as part of the Belt and Road project, aiming to expand Chinese corporate engagement globally by promoting internet connectivity, digital economies, so-called smart cities, and artificial intelligence. Digital infrastructure, from this perspective, is how politicians plan and imagine the future of African cities. Research and media coverage disproportionally focus on Chinese reasons and incentives for the proliferation of surveillance technology (Biryabarema, 2019; Feldstein, 2019; Parkison, Bariyo and Chin, 2019; Mozur, Kessel, and Chan, 2019). This chapter, however, examines Beijing's growing geopolitical footprint on the continent. It investigates the part played by local demand factors that contribute to the growing use of digital surveillance technology. The work lends weight to an examination of the spread of surveillance technologies as a dynamic multilateral social process.

Based on a review of literature, the chapter investigates the impact of Chinese surveillance tools in Africa, focusing on Kenya and Ethiopia's capital cities: Nairobi and Addis Ababa, respectively. Both countries have received substantial financial and technical assistance from China to build their digital infrastructure. In Nairobi the digital infrastructure is Huawei-driven initiatives, consisting of fibre-optic cables, surveillance cameras, interconnected tracking devices, software, and cloud storage systems. The aim is that these digital infrastructures will buttress law and order in an open society. By contrast, Addis Ababa has

DOI: 10.4324/9781003274322-3

sought to expand its digital infrastructure, which consist of fibre-optic cables and cloud storage systems, while maintaining a state monopoly. In both cases, the infrastructure is perceived to be responding to state inefficiency, ambitions, and concerns around state security. The difference in local conditions and political arrangement raises important questions: What effects can be observed as digital infrastructure becomes enmeshed in local technology, discourses, and institutions? What similarities are observable? What differences in application of technology are partly contingent on differences in sociopolitical environments?

The chapter is divided into three parts. I begin with a brief review of the literature. Then, I discuss China's engagement with Africa because of its domestic circumstances and transnational systems of investment. By investigating both cases (Ethiopia and Kenya) and seeking to situate the emergence of digital surveillance technologies in a web of local relations, I aim to illustrate the factors that determine the distribution of technologies and the future of Africa–China relations. Finally, I examine the consequences of China's engagement with Kenya and Ethiopia in digital technologies. I attempt to demonstrate that Chinese companies and government are locally engaged and have agreed to support the visions of the African host countries. This argument challenges the idea that China simply aims to export a model of digital governance and surveillance.

The chapter examines instead how Beijing engages on the terms made available both in Kenya and in Ethiopia. Critically, however, I point out that China's locally responsive engagements do not necessarily result in neutral outcomes. How China chooses to define neutrality is contingent on the promotion of political equality among nations, which aims to maintain economic activity between Africa and China. This posture systematically presents Beijing as an amiable development partner while also de-emphasising its preference for state-driven capital. In the absence of clear and robust privacy and data protection measures, this tendency to privilege state actors regardless of the political regime type leaves many people vulnerable to the misuse of surveillance technologies, even though the Chinese partners profess neutral intentions. Indeed, even in the context of a democratic government, the bolstering of state power reinforces the ambitions of the state towards utilising digital technologies to conduct surveillance for political and economic ends.

3.2 Africa–China Relations

The heightened scholarly attention being paid to Africa–China relations is chiefly inspired by the growing trade, investment, and aid relations. Current research has many threads of thought: one major line considers the contemporary challenges surrounding Africa–China relations. This is best represented by remarks on China's assumed neocolonial motivations that seek to extract mineral resources, which exacerbate inequalities, environmental degradation, and political instability (Ado and Su, 2016; Klare and Volman, 2006; Rich and Recker, 2013; Rotberg, 2009). These authors argue that new aid and investments simply reproduce the same exploitative relations of dependence that characterised Africa's relationship with Europe and the United States. In digital and telecommunication discourses, the discourse is about China's export of an authoritarian version of digital surveillance practices (Biryabarema, 2019; Parkison, Bariyo, and Chin, 2019; Mozur, Kessel, and Chan, 2019). Most accounts presume a coordinated effort between the Chinese Communist Party (CCP) and Huawei. From this vantage point, the adoption of digital surveillance technologies hinges on Beijing's objective to promote its version of digital surveillance via corporate–public partnerships. Yet, critical studies illustrate that there is in fact little evidence that demonstrates Beijing's strict interest in exporting practices and models of development (Brautigam, 2011; Gagliardone, 2019; Mohan and Lampert, 2013).

Other work relates to the agency of African governments in shaping Chinese bilateral relations (Corkin, 2016; Gadzala, 2015; Kragelund, 2015; Mohan and Lampert, 2012; Phillips, 2019). By utilising the concept of agency, literature in this category examines the relationship between enduring geopolitical structures and local efforts in shaping development outcomes. While these studies draw attention to African agency and the asymmetric conditions of China–Africa relations, they tend to ignore non-state actors and unduly focus on Chinese "grand" strategy at the expense of local public and private actors (Mohan, 2015).

Taylor (2006) rejects the idea that China has a grand strategy towards Africa. He asserts that a nuanced analysis of Africa–China relations transcends talk of such a grand "Chinese strategy", which invokes fears among proponents of the liberal order. Indeed, the asymmetric conditions between Africa and China should inspire some scepticism (Chipaike and Knowledge, 2018; Mthembu and Mabera, 2021) – but not a scepticism that is simply contingent on assumed Chinese neocolonial behaviour. Rather, I attempt to explore the degree to which the interests of African digital ecosystem actors are shaping Africa–China relations and yet conditioned by enduring local and global structural arrangements. To presume agency without illuminating the obstacles to its expression romanticises African actors. On the other hand, some recognition of such agency is salient in discourses on structural analyses and representations of Africa and its people. The chapter pays attention to both the broader context of Chinese corporate expansion and the local conditions where multiple actors, discourses, and partnerships work towards establishing digital surveillance practices.

3.3 China's Expansion into Africa

China's expansion into Africa's digital infrastructure sector has been rapid, but not necessarily linear or coordinated in its operations. The push consists of various actors in the public and private arena who have pursued distinct goals. For example, the "Go Out" strategy in 1999, later incorporated into the tenth five-year plan, urged Chinese enterprises to invest abroad as a way to strengthen China's global business presence and to foster Beijing's integration into the global economy

(Wang and Hu, 2017). Drawing on Harvey's (2003) concept of the spatio-temporal "fix", Taylor and Zajontz (2020) interpret China's push abroad via private corporate entities as a necessary element to establish channels for investment as a way to address domestic economic challenges. Precisely, surplus capital was lent abroad to create new commercial and productive enterprises. The promise of higher rates of profit engendered an incentive to support capital flows to Africa. He Yafei, China's Vice Minister of Foreign Affairs, echoed this sentiment in a carefully worded 2014 op-ed piece, when arguing to "'move out' China's economic overcapacity on the basis of its development strategy abroad and foreign policy" (He, 2014).

He Yafei's reading conceptualises the Go Out strategy and the Belt and Road Initiative (BRI) as a push for new markets, consumers, and profit. Beijing's investments in Africa are directed towards infrastructure and extraction to facilitate the needs of its domestic economy. Taylor and Zajontz (2020), like He, see the move to novel geographies as a possible ameliorant to China's own economic challenges. This approach draws attention to the current iteration of global capital and asks how the structural features of the economy motivate Beijing's actions in Africa. This is a salient intervention because many studies decontextualise China's behaviour on the global state; they assume its exceptional quality, while not closely examining the political and economic features that condition its actions.

President Xi Jinping announced the BRI during official visits to Kazakhstan and Indonesia in 2013. Beijing's most ambitious transnational infrastructure building project, according to Huang (2016), includes networks of railways, highways, and energy pipelines. The initiative mainly seeks to expand intercontinental connectivity with China and the circulation of the renminbi, the Chinese currency (Yu, 2018). As a continuation of Beijing's commercial interests abroad, the vast collection of development and investment initiatives stretch from Central Asia to Africa (Cox, 2018). At the same time, Beijing hopes that these global networks will link up with its own neglected Western regions, promoting economic development in places like Xinjiang, which have historically provoked separatist violence (Chatzky and McBride, 2020). This push abroad is in part about ameliorating domestic concerns, while also establishing China's global business presence.

In 2015, Chinese officials began promoting the "Digital Silk Road" (DSR) initiative as a supplementary project to the BRI. The DSR aims to foster internet connectivity, digital economies, smart cities, and artificial intelligence (Hillman, 2021). Reports indicate that five African countries (Angola, Ethiopia, Nigeria, Zambia, and Zimbabwe) have signed DSR agreements with China (Garcia, 2019). Yet, it must be said that the exact number of agreements is hard to verify because many of these memoranda of understandings (MOUs) are unreported (Kurlantzick, 2020). Although BRI and DSR constitute key elements of China's expanding geopolitical footprint, BRI and DSR have no central governing institutions. China has not published a master list of BRI and DRS projects, the terms of which are often negotiated behind closed doors.

Even though natural resources continue to be core interests of China's engagements in Africa, its interests in telecommunications have rapidly expanded. In 2006, the third Forum on China–Africa Cooperation (FOCAC), held in Beijing, marked this diversification of investments. China announced that it would grow its investments in multiple African sectors, including ICT, medicine, and renewable energy (FOCAC, 2006). Alden and Large (2011) claim that China's growing investments and strategic partnerships are not simply a means to secure natural resources and novel consumers, but also a strategy to win favour with African countries. Likewise, Lee (2019) investigates China's diplomatic goodwill efforts in Zambia. Convincingly, she argues that Beijing's ambitions are not always defined by corporate interests or immediate domestic needs. Challenging conventional assumptions about China's strict economic interests in Africa, Lee maintains that the Chinese state capital is also concerned with promoting political goodwill with African governments. Through ethnographic studies of the mining industries of Zambia, Lee (2019) demonstrates how Chinese investors made more compromises to accommodate Zambian state and labour demands than Western private corporations did.

3.4 China's ICT Investments in Africa

Ethiopia and Kenya have limited raw materials bases. Both nations have enjoyed considerable Chinese investments in the ICT sector (Figure 3.1). Regarding digital infrastructure, the evidence suggests that both Chinese companies and government appear to have agreed to support the visions of host African countries. The cases of Kenya and Ethiopia challenge assertions that China seeks to export a model of digital governance and surveillance. It illustrates how China engages

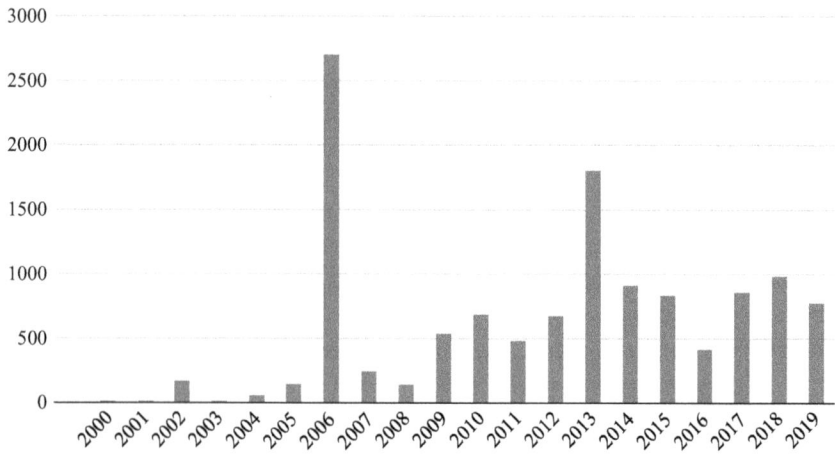

FIGURE 3.1   Chinese ICT Loans to Africa 2000–2019 (USD Million). *Source: China Africa Research Initiative:* https://chinaafricaloandata.bu.edu/.

on the terms made available in local contexts, which result in both locally and globally determined digital infrastructure projects.

For Chinese corporations that have expanded into Africa, profit margins remain relatively high, even in challenging political environments. Surveys conducted on Chinese enterprises in Africa indicate that profit margins are as high as 20%, leading companies like Huawei to expand their operations on the continent. Kirby (2020) contends that Huawei was not shy about pursuing profit in politically challenging environments. Its success was partly contingent on the absence of Western competition, which was averse to African political instabilities. As Ren Zhengfei, the founder of Huawei, put it: "many wars broke out in Africa in the 1990s. All the Western companies pulled out of the market, so we took that opportunity and sold some of our products" (as cited in Kirby, Chan, and Mchugh, 2020, p. 5). Huawei also sold their products 20–30% cheaper than Western companies remaining in Africa. By 2005, Huawei's international sales exceeded its domestic sales. It is these achievements abroad that garnered Beijing's attention (Huawei, 2020). As early as 2004, the China Development Bank opened a USD 10 billion credit line to customers of Huawei's digital products (Hu, 2011). Mackinnon (2019) notes that Huawei has built 70% of Africa's 4G networks, which vastly outpaces Western competitors. A 2016 World Bank report notes that, compared to Huawei, "other foreign firms with shorter time horizons and a higher profit requirement face a unique challenge when competing for contracts in Sub-Saharan Africa" (Sanghi and Johnson, 2016, p. 20).

Chinese loans mostly offered by the EXIM bank amount to USD 9.1 billion in the ICT sector in Africa (CARI, 2018). As shown in Figure 3.1, significant investments were made in 2006 and 2013. The remaining years between 2000 and 2018 were marked by moderate investments. This fluctuating trend is in part a consequence of local interest in digital infrastructure; a conclusion that is antithetical to established presumptions about China's steadily rising investments. Figure 3.2 shows the total number of loans made to Africa in the last two decades. According to SAIS-CARI, China has committed USD 153 billion to Africa between 2000 and 2019. Despite this large economic footprint, there is little data on the specifics of China's lending in the public domain. After rapid growth, annual lending commitments to Africa peaked in 2013, the year the BRI was launched. China's lending to African governments fell by 30% in 2019. China has sharply curtailed lending to the continent partly due to debt sustainability concerns (Song, 2021; Yun, 2020). This observation about the oscillating quantity of ICT loans is reflected in the cases of Ethiopia and Kenya. Both cases show that loans are provided within contexts where Beijing is aiming to advance diplomatic relations with Africa, Chinese corporations are expanding their geopolitical footprint, and local Ethiopian and Kenyan actors are demanding digital infrastructural investments to support development ambitions. I discuss the two cases further in the next section.

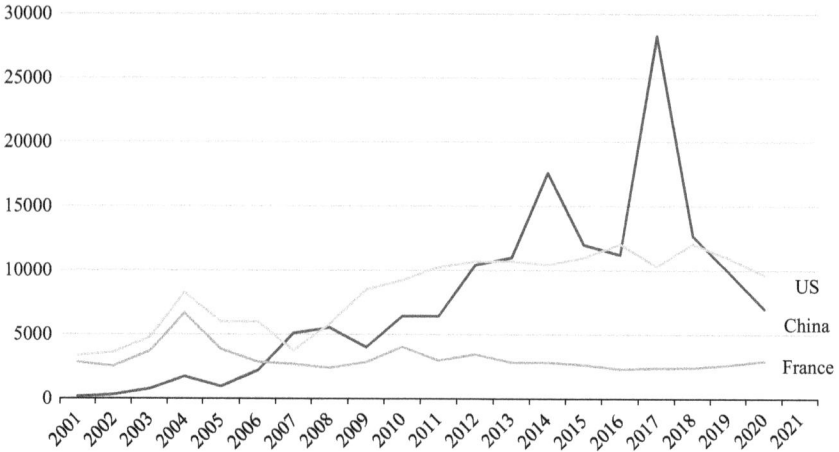

FIGURE 3.2 Total Chinese Loans and U.S. & French Aid to Africa. *Sources: China Africa Research Initiative,* https://chinaafricaloandata.bu.edu/; *OECD Statistics, total official development flows by country and region,* https://stats.oecd.org/Index.aspx?DataSetCode=REF_TOTAL_ODF.

3.5 Ethiopia's Digital Infrastructure Projects

The Bringing Internet to Ethiopia (BITE) initiative launched in 1995 by the Ethiopian government aimed to produce an actionable policy to engender the infrastructure conditions necessary to support connectivity (ITU, 2002). Initial discussions were favourable to a multi-stakeholder approach. However, the Ethiopian People's Revolutionary Democratic Front (EPRDF) rejected the idea of a privately owned internet provider. As a result, a public network service provider was proposed by BITE, which put forward the idea of a not-for-profit service provider with the chief objective of supporting public interest and development goals. The Ethiopian government rejected the BITE initiative and instead decided to lead the development and management of the internet itself. This decision vexed private actors and civil society organisations seeking to import best practices and digital infrastructure (Gagliardone, 2019). Ultimately, the choice was predicated on the government's desire to maintain a monopolistic grip on digital technologies.

In 2006, the Ethiopian Telecommunication Corporation and Chinese telecom giant Zhongxing Telecommunication Equipment Corporation (ZTE) signed the largest agreement in African telecommunication history. Backed by the China Development Bank, ZTE (partially state-owned) offered a loan of USD 1.5 billion to support the replacement and expansion of Ethiopia's telecommunication infrastructure (Dalton, 2014). The loan was disbursed in three phases and expected to be repaid over a 13-year period. The first phase was branded the "Millennium Plan", which implied digital infrastructure with the capacity to make development viable by 11 September 2007, the date marking a new millennium on the Ethiopian calendar (Gagliardone and Brhane, 2021). The first phase was to install around 2,000 kilometres of fibre-optic cable, which aimed to connect Ethiopia's 13 largest cities (Cotterill, 2021; Foster and Morella, 2010; Gagliardone, 2019). The second and third phases expanded coverage to include Ethiopia's rural areas. New digital infrastructure capacity was now able to support a million internet broadband users and 20 million mobile users from an earlier 1.2 million.

In 2011, Ethio-Telecom, the country's sole telecom operator, issued a tender to further augment its network capacity to support around 50 million subscribers by 2015 (Human Rights Watch, 2014). Like ZTE, the tender was contingent on vendor-financing. Unlike in 2006, this time a public tender process was launched. Ethiopia ended ZTE's monopoly by inviting Huawei. The tender was jointly won by the Chinese firms, ZTE and Huawei. Together Huawei and ZTE pledged a total of USD 1.6 billion (Dalton, 2014). This deal was backed by concessionary loans from the EXIM bank. ZTE and Huawei agreed to offer USD 800 million each. Interestingly, it was normal for ZTE and Huawei to compete, especially at home. The Ethiopian government invited Huawei because of its growing reputation on the continent, but also because of ZTE's poor job in 2006 (Dalton, 2014).

The loans are partly provided to support Chinese corporate expansion abroad, but also to improve China's diplomatic efforts in Africa. Beijing appears to present itself as a peaceful rising power and impartial development partner willing to meet the demands of African actors (Jakobson, 2009). The loans are offered without political conditions.[1] This "no strings attached" approach has empowered African partners, like Ethiopia, to utilise Beijing's finance to pursue domestic ICT projects while simultaneously also offering legitimacy to Beijing's affable image. This image is developed in contrast to traditional Western partners, which condition aid and loans, asking African actors to adopt particular market and democratic reforms (Taylor, 2009). The lack of political conditions attached to the loans obscures the impact of Chinese engagement. Chinese state-led financial and technical help tends to benefit state actors over private enterprises. China's seemingly neutral engagement means that it seeks to uphold a strict distinction between political conditions and funding. It does not decide how its technologies are put to commercial and political use.

During this time, Ethiopia was also able to work with partners besides China in establishing its surveillance practices. The work by Citizen Lab, a Canadian information controls laboratory, illustrates Ethiopia's aptitude to combine diversely sourced digital infrastructure and surveillance technology. The government has acquired monitoring tools through various channels, namely, the UK- and German-based Gamma International FinFishers company; Cyberbit, an Israel-based cybersecurity enterprise; and the Italian-based Hacking Team Remote-Control System (Citizen Lab, 2014; Horne, 2014). These systems – as much as any provided by China – boost Ethiopia's governance and surveillance capacities and enable access to files on targeted laptops. They also log keystrokes and passwords to turn on webcams and microphones by stealth. These tools, critically, run on Chinese-funded ICT infrastructure (Human Rights Watch, 2014).

Researchers have studied the Ethiopian government's malware campaign, which targeted activists, lawyers, and political opponents (Citizen Lab, 2017). Reports describe how the state uses emails containing spyware posing as Adobe Flash updates and PDF plugins. Several ethnic Oromo activists like Jawar Mohammed, an Oromo activist and executive director of the US-based Oromia Media Network (OMN), were targeted by the Ethiopian government (Human Rights Watch, 2017). These new digital surveillance practices follow a history of surveillance practices aimed at undermining civil liberties (Hawaz and Xi, 2020; Human Rights Watch, 2014).

Evidence leaked by Edward Snowden indicates that it was not China and Europe alone that supported Ethiopia's surveillance practices. The U.S. National Security Agency (NSA) established the Deployed Signals Intelligence Operations Center in Addis Ababa (Turse, 2017). This began as a meagre counterterrorism undertaking that eventually grew into an operation involving eight U.S. military personnel and 103 Ethiopians surveilling Somalia, Sudan, and Yemen by 2005 (Turse, 2017). In exchange for intelligence and an advantageous location that offered unique access to targets, the NSA provided Ethiopia with training and technology to conduct digital surveillance. This shows Ethiopia's hybridised surveillance system, and its diversely sourced technology from China and the West.

The brief progress made in attaining peace and democratising Ethiopian society by current prime minister Abiy Ahmed is slipping in the face of the 2020 Tigray crisis. Since Ahmed's ascendance to power, Ethiopia has embarked on a series of liberalising reforms that have opened the market. This is exemplified by a bid issued to privatise the state-owned Ethio-Telecom, appointing international firms like KPMG to lead the transformation. This change hinges on the newly awarded operating licence, which was given to a consortium led by Kenya's Safaricom, UK's Vodafone Group, and Japan's Sumitomo that included financing from the U.S. Development Finance Corporation (DFC). The winning bid was an USD 850 million offer with a promise to invest USD 8 billion over the next ten years (Woo and Wexler, 2021). The losing bidder was South Africa's MTN Group whose proposal was financed in part by the Silk Road Fund, a Chinese state investment group. Whether this is indeed an inflection point is a pending matter. The Western-backed consortium marks a push to challenge Beijing's economic influence in Africa (Olander, 2021). It must be made clear that one more licence still needs to be announced. It is widely expected that bids, which include MTN, and Silk Road Fund will be more competitive in the next round. If successful, it is likely that Huawei's digital infrastructure will be used to build the networks.

China has indeed become the largest partner of Ethiopia's ICT development ambitions. Without the EXIM bank's concessionary loans, Ethiopia would not have had the financial means to realise its digital infrastructure monopoly

(Thakur, 2009). Elsewhere on the continent, including Kenya, a liberalisation strategy that relied on multiple private and public partners has driven the establishment of digital infrastructure. China's financial support and Huawei's technical provision have enabled the development of Ethiopia's telecommunication infrastructure, and with it, the State's means to surveil and retain control over the digital infrastructure.

3.6 Kenya's Digital Infrastructure Projects

In the case of Kenya, the Kenya Communication Act of 1998 put an end to the Kenya Posts and Telecommunication Corporation (KPTC), a state-run monopoly (Waema, 2005). This liberalisation strategy allowed the Kenyan state to take a leading role in shaping Information and Communications Technology (ICT) policies that aimed at privatising state-owned enterprises (Waema, 2005). Through the docking of four fibre-optic submarine cables between 2009 and 2011, the government was able to create a relatively competitive telecommunication sector that improved internet connectivity and affordability: competition among local and international firms began driving down the cost of phone calls and made internet services affordable for a larger portion of the population (Lancaster, 2017). Consequently, the sector's regulator reduced interconnection tariffs and instituted a range of regulations aimed at developing further competition.

Despite these policy changes in the ICT sector, the Kenyan government in 2006 did not have the infrastructural capacity to realise these development ambitions. Before 2009, Kenya relied on satellite technology for connectivity, which resulted in limited connectivity and was available at prohibitive costs for most citizens. This necessitated the need to transition from narrowband, which operates on satellite technology, to fibre-optic-powered broadband. China's chief entrance into the Kenyan ICT market came through the docking of fibre-optic cables. Led by Huawei and ZTE, the docking of four fibre-optic submarine cables between 2009 and 2011, enabled the government to create a relatively competitive telecommunication sector that improved internet connectivity and affordability: competition among local and international firms began driving down the cost of phone calls and made internet services affordable for a larger portion of the population (Lancaster, 2017).

Huawei and ZTE were jointly contracted to build new digital infrastructures. The Chinese EXIM bank was instrumental in making this infrastructure financially feasible for Nairobi, as was the case in Ethiopia, where Huawei and ZTE worked to expand internet connectivity. Bidding and winning the contract, the Chinese companies worked with the French corporation Sagem to create Kenya's first National Optic Fibre Backbone Infrastructure (NOFBI), which brought high-speed connectivity to the country's largest cities. The government started by building the NOFBI, initially to interconnect the former provincial headquarters and later to the county headquarters. This novel capacity allowed for e-government projects across the country (ICT Authority, 2021). Each company was expected to manage a different region. Sagem laid the cables for the Coastal and Northeastern region, ZTE worked on the West, and Huawei handled Nairobi and the central parts of the country (Okuttah, 2012; Wahito, 2012). The second phase of extending connectivity was directly funded by the EXIM bank. It offered USD 71 million to cover 36 administrative districts that would provide high-speed internet in rural parts of the country. A condition to this loan was that Huawei had to be the company to build the digital infrastructure.

China's telecommunication companies entered Kenya's ICT sector late and had to navigate a relatively crowded market. National and international companies like MTN from South Africa, Zain from Kuwait, Vodafone from the UK, and Bharti Airtel from India had already entered that market and won shares and customers (Hughes and Lonie, 2007). These corporations localised quickly by shifting from contract-based purchasing plans to prepaid data, calls, and messaging. To go even further, the partly state-owned company Safaricom instigated an initiative intended to expand financial inclusion. Launched in 2007, M-PESA is Safaricom's mobile money transfer and micro-financing service (Avgerou, Hayes, and Rovere, 2016; Morawczynski, 2009). By using funding from the UK's Department for International Development (DFID), Safaricom was able to improve access to financial services for unbanked communities. The Chinese government and companies operating in Kenya adopted a receptive posture towards the wishes of Nairobi and the currents of the business environment. This strategy was similar to their labours in Ethiopia, where China supported the state's ambition to introduce digital infrastructure.

Huawei's 2018 annual report maintained that its Safe Cities project (*anquan chengshi*) serves over 100 countries (Huawei, 2018). According to data collected by the Endowment for International Peace and the Center for Strategic and International Studies, 16 African states have contracted with Huawei to receive digital surveillance and governance technology. These surveillance and governance devices offer multiple services which include smart metering, emergency assessments, and predictive policing. A popular example is the first African safe city system built in Kenya. Huawei was able to connect 1,800 high-definition cameras and 200 high-definition traffic surveillance infrastructures across Nairobi. Additionally, a national police command centre was established to provide support to over 9,000 police officers and 195 police stations (Huawei, 2018). These technologies aim to support crime prevention, accelerated response, and recovery. Due to the dearth of data, the benefits of the Safe City project are hard to verify and appear exaggerated (Epoch Times, 2019; Hillman, 2019). According to Huawei, crime rates from 2014 to 2015 decreased by 46% in areas supported by their technologies in Kenya (Huawei, 2014). But Kenya's National Police Service reports indicate smaller reductions in crime during those years in Nairobi. Nairobi and Mombasa, the two cities with surveillance technologies, have also seen increases in reported crimes in 2017 and 2018.

Equally important, Nairobi's central business district is reliant on digital CCTV cameras purchased from Huawei, but also suppliers like Hikvision, a Chinese state-owned provider of video surveillance technology. The facial recognition technology used on its national borders is powered by Sensetime, a Hongkong-based company. This case, like the example of Ethiopia, also illustrates a hybridised surveillance system that is diversely sourced to establish state security ambitions to manage crime and terror. In particular, Kenya's experience with terrorist attacks by Islamist militants in 2013 has led to the government utilising surveillance technologies and legal powers to manage the threat. Local civil society organisations point out the risks involved in digital surveillance and governance technologies and how the pretext of terror enables the atrophy of personal privacy and extended surveillance practices.

Rather than asserting a Chinese-based vision of digital governance and surveillance in Kenya, Chinese companies and the government have agreed to the propositions of their host. Digital surveillance tools are embedded within state processes that are a result of private–public ventures. Whether operating in Kenya's open market or Ethiopia's closed market, China and its companies have shown dexterity in adapting to local expectations and to sharing the unique vision of the host country. In Ethiopia, Beijing is the largest supporter of Addis Ababa's digital infrastructure projects. Without the EXIM bank's concessionary loans of USD 3.1 billion, the EPRDF would not have been able to realise its state capacity goals. Yet, it is also fair to say that Beijing is not aiming to export a strict normative basis of digital governance and surveillance in Africa. On the contrary, it seems to engage on the terms made available in the local context, which leads to context dependent outcomes. This raises questions about how we should interpret China's adaptive diplomatic strategy and its willingness to meet African states on their terms.

3.7 Conclusion: China's Neutrality

This chapter challenges the conception that China seeks to export a model of surveillance. Chinese companies operating in Africa tend to adapt to local business practices, rather than follow Beijing's supposed geopolitical strategy. Alves and Alden (2008) contend that China's financial and technical support does not result categorically in the exportation of its normative values. The evidence suggests that China helps fortify the political and social processes that were already in place in Ethiopia and Kenya. The lack of a digital governance and surveillance model to export does not negate the possibility of other strategies. Relevant questions, then, are: what kind of political, social, and legal environments are these digital surveillance tools embedding themselves in? How do we interpret China's adaptive diplomatic strategy? How are digital tools being utilised to meet public goals versus other ambitions? China's tendency to privilege state actors over other agents is problematic in the context of authoritarian regimes such as Ethiopia, which has a track record of human rights violations, and the government has shown a predilection towards conducting unwarranted surveillance on citizens. The new technologies enhance the government's capacity. This latter point is not exclusive to authoritarian governments: skewing power towards the state, even in a democracy like Kenya, can result in unwarranted surveillance practices that undermine civil liberties.

China has incessantly repudiated the notion that it is exporting its values and surveillance practices abroad. During the 2018 Beijing Summit of FOCAC, President Xi spoke of the "five no" strategy that shapes its Africa policy: "no interference in the development paths of individual countries; no interference in their internal affairs; no imposition of China's will; no attachment of political strings regarding assistance; and no seeking of selfish political gains in investment and financing cooperation" (Liangyu, 2018). Xi's claims of neutrality do not eliminate concerns or negate the possibilities of recipients of Chinese aid conducting surveillance operations, especially after receiving support to establish digital surveillance capacities. It is clear, however, China's strategy towards Africa has never been explicit, strict, or coercive, but always remunerative in orientation. It is predicated on providing financial support and incentives to promote diplomatic relations. China is not actively promoting surveillance practices and advocating for specific models of development in the same way Western donors explicitly do, where compliance to specific market and democratic reforms is expected. The fact that it financially supports African governments and their ambitions to build digital infrastructure, still, prompts doubts about its neutral impact – and gestures towards a general strategy towards African partners. For these reasons, we must engender more proportional accounts that accent the degree to which African volition is shaping these unfolding relations while also examining the interplay between Chinese tech providers and Beijing's ambitions to promote its interests in Africa.

As I have shown, Beijing's remunerative engagements with Africa reinforce domestic political processes. Beijing's willingness to do business with authoritarian states enables surveillance practices. The way in which China chooses to define neutrality is simply contingent on the promotion of state sovereignty and the absence of political conditions. This framing allows for economic activities to persist while obfuscating the asymmetric conditions that structure relations. But this position also obscures the fact that, while offering aid and loans, China, like others, enables state capacities for surveillance (Jili, 2020). The "no strings attached" approach does not categorically result in neutral outcomes but is a beguiling posture that maintains China's image as a generous development partner, while also deemphasising its tangible impact on the ground. While China's involvement does not actively promote surveillance practices, it does create the conditions for it. How long Beijing maintains this posture of "neutrality" is a paramount matter as it expands its geopolitical footprint. Unfortunately, the few publicly available Chinese state documents remain vague as they pertain to regulating African investments. They lack explicit direction, legally enforceable obligations, and effective accountability measures to mitigate the misuse of digital governance and surveillance infrastructure. It is this lacuna that enables Chinese corporations to adapt to host country ambitions, even at the expense of civil liberties.

Acknowledgements

Without friends and family's companionship, it would have been an arduous task to muster the thew to bring this work to conclusion. It is their love that is the fuel of today, and the harbinger of hope to come.

Note

1 China draws a distinction between political and economic conditions. There are economic conditions associated with Chinese loans. For instance, the resource-backed lending model allows for financing infrastructural projects, which requires borrowing countries to commit future revenues to be earned from its natural resources to pay loans secured from Beijing. This method allows resource-rich and high-risk borrowers to secure needed finance, but it also makes nations more financially vulnerable. With the collapse of volatile commodity prices, the borrower bears all the risk of debt default if the collateral is not enough. To participate in this program, the African countries need to be resource-rich, which obviously excludes Kenya and Ethiopia.

Bibliography

Ado, A., and Zhan S. (2016) 'China in Africa: A critical literature review.' *Critical Perspectives on International Business*, 12 (1), pp. 40–60.

Alden, C., and Large, D. (2011) 'China's exceptionalism and the challenges of delivering difference in Africa.' *Journal of Contemporary China*, 20 (68), pp. 21–38.

Annual Report (2018) Kenya National Police Service. Available at: http://www.nationalpolice.go.ke/crime-statistics.html (Accessed 10 March 2021).

Appel, H. (2019) *The Licit Life of Capitalism: US Oil in Equatorial Guinea*. Durham: Duke University Press.

Avgerou, C., Hayes, N. and La Rovere, R.L. (2016). 'Growth in ICT uptake in developing countries: New users, new uses, new challenges.' *Journal of Information Technology*, 31, pp. 329–333.

Banda, F. (2009) 'China in the African mediascape: A critical injection.' *Journal of African Media Studies*, 1 (3), pp.343–361.

Biryabarema, E. (2019) Uganda's cash-strapped cops spend $126 million on CCTV from Huawei. Reuters, 15 August. Available at: https://www.reuters.com/article/us-uganda-crime/ugandas-cash-strapped-cops-spend-126-million-on-cctv-from-huawei-idUSKCN1V50RF (Accessed 20 June 2021).

Bräutigam, D. (2011) 'Aid 'with Chinese characteristics': Chinese foreign aid and development finance meet the OECD-DAC aid regime.' *Journal of International Development,* 23 (5), pp. 752–764.

Bräutigam, D. and Zhang, H. (2013) 'Green dreams: Myth and reality in China's agricultural investment in Africa.' *Third World Quarterly*, 34 (9), pp. 1676–1696.

Chipaike, R. and Knowledge, M. H. (2018) 'The question of African agency in international relations.' *Cogent Social Sciences*, 4 (1), pp. 1–16.

Comaoff, J., and Comaroff J. (2016) *The Truth About Crime: Sovereignty, Knowledge, Social Order.* Chicago: Chicago University Press.

Corkin, L. (2011) 'Redefining foreign policy impulses toward Africa: The roles of the MFA, the MOFCOM and China Exim Bank.' *Journal of Current Chinese Affairs,* 40 (4), pp. 61–90.

Corkin, L. (2016) *Uncovering African agency: Angola's management of China's credit lines.* New York: Routledge.

Cotterill, J. (2021) Cabling Africa: The great data race to serve the 'last billion.' *Financial Times,* 21 January. Available at: https://www.ft.com/content/adb1130e-2844-4051 -b1df-a691fc8a19b8 (Accessed 10 February 2021).

Dalton, M. (2014) Telecom deal by China's ZTE, Huawei in Ethiopia faces criticism. *The Wall Street Journal,* January. Available at: https://www.wsj.com/articles/SB100014240 52702303653004579212092223818288 (Accessed 30 April 2021).

Feldstein, S. (2019) *The Global Expansion of AI Surveillance.* Carnegie Endowment International Peace, September. Available at: https://blog.fdik.org/2019-09/WP -Feldstein-AISurveillance_final1.pdf (Accessed 5 April 2022).

Feldstein, S. (2020) Hearing on China's strategic aims in Africa, testimony before the U.S.- China Economic and Security Review Commission. May. Available at: https://www.uscc.gov/sites/default/files/Feldstein_Testimon y.pdf (Accessed 10 July 2021).

Feng, D., and Liang H. (2019) *Belt and Road Initiative: Chinese version of Marshall Plan?* Singapore: World Scientific Publishing.

Finnemore, M. (1993) 'International organizations as teachers of norms: The United Nations educational, scientific, and cultural organization and science policy.' *International Organization,* 47 (4), pp. 565–597.

Foster, V., and Elvira, M. (2010) *Ethiopia's Infrastructure: A Continental Perspective.* Washington, DC: World Bank.

Gadzala, A. (2015) *Africa and China: How Africans and Their Governments Are Shaping Relations with China.* Lanham MD: Rowman & Littlefield.

Gagliardone, I. (2019) *China, Africa, and the Future of the Internet.* New York: Zed Books Ltd.

Gagliardone, I. and Brhane, A. (2021) '*Ethiopia digital rights landscape report.*' Institute of Development Studies, pp. 186–208.

Greitens, S. (2019) 'Surveillance with Chinese characteristics: The development & global export of Chinese policing technology.' *Brookings Institute,* pp. 1–15.

Cox, M., Majid, T.S.M., Jie, Y., Yan, J., Hamzah, H., Jusoh, S. and Pongsudhirak, T. (2018) *China's Belt and Road Initiative (BRI) and Southeast Asia.* CIMB ASEAN Research Institute, p. 47.

Hawaz, Y. and Xi, C. (2020) 'The hidden hands of foreign interference and Ethiopia's security challenge, from post 2005 election-2018.' *International Journal of Social Relevance and Concern,* 8 (5), pp. 47–61.

He, Y., (2014) Chin's overcapacity crisis can spur growth through overseas expansion. *South China Morning Post,* January. Available at: https://www.scmp.com/comment /insight-opinion/article/1399681/chinas-overcapacity-crisis-can-spur-growth -through-overseas (Accessed 27 January 2021).

He, X. (1997) 'The market economy and ethnic relations in China', in Ikeo, A. (ed.) *Economic Development in Twentieth Century East Asia: The International Context.* London: Routledge, pp. 190–205.

Horne, F. (2014) How US surveillance helps repressive regimes – the Ethiopia case. *Human Rights Watch,* October. Available at: https://www.hrw.org/news/2017/10/03

/how-us-surveillance-helps-repressive-regimes-ethiopia-case (Accessed 12 January 2021).

Hu, K. (2011) Huawei open letter. *The Wall Street Journal*, February. Available at: https://online.wsj.com/public/resources/documents/Huawei20110205.pdf (Accessed 5 April 2022).

Huang, Y. (2016) 'Understanding China's belt & road initiative: Motivation, framework and assessment.' *China Economic Review*, 40, pp. 314–321.

Huawei (2017) Video surveillance as the foundation of "safe city" in Kenya. *Huawei Industry Insights*, August. Available at: https://www.huawei.com/us/industry-insights/technology/digital-transformation/video/video-surveillance-as-the-foundation-of-safe-city-in-kenya. (Accessed 7 April 2021).

Huawei (2018) *2018 Annual Report*. Huawei, Available at: https://www-file.huawei.com/-/media/corporate/pdf/annual-report/annual_report2018_en.pdf?la=en (Accessed 23 June 2021).

Huawei and Rodland (2018) 'Operators: ICT Infrastructure, investment, innovation, and competition. (运营商: ICT基础设施的投资、创新与竞争) *Huawei and Rodland Berger*, September. Available at: https://www-file.huawei.com/-/media/corporate/pdf/public-policy/huawei_ict_position_paper_cn.pdf (Accessed 5 March 2022).

Hughes, N. and Lonie, S. (2007) 'M-PESA: Mobile money for the 'unbanked' turning cellphones into 24-hour tellers in Kenya.' *Innovations: Technology, Governance, Globalization*, 2 (12), pp. 63–81.

Human Rights Watch (2014) *Ethiopia: Telecom Surveillance Chills Rights*. Human Rights Watch, March. Available at: https://www.hrw.org/news/2014/03/25/ethiopia-telecom-surveillance-chills-rights (Accessed 21 February 2021).

ITU (2002) Internet from the Horn of Africa: Ethiopia case study. *International Telecommunication Union*, July. Available at: https://www.itu.int/osg/spu/casestudies/ETH_CS1.pdf (Accessed 3 March 2021)

Jacques, M. (2009) *When China Rules the World: The End of the Western World and the Birth of a New Global Order*. New York: Penguin Press.

Jili, B. (2020) *Chinese Surveillance Tools in Africa*. China, Law, and Development Project, June. Available at: https://cld.web.ox.ac.uk/files/finaljilipdf (Accessed 5 July 2021)

Kirby, W., Chan B., and Mchugh J. (2020) *Huawei: A Global Tech Giant in the Crossfire of a Digital Cold War*. HBS No. 9-320-089. Boston: Harvard Business School Publishing.

Kragelund, P. (2015) 'Towards convergence and cooperation in the global development finance regime: Closing Africa's policy space?' *Cambridge Review of International Affairs*, 28 (2), pp. 246–262.

Kurlantzick, J. (2020) China's digital silk road initiative: A boon for developing countries or a danger to freedom? *The Diplomat*, December. Available at: https://thediplomat.com/2020/12/chinas-digital-silk-road-initiative-a-boon-for-developing-countries-or-a-danger-to-freedom/ (Accessed 22 July 2021).

Lee, C.K. (2020) *In the Specter of Global China*. Chicago: University of Chicago Press.

Liangyu, (2018) China's five-no approach demonstrates real friendship towards Africa: Kenyan analyst. *Xinhua*, September. Available: http://www.xinhuanet.com/english/2018-09/06/c_137447556.htm (Accessed 3 April 2021).

Marczak B., Guarnieri, C., Marquis-Boire, M., and Scott-Railton, J. (2014) Hacking team and the targeting of Ethiopian journalists. *CitizenLab*, February. Available at: https://citizenlab.ca/2014/02/hacking-team-targeting-ethiopian-journalists/

Marczak, B., Alexander, G., McKune, S., Scott-Railton, J., and Deibert, R. (2017) *Champing at the cyberbit Ethiopian dissidents targeted with new commercial spyware.*

Citizenlab, December. Available at: https://citizenlab.ca/2017/12/champing-cyberbit-ethiopian-dissidents-targeted-commercial-spyware/ (Accessed 6 June 2021).

Mbembé, A. (2001) *On the Postcolony.* Berkeley: University of California Press.

McBride J., Chatzky, A. and Siripurapu, A. (2020) *The National Debt Dilemma.* Council on Foreign Relations. Available at: https://www.cfr.org/backgrounder/national-debt-dilemma (Accessed 12 February 2021).

Mohan, G. (2015) 'Queuing up for Africa: The geoeconomics of Africa's growth and the politics of African agency', *International Development Policy Review,* 37 (1), pp. 45–52.

Mohan, G., and Lampert B. (2013) 'Negotiating China: Reinserting African agency into China–Africa relations.' *African Affairs,* 112 (446), pp. 92–110.

Morawczynski, O. (2009) 'Exploring the usage and impact of 'transformational' mobile financial services: The case of M-PESA in Kenya.' *Journal of Eastern African Studies,* 3(3), pp. 509–525.

Mozur, P. (2019) Made in China, exported to the world: The surveillance state. *The New York Times,* April. Available at: https://www.nytimes.com/2019/04/24/technology/ecuador-surveillance-cameras-police-government.html (Accessed 23 January 2021).

Okuttah, M. (2012) M-Pesa drives safaricom as profit declines to Sh12. 8bn, *Business Daily.*

Parkinson J., Bariyo N., and Chin J. (2019) Huawei technicians helped African governments spy on political opponents. *Wall Street Journal,* August. Available at: https://www.wsj.com/articles/huawei-technicians-helped-african-governments-spy-on-political-opponents-11565793017 (Accessed 4 April 2021).

Rich, S. and Recker S. (2013) 'Understanding Sino-African relations: Neocolonialism or a new era?' *Journal of International and Area Studies,* 20 (1), pp. 61–76.

Rodney, W. (2018) *How Europe Underdeveloped Africa.* New York: Verso Trade.

Rotberg, R. (2009) *China into Africa: Trade, Aid, and Influence.* Washington, DC: Brookings Institution Press.

Sanghi, A. and Johnson, D. (2016) *Deal or No Deal: Strictly Business for China in Kenya?* Washington, DC: The World Bank.

Snow, P. (1995) China and Africa: Consensus and Camouflage, in Thomas Robinson and David Shambaugh (eds) *Chinese Foreign Policy: Theory and Practice.* Oxford: Oxford University Press, pp. 283–321.

Song, W. (2021) Decline in China's lending to Africa doesn't tell full picture of cooperation. *Global Times,* March. Available at: https://www.globaltimes.cn/page/202103/1219995.shtml (Accessed 11 February 2021).

Taylor, I. (2006) China's oil diplomacy in Africa. *International Affairs,* 82(5), pp. 937–959.

Taylor, I. (2009) *China's New Role in Africa.* Boulder: Lynne Rienner Publishers.

Taylor, I. (2014) *Africa Rising? BRICS-diversifying Dependency.* Oxford: James Currey.

Taylor, I. and Zajontz, T. (2020) 'In a fix: Africa's place in the Belt and Road Initiative and the reproduction of dependency.' *South African Journal of International Affairs,* 27(3), pp. 277–295.

Thakur, M. (2009) 'Building on progress? Chinese engagement in Ethiopia.' *South African Institute of International Affairs,* 38, pp. 4–23.

Turse, N. (2017) *How the NSA Built a Secret Surveillance Network for Ethiopia.* The Intercept, September. Available at: https://theintercept.com/2017/09/13/nsa-ethiopia-surveillance-human-rights/ (Accessed 21 March 2021).

Wahito, M. (2012) *Kenya: China to fund Kenya's Fibre Optic Project.* Capital FM.

Wang, H., and XueYing H. (2017) 'China's 'going-out' strategy and corporate social responsibility: Preliminary evidence of a 'boomerang effect'.' *Journal of Contemporary China,* 26 (108), pp. 820–833.

Wang, Y. (2017) *China Connects the World: What Behind the Belt and Road Initiative.* Beijing: China Intercontinental Press.

Xinhua (2017) 8 Quick facts about Kenya's standard gauge railway. *Xinhua,* May. Available at: http://www.xinhuanet.com/english/2017-05/31/c_136328584.htm (Accessed 30 February 2021).

Yu, J. (2018) 'The Belt and Road Initiative: Domestic interests, bureaucratic politics and the EU-China Relations.' *Asia Europe Journal,* 16 (3), pp. 223–236.

Yun, S. (2020) China and Africa's debt: Yes to relief, no to blanket forgiveness. *Brookings,* April. Available at: https://www.brookings.edu/blog/africa-in-focus/2020/04/20/china-and-africas-debt-yes-to-relief-no-to-blanket-forgiveness/ (Accessed 2 May 2021).

4

THE ARTIFICIAL INTELLIGENCE – BIOTECH REVOLUTION IN AFRICA

Eleonore Pauwels and Klaus Tilmes

4.1 Introduction

African nations increasingly recognise that the convergence of Artificial Intelligence (AI) and modern biotechnologies is not only becoming a strategic societal and welfare asset, but also a powerful driver to preserve national security and exert sovereignty over Africa's genomic wealth (African Union and African CDC, 2020, East African Community, 2021).

The current COVID-19 pandemic serves as a wake-up call across the world of our shared vulnerability to biothreats and the crucial importance of bio-medicine and biodefence programmes for threat mitigation. The combination of genomics surveillance, AI, and advanced bioinformatics has drastically bol-stered the ability to track the spread of SARS-CoV-2 variants and decipher transmission dynamics in real time (Giandhari et al., 2020). Technological con-vergence has also aided in the development of timely diagnostics tools and accelerated the synthesis of vaccines. Global disease control programmes, such as those for tuberculosis, malaria, HIV, foodborne pathogens, and antibiotic resistance, now recommend genomics-based surveillance as a vital component (WHO, 2019).

Africa records the lowest human capital score and carries the world's high-est disease burden. The pandemic has highlighted the critical need to improve Africa's epidemic preparedness and surveillance capabilities (EIB, 2020), estab-lish biobanks (Peeling et al., 2020), and expand local diagnostics, treatment, and manufacturing capacity (Nkengasong, 2020). The key question is whether the accelerating global wave of health care innovations, propelled by the rapid convergence of digital, bio-, nano-, and cognitive technologies, will engage or bypass Africa – both as contributor and as beneficiary. The stakes are high: with all modern non-African populations substantially descending from Africa,

DOI: 10.4324/9781003274322-4

the continent's largely unexplored genomic code can help unlock much of the world's global genomic goods.

Given this challenging context, how can African nations assume a leadership role in this era of genomics and maximise the benefits of modern biotechnologies for the prevention, diagnosis, and treatment of diseases? Given the scientific discoveries and geopolitical stakes involved, what are the pathways and prospects for the European Union (EU) to expand its collaboration with Africa to convert these genomic possibilities into accessible and affordable solutions for all of humanity?

To explore these issues, the next section illustrates how the convergence of AI and modern biotechnologies can be applied to infectious diseases prevention and biothreat monitoring – two shared priorities for African and European leaders to combat the proliferation of pathogens. Section 4.3 offers a comprehensive mapping of Africa's genomics and bioinformatics landscape. By highlighting promising genomics ventures that reflect the scope of Africa's biotechnology aspirations, this section underscores the value of long-term scientific partnerships and funding commitments – two potential avenues for EU–Africa genomics cooperation. This is followed by a discussion of the geopolitical positioning of other nations, notably China and the United States, to compete with the EU in AI and genomics. In this perspective, we highlight some of the EU's strategic strengths but also innovation hurdles and coordination delays. We conclude with an outlook section that provides entry points for EU–Africa cooperation on AI and genomics to augment both regions' biotechnology economies.

4.2 A New Era of Genomics and AI Convergence

4.2.1 The State of Biotechnology – from Analogue to Digital

In the last two decades, the state of biotechnology has moved from analogue to digital. Bioinformatics, which involves analytical methods for understanding large biological datasets, has enabled advances in biosciences thanks to accelerating computing and data processing capabilities. These developments are critical to genomic analysis – an interdisciplinary field which focuses on the structure, function, evolution, mapping, and editing of genomes across different domains, ranging from biomedicine and biotechnology to biosecurity. Insofar as the underlying datasets accurately represent real-world phenomena, AI-based applications can provide useful tools for identifying patterns and automating intelligent actions to address a complex issue or solve a specific problem that would otherwise require considerable time and mental effort. This technological convergence of AI with biosciences is not only extending across the economic sphere, from healthcare and agriculture to industrial biotechnology (Chui et al., 2020), but is already transforming how public and private sector actors monitor and seek to prevent the proliferation of new biosecurity threats, from illicit gene-synthesis and gain-of-function research to epidemic surveillance (Pauwels, 2021).

This accelerating convergence has already proven to be fundamental during the fight against COVID-19, with applications ranging from improved disease surveillance to AI-enabled clinical research and treatment, and optimisation of health operations. Future prosperity, health, and security of African populations critically depend on how governments will develop, master, secure, or outsource capacities at the confluence of AI and biosciences. Two strategic examples – precision public health and biothreat prevention – illustrate the transformational implications.

4.2.2 Genomics and Bioinformatics for the Prevention of Infectious Diseases

The integration of AI computing within modern biomedicine allows researchers to rely on synthetic datasets and predictive methods to produce actionable knowledge in a genome's biology and assess its clinical value. AI computing also creates increased potential for monitoring and optimising data analytics across the multimodal datasets that constitute the complete genetic or molecular profiles of humans, animals, and pathogens. A significant advantage that AI computing could bring to public health and clinical research is to process simultaneously massive amounts of genomic, physiological, health, ecosystem, and lifestyle data about populations in their environment. These approaches are crucial to improving our understanding of genomics and biological processes related to human and animal pathologies, including infectious diseases.

The convergence of AI with biotechnology could help identify which genetic functions are key to augmenting the capacity of a pathogen to infect a host, evade the immune system, spread among subpopulations, or resist vaccines and antibiotics. Predictive modelling is important for real-time disease surveillance and for monitoring and preventing future zoonotic spill-overs using advanced bio-forensics and sensing capacity for detecting pathogens. The fast production of medical countermeasures (such as immunoassay diagnostic tests for detecting the antigen or antibody properties of certain proteins, liquid biopsies, and vaccines) also increasingly depends on advances at the intersection of genomics, AI, and bioinformatics.

The COVID-19 pandemic serves as a prime example of how emerging "in silico" capacities in pathogen genomics are key for developing rapid medical countermeasures. In 2020, at the onset of the pandemic, scientists designed a platform to automate the synthesis of existing RNA viruses, which are estimated to make up 44% of all emerging infectious diseases (Thi Nhu Thao et al., 2020). Using this platform, they were able to synthetise clones of the SARS-COVID-2 virus a week after receiving the synthetic DNA fragments. Such technical advances enable both the real-time genotypic detection of viral traits and the modelling of the pathogen's mutational landscape.

Until recently, most health genomics research has been conducted in northern hemisphere clinical settings, with African populations being severely under-represented. Thus, there is an urgent need to undertake research with African populations to ensure that genomic medicine solutions are tailored to African patients (Mulder, 2017). Considering Africa's genetic diversity, it is highly likely that the application of precise and predictive diagnoses considerably advances medical treatment on a global level (Pereira et al., 2021).

4.2.3 Transformational Opportunities for Biothreats Monitoring in Africa

Considering Africa's disproportionate burden of infectious diseases, the combination of AI, bioinformatics, and genomics research can accelerate the discovery of new treatment options for malaria, tuberculosis, HIV/AIDS, Ebola virus, and Lassa fever (Bah et al., 2018).

A total of 140 disease outbreaks are anticipated to occur each year on the African continent (WHO, 2020a). These outbreaks pose additional threats to existing endemic infectious diseases, which account for at least 35% of the continent's 10 million annual deaths (Roser, 2016). AI-enabled genomic surveillance programmes can play a critical role in the prevention, control, and elimination of new, re-emerging, and endemic infectious diseases. Genomic-informed pathogen surveillance has already demonstrated its critical efficiency, including the 2018 outbreak of Lassa fever virus in Nigeria (Siddle et al., 2018) and the Ebola virus outbreaks in the Democratic Republic of the Congo (2018–2020). During these outbreaks, the combination of genomic data with an array of population datasets has helped stress-test the effectiveness of diagnostics, transmission patterns, and medical countermeasures (Gardy and Loman, 2018). During the SARS-CoV-2 pandemic, the combination of pathogen genomic data and population datasets has allowed to track more efficiently the spread of new variants, including the spread of B.1.351 (N501Y.V2) in South Africa, which have high transmission rates and the potential to affect COVID-19 medical countermeasures (WHO, 2020b). Adding new surveillance strategies with pathogen genomics sequencing tools can help with early detection and prevention of zoonotic diseases' spill-overs to human populations (Armstrong et al., 2019).

Biothreat monitoring in Africa could be transformed by increasingly allying advanced bioinformatics tools with next-generation sequencing (NGS) equipment capable of high pathogen resolution at relatively low costs. However, the integration of AI, bioinformatics capacities, and NGS is lagging behind in Africa, despite the urgent need for rapid and in-depth pathogen characterisation that could lead to more targeted and robust disease threat control (Makoni, 2020). Managing the sweeping technological advances now underway will require new prevention capacities, foresight, and governance structures that draw on cross-sectoral expertise from industry, academia, politics, and defence. A good example is the United States' Biomedical Advanced Research and Development

Authority (BARDA), whose dual mission is not only to support research and bring medical countermeasures to the market but also to collaborate with businesses on initiatives that are not always on big pharma's or biotech's radar screens. For instance, over the last decade BARDA has been collaborating with pharmaceutical companies, such as Merck, to develop a single-shot vaccine against Ebola and other forms of multidrug resistance (Miles, 2018). In 2020, the von der Leyen Commission rightly called for a European BARDA to fill a critical institutional gap that can serve as an accelerator of public–private partnerships and a defence shield against future natural and engineered biothreats (Zubascu, 2020). Such an initiative could be developed in partnership with the African region. By working together and investing in the capacities of private companies at the confluence of AI, bioinformatics, and genomics, a European-style BARDA could boost Africa's ability to develop and manufacture new vaccines.

4.3 Mapping Africa's Landscape of Genomics and Bioinformatics

Globally, the generation of human genome data is undergoing a period of exponential growth. Countries are beginning to recognise the potential technological and system-level healthcare benefits of genomic data and have announced mass full genome sequencing initiatives.[1] In a future scenario, in which these efforts succeed in capturing the world's full genomic diversity and are linked together thanks to new governance arrangements, shared data standards, and secure cross-border exchange,[2] genomics could generate valuable global public goods for all of humanity (Munshi, 2020).

Africa holds more genomic diversity than any other continent. Yet, most of it remains untapped. With more than a million individual genomes having been sequenced so far worldwide, a mere 1.5–2% originate from Africa compared with ~80% from European descendants. A recently published study covering 426 individuals from 50 ethnic groups in Africa reported three million previously undescribed variants (Choudhury et al., 2020). A similar pattern applies to disease-specific datasets, of which more than half focus on oncology, 13% on rare diseases, and 10% on neurological disorders. Most genomics-enabled drug discovery programmes deal with rare genetic variants. Yet, despite this immense potential, Africa accounts for less than 1% of the global investment in genomics research and clinical studies (Pennisi, 2021). An inventory of 187 genomic initiatives showed that 50% are located in the United States and 19% in Europe, while Africa is represented with just four initiatives (IQVIA, 2020). With negligible research and development (R&D) investments by African governments and biotech/pharma companies, genomic research depends mainly on funding from international research institutions. The National Institutes of Health (NIH) (with 75% of allocated funds) and the UK's Medical Research Council and Wellcome Trust (with 21%) are funding the largest share of genomic projects in Africa, which stands in sharp contrast to funding from the EU (1.4%) (Hamdi et al., 2021).[3]

Today, a growing number of African scientists and institutions are leading genomic research (Pennisi, 2021). A closer look at path-breaking genomic initiatives in Africa provides insights into progress and remaining challenges and highlights promising opportunities for expanded collaboration with EU-based institutions.

The Human Heredity & Health in Africa (H3Africa) Consortium, created in 2012, has ushered in a new era of genomics and life sciences research that aspires to be locally productive and globally competitive. Partnering with the African Society of Human Genetics and provisioned with a ten-year funding commitment of USD 180 million from the NIH and the UK's Wellcome Trust, H3Africa aims to build clinical research capabilities and foster collaborative networks within the African scientific community. The H3Africa programme consists of multiple projects and sites distributed across 30 countries. These generate genomic data and research outputs linked to specific diseases, such as the genetic causes of blindness, Alzheimer's, cancer, kidney failure, and sickle disease. A core tenet is that research teams must deposit any project data into a shared, pan-African repository (H3ABioNet) (Mulder et al., 2017). H3ABioNet ensures ethical security compliance and facilitates the data flow between researchers and the European Genome-phenome Archive and other public depositories.

Building on H3Africa's foundation, the NIH announced in October 2022 a five-year, USD 75 million award to harness Data Science for Health Discovery and Innovation in Africa (DS-I Africa). Research centres are set to validate AI models to improve pregnancy outcomes and mental health (Kenya), study pandemic preparedness (Nigeria), diagnose eye disease and cervical cancer (Uganda), improve access to surgical care (Cameroon), and develop innovative solutions to mitigate health impacts of climate change (South Africa). This long-term commitment to co-develop solutions to Africa's most pressing public health problems can serve as a blueprint for similar genomic partnerships with the EU.

Another aspirational project is the Three Million African Genomes (3MAG) project – a continent-wide endeavour to build a representative human reference genome (Wonkam, 2021). By sequencing the full scope of Africa's genetic variation, the goal is to understand immunity to infection for the benefit of Africans and non-Africans alike and correct faulty medical diagnoses for people of African descent. Estimated funding of USD 4.5 billion over the span of a decade requires the support of African governments, academia, industry, and international organisations. The knowledge generated by 3MAG will raise profound ethical issues, such as informed consent, the role of communities, privacy, and confidentiality of genetic information, as well as benefit-sharing and the commercialisation of research results. Interestingly, the EU's 1+ Million Genomes initiative aims to make genomes accessible by 2022 and position the EU as a global player (European Commission, 2021a). The close alignment of this EU initiative and 3MAG, namely, to develop targeted medicines, boost prevention, and improve health systems, may yield new opportunities for expanded collaboration.

The African Pathogen Genomics Initiative (Africa PGI) aims to become the first public health surveillance system (Africa CDC, 2021). In October 2020, the African Centers for Disease Control and Prevention (Africa CDC) announced the launch of a four-year initiative to build a continent-wide pathogen genomics network of laboratories, bioinformatics capabilities, data systems, and expert personnel. Partners in this USD 100 million public–private non-profit consortium include the US CDC, the Gates Foundation, genomics sequencing company Illumina, UK-based biotechnology company Oxford Nanopore Technologies, and Microsoft's Azure cloud platform. Complementing this initiative, the European Center for Disease Prevention and Disease Control and Africa CDC launched a new €10 million partnership in December 2020 to facilitate harmonised surveillance and disease intelligence and implement a public health workforce strategy (Africa CDC, 2020).

To realise the Africa PGI vision several key challenges need to be overcome. To start with, around 70% of next-generation sequencers are concentrated in just five countries (South Africa, Kenya, Nigeria, Morocco, Egypt), leaving gaps in genomic data sourced from North and Central Africa (Hamdi, 2021). Moreover, with only 17% of all genome sequencers installed in public health institutes, increasing public sector capacities and creating functional networks with research facilities in countries are top priorities. Multi-pathogen laboratories, strategically located across Africa, would optimise scarce capacity, strengthen surveillance of neglected diseases, and support public health institutes. A tiered network of regional, national, and specialised laboratories would facilitate the gradual adoption of standardised tools and quality assurance systems to resolve ethical, legal, and socioeconomic challenges, including validating collaboration, intellectual property rights, and community engagement and preventing genetic stigmatisation. Integrating genomic surveillance into public health systems will require enabling policies and adoption of good practices for the collection, analysis, and cross-border sharing of genomic data.[4] Bulk procurement at continental level would reduce the high cost of genomic sampling for routine use by national health institutes and disease programmes.

Diverse expertise is needed to support genomic surveillance. Training programmes and professional networks[5] have begun to expand Africa's genomic workforce but need to be supplemented by mentorship, career incentives, idea generation, and research opportunities for African scientists, signalling promising entry points for joint research programmes, academic scholarships, and institutional support from the EU and bilateral partners (Nyirenda, 2021). Global research collaboration, through long-term partnerships and networks, is an effective way to deliver impactful research, build human capital, and strengthen institutional capacities. The European and Developing Countries Clinical Trials Partnership (EDCTP) is a marquee programme which has promoted the strong involvement of African scientists, supported local ownership, and funded the establishment of four regional networks of excellence, including on TB, HIV/AIDS, and malaria. To date, EDCTP-funded programmes, totalling more than

€720 million since 2014, have enabled hundreds of researchers in 238 African institutions and 163 European institutions to participate in multi-centre, multi-national clinical studies and promote greater self-reliance in health research and limit brain drain.

54Gene (https://54gene.com/) is a genomic start-up which pursues an alternative path to close Africa's genomic gaps and compensate for the lack of dedicated public R&D funding. Positioned as a genetic technology platform, the company aims to build Africa's largest for-profit biobank and translate its research into potential drugs and molecular diagnostics to reshape the trajectory of Africa's healthcare ecosystem and global drug discovery (Kene-Okafor, 2020). Founded in 2019 by a Nigerian biotech entrepreneur, 54Gene has attracted financial backing by Silicon Valley venture firms, the World Bank's IFC, Novartis, and the Gates Foundation (Maxmen, 2020). The goal of the initial phase is to aggregate and analyse the genomes of 100,000 Nigerians, with plans to expand to other African countries. Operating under explicit protocols for data collection, informed consent, and privacy, the company has set up a network of Nigerian hospitals and regulators to gather samples. The business model for 54Gene is to charge drug-development firms for access to the genetic data in the company's biobank and offer low-cost genetic tests.

4.4 Competitive Dynamics and Geostrategic Considerations

China is pursuing a long game to expand its influence in Africa. For decades, China has nurtured relationships with political elites of several African countries, especially those with strategic mineral and biological resources (Albert, 2017). Starting in 2013, ad hoc collaborations gradually turned into an ever-expanding network of Sino-African science and technology agreements as part of President Xi Jinping's globe-spanning infrastructure-development programme, the USD 1 trillion Belt and Road Initiative (BRI) (Masood, 2019). The African Union Commission and 40 African countries have signed BRI-scientific development agreements, ranging from AI and satellite imagery projects to genomics (Roussi, 2019). Along the way, China has become the largest investor in Africa's critical digital infrastructure and a partner of choice for research and education with thousands of scholarships offered each year to African PhD students.

In the wake of the COVID-19 pandemic, President Xi Jinping's ambitions for a "Health Silk Road" accelerated to put China in a position to project and shape global health, medical and biosecurity leadership (Lancaster, 2020; Brînză, 2020). This ambitious initiative underscores Africa's importance for China's geostrategic positioning to gain access and control over critical information infrastructure and transnational biological data-reservoirs (Pauwels, 2020). Mining the genotypes and phenotypes of large population groups will help fuel China's AI and genomics research and translate into significant economic and security assets. The Beijing Genomics Institute (BGI), the world's largest genetic research centre, is providing sequencing services to health and biotech groups in more than 60 countries, thereby achieving unrivalled access to their genomic data (MGI News, 2019; Lynch, 2017; Needham and Baldwin, 2021). China also owns Genuity Science, the largest global genomic data platform, to better diagnose diseases and design tailored therapeutics (Genuity Science, n.d.).

How well is the EU positioned in this competition? When looking at the raw figures alone, the EU should be a global leader in developing breakthrough health care solutions (European Commission, 2019). The biotech and pharma sectors are cornerstones of Europe's knowledge-based economy. The EU, which accounts for a quarter of global public R&D, can draw on 1.8 million researchers compared to 1.6 million in China and 1.3 million in the United States. However, the EU has been unable to capitalise fully on these strengths due to lower investments in R&D-intensive businesses, weaker knowledge connections across the health ecosystem, a fragmented health care system, uneven regulatory procedures, and high market entry barriers for small and medium-sized enterprises (SMEs).[6] Healthcare innovations in leading European countries (Germany, the Netherlands) encounter difficulties during ideation and testing stages due to heavily regulated genomics research and public scepticism about new solutions. By comparison, frontier African countries (South Africa, Kenya) exhibit strengths by relying on frugal innovations to address local problems, but experience difficulties in reaching scale due to weak IP systems, mismanagement, infrastructure deficits, and pervasive skill gaps (Schee genannt Halfmann, 2018). In terms of overall R&D investments, China is poised to overtake both the EU and the United States in areas such as AI and genomic research, which are set to generate significant productivity gains in health care. In a rapidly changing landscape of gene and cell-based health innovations, new clinical trials have increased by 36% in the United States and 28% in Asia, compared with less than 2% in Europe between 2014 and 2019. With the global health data market projected to increase fivefold to reach USD 70 billion by 2025, the EU needs to react strategically and adjust its innovation culture to ensure its current health data market retains its sovereignty and captures a fair share of future growth.

Set against this background, public–private partnerships (PPP) between governments, research universities, and private companies offer one pathway to accelerate innovations by combining public and private expertise and funding. The EU's Innovative Medicine Initiative (IMI) (https://www.imi.europa.eu/), the world's largest public–private partnership in life sciences, has attracted significant private investment and gained international recognition for facilitating collaboration among multinational companies and the sharing of data. Among its successes, IMI created a simple diagnostic device and vaccine against the Ebola virus. For their part, African countries are increasingly recognising the importance of strategic PPP alliances to address health challenges. Without collaborations between stakeholders, innovation can often not be realised. In Kenya, universities and small companies have joined forces with government institutions and foreign international companies, such as IBM and Philips, which have opened research and innovation centres for healthcare in Nairobi.

The political priorities of the von der Leyen Commission signal an emphasis on mission-driven research and industrial strategy: e-health to provide high-quality health care; faster cancer diagnosis and treatment; and development of affordable medicines. The EU's *Innovative Health Initiative* would support R&D activities to address global challenges and Europe's industrial competitiveness through the discovery and launch of innovative health products. The second pillar is the *EU–Africa Global Health Partnership*, which aims to increase health security in sub-Saharan Africa and reduce the risks of global pandemics and antimicrobial resistance (through rapid testing centres, anti-disinformation campaigns, and community engagement). However, except for a single proposal to support poverty-related disease research in Africa, the entire field of genomics and AI-related health had been noticeably missing from the EU-Africa Health programme until recently.

How will this competitive dynamic play out against Africa's near-complete dependency on vaccine imports and the AU's stated objective of having 60% of routine vaccines produced locally by 2040? The EU-sponsored vaccine manufacturing initiative of €1 billion for Africa, announced during the 2020 Global Health Summit, is promising relief. The Senegalese government has signed agreements to build the first manufacturing hub for COVID-19 and other vaccines at an estimated cost of USD 200 million, financed by European and US governments, with production set to start by end-2022 (African Business, 2021). In July 2021, European Commission president von der Leyen announced a new initiative to develop mRNA vaccines against malaria, enlisting BioNTech and the European Investment Bank (EIB) to support manufacturing facilities in Rwanda and Senegal (European Commission, 2021b). Simultaneously, the WHO established an mRNA vaccine technology transfer hub, the African Development Bank committed to creating two vaccine technology transfer platforms, and the World Trade Organization expressed support for regional vaccine manufacturing hubs. In a sign of increasing competition for gaining a foothold in Africa's underserved market for vaccines, the Egyptian government will produce Chinese Sinovac and is pursuing manufacturing agreements for Russia's Sputnik V vaccine (Ovadia, 2021).

Whoever gains a dominant position to control these powerful resources may well be able to influence the well-being of entire populations and impact innovation in allied countries. Inequality between countries that are tech-leaders and those that are tech-takers may rise if new forms of data-exploitation happen without a parallel transfer of technological skills, capacity-building and financial benefit-sharing with local populations (Pauwels, 2019). The Nagoya Protocol on *Access to Genetic Resources and the Fair and Equitable Sharing of Benefits from Their Utilisation* creates an overall legal framework and a commitment to transparency for both providers and users of genetic resources to operate under (Convention on Biological Diversity, 2015). Earlier this year, the African Academy of Sciences issued *Recommendations for Data and Biospecimen Governance in Africa* (The African Academy of Sciences, 2021) by introducing a "tiered" consent whereby research participants could select from a list of options they consent to their data being used for.[7] It remains to be seen whether this proposal gives Africans more say in how their genomic data is being used or whether opting out of broad consent as the default option could put African countries at odds with other nations in genomic research, curtail R&D investments, and complicate the storage of biological samples. This set of issues is closely intertwined with questions about personal data protection and the wider debate about digital sovereignty, cross-border data flows, and data localisation in Africa and in Europe. Without doubt, these issues will need to be tackled as part of any future genomic collaboration.

4.5 Conclusion and Outlook

Africa's genomic resources hold enormous potential for improving disease surveillance, targeting pandemic response, and alleviating the continent's high disease burden. This puts Africa in a unique position to contribute to the creation of a new class of global genomic goods that, if managed responsibly, could benefit humanity. However, relative to biotechnology advances in frontier regions (the United States, China, Europe), Africa finds itself in a catch-up mode, as is evident in the near-complete vaccine dependency from abroad.

This chapter showed that the key building blocks for Africa's genomic future have been put into place over the last decade, setting Africa's genomic prospects on a path for expansion and take-off. Strong scientific leadership paired with long-term strategic funding from public and philanthropic sources and a deep commitment to create collaborative networks with research institutes across the continent and internationally occupy a central role in building ownership and momentum for pursuing an Africa-wide biotechnology strategy.

Looking at the prospects of EU–Africa cooperation in modern biosciences, the chapter offers several important lessons. First, the COVID-19 pandemic has added urgency for a continental strategy on genomics, in particular for infectious diseases prevention and biothreat monitoring (African Union and African CDC, 2020). In this regard, the EU has launched several key initiatives to expand collaboration in Africa and mobilise private sector investments, notably in vaccine production and research. PPP arrangements backed by innovative funding models and government support in frontier countries are playing a prominent role. Second, while Europe used to be the source of breakthrough scientific development in genomics, it is now at risk of falling behind other regions globally in realising the potential at the confluence of AI, bioinformatics, and genomics. To overcome the slow adoption and integration of converging tools in data-optimisation and AI-led computing, Africa's vibrant bio-ecosystem can provide new impulses for innovation that Europe would be well advised to support and draw on. Third, the EU is well positioned to seize the opportunity and connect its genomic strategy with the growing bioeconomy potential across Africa – and demonstrate how such a collaboration would be beneficial to the populations of both continents. Finally, for such opportunities to materialise, critical issues related to digital sovereignty and data governance need to be discussed and harmonised at the highest EU–Africa levels as well as between Member States and regional organisations.

The agenda for turning genomic advances into innovative health solutions over the coming decade is long and ambitious. Drawing on promising initiatives and blueprints outlined in this chapter, an appropriate strategic funding commitment from the EU and private companies would signal a long-term engagement and leverage the existing capacity, expertise, and institutional infrastructure. Joint pronouncements by European and African leaders to invest in local production capacity (for vaccines and reagents) and genomics centres to overcome Africa's vaccine dependency are setting a new direction and need to be followed with concrete implementation milestones. In parallel, it is critical to strengthen the resilience of supply chains and financing models that would allow further integration of genomics in public health systems and programs. This will also open new possibilities for supporting the rapidly growing start-up ecosystem for converging healthcare and data science applications in both Africa and Europe and strengthen the pipelines for scalable innovations. To ensure an equitable distribution of capacity and benefits across the continent, special attention is needed to avoid North–South or East–West gaps. The expansion of funding opportunities to promote African science training, technology cooperation, and international partnerships with leading public and private genomic institutes is essential for increased mentorship and multidisciplinary scholarship. Cross-border sharing of data and genomic samples needs to be facilitated by clear guidelines and regulatory oversight, accompanied by investments in digital connectivity to make bioinformatics and databases widely accessible. The ultimate test will be to gain the public's buy-in and trust through easily accessible, affordable, and effective healthcare solutions that reduce the risk of future pandemics and lower Africa's staggering disease burden.

These priorities mark clear entry points for EU–Africa cooperation going forward. The opportunity for the EU to engage fully is now.

Notes

1 Publicly funded initiatives include Genomics England, which is pursuing a target of 5 million genomes. Dubai Genomics states that it will undertake whole genome sequencing of the entire population of 2.8 million. The most ambitious sequencing program is from China, where a target of 100 million genomes by 2030 was announced as part of China's Precision Medicines initiative. Privately owned companies with very large genomic databases include Ancestry.com (with a current cohort of 15 million genotypes) and 23andMe (10 million genotypes).

2 In 2018, the European Union announced that 13 European countries would cooperate in linking genomic databases, permitting greater representation across populations and expanded genomic research.

3 Of note, in preparation for the forthcoming EU-Africa Global Health Partnership, the European Commission requested a review of the *European and Developing Countries Clinic Trials Partnership Program (EDCTP2)* ("edctp3_draft_proposal_14_august_202

0.pdf," n.d.). Between 2014 and 2019, the EDCTP2 awarded € 699 million to clinical studies, clinical research capacity, and fellowship programs. However, the EDCTP2 program does not appear to include funding for genomic research, networks, policy development, and capacity building.

4 The Nagoya Protocol offers a useful framework for the fair and equitable sharing of benefits of genetic resources (Nagoya Protocol, 2021).

5 In addition to the H3Africa bioinformatics network, other initiatives include the African Genomic Medicine Training Initiative, the Developing Excellence in Leadership and Genetics Training for Malaria Elimination (supported by the Wellcome Trust), programs offered by the South African National Bioinformatics Institute and other universities, training programmes by genomics institutions such as the African Center of Excellence for Genomics of Infectious Disease (ACEGID), and the Medical Research Council-The Gambia, among others.

6 A recent McKinsey report (McKinsey, 2021) also confirms that Europe's world-class science and innovation need to be matched with stronger scale-up capabilities and a broader funding base if Europe is to emerge as a leader in biotech. Among the recommendations, three stand out: "go global"; "incubate innovation"; and "invigorate public markets" to combat market fragmentation and maximise knowledge sharing to make private- and public-funding schemes globally competitive.

7 For example, they could opt for their data be used only for the specific study for which it was collected; alternatively, they could allow data to be used in future studies relating to a specific disease. A third tier could allow research to use the data for any health-related study, which would be similar to broad consent.

References

Africa CDC, 2021. Genomic-informed pathogen surveillance in Africa: Opportunities and challenges. https://doi.org/10.1016/S1473-3099(20)30939-7

Africa CDC, 2020. European Union and African Union sign partnership to scale up preparedness for health emergencies. https://africacdc.org/news-item/european -union-and-african-union-sign-partnership-to-scale-up-preparedness-for-health -emergencies/ (accessed 10.11.21).

African Business, 2021. *Senegal Plans "Africa's First" Covid-19 Vaccine Manufacturing Hub.* https://african.business/2021/07/technology-information/senegal-to-build-200m- vaccine-manufacturing-plant/ (accessed 7.31.21).

African Union, African CDC, 2020. *Africa Joint Continental Strategy for COVID-19 Outbreak.* https://africacdc.org/download/africa-joint-continental-strategy-for-covid -19-outbreak/ (accessed 11.10.21).

Albert, E., 2017. China in Africa [WWW Document]. Council on Foreign Relations. https://www.cfr.org/backgrounder/china-africa (accessed 8.12.21).

Armstrong, G.L., MacCannell, D.R., Taylor, J., Carleton, et al., 2019. Pathogen genomics in public health. *New England Journal of Medicine.* 381, 2569–2580. https://doi.org/10 .1056/NEJMsr1813907

Bah, S.Y., Morang'a, C.M., Kengne-Ouafo, J.A. et al., 2018. Highlights on the application of genomics and bioinformatics in the fight against infectious diseases: Challenges and opportunities in Africa. *Front. Genet.* https://doi.org/10.3389/fgene .2018.00575

Brînză, A., 2020. Some say China's belt and road helped create this pandemic. Can it prevent the next one? https://thediplomat.com/2020/04/some-say-chinas-belt -and-road-helped-create-this-pandemic-can-it-prevent-the-next-one/ (accessed 8.12.21).

Choudhury, A., Aron, S., Botigué, L.R., et al., 2020. High-depth African Genomes inform human migration and health. *Nature* 586, 741–748. https://doi.org/10.1038/s41586-020-2859-7

Chui, M., Evers, M., Manyika, J., Zheng, A., et al., 2020. The bio revolution: Innovations transforming economies, societies, and our lives | McKinsey. https://www.mckinsey.com/industries/pharmaceuticals-and-medical-products/our-insights/the-bio-revolution-innovations-transforming-economies-societies-and-our-lives (accessed 8.4.21).

Convention on Biological Diversity, 2015. About the Nagoya protocol. https://www.cbd.int/abs/about/ (accessed 10.12.21).

East African Community, 2021. Africa's largest convening on bioeconomy. http://www.publicnow.com/view/029483AEF332201FA6034F2EC0D5DBD467E2F347 (accessed 11.10.21). edctp3_draft_proposal_14_august_2020.pdf, n.d.

EIB, 2020. Africa's digital solutions to tackle COVID-19. https://www.eib.org/en/publications/african-digital-best-practice-to-tackle-covid-19 (accessed 8.4.21).

European Commission, 2021a. 1+ Million genomes | Shaping Europe's digital future https://digital-strategy.ec.europa.eu/en/policies/1-million-genomes (accessed 10.11.21).

European Commission, 2021b. Fighting infectious diseases: Focus on Africa. https://ec.europa.eu/commission/presscorner/detail/en/SPEECH_21_3864 (accessed 8.5.21).

European Commission | EU-Africa Global Health Partnership, 2019. EU-Africa global health partnership (Horizon Europe programme) https://ec.europa.eu/info/law/better-regulation/have-your-say/initiatives/11907-EU-Africa-Global-Health-Partnership-Horizon-Europe-programme-_en (accessed 8.6.21).

Gardy, J.L., Loman, N., 2018. Towards a genomics-informed, real-time, global pathogen surveillance system. *Nature Review Genetics.* 19, 9–20. https://doi.org/10.1038/nrg.2017.88

Genuity Science | Biological Data Insights to Power Health Discovery, n.d. https://genuitysci.com/ (accessed 8.12.21).

Giandhari, J., Pillay, S., Wilkinson, E. et al., 2020. *Early transmission of SARS-CoV-2 in South Africa: An epidemiological and phylogenetic report.* medRxiv 2020.05.29.20116376. https://doi.org/10.1101/2020.05.29.20116376

Hamdi, Y., Zass, L., Othman, H., et.al., 2021. Human OMICs and computational biology research in Africa: Current challenges and prospects. *Omics J. Integr. Biol.* 25, 213–233. https://doi.org/10.1089/omi.2021.0004

IQVIA Institute for Human Data Science, 2020. *Understanding the Global Landscape of Genomic Initiatives.* https://www.iqvia.com/insights/the-iqvia-institute/reports/understanding-the-global-landscape-of-genomic-initiatives (accessed 8.3.21).

Kene-Okafor, T., 2020. What 54gene actually does and why you should care, as told by COO, Delali Attipoe. Techpoint Africa. https://techpoint.africa/2020/12/22/what-54gene-actually-does-delali-attipoe/ (accessed 8.5.21).

Lancaster, K., Rubin, M., Rapp-Hooper, M., 2020. *Mapping China's Health Silk Road.* Council on Foreign Relations. https://www.cfr.org/blog/mapping-chinas-health-silk-road (accessed 8.12.21).

Lynch, D.J., 2017. Biotechnology: The US-China dispute over genetic data. *Financial Times.*

Makoni, M., 2020. Africa's $100-million pathogen genomics initiative. *Lancet Microbe* 1, e318. https://doi.org/10.1016/S2666-5247(20)30206-8

Masood, E., 2019. How China is redrawing the map of world science. https://www.nature.com/articles/d41586-019-01124-7 (accessed 8.12.21).

Maxmen, A., 2020. The next chapter for African genomics. https://www.nature.com/articles/d41586-020-00454-1 (accessed 8.5.21).

McKinsey, 2021. *Can European Biotechs Achieve Greater Scale in a Fragmented Landscape?.* https://www.mckinsey.com/industries/pharmaceuticals-and-medical-products/our-insights/can-european-biotechs-achieve-greater-scale-in-a-fragmented-landscape (accessed 8.6.21).

MGI News, 2019. *Africa's First High-throughput Genome Sequencing Center Is Launched.* https://en.mgi-tech.com/News/info/id/15 (accessed 8.12.21).

Miles, T., 2018. WHO Sends First Doses of Experimental Vaccine to Tackle Congo Ebola Outbreak. *Reuters,* 16 mai 2018. https://www.reuters.com/article/health-ebola-idUSL5N1SN35L.

Mulder, N., 2017. Development to enable precision medicine in Africa. *Pers. Med.* 14, 467–470. https://doi.org/10.2217/pme-2017-0055

Mulder, N.J., Adebiyi, E., Adebiyi, M., et al., 2017. Development of bioinformatics infrastructure for genomics research. *Glob. Heart* 12, 91–98. https://doi.org/10.1016/j.gheart.2017.01.005

Munshi, N., 2020. How unlocking the secrets of African DNA could change the world. *Financial Times.*

Nagoya Protocol, B., 2021. *The Nagoya Protocol on Access and Benefit-sharing.* https://www.cbd.int/abs/ (accessed 8.6.21).

Needham, K., Baldwin, C., 2021. *China's Gene Giant Harvests Data from Millions of Pregnant Women.* Reuters.

Nkengasong, J., 2020. Let Africa into the market for COVID-19 diagnostics. *Nature* 580, 565–565. https://doi.org/10.1038/d41586-020-01265-0

Nyirenda, T., Bockarie, M., Machingaidze, et.al., 2021. Strengthening capacity for clinical research in sub-Saharan Africa: Partnerships and networks. *Int. J. Infect. Dis.* 110, 54–61. https://doi.org/10.1016/j.ijid.2021.06.061

Ovadia, Z.U., 2021. Is there any COVID-19 vaccine production in Africa? *Carnegie Endow. Int. Peace.* https://carnegieendowment.org/2021/09/13/is-there-any-covid-19-vaccine-production-in-africa-pub-85320 (accessed 10.12.21).

Pauwels, 2019. The new geopolitics of converging risks: The UN and prevention in the era of AI - United Nations University Centre for Policy Research. https://cpr.unu.edu/research/projects/the-new-geopolitics-of-converging-risks-the-un-and-prevention-in-the-era-of-ai.html#outline (accessed 8.4.21).

Pauwels, E., 2021. Hybrid CoE *Strategic Analysis* 26: Cyber-biosecurity: How to protect biotechnology from adversarial AI attacks. *Hybrid CoE–Eur. Cent. Excell. Countering Hybrid Threats.* https://www.hybridcoe.fi/publications/cyber-biosecurity-how-to-protect-biotechnology-from-adversarial-ai-attacks/ (accessed 8.4.21).

Pauwels, E., 2020. The anatomy of information disorders in Africa https://www.kas.de/en/web/newyork/single-title/-/content/the-anatomy-of-information-disorders-in-africa (accessed 8.12.21).

Peeling, R.W., Boeras, D., Wilder-Smith, A., Sall, A., Nkengasong, J., 2020. Need for sustainable biobanking networks for COVID-19 and other diseases of epidemic potential. *Lancet Infect. Dis.* 20, e268–e273. https://doi.org/10.1016/S1473-3099(20)30461-8

Pennisi, E., 2021. Africans begin to take the reins of research into their own genomes. https://www.sciencemag.org/news/2021/02/africans-begin-take-reins-research-their-own-genomes (accessed 7.30.21).

Pereira, L., Mutesa, L., Tindana, P., Ramsay, M., 2021. African genetic diversity and adaptation inform a precision medicine agenda. *Nat. Rev. Genet.* 22, 284–306. https://doi.org/10.1038/s41576-020-00306-8

Roser, M., Ritchie, H., 2016. *Burden of Disease. Our World Data.*

Roussi, A., 2019. Chinese investments fuel growth in African science. https://www.nature.com/articles/d41586-019-01398-x (accessed 8.12.21).

Schee genannt Halfmann, S., Evangelatos, N., Kweyu, E., et.al., 2018. The creation and management of innovations in healthcare and ICT: The European and African experience. *Public Health Genomics* 21, 197–206. https://doi.org/10.1159/000499853

Siddle, K.J., Eromon, P., Barnes, K.G., et al., 2018. Genomic analysis of Lassa Virus during an increase in cases in Nigeria in 2018. *N. Engl. J. Med.* 379, 1745–1753. https://doi.org/10.1056/NEJMoa1804498

The African Academy of Sciences, 2021. *Policy Paper: Recommendations for Data and Biospecimen Governance in Africa.* https://www.aasciences.africa/publications/policy-paper-recommendations-data-and-biospecimen-governance-africa (accessed 8.1.21).

Thi Nhu Thao, T., Labroussaa, F., Ebert, N., et al., 2020. Rapid reconstruction of SARS-CoV-2 using a synthetic genomics platform. *Nature* 582, 561–565. https://doi.org/10.1038/s41586-020-2294-9

WHO, 2020a. *Emergency Operations Annual Report: Saving Lives and Reducing Suffering WHO's Work in Emergency Response Operations in the WHO African Region in 2018.* World Health Organization.

WHO, 2020b. SARS-CoV-2 Variants. https://www.who.int/emergencies/disease-outbreak-news/item/2020-DON305 (accessed 8.4.21).

WHO, 2019. *HIV Drug Resistance Report 2019.* https://www.who.int/publications-detail-redirect/WHO-CDS-HIV-19.21 (accessed 8.4.21).

Wonkam, A., 2021. Sequence three million genomes across Africa. *Nature* 590, 209–211. https://doi.org/10.1038/d41586-021-00313-7

Zubascu, F., 2020. EU to set up BARDA-style biomedical research agency in 2021 [WWW Document]. *Science|Business.* https://sciencebusiness.net/news/eu-set-barda-style-biomedical-research-agency-2021 (accessed 8.4.21).

5

AFRICAN MICRO, SMALL, AND MEDIUM ENTERPRISES NEED TO DIGITALLY TRANSFORM TO BENEFIT FROM THE AFRICA CONTINENTAL FREE TRADE AREA (AFCFTA)

Tunde Fafunwa and Fola Odufuwa

5.1 Introduction

While there is no standard definition for micro, small, and medium-sized enterprises (MSMEs), the World Trade Organization (WTO) defines small to medium-sized enterprises as companies with 10–250 employees, and companies with less than 10 employees as micro enterprises. The overwhelming numbers of businesses in the MSME category are micro and small (less than 100 employees). Micro, small, and medium-sized enterprises (MSMEs) account for up to 70% of total employment and 50% of GDP in African countries (UN 2021). Successful digitalisation of MSMEs would have extraordinary direct and indirect benefits for job growth and economic gains.

This chapter examines how the digital transformation of African micro, small, and medium-sized enterprises (MSMEs) would allow them to benefit from the AfCFTA. It investigates the current state of digitalisation in MSMEs and the sophistication and complexity of the AfCFTA protocols. The necessity of digitalising for MSMEs to participate and benefit from the reduced trade barriers that the AfCFTA offers is explored. The example of the South African Development Community (SADC) is used to illustrate the benefits of regional cooperation in unlocking the benefits of the AfCFTA for MSMEs. Finally, the value of EU–Africa cooperation to open African markets and platforms for MSME participation is addressed.

Section 5.2 reviews the basis of the AfCFTA and its relationship to businesses. The AfCFTA is an agreement to boost trade between African countries by reducing trade barriers. The treaty came into force as an agreement of 54 African governments in 2019. Initial trading under the agreement commenced in January 2021, with the completion of an e-commerce protocol expected in 2022. The AfCFTA holds great promise as a marquee for driving the next wave of Africa's

DOI: 10.4324/9781003274322-5

growth. Anchored on the prioritisation of intra-African trade, regional collaboration, industrialisation, and economic diversification, the free trade agreement could consolidate the continent's markets by developing regional and specific value chains. It could also offer new opportunities to the private sector and MSMEs in particular to scale their businesses and access large and more lucrative African markets.

Section 5.3 examines the current state of digitalisation in MSMEs and the role that regional bodies such as the SADC can play. MSMEs make up 90% of firms and 60% of all private-sector employment in Africa (ITC 2020). The vision of the AfCFTA is to "create one African market" and encourage MSMEs and large producers to originate and conclude deals among themselves. For this vision to be realised, MSMEs must have digital ecosystems, including e-payments, and a wholesale marketplace (Business to Business (B2B)) such as Alibaba and others. Through collaborative platforms like these, suppliers and buyers could have a "say" in the operation of the system, and an "ownership stake" in the long-term benefits. This section examines a dilemma: while the AfCFTA is designed to get African countries to trade in goods, the continent's manufacturing base is weak. Currently, South Africa, Egypt, and Nigeria together control 56% of the share of manufacturing in African GDP (Signé, 2018). African economies are dominated by highly fragmented MSMEs and a public sector that struggles to implement progressive policies even when formulated. National digital ecosystems are underdeveloped in most African markets.

Notwithstanding these challenges, Section 5.3 argues that digitalisation can enable MSMEs to seize the unprecedented opportunity that the AfCFTA represents. Digitalisation, in our view, is the transformation of a capacity, process, or sector through digital processes or technologies to provide new value or benefits. The implementation of the AfCFTA will open new possibilities in digitalisation for the African continent.

The last section issues a set of recommendations for policymakers and addresses the role of EU–Africa cooperation. The section engages notably with the value of EU–Africa cooperation in MSME capacity development and supporting access to African markets and platforms.

5.2 The AfCFTA and African Enterprises

5.2.1 The Promise of the AfCFTA

The AfCFTA architecture consists of a solid set of negotiated agreements and protocols which intend to create a liberalised single market for African goods and services (AU, 2018). The agreement lays the basis for the structural transformation and diversification of African economies, and the competitiveness of the public and private sectors. The AfCFTA seeks to promote, inter alia, regional integration and collaboration, the development of new value chains, and the establishment of a Digital Single Market (DMS). Following the finalisation of Phase I negotiations the Protocol on Trade in Goods, the Protocol on Trade in Services, and the Protocol on the Rules and Procedures on the Settlement of Disputes were ratified. Phase II negotiations are still ongoing and focus on Protocols on Investment, Competition, and Intellectual Property Rights (AU, 2020b). The African Union (AU) further mandated negotiations on an E-Commerce Protocol for Phase III. In light of the COVID-19 pandemic and the heightened importance of online, virtual, and digital services, the AU stated that the protocol would be completed by December 2021. However, as of January 2022, Phase II negotiations were widely reported to be well advanced, but not complete, with Phase III yet to be fully underway.

However, the AfCFTA is much more than an agreement between nations on trade liberalisation. It is bringing about deep and unprecedented commercial and regulatory arrangements between nations on real-world and digital trade which, as they materialise, will be a watershed achievement for the African continent. Presently, there is no single platform, digital or physical, connecting 1.2 billion Africans through which African buyers can purchase goods or services from African sellers. Overall, e-commerce is limited. Though Nigeria, South Africa, and Kenya account for 50% of online retail sales (ITC, 2020, p. 2), only 1% of Africa's e-commerce marketplaces are responsible for 60% of website visits (ITC, 2020, p. 8). Furthermore, only 11% of African marketplace websites allow for financial transactions. The AfCFTA could thus lead to a significant boost to African e-commerce through its intergovernmental structures and provisions for digital identities, cross-border payments, and mutual recognition, among others.

The AfCFTA came into force on 1 January 2021. However, early adoption is slow as the agreement's protocols are still being negotiated. Various optimistic models estimate that the AfCFTA's positive impacts within the first ten years of implementation could include a 52% rise in intra-African trade (Fofack, 2020), annual growth in GDP of up to 0.97% for the region (Mesut, Peters and Knebel, 2018), and that consumer and business spending could reach a combined value of USD 6.7 trillion (Signé and van der Ven, 2019). African countries are projected to achieve gains from exports of up to 2.2% or USD 56 billion by 2040 (ECA, 2020c).

5.2.2 Characterising African Enterprises

AfCFTA's post-implementation success critically depends on the involvement and active participation of the private sector, which drives the economic growth and development of African countries (ECA, 2020a). Developing and digitally enabling this pivotal sector and onboarding informal MSMEs are essential to improve the quality of life for Africa's citizens as envisaged through the AfCFTA.

According to the International Finance Corporation (IFC 2020), 1,100 companies with annual revenues over USD 500 million are operating in Africa. These large corporations are likely to be early players in the AfCFTA as they have the capacity and resources to access and exploit new opportunities across a wider array of markets. However, most private businesses are not at this scale and fall within the band of MSMEs. Yet, these smaller firms constitute the real backbone of African economies as they make up at least 90% of businesses and 60% of jobs on the continent (ITC, 2018b).

Due to their smaller sizes and restricted ability to scale, MSMEs generally work under tough conditions and business environments. The vast majority falls within the informal sector, which further impedes their capacity and capability to participate in the AfCFTA. The informal sector is generally defined as the segment of the economy that is neither taxed nor monitored by the government (ILO, 2017, p. 11). In Southern Africa, an average of 83% of all enterprises are informal (Table 5.1).

Constraints in the business environment hinder value-adding activities, limit growth, and thus impede many micro and small operators' development into medium-sized or large enterprises. The contrast of an exceedingly large number of smaller firms set against a rather small number of medium or large corporations is a phenomenon described in a UNECA report as the "missing middle" (ECA, 2020a).

Despite these limiting factors, MSMEs make a significant contribution to SADC economies reaching up to 70% in Zambia, 50% in Zimbabwe, 40% in Mauritius, and 34% in South Africa (ECA, 2020b). Lower numbers reflect economies with less dependence on MSMEs. According to OECD, 22% of new jobs in Africa are being created by smaller businesses that have been formed in the last five years (AUC and OECD, 2019).

5.3 Digitalisation and MSMEs

5.3.1 The Function of Digitalisation

The AfCFTA strongly depends on the digitalisation of the public and private sectors. Digitalising the national economy improves public and private access to platforms, data services, and online applications. A digitalised public sector will in turn facilitate crosscutting support for value chains and critical areas of

TABLE 5.1 MSMEs in Southern Africa

No. of MSMEs		Percentage of unregistered MSMEs	
South Africa	5.8 m	Zambia	90
Zimbabwe	3.5 m	Malawi	89
Tanzania	3.1 m	Mozambique	87
Malawi	1.6 m	Tanzania	86
Lesotho	76,068	Zimbabwe	85
Eswatini	68,000	South Africa	84
		Lesotho	81
		Eswatini	75
		Mauritius	70

Sources: Finmark, 2012; 2015; 2017; 2019; IFC 2018; MCTA 2008; MTI 2012

the economy including agriculture, education, finance, and health – to list a few. In the private sector, there is mounting evidence that digitalisation and digital business solutions increase the productivity, capital, and revenue of enterprises (World Bank, 2020). Digitalisation has been proven to transform industries, value chains, and economic segments including the MSME sector (Disse and Summer, 2020). A recent study using World Bank Enterprise data for 266 economies demonstrated that the business use of email in communicating with suppliers and clients, ownership of a business website, or newer equipment or technologies by medium-sized enterprises had positive effects on employment growth (Ndiaye et al, 2018).

The Digital Transformation Strategy for Africa (DTS) (2020-2030) (AU, 2020a) was adopted at the February 2020 AU Summit in Addis Ababa. The strategy identifies several key pillars and crosscutting areas required for digital transformation on the continent. These include skills, infrastructure, regulation, innovation and entrepreneurship, and identification, amongst others. The innovation and entrepreneurship pillar focuses on the importance of MSMEs.

Yet, central to the DTS is the need for mutual recognition, regional integration, and standardisation of existing digital projects and systems. Electronic trust networks are a key enabler of secure cross-border digital interactions and a main building block of the Digital Single Market (DSM) that is hoped will result from the implementation of the AfCFTA.

Evidence suggests that the growing use of digital tools by MSMEs is driven by the penetration of mobile networks and the increasing popularity of platforms and social media (Partnership for Finance in a Digital Africa, 2019). However, it appears that MSME digitalisation is not yet sufficiently developed to positively affect the participation of MSMEs in the AfCFTA in any significant way. Although government policies favour technology adoption and many private sector actors are developing digital capacity programmes, MSME penetration of these initiatives is relatively slim. The lacuna in MSME participation in the continental trade agreement is therefore a *real possibility* that needs to be envisaged and resolved through proactive policymaking.

Digitalisation can help businesses that want to formalise by facilitating the identification and verification of informal enterprises and improving how national agencies responsible for MSME development access them. It can reduce the distances MSMEs travel to reach the nearest registration office, which can be hundreds of kilometres in rural Africa. A Banque de France study from 2019 on the impact of mobile financial services found that the adoption of mobile money and money credit by MSMEs decreased the size of the informal sector by 2.4–4.3 percentage points of GDP between 2000 and 2015 in 101 developing and emerging countries – a third of which are in Africa (Jacolin et al., 2019). A non-representative survey of 500 SMEs in Nigeria concluded that digitalisation has a significant impact on small and medium-sized businesses that participated in the study. The effects of SME digitalisation included job creation, poverty reduction, and the opening up of new business opportunities (Shettima and Sharma, 2018). Furthermore, there is a positive correlation between the use of smartphones by Senegalese MSMEs and exporting (Atiyas and Dutz, 2021). A 2019 survey of Kenyan micro-businesses found increasing use of contemporary digital tools and platforms by MSMEs in their day-to-day business activities resulting in new opportunities and challenges for their economic and financial inclusion (Partnership for Finance in a Digital Africa, 2019). Kenyan MSMEs use e-commerce marketplaces (Alibaba, Amazon), social media (Instagram, WhatsApp, Facebook), and learning channels (YouTube) to source goods, push sales, and create better products and services (Gachoka and Won, 2019).

This trend is not unique to Kenyan MSMEs. Across Africa, MSMEs are going online, with the distinction between their online and offline business activities gradually narrowing. According to the World Bank (2019), 29% of MSMEs in DR Congo use information and communications technology (ICT) to improve business visibility through websites, social media (9%), online training (7%), and digital tools to support operations (6%). More than half of Zambia's SMEs in support services report access to a good-quality internet link. This in turn aids the use of social media for business promotion (56%) and the development of company websites (44%) (ITC, 2018). Around 86% of SMEs that participated in a 2018 survey of 1,000 business owners in South Africa regularly use smartphones, cloud services (22%), and e-commerce (20%) to conduct business (SME Africa, 2018). In a more recent report, 97% of South African small businesses reported that they had invested in new technologies in 2019, with 53% of them citing evidence of significant increases in profitability (Xero, 2020). The use of accounting cloud packages among the same SMEs rose from 13% in 2017 to 61% in 2019, further demonstrating smaller businesses' growing appetite for digital solutions.

This is, however, not the whole story. Despite the emerging shift, MSMEs are generally not taking full advantage of digitalisation. Financial Inclusion on Business Runways (FIBR, 2018) posits that only a few MSMEs are using advanced digital tools such as subscription services in Tanzania, Ghana, and Kenya. A third of South African SMEs that participated in a 2019 survey are apprehensive of "being left behind" due to new developments in technology (Xero, 2020). Stakeholders point to increasing exposure by MSMEs to online fraud, misinformation, and disinformation as challenges to digital adoption by smaller enterprises.

The use of digital tools by MSMEs appears to be driven by the penetration of mobile networks, the increasing popularity of platforms and social media as well as government policies that may favour technology diffusion. MSMEs' adoption of digital technologies relevant to the AfCFTA, however, is relatively thin – even in the leading countries. In addition, although MSME-development strategies based on ICTs, technology, or digitalisation may be referenced in national MSME policy documents, active measures to aid the digitalisation of MSMEs tends to be ineffective; if they are implemented at all. Presently, there is a widening gap between countries with significant advancements in legislation, policies, and infrastructure promoting the digital economy and those that are trailing.

Countries that have embraced digital realities such as Mauritius, Kenya, Nigeria, South Africa, and Rwanda are making good strides to reform their respective national economies. They are implementing policies that promote growth in private sector investments, ease of doing business, ecosystems of innovation, infrastructure implementations, and take-up of digital services by the population. For instance, internet penetration in Northern and Southern Africa is presently 50% and 51% respectively. In contrast, this figure is just 12% for Central Africa, meaning that more work needs to be done by way of policy formulation and infrastructure implementations to lift that region into the digital economy (Hootsuite, 2019). Indeed, perhaps due to digital under-development and other factors, many private enterprises are not currently informed of the imminent implementation of the AfCFTA. A 2020 survey of MSMEs in manufacturing, wholesale/retail, agriculture, and services in Nigeria found that 75% are not aware of AfCFTA (NACCIMA, 2020), signifying acute policy gaps in communication and engagement that need to be addressed if the continental agenda shall be successful from the onset.

This discussion notwithstanding, digitalisation alone cannot resolve all challenges that MSMEs in Africa face. According to Gillwald, Moyo, and Stork (2012), digitalisation usually occurs within the context of a national digital ecosystem enabled by coherent policies. This creates a universe of high-quality interconnected networks, services, applications, and content that are available for different types of users and uses. This ecosystem should create (or update) digital skills, digital workers, and digital communities of innovation and local entrepreneurship – together with enhanced capacities for digital regulations and policy-making. When combined with a complementary suite of policies and incentives that overcome regulatory challenges, digitalisation can create an unprecedented opportunity for governments to formalise and upgrade the MSME sector. Incentive-based online platforms can be created to make the registration of informal enterprises easier. For illustration, Benin increased the registration of informal businesses by 16.3% by offering free training programmes with online bank account opening (IMF, 2020).

5.4 Building Africa's Manufacturing Capabilities

Digitalisation and the implementation of the AfCFTA will improve the competitiveness of African manufacturing. The literature posits that African manufacturing is presently weak and non-competitive (Lopes and Willem te Velde, 2021). This is not the case with African commodities – as most economies are yet to diversify from their high resource- or agriculture-bases. For example, Zambia assessed the readiness of the country's exporters for the AfCFTA and reported that "the greatest limitation to export growth is not market opportunity but limited domestic supply capacity" (MCTI Zambia, 2020). This rings true for much of Africa. Africa's manufacturing value added (MVA) slipped from 16.3% to 9.7% in the 20 years from 1990 to 2010 and currently stands at

11.3% (World Bank, 2021). SADC manufacturing value-added as a proportion of GDP has similarly declined from 12.4% in 2009 to 10.9% in 2019 with Botswana, Zambia, Angola, and Tanzania lagging (SADC, 2021). Though South Africa is the dominant economy in the region with a well-developed telecom, energy, and physical (road, water, and train) infrastructure, the growth of its manufacturing sector has been almost negligible in recent years (SADC, 2021).

There is a growing use of ICTs in manufacturing in many countries. It would appear that this rise is due to an adaptation by local enterprises to global trends rather than a response to any explicit digital policies that specifically promote digital manufacturing. Yet, the AfCFTA depends on the industrialisation of Africa and the domestic production of local "Made in Africa" goods, which must be competitive to thrive in cross-border markets. Diversified economies with a solid industrial base producing locally manufactured goods will be the early beneficiaries of the AfCFTA (UNCTAD, 2019).

5.5 COVID-19 and Digitalisation

While COVID-19 has posed a huge challenge in every area of life, the pandemic is accelerating the digitalisation of businesses through increased uptake of digital tools and remote working. Much of the digitalisation of society and enterprises is taking place regardless of government policy. Since the start of the pandemic, digital adoption is estimated to have jumped ahead to where it was expected to be in 2023 or even 2024. Apart from the well-known examples of education moving into the virtual space, the adoption of digital technologies, including basic e-commerce, and digital payments by the African private sector, has also significantly increased. Twenty-five per cent of Africa's MSMEs scaled up their use of digital tools during the pandemic, with women-owned MSMEs demonstrating as much interest in digitalisation and digital upskilling as MSMEs led by men (IFC, 20201).

In an ECA business survey conducted in March 2021, 61% of firms reported an increase in online sales since the start of COVID-19. In reaction to the crisis, 61% of micro-sized enterprises and 75% of businesses in the goods sector identified online selling as a major new opportunity area (ECA, 2021). Although COVID-19 exacerbated the vulnerability of the private sector and MSMEs, the increased digitalisation spurred by the outbreak appears long-lasting. Accordingly, it leads to greater use of technology which may result in advantages in new business models and practices, and help African economies to build back better.

Based on these developments, two key questions arise:

(1) How to sustain MSMEs' transition to digitalisation that arose from the shock and realities of the pandemic?
(2) How to provide institutional support to African economies to help them build back better?

COVID-19 is an opportunity to accelerate the digitalisation of MSMEs. Governments should seize this opportunity and offer financial support and incentives, online information services, and toolkits; set up digital teams to directly assist MSMEs with digitalisation and formalisation; and develop capacity building and training programmes to help businesses overcome the challenges created by the pandemic. As a result, increased digitalisation of MSMEs, arising from the outbreak of COVID-19, could become long-lasting and lead to greater use of technology, new business models, and sustainable trade practices.

5.6 MSMEs and the AfCFTA

5.6.1 Integrating African MSMEs into the AfCFTA

Although the AfCFTA is designed to bring African countries together in a way never seen before, there are presently no direct provisions or institutional arrangements particularly targeted at the inclusion of MSMEs in the continental single market. Therefore, MSMEs may find it difficult to participate and take advantage of the AfCFTA without significant digitalisation upgrades, capacity development, and institutional support, leading to the removal of barriers to doing business across borders.

From a review of the agreement and negotiated protocols, the AfCFTA provisions for MSMEs appear elementary rather than revolutionary. For instance, the Protocol on Trade in Services seeks to channel the potential and capacities of MSMEs to participate in regional and global value chains but the strategies detailing how this would be done are not clear. Article 27 (2d) of the Protocol directly mandates countries to give specific attention to formal and informal MSME service suppliers, especially those owned by women and youth (African Union, 2018). But the national or regional mechanisms to implement this policy are not specified and still need to be worked out. It is thus not clear how informal MSMEs could *actually* participate in the AfCFTA.

The ability of African MSMEs to participate in the AfCFTA (even if they digitalise) is presently limited by different critical factors:

- The high costs of doing business at home, which are partly due to the overbearing way MSMEs are licensed, taxed, and regulated particularly, which altogether lead to high input costs.
- The limitations and barriers encountered in cross-border trading. The movement of goods and services between countries – a central premise of the AfCFTA – is presently affected by the prevalence of Non-Tariff Barriers (NTBs) and Non-Tariff Measures (NTMs) in most countries. Across Africa, there are trade disputes between countries leading to the closure of borders and restriction of trade, which, if unresolved, will continue to affect MSMEs and intra-Africa trade in undesirable ways. African governments are generally reluctant to open up their domestic markets to external competition or

players from other African countries. For example, cabotage restrictions that limit the ability of a company to move goods and services into another country will prevent e-hauling tech companies that facilitate factory-to-retail distribution from scaling across borders contrary to the goals of the AfCFTA.

Liberalisation will positively lift national e-commerce ambitions by enabling a coordinated flow of cross-border goods, allowing consumers in one country to be able to purchase goods and services from another country. These cross-border exchanges are presently not possible under existing business and regulatory environments.

- Inadequate business support and trade facilitation. More importantly, although AfCFTA was designed to enable African enterprises to do business among themselves, there is an underlying assumption that MSMEs can and want to internationalise. However, evidence suggests that MSMEs may not be able to trade across borders on their own, even if they digitalise, without significant assistance in digital upskilling, trade facilitation, e-commerce policy support, and access to finance. Likewise, they will need access to information exchanges for price and opportunity discovery, and infrastructure improvements to aid cross-border logistics.

African policymakers are in uncharted territory concerning the implementation of the AfCFTA. All the AfCFTA agreements and negotiated protocols should contribute to the reform of the public and private sectors and positively affect MSMEs when operationalised. Still, MSME-focused institutional coverage is required, and the interests of MSMEs need to be directly acknowledged and considered in the development of regional and national strategies for implementing the free trade agreement. MSMEs need external help in virtually all African countries without which their participation in the AfCFTA is likely going to be feeble. The assumption that MSMEs will automatically participate in the AfCFTA when countries improve their domestic business environments may be overly simplistic or even far-fetched.

5.7 Recommendations for Policymakers

5.7.1 Supporting African Policymaking Bodies to Aachieve AfCFTA – MSME Connections

The success of the AfCFTA depends heavily on African national governments liberalising their markets and adopting digitally biased MSME policies. There is overwhelming evidence of a disconnect between the apparent sound commitment by many African governments to good policies and the practical implementation of those policies, attributed to ineffective institutional capacity or weak political economy environments (Lopes and Willem te Velde, 2021).

Nearly all African countries have established MSME policies and business development and support programmes, but implementation and practice often fall *way behind* government objectives. Furthermore, most national MSME policies were developed pre-AfCFTA and need to be updated to get them fit-for-purpose for the continental trade arrangements. There is a real possibility that MSMEs may be unwittingly "left behind" as the operationalisation of the AfCFTA goes forward. There is thus a case to be made for the creation of institutional structures to support the integration of MSMEs into the AfCFTA – though the form and nature of how to do this may be debated. It appears that without such structures the AfCFTA's potential to benefit MSMEs will be significantly reduced. Consequently, to effectively support the development and digitalisation of the MSME sector, it does not suffice to anchor AfCFTA implementation on a business-as-usual policy approach.

5.7.2 Going Forward

Four areas need to be addressed to guarantee the AfCFTA's success in accelerating digital transformation. First, it is essential to resolve incoherence and inconsistencies within and between national regulatory systems relating to e-commerce. Key areas for creating an enabling digital environment are eTransactions, ePayments, Data Protection, and Cybersecurity. According to the World Bank (2021), most lower- and middle-income countries have deficiencies in one or more of these areas. National reform addressing these deficiencies could then fit into making the AfCFTA work at the continental level.

New frameworks are emerging to develop digital regulatory environments that are progressive, holistic, and collaborative. These new approaches recognise the complex, fast-changing, and often confusing environment in which technological innovation and digital services are created, managed, and controlled. In addition, collaboration across public, private, and civil sectors plays a pivotal role in delivering and generating a successful and inclusive regulatory environment. Most importantly, these new frameworks put people and the common good closer to the central purpose of regulation.

One such framework is the International Telecommunications Union's (ITU) G5 (fifth generation) regulation (ITU, 2020b). The ITU's G5 benchmark for collaborative regulation provides new regulatory perspectives and tools, roadmaps for navigating digital transformation, and evidence-based exploration of the future of markets and regulation. The G5 approach supports "leap-frogging" over previous generations of regulation, particularly G3 (third generation), which emphasises a siloed approach to access, innovation, investment, competition, and consumer protection. The ITU identified several African countries that successfully forged ahead in specific areas or overall, including Kenya, Morocco, and Botswana. Regional bodies such as the AU and the UN Economic Commission for Africa (ECA) can play a significant role as facilitators and enablers of solutions of this nature, by using their convening power to engage and support the member states actively.

Second, a cohesive, standards-based purchasing initiative should be modelled on the digital online trading platform approach of the African Medical Supply

Platform (AMSP). AMSP was created in mid-2020 and is run by the Africa Centres for Disease Control and Prevention through the AU, with support from the UN ECA. It receives funding from the African Export-Import Bank.

AMSP has created a bulk online purchasing power platform for African governments to secure medical supplies. At a time when the price of medical masks increased sixfold, AMSP was able to offer producers larger, more reliable, orders, while simultaneously offering buyers stable lower prices. This could be achieved by automating the aggregation of orders, digitalising back-end processes, providing transparency, and creating a "trusted" environment for African countries to effectively compete for goods while benefiting from competitive wholesale prices. Practical AfCFTA complexities as to how one country will recognise and allow MSMEs in another to play in its markets may be better treated under this kind of platform approach.

AMSP has shown that when African countries come together, significant breakthrough initiatives can be achieved. There is reason to believe that no single nation would have been able on its own to successfully handle the outbreak of COVID-19 without the sort of resources and institutional arrangements that AMSP made available for the entire continent. In unlocking the digital transformation, there is much to be learned from this unique crisis-driven innovation. It created a continent-wide digital platform, including a "made in Africa" section, all virtually, without any in-person meetings.

Third, a sustained "mass market" approach to bringing MSMEs online and into the formal economy is needed. Efforts by Microsoft, Cisco, and others to onboard MSMEs onto the web and e-commerce should be expanded to also include African platforms. For example, Microsoft's 4Afrika initiative invests in start-ups, partners, small-to-medium enterprises, and youth and claims to have trained 1.6m individuals across Africa to date since 2013 (Microsoft, 2021). Cisco has shown a commitment to training students on its technology, with almost 700,000 students trained since 1998, and a further commitment to training an additional one million students between 2020 and 2025 (Cisco, 2019).

More recently, social enterprises like Potential.com, are making a broad set of business, management, and e-commerce tools and capabilities available to SMEs for free. This effort, if expanded and combined with the establishment of local SME hubs as proposed by the International Chambers of Commerce (ICC) and sustained over the medium term, could also provide the kind of scale required for a mass migration of SMEs online.

Finally, direct linkages between the state, private sector, and civil society are required. Public–private partnerships (PPP) can be a critical mechanism to leverage scarce public funding, with private sector capital and innovation. The need to balance the PPPs' public benefits with private profits is well understood. However, the opportunity to both validate the public benefit and deepen it by adding civil society operating at the community level is frequently overlooked. Civil society organisations (CSOs) provide two vital and unique success factors. First, they are typically integrated or embedded with different communities and therefore can better represent and articulate their needs. Second, CSOs can play a critical role in validating the expected benefits of the implementation mechanisms and programs. Therefore, CSOs constitute the critical "third leg" required for sustainable success. Digital tools and services including moderated chat groups, online workshops, webinars, and communication platforms can facilitate engagement and dialogue between stakeholders. The public sector must retain leadership, accountability, and oversight capabilities for creating an enabling environment and ecosystem. Meanwhile, the private sector has a crucial role in the design, management, operations, and delivery of digital systems. The participation of civil society in the design and monitoring of how these systems are utilised is critical. Without CSOs as the essential "third leg", any recommendation for an inclusive continent-wide strategy may not work.

5.8 EU–Africa Cooperation

EU–Africa cooperation could play a fundamental role in accelerating digital transformation through the AfCFTA. SMEs form the core of the EU economy. In the EU they employ more than 100 million people, account for 99% of all businesses, and generate more than 50% of the region's gross domestic product, with high priority given by European policymakers to both digitalisation and access to global markets (European Commission, 2021). The EU Digital Services Act and Digital Markets Act aim to put people first in policies and frameworks for fair, interoperable platforms. This is also consistent with the European Digital SME Alliance, whose principles seek to ensure that SMEs can benefit from and compete online via a level playing field. Therefore the EU brings a deep understanding of the vital role SMEs play in economic growth and prosperity. At the same time, according to Eurostat (2021), Europe was Africa's largest trade partner with a 28% share of exports and imports. Much of this trade entails the export of commodities and primary goods from Africa to Europe and import into Africa of manufactured goods. While the amount and percentage of digital transactions are difficult to ascertain, most indications are that these currently make up a small part of EU–Africa trade, but this is likely to grow significantly going forward.

However, for EU–Africa digital trade to grow significantly, several barriers must be overcome. One of the critical barriers that African businesses must navigate and master to do business with the EU is data protection, notably the EU's General Data Protection Regulation (GDPR). While the EU is a frontrunner for personal privacy and data protection, the regulatory environment is complex, challenging, and time-consuming to master, and requires significant resources to build and maintain compliance. For data services and transactions, these rules are non-negotiable. EU–Africa cooperation could provide a facility to support the training, access to resources, and compliance certification for African MSME businesses. Online self-paced tutorials and training modules, particularly in local languages, and an interactive tool for checking compliance would go a long way to getting MSMEs over the digital business divide.

Many policymakers in Africa find the dynamic, complex, constantly evolving data and technology environment daunting. EU–Africa cooperation could provide an interactive channel for sister institutions and policymakers in the EU and Africa to engage in a constructive dialogue, and jointly explore how to regulate digital technology for the common good. In doing this, it is vital to guard against isomorphic mimicry (Andrews et al., 2017) – a situation where "best practices" are replicated in form but not in function. Unfortunately, this situation is all too common where processes and institutions are copied but lack the necessary depth of experience, expertise, and independent authority to make them truly successful. What is needed is to fund platforms and frameworks that enable policymakers to meet, engage, and interact in structured peer learning exchanges. Well-structured peer exchanges with expert input and two-way dialogue that interrogates complex digital policy issues among practicing policymakers are essential to creating successful "African solutions to African problems".

Policies and regulations are only part of the picture; investment is needed to create and extend digital infrastructure, digital services, and digital innovation. On the continent, there are more than 630 tech and innovation hubs and a vigorous fintech sector. Innovation is required, particularly for interconnected e-payments systems and digital services. The EU–Africa cooperation can encourage Series A and B funding and spur private equity investment by supporting the dissemination of factual data, to counter some of the risk premium generated due to the information gap that exists for potential investors.

Innovative funding models are already emerging, such as from the World Economic Forum (WEF). WEF created the EDISON Alliance, a large global alliance to improve the lives of one billion people globally through affordable and accessible digital solutions. As part of this initiative, the green and sustainable bond framework was adopted as a template to create a Guidebook to Digital Inclusion Bond Financing (WEF, 2021). The guidebook supports companies in raising money for projects around digital infrastructure and services by issuing digital inclusion bonds specifically for that purpose. EU–Africa cooperation initiatives could advocate this approach with a focus on collaborative B2B platforms that bring a broad range of MSMEs into the digital and e-commerce marketplace.

Finally, the creation of a DSM is a stated priority of the African Digital Transformation Strategy, the African Union, the ECA, and is supported by the EU. A DSM could help overcome the small market sizes, and differing regulations, that currently constrain investment in many African tech businesses. Providing financing instruments, such as guarantees and blended finance, for cross-border digital investments, and improving links to the EU single market would go a long way to accelerating the DSM (Daniels et al., 2020).

References

AU (African Union) (2018) *Agreement establishing the African Continental Free Trade Area.* Addis Ababa: African Union.

African Union (2020a) *Digital Transformation Strategy for Africa (2020–2030)*. Addis Ababa: African Union.

African Union (2020b) *Decision on the African Continental Free Trade Area (AfCFTA). Assembly/AU/Dec.751(XXXIII)*. African Union. Available at: https://www.tralac.org/documents/resources/cfta/3176-au-assembly-decision-on-the-afcfta-february-2020/file.html. (Accessed: 9 June 2021).

Andrews, M., Pritchett, L. and Woolcock, M. (2017) *Looking Like a State: The Seduction of Isomorphic Mimicry*. Oxford: Oxford Scholarship Online.

Atiyas, I. and Dutz, M. (2021) *Digital Technology Uses Among Informal Micro-sized Firms Productivity and Jobs Outcomes in Senegal*. Washington, DC: World Bank.

AUC and OECD (2019) *Africa's Development Dynamics 2019: Achieving Productive Transformation*. Addis Ababa: African Union.

Cisco (2019) *Cisco Reinforces Commitment to Africa: Training 1 Million New Members of Africa's Digital Workforce and Expanding Support for SMBs"*. Available at: https://newsroom.cisco.com/press-release-content?type=webcontent&articleId=1988801 (Accessed: 3 June 2021).

Daniels, C., Erforth, B., Floyd, R., and Teevan, C. (2020) *Strengthening the Digital Partnership Between Africa and Europe*. Brussels: European Think Tanks Group (ETTG).

Disse, S. and Summer, C. (2020) *Digitalization and Its Impact on SME Finance in Sub-Saharan Africa: Reviewing the Hype and Actual Developments*. Bonn: German Development Institute.

ECA (2020a) *Innovative Finance for Private Sector Development in Africa*. Addis Ababa: Economic Commission for Africa.

ECA (2020b) *Strategies and Policies for the Integration of Micro, Small and Medium-sized Enterprises into the Industrialization Process in Southern Africa*. Addis Ababa: Economic Commission for Africa.

ECA (2020c) *An Empirical Assessment of the African Continental Free Trade Area Modalities on Goods*. Addis Ababa: Economic Commission for Africa.

ECA (2021) *Reactions and Outlook to COVID-19 in Southern Africa*. Addis Ababa: Economic Commission for Africa.

European Commission (2021) *Internal Market, Industry, Entrepreneurship and SMEs*. Available at https://single-market-economy.ec.europa.eu/smes_en

Eurostat (2021) *Africa-EU: International Trade in Goods Statistics. Eurostat Statistics Explained*. Brussels: European Union.

FIBR (2018) *Superplatforms: Unlocking the Potential of Merchants, E-Commerce and Financial Services in Africa*. Cambridge: BFA Global.

Finmark (2012) *FinScope MSME survey Zimbabwe 2012*. Johannesburg: Finmark Trust.

Finmark (2015) *FinScope MSME Lesotho*. Johannesburg: Finmark Trust.

Finmark (2017) *Micro, Small and Medium Enterprise Survey Eswatini 2017 Report*. Johannesburg: Finmark Trust.

Finmark (2019) *FinScope Malawi 2019 micro, small and medium enterprise survey*. Johannesburg: Finmark Trust.

Fofack, H. (2020) *Making the AfCFTA Work for the Africa We Want*. Washington, DC: Africa Growth Initiative at Brookings Policy Brief.

Gachoka, A. and Won, J. (2019) *How Small Merchants in Africa Are Using Superplatforms*. presented at the FiBR Webinar, February 28, 2019. Available at https://www.dropbox.com/s/wg6c2g8c0tjb8p8/FIBR%20Webinar_%20Superplatforms%20and%20MSMEs.pdf?dl=0. .

Gillwald, A., Moyo, M., and Stork, C. (2012) *Understanding What Is Happening in ICT in South Africa, Policy Paper 7*. Cape Town: Research ICT Africa.

Hootsuite (2019) *Digital 2019: Essential Insights into How People Around the World Use the Internet, Mobile Devices, Social Media, and e-commerce.* Vancouver: Hootsuite.

IFC (2018) *The Unseen Sector: A Report on the MSME Opportunity in South Africa.* Washington, DC: International Finance Corporation.

IFC (2020), *e-Conomy Africa 2020: Africa's $180 Billion Internet Economy future.* Washington, DC: International Finance Corporation.

ILO (2017) *Transition from the informal to the formal economy recommendation, 2015 (No. 204): Workers' Guide.* Geneva: International Labour Office.

IMF (2020) *Digitalisation in Sub-saharan Africa.* Washington, DC: International Monetary Fund.

ITC (2018) *Promoting SME Competitiveness in Zambia.* Geneva: International Trade Centre.

ITC (2020) *Business and Policy Insights: Mapping e-Marketplaces in Africa Publisher.* Geneva: International Trade Centre.

ITU (2020a) *Measuring Digital Development: Facts and Figures 2020.* Geneva: International Telecommunication Union.

ITU (2020b) *Global ICT Regulatory Outlook 2020. Pointing the Way Forward to Collaborative Regulation.* Geneva: International Telecommunication Union.

Jacolin L., Massil J. K., and Noah A. (2019) *Informal Sector and Mobile Financial Services in Developing Countries: Does Financial Innovation Matter?* Paris: Banque de France.

Lopes, C., and Willem te Velde, D. (2021) *Structural Transformation, Economic Development and Industrialization in post-Covid-19 Africa.* New York: Institute for New Economic Thinking.

MCTI (2008) *Revised Small, Micro, & Medium Enterprise Policy Of Eswatini.* Mbabane: Ministry of Commerce, Trade & Industry.

MCTI Zambia (2020) *National Strategy for Implementation of the African Continental Free Trade Area Agreement.* Lusaka: Ministry of Commerce, Trade & Industry.

Mesut, S., Peters, R. and Knebel, C. (2018) African Continental Free Trade Area: challenges and opportunities of tariff reductions. UNCTAD Research Paper No. 15. *Division on International Trade in Goods and Services, and Commodities, UNCTAD.* Available at: https://unctad.org/en/PublicationsLibrary/ser-rp-2017d15_en.pdf (Accessed: 8 June 2021).

Microsoft (2021) *The Microsoft 4Afrika journey in Africa.* Available at: https://query.prod.cms.rt.microsoft.com/cms/api/am/binary/RWCYLh. (Accessed: 4 June 2021).

MTI (2012) *National Baseline Survey Report: Micro, Small and Medium Enterprises in Tanzania.* Dodoma: Ministry of Trade & Industry.

NACCIMA (2020) *Impact of the African Continental Free Trade Area on Nigerian Micro, Small, and Medium Enterprises.* Lagos: Nigerian Association of Chamber of Commerce, Industry, Mines, and Agriculture.

Ndiaye, N., Razak, L.A., Nagayev, R., and Ng, A. (2018) *Demystifying Small & Medium Enterprises' Performance in Emerging and Developing Economies.* Available at: www.elsevier.com/journals/borsa-istanbul-review/2214-8450 (Accessed: 9 June 2021).

Partnership for Finance in a Digital Africa (2019) *Micro-Entrepreneurs in a Platform Era.* Surrey: Partnership for Finance in a Digital Africa.

SADC (2021) *SADC Selected Economic and Social Indicators 2019.* Gaborone: Southern Africa Development Community.

Signé, L. (2018) *The Potential of Manufacturing and Industrialization in Africa: Trends, Opportunities, and Strategies.* Washington, DC: Brookings Institution.

Signé, L. and van der Ven, C. (2019) *Key to Success for the AfCFTA Negotiations.* Washington, DC: Africa Growth Initiative at Brookings Policy Brief.

Shettima, M.B., and Sharma, N. (2018) *Impact of Digitalization on Small and Medium Enterprises in Nigeria.* Chennai: Indian Journal of Science & Technology.

SME Africa (2018) *An Assessment of South Africa's SME Landscape Challenges, Opportunities, Risks & Next Steps.* Johannesburg: SME Africa.

United Nations (2021) *MSME 2021: Key to an Inclusive and Sustainable Recovery.* Geneva: United Nations.

UNCTAD (2019) *Economic Development in Africa Report 2019 Made in Africa – Rules of Origin for Enhanced Intra-African Trade.* Geneva: SADC.

World Bank (2019) *Scaling up Ecosystems for Small Businesses in the Democratic Republic of Congo.* Washington, DC: World Bank.

World Bank (2020) *Africa's Pulse: Charting the Road to Recovery.* Washington, DC: World Bank.

World Bank (2021) *World Development Indicators.* Washington, DC: World Bank.

WEF (2021) *Guidebook to Digital Inclusion Bond Financing - The EDISON Alliance.* Geneva: World Economic Forum.

Xero (2020) *RE: START 2020: The State of South African Small Business: The Trends Set to Shape Recovery.* Cape Town.

6

DIGITALISATION, GLOBALISATION, AND COVID-19

Unpacking the Opportunities for African Labour Markets

Karishma Banga

6.1 Introduction

The African economy has been hard-hit by the COVID-19 pandemic; real GDP in Africa was projected to grow by 3.4% in 2021, after contracting by 2.1% in 2020 due to COVID-19. In the same year (2020), working hours across the continent declined by 7.7%, and an estimated 29 million African jobs may have been lost (World Bank, 2021). Amidst this downwards trend, some segments of the global economy have been worse hit than others – particularly the informal sector, labour-intensive manufacturing, and micro, small and medium-sized enterprises (MSMEs). In contrast, COVID-19 has given a boost to the demand for ICT and ICT-enabled services, with global ICT services exports reaching USD 676 billion in 2020 (UNCTAD, 2021). Leveraging digital transformation and digital trade in Africa has been increasingly touted as a crucial mitigating pathway from the economic effects of COVID-19. Digitalisation in sub-Saharan Africa (SSA), for instance, is estimated to increase growth by nearly two percentage points and reduce poverty by one percentage point a year (World Bank, 2019), with the effect being doubled if paired with stronger investments in human capital.

The EU has historically been an important economic partner for Africa; it is the largest investor, with its foreign direct investment stock in Africa reaching EUR 222 billion (UNCTAD, 2018). The post-COVID-19 recovery of African trade is also significantly linked to European production and trade recovery, given the close integration of African firms within Europe-led supply chains. Of all African value added in exports, a sizeable 62.8% is embedded within EU exports (Figure 6.1). The EU is also an important partner for trade in services for Africa, accounting for 32% of Africa's total services exports and 44% of information and communications technology (ICT) exports (Figure 6.2). The digital

DOI: 10.4324/9781003274322-6

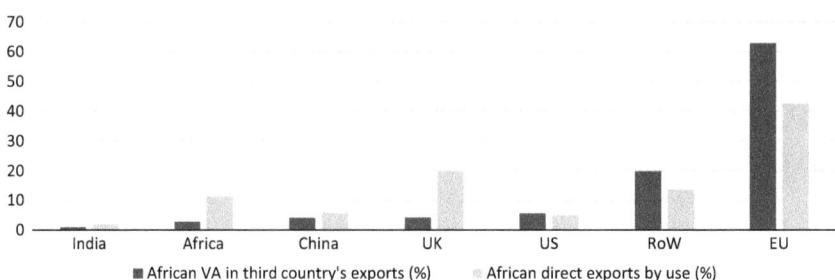

FIGURE 6.1 African VA, by Partner Economies. *Source: Data from Banga et al. (2020). VA is value-added.*

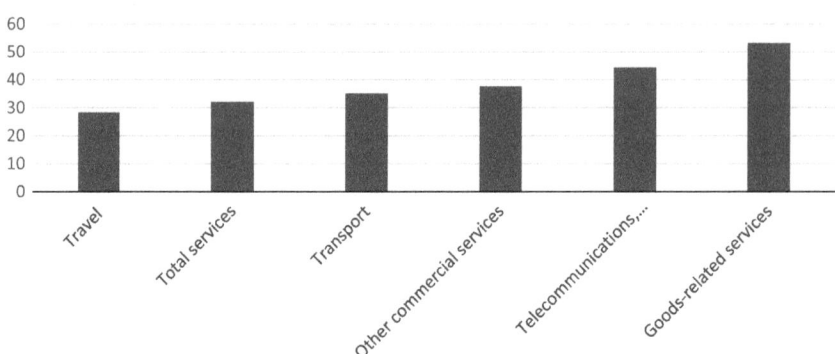

FIGURE 6.2 EU's Share in Africa's Export of Services. Source: Author, constructed from BaTIS.

sector in Africa has, however, been dominated by China's presence; around 70% of the continent's 4G networks, for instance, have been supported by Chinese investment (Mackinnon 2019).

There is much scope for developing an effective cooperation between the European Union (EU) and African Union (AU) in supporting digital transformation on the continent. The EU has identified digitalisation as an important area in development cooperation and recognised the need for mainstreaming digital technologies and services in EU development policy (ETTG, 2020). In particular, the Joint Communication by the European Commission to the European Parliament and the Council in 2020 proposed action on partnering with Africa to boost the continent's digital transformation (EU, 2020). The Joint Communication recognised the need for the EU–AU partnership to leverage its close ties and geographic proximity to enhance economic opportunities and decent job creation on both continents, including through boosting trade and sustainable investments in Africa and advancing regional and continental economic integration (EU, 2020). The increased interest in the digital economy on the African continent due to economic effects from COVID-19, coupled with the upcoming e-commerce negotiations in the AfCFTA, presents a unique opportunity for the EU to share lessons on creation of digital single markets and regulatory frameworks and to build digital cooperation with the AU. Several EU member states have already committed to supporting the growth of e-commerce in Africa, as noted in their Digital for Development (D4D) strategies. For instance, Germany and the Netherlands are supporting UNCTAD's *Rapid eTrade Readiness Assessments of Least Developed Countries* programme, which aims to help countries in identifying barriers to e-commerce development and proposes tailored solutions. *Make-IT in Africa*, funded by the German Federal Ministry for Economic Cooperation and Development (BMZ), is another good example of a tech entrepreneurship initiative promoting digital innovation for sustainable and inclusive development in Africa by facilitating better access to finance, markets and skills. At the continental level, the recently launched D4D Hub emphasises the need for an African Digital Single market, while GIZ has partnered with the AU on another project called Data-Cipation, which takes a citizen-centric approach in digital projects for facilitating good governance (GIZ, 2018).

But digital transformation in Africa will require more targeted investments, informed by careful analysis of policy and regulatory readiness for technology sustainability and its inclusive engagement. There is a persistent digital divide, in both access and use of technology; for instance, 82.5% of Europeans had access to the internet in 2019, but this falls to less than 30% of the African population (ETTG, 2020). Even at the same level of internet penetration, SSA countries benefit less in terms of manufacturing productivity gains, due to an overall lack of physical infrastructure and absorptive capacity (Banga and te Velde, 2018). This two-pronged digital divide is likely to have important distributional effects in terms of exacerbating the existing socio-economic divides, both between Africa and the rest of the world, and within African countries.

This chapter focuses on leveraging the EU–AU partnership for targeted digital interventions that can boost job creation in Africa. It provides a holistic and nuanced understanding as to how labour markets in African countries are changing against the backdrop of digitalisation, globalisation, and COVID-19, with the aim of identifying critical and concrete areas of intervention for the EU–AU digital cooperation. This is done by examining the challenges and opportunities presented by digital technologies in all three sectors – agriculture, manufacturing, and services – and analysing how the EU–AU digital cooperation can facilitate structural transformation on the African continent by increasing both within-sector and across-sector productivity gains. Such structural transformation is critical for the creation of more productive and decent jobs in Africa (Oqubay and Ohno, 2019). Section 2 examines the role of digital transformation in boosting job creation in the agricultural sector. Section 3 analyses the potential of manufacturing-led recovery, while Section 4 identifies new avenues unlocked in the services sector due to digitalisation, further accelerated by the pandemic. Section 5 presents concluding remarks.

6.2 Digitalisation and Agriculture-led Employment Growth in Africa Post-COVID-19

Agriculture historically accounts for a large share of export earnings in many African countries– for instance, 65% in Kenya and 84% in Ethiopia – as well as of employment. While the agricultural sector continues to account for more than 50% of the sub-Saharan African workforce, employment in the sector has declined by roughly 18% over the last 20 years (World Development Indicators, 2021). The agricultural sector in African countries has also witnessed several supply-side shocks during the pandemic; including (a) lower access to markets due to restrictions on movement, closure of markets and business, and serious declines in household incomes across communities; (b) lower access to labour during lockdown; (c) loss of land for farming due to inability to afford rent; and (d) inability to top-up mobile phones with credit due to travel restrictions (ibid.). Given that the agricultural sector in Africa has traditionally catered to the domestic market rather than the export market, it has been relatively less affected by adverse demand shocks from the pandemic. In fact, as per World Bank (2021), household employment in agriculture has risen in Uganda, Nigeria, and Malawi since the beginning of the COVID-19 pandemic, with people previously not engaged in agricultural activities moving into the sector, particularly into crop farming (World Bank, 2021). However, in some countries, such as Uganda, there has been a shift towards subsistence farming due to the pandemic (Banga et al., 2021).

6.2.1 Ag-platforms: Opportunities and Challenges

Leveraging digitalisation for increasing value from the agricultural sector holds significant potential for boosting employment generation, particularly for post-COVID-19 recovery on the continent. Digitalisation of the sector can further facilitate linkages between the less-formal segments of the sector with more formal and productive segments.

Digital technologies operating in the African agricultural sector can be broadly classified under five categories;

- agricultural digital platforms, primarily driven by software development;
- agricultural biotechnology, harnessing the strengths of biotech and bioengineering;
- innovative food and farming, which unlock new systems of plantation and food alternatives;
- farm robotics and automation, drawing on mechanical and electronic engineering coupled with artificial intelligence (AI); and
- smart warehousing and logistics, consisting of the use of blockchains, fleet optimisation software and economic resource planning (ERP).

Among the five sets of technologies, agricultural digital platforms (here on in ag-platforms) have the highest uptake on the continent and therefore hold the most potential in transforming the African agricultural sector and creating new employment opportunities (see Table 6.1). The prioritisation of digital platforms over other technologies in agricultural value chains has been corroborated by Krishnan et al. (2020) in their study of digitalisation in the East African agricultural sector. The authors find that the majority of the agri-businesses in East Africa – between 66% and 86% of firms – are using data-connected devices, such as mobile and web apps, to facilitate information, financial and commodity transaction processes along agricultural value chains. However, the use of digital platforms on the continent remains fragmented. As of January 2021, there were 1,200 digital platforms in Africa, with only five African countries – Nigeria, South Africa, Kenya, Egypt, and Ghana – accounting for 80% of these (GSMA, 2021).

Digital platformisation of the African agricultural sector, whilst holding significant potential to transform the sector, could exacerbate existing socio-economic inequalities (Krishnan et al., 2020; Banga et al., 2021). Farmers on ag-platforms in Uganda[1] did better, in terms of access to trainings and access to decent work, but a gender digital divide still persisted (Krishnan et al., 2020). Female farmers not only had lower access to the internet than men, but also had lower productivity than male farmers, even when using the same platforms.

TABLE 6.1 Digital Platforms in Agriculture: Pathways for Growth and Job Creation

Pathway	Potential impact on business growth and employment
Platforms for digital value chain management	Enabling agribusinesses, cooperatives, nucleus farms and input agro-dealers to connect with smallholder farmers; creating efficiencies in the supply chains. Improvements in value chain quality through enabling higher traceability and accountability.
E-commerce platforms	Lower transaction costs and information asymmetries; connecting smallholder farmers with commercial players. Digital platforms can link the informal agricultural sector to more productive sectors of the economy and to potential markets and lead to increased agricultural regional trade, and subsequently jobs.
Digital financial platforms	Increased resource flows due to mobile technologies in farming can increase demand for labour and employment; for instance employment increased by 12 percentage points in Kenya due to M-Pesa.
Platforms for information exchange	Access to real-time data, land and weather mapping ag-platforms can increase value-addition and diversification of functions, creating new and more skilled jobs.
Digital trade facilitation	Introduction of single window for trade facilitation, digital certificates of origins, electronic cargo tracking and development of apps such as Sauti, targeting cross-border trade.

Source: Author, based on a review of literature

Ag-platforms also seemed to have increased access to formal work for women and youth – i.e. a higher share of platformised women and young farmers received a contract for their work than those that were off platforms (ibid.). However, numbers remained critically low, indicating that buyer–farmer relationships have not yet formalised to the extent of providing contracts, implying low trust in online services and e-commerce as well as limited cohesion in the relationship (ibid.). Furthermore, digital farming apps are currently unable to live up to their promise of providing real-time information on weather, soil, pests, and other natural factors (an in-turn productivity gains) due to a limited number of mobile towers in African rural areas (ibid.).

A different survey of 400 Ugandan ag-entrepreneurs revealed that a majority of digital platform users reported a spike in their use of the platform after COVID hit, primarily for searching more information on COVID support and to access farming inputs, such as seeds and fertilisers, during the lockdown (Banga et al, 2021). Alarmingly, however, less than 5% of the sample was found to be engaged with digital platforms, largely due to a lack of awareness of such platforms (reported by over 70% of non-users), followed by high access costs and a lack of support in using these platforms, in addition to lagging digital infrastructure and low internet penetration in rural areas (ibid.). Those who did use such platforms reported farm group leaders and cooperatives as their main support in using the platforms (29% of users), followed by extension officers (24%), and trainings by the platform itself (24%).

6.2.2 Role of EU–AU Digital Cooperation

Ag-platforms are clearly important avenues for accessing information and inputs – particularly during COVID-19 – and provide valuable opportunities to women and youth in terms of access to decent work and productivity gains. There is significant potential of leveraging these platforms for job creation, but this requires *targeted investments by the EU–AU partnership in digital infrastructure development, particularly in rural areas*. As part of the Africa-Europe Alliance for Sustainable Investment and Jobs, an EU–AU Digital Economy Task Force (DETF) was established in 2020, followed by the establishment of the EU D4D Hub in 2020 to develop a tangible and joined-up approach towards implementation aspects between EU partners (Jones and Teevan 2021). An important recommendation of the DETF report (European Commission, 2020) is expanding digital connectivity to rural areas in African countries, with the recently launched "Rural Connectivity Toolkit" from the European Investment Bank (2021), offering technical assistance on improving telecom projects and establishing innovative financial tools to increase affordability of digital connectivity. In mature markets such as Morocco, Egypt, and South Africa, African governments can further increase network capacity by granting mobile Virtual Network Operating Licenses (MVNO) to more African telecom firms. The licences will enable them to partner with EU telecom providers that have spare network capacity and are looking to expand the geographical scope of their network coverage in African countries, thus creating a win-win situation.

A second area of EU–AU digital cooperation includes coordinating and scaling capacity and awareness-building programmes that are aimed at increasing awareness of digital platforms and models of use and their benefits, particularly for African youth and ag-entrepreneurs. In facilitating the uptake and use of digital platforms, special attention needs to be paid to ensure that existing socio-economic divides are not replicated. The digital cooperation partnership therefore should focus on increasing women's access to technology, going beyond expanding access to mobile phones to facilitating ownership of mobile phones and other digital capital, potentially through funding innovative finance schemes to help split the cost of mobile ownership through time (GSMA, 2019). The EU–AU digital cooperation should also support programmes that promote the involvement of women in the design, development, and production stages of ag-platforms targeted funding to apps or by offering support to specific programmes that aim at increasing enrolment of women in Technical and Vocational Education and Training (TVET) subjects. Supporting longer-term trainings and mentorship programmes as well as gender budgeting in training and upskilling programmes can also help[2] (Banga et al., 2021). The information and training material needs to be comprehensible to farmers and women with low to moderate literacy levels, potentially through making use of storyboards, simple language, and integrating feedback from focus groups testing the resources.

6.3 Digitalisation and Manufacturing-led Employment Growth in Africa Post-COVID-19

Compared to the 1990s, Africa's growth rate in the 2000s doubled. Nonetheless, attempts by African countries to industrialise have not materialised, and most African countries remain locked into providing primary commodities with limited value-addition (Lopes, 2019). In the case of manufacturing trade, Africa remains a peripheral player, and there are rising concerns around premature de-industrialisation (Rodrik, 2016) and "jobless growth". As seen from Figure 6.3, the share of industry in Africa's GDP has declined in the period 1990–2019, from 29.9% to 26.8%. This has largely been due to a surge in the share of services in Africa's GDP at a time when there was a global expansion of service activities, accelerated through mobile telephony, reduction in ICT costs and financial services. Recently, however, there has been a renewed focus on industrial development and manufacturing-led growth and employment in Africa, with new studies debunking "de-industralisation in Africa". For instance, in SSA, the share of workers in manufacturing is found to have risen by 1.2 percentage points from 7.2% to 8.4% between 2010 and 2018 (Kruse et al., 2021). Industrialisation in SSA appears to have been spurred by unregistered, small businesses producing low-quality goods for domestic markets (ibid.).

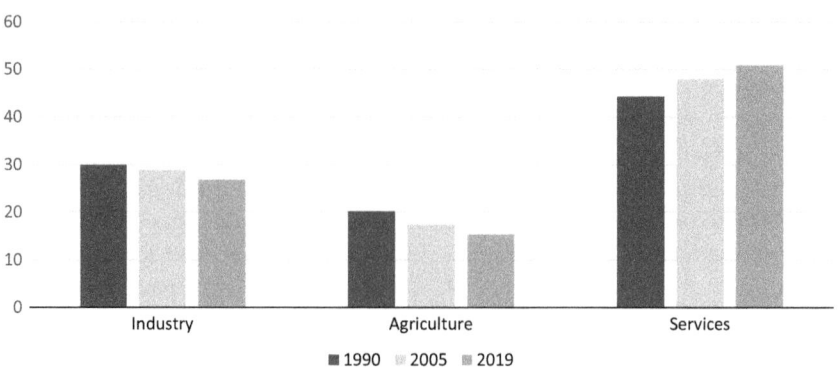

FIGURE 6.3 Sectoral Share of Africa's GDP (%). Source: Author, constructed from World Development Indicators database (2021).

6.3.1 Automation and COVID-19: A Twofold Blow to Manufacturing?

The increasing automation of global manufacturing, coupled with adverse economic effects of the COVID-19 crisis, has served a twofold blow to the manufacturing sector in Africa. Consider the case of robotics. In 2015, Africa's share in robots sold was just 0.2% of global sales, and 15 times lower than its own share in world GDP (around 3%) (Banga and te Velde, 2018). In the context of such a digital divide, increasing automation and digitalisation of global manufacturing production could create incentives for lead firms in developed economies, including the EU, to re-shore manufacturing jobs from Africa or limit future offshoring, leading to a loss of "could-have-been" jobs in Africa. A 10% growth in robotics investment, for instance, corresponds to a 0.54% drop in offshoring, with a higher (negative) correlation for labour-intensive jobs (De Backer et al., 2018). There may still be a "window of opportunity" for African countries to develop export capabilities in less-automated sectors, such as paper and paper products, food products, wood and wood products, but this window is also narrowing (Banga and te Velde, 2018). For instance, in the case of furniture manufacturing, the cost of operating a robot in the United States becomes cheaper than Kenyan formal labour in 2033 (ibid.).

COVID-19 has further worsened prospects of manufacturing-led development in Africa. On the one hand, manufacturing has been hard-hit through supply-side disruptions, including shortages of inputs, closure of factories, and shortages in the workforce. On the other hand, African manufacturing firms also faced demand-side disruptions during the pandemic due to cancellation of export orders from companies in the United States and EU due to national lockdowns in these economies. Within manufacturing, the automotive and the textile and garments sectors were the worst hit; these segments represent most noteworthy shares of global innovation and are also labour intensive. Pre-COVID, the automotive sector in South Africa, for instance, contributed to about 6.9% of the country's GDP in 2019, employing around 120,000 people, and exporting close to 390,000 vehicles (Lopes and te Velde, 2021). New vehicle sales in South Africa, for the second quarter of 2020, witnessed a whopping decline of 63.4% (Gilham, 2020) and a 40% decline in export sales in the first eight months of 2020 compared to the same period in 2019 (Furlongher, 2020). Similarly, garments form an important sector for both Ethiopia and Kenya, accounting for roughly 38,000 formal jobs, employed by over 200 firms, with an additional 75,000 small and medium-sized enterprises (SMEs) aggregated within the textile and garments value chains (UNECA, 2020). In a survey by the Kenyan Association of Manufacturers, 87% of domestic producers in Kenya reported a shortage of raw materials owing to reduced supply from China, and 23% reported downsizing (KEPSA, 2020). COVID-19 has also accelerated the digitalisation of production globally; to mitigate supply chain risk, lead firms may increasingly rely on automation and digital technologies along their supply chains (Seric and Winkler, 2020).

African manufacturing firms could benefit by moving from a passive to an active approach towards digitalisation, which in itself can create new employment opportunities. Evidence from Kenya suggests that digitalisation can open up new opportunities within manufacturing in terms of increases in efficiency, diversification into more value-added products, expansion in regional and global trade, lowering production costs, and increasing export competitiveness (Banga and te Velde, 2018). A case study of the A-to-Z garments factory in Tanzania further demonstrates how investment in the digital technologies of CNC (computer numerical control) cutting has created new employment opportunities through increases in overall productivity, and the related expansion in output and exports. Installing CNC lasers has led to some job losses in cutting tasks but increased overall jobs in the next task of stitching, which is more skilled and ranks relatively lower on technical and economic feasibility of automation (Minian et al., 2016; Berg et al., 2017). Adopting digitalisation in certain segments of manufacturing has also made African countries more competitive and resilient to the pandemic. Banga and Banga's forthcoming analysis using the World Bank's "Impact of COVID survey" Round 1 for the year 2020 finds that African firms with a digital response to COVID-19 fared better in terms of economic performance and resilience compared to firms that did not adopt a digital response. While 70% of firms without a digital response to the pandemic witnessed a decrease in total hours worked per week, only 56% of firms employing a digital response reported the same negative trend. Similarly, a higher share of firms with a digital response (43%) reported no changes to hours worked than those without a digital response (29%).

6.3.2 Role of the EU–AU Digital Cooperation

Based on clear demand from African countries, targeted and strategic investment by the EU can support digital transformation of the manufacturing sector in Africa and increase competitiveness of African manufacturing firms, creating much-needed employment gains. There is a strong focus in the EU on leveraging investment through blended finance and loan guarantees under the European Fund for Sustainable Development Plus (EFSD+). One of the areas where this investment can be focused is the *creation of or support towards the development of African digital and manufacturing start-ups and technology and innovation hubs that are well integrated into the domestic economy.* This can be further promoted through the EU–AU Innovation Bridge – one of the flagships of the D4D Hub, which aims at developing digital innovation ecosystems, strengthening the collaboration and fostering exchanges between neighbouring continents (D4D Hub, 2020). Second, there is a need *to facilitate domestic integration of large productive digitalised firms in Africa with local firms and suppliers for large-scale employment generation* (Rodrik, 2018). For the EU, this can give a boost to EU member states' exports of capital goods and machinery to African firms, as well as a boost to export of services, such as repair and maintenance.

Third, the EU–AU digital cooperation needs to invest in targeted skills development in African countries, with much scope for sharing best practices on digital skills development by EU firms. As per cross-sector data from the World Business Environment Survey (WBES), less than 50% of firms surveyed across several developing countries are offering any sort of formal training to workers (Banga and te Velde, 2020). In Africa, employer-led training tends to be without certification or informal apprenticeships, whereas in Austria, Denmark, Germany, and the UK, work-based training comprises a formal apprenticeship that offers young people a programme of structured on-the-job learning. Fourth, the EU, the AU, and other development partners can work with the private sector *to develop a re-tooling programme, which can enable African manufacturing firms to make use of digitalisation in re-tooling production towards the supply of essential commodities during the pandemic.* The EU–AU partnership should support such re-tooling programmes, including those that use digitalisation to diversify into different product lines and functions.

A good example is H&M coordinating with the EU to re-tool its supply chains (Ecotextile News, 2020). The company has also signed an agreement with IndustriALL Global Union to engage in responsible purchasing practices with suppliers, including in Ethiopia and Kenya, through stable orders, fulfilling agreed payment terms and by fostering conditions that allow suppliers to protect jobs and workers' wages (Ecotextile News, 2021). Lastly, if the EU is serious about promoting a human-centric approach to digitalisation and working with African countries on promoting their digital sovereignty, then *investment into building local and regional data centres on the continent is key.* This needs to be accompanied by investment into building data processing capacities on the continent through support to "local infomediaries" – firms that act as data intermediaries and can turn data into actionable information – and national and regional skill-development initiatives on data analysis and processing (Banga and Hernandez, forthcoming).

6.4 Digitalisation and Services-led Employment Growth in Africa Post-COVID-19

Digitalisation of manufacturing supply chains, accelerated by COVID-19, and potential re-shoring of manufacturing jobs have increased concerns regarding the potential of manufacturing-led development for job creation in Africa. Accordingly, increasing attention is being given across African countries to a services-led transformation. As seen from Figure 6.3, services account for a majority (almost 51%) of Africa's GDP, and represent a growing share of total exports for many African countries. For Ethiopia, Mauritius, Kenya, Morocco, and Uganda, services represented more than 40% of exports on average for the period 2014–2018 (Mendez-Parra, 2020). Digital technologies are further opening new avenues of value-added in the services sector, including in information technology (IT) or IT-enabled services, such as business and financial services (Newfarmer et al., 2019; Gollin, 2018). These services, however, may not be very employment-intensive since highly productive and tradable services, such as IT services, require highly skilled workers (Schlogl and Sumner, 2020).

The pandemic adversely affected international trade in services, with the World Trade Organization's (WTO) global services trade barometer registering a sharp decline in 2020, followed by a strong bounce back of trade in services in 2021. The demand for ICT and ICT-enabled services has, however, increased globally, with more and more businesses in traditional sectors, such as garments, shifting online and workers working from home. New economic opportunities include an increased offer of digital services (e.g. cloud computing) and digitally deliverable services (i.e. that can be carried out online, e.g. legal services), e-commerce, and online work. Digitalisation has also increased demand for workers in service sectors, such as maintenance and repair, delivery and postal services, along with changing the nature of work through digital platforms and the rise of online work.

6.4.1 Potential for an ICT and E-commerce-enabled Recovery

Digitally deliverable services (DDS), defined as an aggregation of ICT services, as well as those services which can be digitally delivered, such as insurance and pension services, financial services, charges for the use of intellectual property, and other business services and audiovisual and related services,[3] are likely to be more resilient to the pandemic than services which cannot go digital, such as transport and tourism. But the latter set of services accounts for the highest share in traded services in Africa (UNCTAD, 2022). Moreover, while DDS trade in Africa is a sizeable USD 24.3 billion, it is driven by a handful of countries – Ghana (25% of Africa's DDS trade), Morocco (18%), South Africa (15%), Algeria (7%), Kenya (5%), and Nigeria (4%) (Banga and Banga, forthcoming). On average, DDS form less than 30% of African countries' services trade, with the share of DDS trade in total services being less than 10% in some African countries such as Tanzania, Ethiopia, Mozambique, Ethiopia, Gambia, and Namibia (ibid.).

Examining the actual mode of supply of services in African countries, Banga and Banga (2022) find that the share of services being delivered digitally (online) is less than 40% in Uganda, Botswana, Nigeria, the Comoros, Mauritius, Namibia, Egypt, and Sudan. Even in the countries where majority of services are supplied through Mode1 (cross-border online supply), such as Ghana, the resilience to economic shocks, such as the pandemic, is contingent on good and reliable access to the internet as well as appropriate ICT regulatory frameworks. There may be a new opportunity, in the form of jobs in the cloud services and data hosting category for African countries that have supportive data and privacy frameworks. The EU can play an important role in this, since it accounts for 32% of Africa's total services exports and 44% of ICT exports. But access to and usage of cloud and data hosting services in emerging African markets currently tend to rely on data centres outside their local markets, with limited domestic capabilities. Several African countries do not have broadband speeds adequate and affordable enough to support reliable cloud service usage, and these have further declined during the lockdown (Banga and Banga, 2022).

Another new employment opportunity could emanate from e-commerce value chains, including jobs related to supply chain management, logistics, and delivery. COVID-19 has given a boost to e-commerce globally, but the accelerating impact of COVID-19 on e-commerce in Africa has been constrained by persisting weaknesses in the continent's digital economy that continue to frustrate e-commerce development (Futi and Macleod, 2021). These include high internet costs, weaknesses in postal services and capacities, cross-border trade costs, and the limited uptake of electronic and digital payment systems (ibid.). There have also been supply-side disruptions to African e-commerce in the form of travel disruptions, delays in parcel delivery due to cargo, air, and transport disruptions, increasing airfreight prices due to the cancellation of flights, in addition to shortages of qualified workers, data safe packaging, and poor delivery infrastructure. Banga et al.'s (2021) survey and follow-up interviews with 31 African e-commerce businesses indicate that over 62% of firms witnessed an increase in e-commerce since the start of the pandemic. However, over 60% of the firms surveyed are selling through their own e-commerce websites. Third-party e-commerce platforms charge 10–15% of commission on product sales, thus discouraging African sellers. Cross-border e-commerce in Africa is further limited for various reasons: (i) postal competence and delivery and transport costs; (ii) issues of taxation, including foreign taxation, double taxation, and VAT regulations; (iii) lack of reliable payment solutions; (iv) lack of awareness of national and regional rules; and (v) custom duties and custom procedures (ibid.).

6.4.2 The Role of EU–AU Digital Cooperation

Under the EFSD+, *the EU should target investment towards improving digital infra- structure in Africa including by improving access to broadband and cloud infrastructure.* An important initiative in progress includes the EU-AU-ITU project Policy and Regulation Initiative for Digital Africa (PRIDA),[4] which is working on har- monising spectrum utilisation and also governance frameworks across the con- tinent. Improving broadband access and mobile data costs in African countries can in turn increase their competitiveness, facilitating cost-competitive link- ages between African firms, from countries such as Senegal and Uganda, and the European business process outsourcing (BPO) market (CBI 2020). There is much scope for *fast-tracking and supporting the adoption of existing regional initiatives in Africa, such as the One Network Area (ONA) which aims to reduce high roaming charges and interconnection rates in East Africa.*

The majority of the existing digital apps in Africa are oriented towards the domestic market, with few digital apps targeting cross-border e-commerce. Under the EU–AU partnership, *seed investment and support for scaling should be targeted towards those initiatives and start-ups that offer broad-ranging suppor*t (e.g. on logistics and storage) to firms or initiatives that have greater financial interoper- ability and those that lower cross-platform and cross-border transaction fees. A good example of a cross-border e-commerce app is Sauti, which is specifi- cally reducing gendered barriers to cross-border trade. Interventions regarding e-commerce-related tools in Africa are important; these can include financial support to the development of websites and digital tools that capture the presence and implementation status of soft digital infrastructure policies across countries. This will create awareness of policies and of the gaps in coherence across national and regional rules – an important obstacle in cross-border e-commerce trade.

6.5 Conclusion

This chapter highlights the importance of steering EU–AU digital cooperation towards facilitating structural transformation on the African continent through (a) increasing within-sector productivity gains, particularly in the agricultural sector; and (b) increasing across-sector productivity gains by shifting labour towards more productive manufacturing and services sectors. There is strong potential for digital platforms in the agricultural sector to boost productivity and generate employment in African countries, but large-scale gains have not been realised yet. There is a renewed focus on industrial development and man- ufacturing-led growth and employment in Africa, with new studies debunking "de-industrialisation in Africa" (Kruse et al., 2021). This is particularly important from the AU–EU partnership point of view since the COVID-19 recovery of African trade is significantly linked to European production and trade recov- ery, given the close integration of African firms within European supply chains. However, COVID-19 is accelerating digitalisation of global manufacturing production. In the context of a persistent digital divide between Africa and the EU, this raises concerns about limited offshoring of manufacturing jobs from the EU to Africa in the future. A two-pronged digital divide plagues African countries: not only do they have lower access to digital technologies, but the manufacturing productivity benefits from digital technologies are also lower in these countries, potentially due to an overall lack of absorptive capacity in the workforce. New jobs may arise in e-commerce value chains and in services sectors such as cloud computing and data hosting in African countries with good privacy and regulatory frameworks and a relatively skilled workforce.

Four key findings emerge from this chapter for the EU–AU digital cooperation. First, ag-platforms can increase productivity gains and access to decent work for African farmers, but there is a need for EU–AU digital cooperation to facilitate digital infrastructure development in rural areas. There is also a need to (a) coordinate and scale capacity-building and awareness-building programmes for models and benefits of digital platforms; and (b) target women's access to technology in Africa and their involvement in the design, development, and production stages. The recent launch of the EU's D4D Hub and its regional component – the AU–EU D4D Hub – is timely, as it can provide a useful platform for European and African public and private actors to collaborate and coordinate their digitalisation initiatives on these issues.

Second, targeted and strategic investments by the EU under the EFSD+ can support digital transformation of the manufacturing sector in Africa. The EU–AU cooperation should promote African digital and manufacturing start-ups and technology and innovation hubs that are well integrated into the domestic economy and facilitate domestic integration of large productive digitalised firms with local firms and suppliers for large-scale employment generation. For the EU, this can give a boost to EU member states' exports of capital goods and machinery to African firms, as well as a boost to export of services, such as repair and maintenance.

Third, to capitalise on new employment opportunities arising in services sectors such as e-commerce, cloud computing, and data hosting, the EU–AU partnership should further target improving digital infrastructure in Africa through access to broadband and cloud infrastructure. It is important to support the development of local and regional data centres on the continent, as well as building data processing capacities through support to local infomediaries and national and regional skill-development initiatives on data analysis and processing.

Fourth, seed investment and support for scaling needs to be targeted towards those initiatives and start-ups that offer broad-ranging support to farmers and firms or initiatives that have greater financial interoperability and those that lower cross-platform and cross-border transaction fees. The partnership should facilitate linkages of African MSMEs with platforms through improving access to working capital to pay the transaction fees or through incubators which provide subsidised access to these e-commerce platforms and trainings on how to use them.

Notes

1 Broadly classified as those that are using (a) digital platforms such as Facebook/ WhatsApp; (b) Android-based digital apps for agriculture; or (c) accessing information via USSD or SMS.
2 This means setting aside a proportion of the budget for any initiative on youth to effectively target women's uptake of the programme. This ranges from advertising the programme to hiring female trainers and ensuring high enrolment and completion of the training by women.
3 The digitally deliverable services series is based on the concept of potentially ICT-enabled services as developed by UNCTAD in a technical note in 2015 as well as in a report of the 47th United Nations Statistical Commission in 2016.
4 https://www.itu.int/en/ITU-D/Projects/ITU-EC-ACP/PRIDA/Pages/default .aspx

References

Banga, K. and te Velde, D.W. (2018). *Digitalization and the Future of Manufacturing in Africa.* London: Supporting Economic Transformation.
Banga, K., Gharib, M., Mendez-Parra, M and Macleod, J. (2021). *E-commerce in Preferential Trade Agreements Implications for African Firms and the AfCFTA.* ODI report. London. Available at: https://cdn.odi.org/media/documents/e-commerce_in_preferential _trade_agreements_report.pdf (Accessed: 29 March 2022).
Banga, K., Keane, J., Mendez-Parra, M., Pettinotti, L. and Sommer, L. (2020). *Africa Trade and Covid19: The Supply-Chain Dimension.* ODI working paper. Available at   https://odi.org/en/publications/africa-trade-and-covid19-the-supply-chain -dimension/
Banga, R. and Banga, K. (2022). Scoping the Potential for a Digital Led Recovery from COVID-19 in Africa. *Journal of African Trade* pp. 1–24.
Berg, A., Hedrich, S., Lange, T., Magnus, K. and Mathews, B. (2017). *The Apparel Sourcing Caravan's Next Stop: Digitization (McKinsey Apparel CPO Survey 2017).* London: McKinsey Apparel, Fashion & Luxury Group.
CBI (2020). The European market for IT-enabled services and business process outsourcing in Senegal and Uganda. Available at https://www.cbi.eu/market-information/ outsourcing-itobpo/bpo-senegal-uganda#part-ii-european-opportunities-and-obstacles-for-specific-ites-and-bpo-in-senegal-and-uganda
D4D Hub (2020). *Flagship: African-European Digital Innovation Bridge (AEDIB).* European Commission. Available at: https://futurium.ec.europa.eu/en/Digital4Development/ discussion/flagship-african-european-digital-innovation-bridge-aedib?language=fr (Accessed 29 March 2022).
De Backer, K., DeStefano, T., Menon, C. and Suh, J.R. (2018). *Industrial Robotics and the Global Organisation of Production.* Working Paper. Paris: OECD.
Ecotextiles News (2020). H&M suppliers to make PPE to tackle COVID-19. Available at https://www.ecotextile.com/2020032225865/fashion-retail-news/h-m-suppliers-to -make-ppe-to-tackle-covid-19.html
Ecotextiles News (2021). H&M to work with suppliers on COVID recovery. Available at: https://www.ecotextile.com/2021031627543/fashion-retail-news/h-m-to-work -with-suppliers-on-covid-recovery.html (Accessed: 29 March 2021).
ETTG (2020). Strengthening the digital partnership between Africa and Europe. Available   at   https://ettg.eu/wp-content/uploads/2020/10/ETTG-Publication

-Strengthening-the-digital-partnership-between-Africa-and-Europe.pdf (Accessed 29.03.2021).

EU (2020). Joint communication to the European parliament and the council. Available at https://ec.europa.eu/international-partnerships/system/files/communication-eu-africa-strategy-join-2020-4-final_en.pdf (Accessed 29 March 2022).

European Commission (2020). Africa-EU partnership. Available at: https://ec.europa.eu/international-partnerships/africa-eu-partnership

European Investment Bank (2021). Rural connectivity toolkit. Available at: https://www.eib.org/en/publications/rural-connectivity-toolkit (Accessed: 29 March 2021).

Ezeomah, B. and Duncombe, R. (2019). The role of digital platforms in disrupting agricultural value chains in developing countries. In International Conference on Social Implications of Computers in Developing Countries(pp. 231–247). Cham: Springer.

Furlongher, D. (2020) New vehicles sales set off on a long and slow road to recovery. *Business Day*, 1st September 2020, https://www.businesslive.co.za/bd/economy/2020-09-01-new-vehicle-sales-setoff-on-a-long-and-slow-road-to-recovery/ (Accessed: 29 March 2021).

Futi, G. and Macleod, J. (2021). Covid-19 impact on E-Commerce: Africa. *United Nations. Economic Commission for Africa; United Nations.* Economic Commission for Africa (2021–02). Addis Ababa. Available at: https://repository.uneca.org/handle/10855/43939

Gilham, S. (2020). Naamsa: Vehicle sales in SA plunge to biggest quarterly decline on record. *The South African*, July 2020, https://www.thesouthafrican.com/motoring/naamsa-vehicle-sales-july-2020/ (Accessed 29. March 2022).

GIZ (2018). GIZ African Union Office. Available at: https://www.giz.de/de/downloads/giz2018-EN-African-Union-Office-Annual-Report.pdf (Accessed: 29 March 2022).

Gollin, D. (2018). *Structural Transformation without Industrialization. Pathways for Prosperity Commission Background Paper Series no. 2.* University of Oxford.

GSMA (2019). The digital lives of refugees: How displaced populations use mobile phones and what gets in the way. Available at: https://www.gsma.com/mobilefordevelopment/wp-content/uploads/2019/07/The-Digital-Lives-of-Refugees.pdf (Accessed 29.03.2021).

GSMA (2021). The mobile economy Sub-Saharan Africa. Available at https://www.gsma.com/mobileeconomy/sub-saharan-africa/ (Accessed 29 March 2022).

Jones, A. and Teevan, C. (2021). Team Europe: Up to the challenge? *ECDPM.* Policy Brief No. 128. January 2021.

KEPSA – Kenya Private Sector Alliance (2020). Business perspectives on the impact of the coronavirus on Kenya's economy. Arusha: East African Business Council (www.eabc-online.com/membership/ matrix-of-issues?id=260).

Koskinen, K., Bonina, C. and Eaton, B. (2019). May. Digital platforms in the global south: Foundations and research agenda. In *International Conference on Social Implications of Computers in Developing Countries* (pp. 319–330). Springer, Cham.

Krishnan, A., Banga, K., Raga, S., Pettinotti, L. and Mendez-Parra, M. (2020). Ag-platforms as disruptors in value-chains; evidence from Uganda. ODI working paper series.

Kruse et al. (2021). A manufacturing renaissance? Industrialization trends in the developing world. Available at: https://www.wider.unu.edu/publication/manufacturing-renaissance-industrialization-trends-developing-world (Accessed: 29. March 2022).

Lopes, C. (2019). Structural transformation through industrialisation. In *Africa in Transformation* (pp. 65–82). Palgrave Macmillan, Cham.

Lopes, C. and Willem te Velde, D. (2021). *Structural Transformation, Economic Development and Industrialization in Post-Covid-19 Africa*. New York: Institute for New Economic Thinking.

Mackinnon, A. (2019). For Africa, Chinese-Built internet is better than no internet at all. *Foreign Policy*. Available at: https://foreignpolicy.com/2019/03/19/for-africa-chinese-built-internet-is-better-than-no-internet-at-all/ (Accessed 29 March 2022).

Mendez-Parra, M. (2020b) *Trade in Services and the Coronavirus: Many Developing Countries Are at Risk*. SET Paper. London: ODI. https://set.odi.org/wp-content/uploads/2020/03/Trade-in-servicesand-the-coronavirus-many-developing-countries-are-at-risk.pdf

Minian, I., Martinez, A. and Ibanez, J. (2016) Technological change and the relocation of the apparel industry. *Problemas del Desarrollo. Revista Latinoamericana de Economía* 48(88), pp. 139–164.

Newfarmer, R., Page, J. and Tarp, F. (2019). *Industries Without Smokestacks: Industrialization in Africa Reconsidered* (p. 480). Oxford University Press.

Oqubay, A. and Ohno, K. (2019). *How Nations Learn: Technological Learning, Industrial Policy, and Catch-up* (p. 368). Oxford University Press.

Rodrik, D. (2016). Premature deindustrialization. *Journal of Economic Growth* 21(1), pp. 1–33.

Rodrik, D. (2018). *New Technologies, Global Value Chains, and Developing Economies* (No. w25164). National Bureau of Economic Research.

Schlogl, L. and Sumner, A. (2020). *Disrupted Development and the Future of Inequality in the Age of Automation* (p. 102). Springer Nature.

Seric, A. and Winkler, D. (2020). COVID-19 could spur automation and reverse globalisation – to some extent. Available at: https://voxeu.org/article/covid-19-couldspur-automation-and-reverse-globalisation-some-extent (Accessed: 29. March 2022).

UNCTAD (2018). *World Investment Report*. United Nations Conference on Trade and Development.

UNCTAD (2021). Impact of the covid-19 pandemic on trade in the digital economy. *UNCTAD Technical Notes on ICT for Development No. 19*. United Nations. Available at: https://unctad.org/system/files/official-document/tn_unctad_ict4d19_en.pdf (Accessed: 29 March 2022).

UNCTAD (2022). Economic Development in Africa report. United Nations. Available at https://unctad.org/system/files/official-document/aldcafrica2022_Ch2_en.pdf.

UNECA (2020). COVID-19 in Africa. United Nations. Available at https://archive.uneca.org/sites/default/files/PublicationFiles/eca_covid_report_en_24apr_web1.pdf.

World Bank (2019). *Africa's Pulse*. World Bank Group.

World Bank (2021). *Global Economic Prospects*. World Bank.

World Development Indicators (2021). *Employment in Agriculture*. Available at: https://data.worldbank.org/indicator/SL.AGR.EMPL.ZS?locations=ZG (Accessed 29 March 2022).

7

DIGITALISE TO INDUSTRIALISE

Egypt, Morocco, Tunisia, and the Africa–Europe Partnership

Karim El Aynaoui, Larabi Jaïdi, and Akram Zaoui

7.1 Introduction

Since the mid-2010s, North African countries have been pursuing what some observers have called a "return to Africa" (Dworkin, 2020). Egypt, Morocco, and Tunisia have attempted to position themselves as major components of Europe-Mediterranean-Africa infrastructure and supply chains corridors (Tanchum, 2020). The three countries are trying to act as bridges between Africa and Europe amid discussions on the evolution of the partnership between the African Union (AU) and the European Union (EU). These efforts have taken place in a global context marked by a "rebirth of industrial policy" (Aiginger & Rodrik, 2020). Discussions around industrial policy, nearshoring, and reshoring have intensified as a result of the COVID-19 pandemic, which is presented as not only an economic challenge, but also as an opportunity for industrialisation on both sides of the Mediterranean.

In recent years, the official agendas of the AU and the EU have prioritised digital, innovation, and industrialisation – as both continents focus on deepening economic progress. Against this backdrop, Egypt, Morocco, and Tunisia have attempted, with varying levels of success, to refine their digital ecosystems, innovation policies, and industrial strategies. In particular, the digitalisation of the manufacturing sector and Industry 4.0 (I4.0) increasingly appears in official discourses. The digital revolution is indeed bringing fresh transformations and challenges to the industrial sector with the emergence of new transformative technologies such as the Internet of Things (IoT), Artificial Intelligence (AI), robotics, and additive manufacturing (3D printing). Manufacturing processes and the organisation of production, notably within Global Value Chains (GVCs), are already experiencing changes. For example, digitalisation has increased both the participation of small and medium enterprises (SMEs) in

DOI: 10.4324/9781003274322-7

GVCs (Lanz et al., 2018) and the share of services embodied in manufactured goods (Görlich, 2021).

In light of strong competition from Asia and the probable further concentration of industrial production that the Fourth Industrial Revolution (4IR) could bring (Schwab, 2016); the digital revolution constitutes both an opportunity and a potential threat for Egypt, Morocco, and Tunisia. Digitalisation can help industries increase their productivity and better respond to emerging trends and clients' needs through the improvement of their own processes. If North African industries reach higher degrees of digitalisation, they can strengthen their competitiveness and the favourable position they already enjoy for exporting and value chains participation in view of their geographic proximity to the EU market and manufacturing fabric.

Digital matters are one of the five key partnership areas proposed in the EU's Comprehensive Strategy with Africa (EC, 2020). Nevertheless, the fact that the AU–EU Digital Economy Task Force barely mentions manufacturing as an area of potential collaboration (EU–AU DETF, 2019) shows that the focus on the intersection between digitalisation and the manufacturing sector is still minimal in Union-to-Union digital-related discussions. The AU's Digital Transformation Strategy for Africa 2020–2030 (DTS) provides greater emphasis on topics such as the 4IR, 3D printing, and AI (AU, 2020).

In this chapter, we argue that the digitalisation of the manufacturing sector should be further prioritised both within Egypt, Morocco, and Tunisia and in discussions between the EU and its African partners. Industrialisation – which is the avenue favoured by the three North African nations to ensure structural transformation – should be supported by smart digital and industrial policies. To this end, there is a need for a greater emphasis on the digital sector. An industrial policy can be defined as "any type of intervention or government policy that attempts to improve the business environment or to alter the structure of economic activity towards sectors, technologies or tasks" (Warwick, 2013). Across the world, such policies now need to be refined to embrace the challenges brought by new technologies. Policies should encourage further digitalisation of the industrial private sector. EU support to its Southern Neighbourhood's manufacturing sector has already materialised in the past, but should be deepened, expanded, and refined, particularly when it comes to digitalisation. On the African level and in the framework of the AU–EU partnership, we advocate stronger synergies between the various levels of engagement to support the establishment and reinforcement of Regional Value Chains (RVCs).

First, we assess the current levels of industrialisation in Egypt, Morocco, and Tunisia as well as the policies these countries have implemented in relation to industrialisation. This is required to understand how digitalisation can help consolidate the existing capabilities accumulated in the three countries.

Second, we evaluate the current levels of digitalisation in Egypt, Morocco, and Tunisia, and critically review the digital strategies that the three countries have implemented during the past two decades. This enables us to establish on what ground we can build further policies.

Third, we examine initiatives in Egypt, Morocco, and Tunisia that relate to the digitalisation of their industry and I4.0. Many of these initiatives are still in their infancy but should be encouraged going forward.

Fourth, we explore ways that Egypt, Morocco, and Tunisia can strengthen their integration into the European industrial fabric, which could go through a better inclusion in European initiatives, programmes, and strategies that relate to infrastructure, manufacturing, and research and innovation (R&I). The digitalisation of North African industries can play a part in realising this objective.

7.2 Digitalise to Industrialise in Egypt, Morocco, and Tunisia

Awareness of the necessity to adapt to the transformations of industry, notably those caused by the digitalisation of production, has been increasing during the past three decades in Egypt, Morocco, and Tunisia. It has been further boosted during the past decade by the roles that digital technologies are playing in the global economy and, more recently, by the COVID-19 pandemic. Foreign direct investment (FDI) from, and exports to the EU, coupled with adequate industrial policies focusing on upgrading the processes of industrial companies, have helped the three countries boost their manufacturing fabric. Manufacturing is thus a key component of trade between the three North African nations and the EU. Nevertheless, incentives for industrial companies to upgrade their use of digital tools have borne limited results, and the lack of adoption of such tools could constitute a potential threat to their manufacturing sector as a whole.

Industrialisation has been a priority in Egypt, Morocco, and Tunisia since the three countries fully reclaimed their sovereignty in the 1950s, and the trade relationship with Europe was key to the industrial development of the three countries. The 1990s and 2000s marked a turning point in the intensification of industrial relations between North Africa and Europe. Two factors help explain this. First, in the wake of a global outsourcing movement, FDI from industrial economies to developing countries increased. This increase was notably made possible by the emergence of new Information and Communication Technologies (ICTs). Second, free trade agreements (FTAs) between Egypt, Morocco, Tunisia, and the EU gradually entered into force. These FTAs, which came with Association Agreements (AAs), sought to remove tariffs on industrial products. Entering into force between 1998 and 2004, the AAs pushed Egypt, Morocco, and Tunisia to enact more refined industrial strategies and pursue upgrading efforts for their production. The countries reacted by protecting their industrial fabric from European competition. They sought to help businesses take advantage of the opening of European markets and attract FDI (Bianchi et al., 2018). Consequently, from the 1990s onwards, the three countries launched a new generation of industrial strategies.

One of the priorities of these renewed strategies has been to upgrade the manufacturing fabric, notably in terms of adoption of digital technologies. This was demonstrated by the launching of the Tunisian upgrading programme (or PMN) in 1995 and of the Industrial Modernisation Centre (IMC) in 2000 in Egypt. Both instruments have included a focus on the digitalisation of manufacturing companies. Similarly, in Morocco, the National Pact for Industrial Emergence (2009–2014), an industrial strategy, created "Moussanada TI", a programme aimed at boosting the adoption of information systems by Moroccan SMEs.

7.2.1 Links with Europe

Egypt, Morocco, and Tunisia have economies that are amongst the most complex in Africa. According to the Economic Complexity Index, "economic complexity expresses the diversity and sophistication of the productive capabilities embedded in the exports of each country". (Economic Complexity Index, 2019). The EU is the first trade partner for the three countries. As Table 7.1 shows, manufacturing represents a sizeable share of this trade and the economies of the three countries, accounting for between 14 and 16% of their GDPs (World Bank,

TABLE 7.1 Trade Relations between the EU and the Three Studied Countries at a Glance

	Egypt	*Morocco*	*Tunisia*
Share of manufacturing in GDP	15.9%	14.9%	14.8%
Ranking in Africa in terms of economic complexity	3rd	12th	1st
Date of signing of the FTA with the EU	2001	1996	1995
Date of entry into force of the FTA with the EU	2004	1997	2000
Subcommittees with the Association Councils dealing with industry and R&I	Industry, trade, services and investment	Industry, trade, and services Research and innovation	Industry, trade, and services Research and innovation
Date of creation of the subcommittees	2007	2003	2003
Share of total imports coming from the EU	25.8%	51%	48.3%
Share of total exports going to the EU	21.8%	64%	70.9%
Share of manufactures in exports to the EU	44.2%	71.7%	85.7%
Share of manufactures in imports from the EU	70.8%	73.8%	79.7%

Sources: based on World Bank, 2019; Economic Complexity Index, 2019; EC, 2020

2019). Manufacturing, therefore, provides a good basis on which to build cooperation on digitalisation and reinforce cross-Mediterranean RVCs.

7.3 Egypt, Morocco, and Tunisia: Reaping the Benefits of Digitalisation

North African economies appear as African leaders in terms of use of the internet both by citizens and by companies. Nevertheless, their start-up ecosystems perform more poorly than certain sub-Saharan African economies, such as Nigeria, Kenya, and South Africa, and should be reinforced. Stronger ecosystems could help provide the domestic manufacturing sectors of Egypt, Morocco, and Tunisia with adequate digital solutions to improve their performance, and introduce positive spill-over effects in terms of innovation and productivity. Overall, in spite of the fact that many positive developments can be observed in Egypt, Morocco, and Tunisia, results remain rather mixed and more should be done for the economies and societies to further reap the fruits of digitalisation.

Assessing overall digitalisation in a country is important because it shows to what extent the economy and society have adopted and use digital technologies, with possible positive spill-over effects on production. In North Africa, 4G coverage has increased dramatically, rising from 35% to about 84% of the population in five years. International internet bandwidth per internet user more than tripled in half a decade. In 2018, 57% of North Africa's formal sector companies had a website, as opposed to only 31% Africa-wide. Eighty-two per cent of formal sector firms in North Africa now use emails to interact with their clients and suppliers, while only 39% of them did five years ago (AUC/OECD, 2021).

Within North Africa, Morocco, and Tunisia are leaders in the use of the internet by companies, and their advantage is even clearer when it comes to small enterprises (see Table 7.2). Websites allow companies to target new potential customers, but many North African companies need to update their websites to ensure better impact and help enlarge their customer base.

The United Nations Conference on Trade and Development (UNCTAD) B2C E-Commerce Index confirms Morocco's and Tunisia's lead in terms of economic use of digital tools, as they are amongst the best positioned nations in terms of e-commerce (Table 7.3). Nevertheless, the Index also shows that there was no real North African advance in terms of e-commerce in 2019. As stated

TABLE 7.2 Companies and SMEs with a Website in Egypt, Morocco, and Tunisia

	Egypt	*Morocco*	*Tunisia*
Share of companies with a website	52%	69%	66%
Share of small enterprises with a website	38%	67%	59%

Source: AUC/OECD, 2021

TABLE 7.3 B2C E-Commerce Index Scores of Selected African Countries

	Côte d'Ivoire	Egypt	Ghana	Morocco	Nigeria	Senegal	Tunisia
B2C E-Commerce Index	31.3	39.4	42.8	43.4	53.2	42.7	58.1

Source: UNCTAD, 2019

above, e-commerce can be an important driver of growth as it can have positive effects on cost-reduction, sales growth, exports, and participation in GVCs, especially for SMEs (Lanz et al., 2018).

Overall, digitalisation does not constitute a tool for boosting employment yet in Egypt, Morocco, and Tunisia. According to Crunchbase, only 92 start-ups have been able to raise more than USD 100,000 in Egypt between 2011 and 2020. The figure was even lower in Morocco and Tunisia, with only 13 start-ups each reaching that target during the same period. Although employment is not the only outcome that can be expected from start-ups, it is clear these levels of funding indicate small positive spill-over effects from local start-ups to the rest of the economy (AUC/OECD, 2021).

7.3.1 Government Initiatives, Interventions, Strategies, and Policy Instruments on Digitalisation

Egypt, Morocco, and Tunisia have co-developed their industrial and digital strategies. The highest authorities in each of the three states have shown keen interest in ICTs. For instance, Tunisia was the organiser of the World Summit for the Information Society in 2005, and several ministers were assigned to ICTs since the 2010–2011 revolution, reflecting awareness amongst the political elite about the importance of this matter for the Tunisian economy. Morocco started adopting digital-related strategies in the late 1990s with the 1999–2003 five-year plan, followed by "e-Maroc 2010" (2005–2010) and the "National Strategy for the Information Society and Digital economy" (2009–2013), often referred to as "Maroc Numeric 2013". As for Egypt, it has also produced multiple digital-related strategies during the past few decades. A Ministry of Communications and Information Technology was established in 1999 and national strategies include Egypt's Vision of the Information Society (2003) as well as two ICT Strategies (2007–2010 and 2014–2020). However, in the three countries, these strategies have failed to achieve the expected results. For instance, "e-Maroc 2010" was never evaluated, and a report by the Moroccan Court of Auditors reveals that "Maroc Numeric 2013" ended in a clear underperformance. Only 295 Moroccan companies benefitted from the support of "Moussanada TI" to get equipped with professional information systems, far from the 3,000 targets that "Maroc Numeric 2013" had planned for (Cour des Comptes, 2014).

7.3.2 Egypt

With regard to innovation-driven entrepreneurship ecosystems, Egypt is clearly ahead when compared to Morocco and Tunisia. This can be mainly explained by its stronger domestic customer base (the 2nd population in Africa after Ethiopia and the 14th worldwide) and close connections with the Middle East. As shown in Table 7.4, Cairo is one of the five most important start-up ecosystems on the continent (AUC/OECD, 2019).

Equity Venture Capital (VC) funding shows that Egypt is performing much better than Morocco and Tunisia in innovative entrepreneurship. Egypt was also the third largest market in the continent in terms of VC funding with USD 269 million of investments over USD 200,000 in tech and digital start-ups, marking a strong growth in recent years as equity investments stood at USD 9 million in 2017 and 59 million in 2018 (AUC/OECD, 2021).

7.3.3 Morocco

Despite adopting a number of policies to support the innovation and entre-preneurship ecosystem, Moroccan entrepreneurs face difficulties in accessing funds and in growing their businesses. In 2016, the then Moroccan Minister of Industry, Trade, and the Green and Digital Economy, Moulay Hafid El Alamy, announced a new Plan called "Maroc Digital 2020". One year later the Agency for the Development of the Digital sector (ADD) was created and placed under the authority of Mr. El Alamy's Ministry. The Agency adopted a roadmap (2020–2025) comprising 15 actions including the support to smart factories and industry 4.0, the digitalisation of SMEs, digital entrepreneurship, AI, a national programme for digital training, digital infrastructure, and the creation of a dig-ital park. Other mechanisms were created under the purview of the Agency in charge of SMEs ("Maroc PME") such as "INCUB-IDEA" and "INCUB-STARTUP", helping entrepreneurs conceive and launch their companies. The Central Guarantee Fund also launched a dedicated vehicle called "Innov-Invest" and supported by the aforementioned PACC (about EUR 12.5 million were pledged), with the objective to fund 300 start-ups between 2017 and 2022 (170 have received support so far). That being said, one of the main challenges that remain for Moroccan entrepreneurs is a staggering lack of funding. Investment continues to be dominated by lending, with significant guarantees expected

TABLE 7.4 Share of the Total Number of Start-ups in Africa in Selected Cities

	Cairo	Cape Town	Johannesburg	Lagos	Nairobi
Share of the total number of start-ups in Africa by location	6.9%	12.5%	10.1%	10.3%	8.8%

Source: AUC/OECD, 2019

from entrepreneurs. Moroccan start-ups find it difficult to scale up and reach maturity, as most projects funded by local VC companies focus on the pre-seed, seed, and series A stages.

7.3.4 Tunisia

Tunisia has similarly introduced a number of measures to support its digital eco-system, but it is still unclear if these measures have been successful, while the wider economic climate in Tunisia poses problems for entrepreneurs. In 2014, Tunisia adopted a National Strategy called "Digital Tunisia 2020" followed by a National Strategy for Numeric Transformation (2021–2025) that was announced during the Tunisia Digital Summit in October 2020. More recently, a regulation on drones was announced by the Minister of Transportation in February 2021. The Tunisian Institute for Strategic Studies, a think tank under the aegis of the Tunisian presidency of the Republic, published a report in 2018 proposing the adoption of a strategy on IoT. As for Tunisia's start-up ecosystem, it is now sup-ported by a series of measures. The most noteworthy one was the adoption of the Startup Act in 2018. This law allows innovative companies responding to cer-tain criteria and their founders to benefit from financial and fiscal advantages in order to develop their operations. The law is part of the Startup Tunisia National Strategy. The strategy includes two other components: Startup Invest and Startup Ecosystem.

The Startup Invest pillar notably included the launch of a "fund of funds" called ANAVA ("forward" in Tunisian Arabic). ANAVA aims to reach an invest-ment capacity of EUR 200 million that would be injected into more than 13 VC funds dedicated to start-ups at every stage of their development (pre-seed and seed, early and late stages). ANAVA was officially launched in March 2021 and benefits from a USD 75 million investment from the World Bank. It should be complemented by an incubator for VC companies (VC Lab) and a Guarantee Fund. As for the Ecosystem Pillar, it aims at funding start-ups and entrepreneur-ial hubs in Tunisia through a multiplicity of financial instruments available for all the different stages of a start-up's development. Lastly, in June 2021, Tunisia's Parliament unanimously adopted a law on crowdfunding as a complement to the Startup Act.

TABLE 7.5 Total VC Funding for Deals over 200,000 USD (Million USD).

	Egypt	Ghana	Kenya	Morocco	Nigeria	Senegal	South Africa	Tunisia
Total VC funding for deals over 200,000 USD (million USD)	269	111	305	11.2	307	8.8	259	3.4

Source: AUC/OECD, 2021

7.4 Strengthening the Linkage between Digital and Industry in North Africa

In this section we discuss possible avenues to strengthen the linkages between digital and industry in North Africa, focusing on our three case countries: Tunisia, Egypt, and Morocco.

7.4.1 Tunisia

Tunisia has undertaken a series of policies to move to I4.0. Although the country managed to upgrade the digitalisation of its industrial companies, results reached in the adoption of advanced digital technologies have been rather mixed. The PMN has helped digitalise manufacturing companies by boosting their adoption of digital technologies by 64%. Results are even higher for manufacturing SMEs (70%), which indicates that the PMN contributed to the reduction of the digital gap between SMEs and bigger companies. Nevertheless, the adoption of advanced non-specific software tools (enterprise resource planning, knowledge management systems, customer relationship management, and supply chain management) remains low in Tunisia, and the digital gap remains strong between coastal regions and interior regions (Ben Khalifa, 2020). Public support to SMEs therefore proves to be of paramount importance to help industrial companies improve their use of ICTs. This is all the more important as companies either lack awareness of the necessity to go digital or lack the financial means to invest in this matter.

As for the start-ups ecosystem applied to industry, Tunisia has tried to integrate existing infrastructure with innovative companies. For instance, Novation City, a "cluster of competitiveness" based in Sousse (northeast) focusing on electronics and mechatronics and created in the mid-2000s, recently launched Starti4, an incubation and acceleration programme with a focus on I4.0. The project was set up in collaboration with Innov'i – EU4Innovation programme, which was launched in 2019 and received EUR 14.5 million from the EU to invest in innovative companies in 21 governorates across Tunisia during the period 2019–2024. Starti4 aims at connecting industrialists, start-ups, and academia. A growing interest in I4.0 was also demonstrated by the organisation of the "Smart Industrie" event that took place in 2017 and 2020 under the supervision of the Tunisian Agency for the Promotion of Industry and Innovation and which was specifically dedicated to the 4IR.

7.4.2 Morocco

In Morocco, the rhythm of adoption of programmes focused on the digitalisation of industrial companies has tended to increase during the past few years, and authorities are pushing the private sector, and notably SMEs to further embrace digital technologies. A particularity of Morocco is that private sector–funded academic institutions are playing a key role in that push. Morocco also adopted mechanisms under the purview of "Maroc PME" and the ADD. These include "Tatwir Startups" which was launched in February 2021. This programme aims at supporting start-ups of relevance to the Moroccan industry and is part of the Industrial Recovery Plan (2021–2023) that was inaugurated by the Ministry of Industry to face the economic crisis induced by the COVID-19 pandemic. The University Mohammed VI Polytechnic, an academic institution with premises in different cities in Morocco and funded by the OCP Group, the first industrial group in Morocco, inaugurated in February 2021 a data centre and the most powerful supercomputer in Africa. It also hosts an Innovation Lab for Operations focusing on solutions for industrial digitalisation. Another initiative is the recent Memorandum of Understanding (MoU) between the Ministry of Industry, the ADD, the Euro-Mediterranean University in Fez (EMUF) and the Project Consortium "Fez Smart Factory" to develop I4.0 projects and encourage the digitalisation of industrial SMEs in the Fez region (centre-north). The MoU thus bridges the ADD's "Smart Factory" project and the EMUF's "Fez Smart Factory Project", seeking to create an integrated and sustainable zone for industrialists wishing to digitalise and modernise their activities in the Fez region. EMUF, which has received funding from the Union for the Mediterranean (UfM) and the EU, was also the venue chosen for the second edition of the Global Industry Conference 4.0 in 2021 (the first edition took place in 2019), an event placed under the aegis of the Ministry of Industry. Non-academic stakeholders pertaining to the sphere of professional organisations are also engaged in adapting the workforce to the digital era. Thus, the Moroccan Federation of Information Technology, Telecommunications and Offshoring is associated with the National Agency for the Promotion of Employment and Skills to create vocational training programmes in digital matters (AUC/OECD, 2021).

7.4.3 Egypt

Egypt has worked to adapt its policies, the IMC, the private sector, and international institutions to boost the digitalisation of its manufacturing fabric. Thus, the IMC launched the Digital Transformation and Technology Support Programme Action Plan 2019–2021 to support the digitalisation of production in different industries. The country's first I4.0 Innovation Centre was inaugurated in April 2021 following a MoU between the Information Technology Development Agency, the IMC, and Siemens Egypt. It will be headquartered in the Knowledge City at the New Administrative Capital. The Knowledge City was precisely designed to concentrate higher-education institutions and ensure better transfer of technology and know-how to the private sector. Like Morocco, Egypt also expressed interest in I4.0 in the framework of the Programmes for Country Partnerships (PCPs) led by the United Nations Industrial Development Organisation (UNIDO), which aim at accelerating inclusive and sustainable industrial development among member states.

To summarise, we note that for I4.0 to succeed in the three countries, several stumbling blocks would need to be addressed. First, VC vehicles tend to prioritise services, marketplaces, and Software as a Service investments over I4.0 and robotics. Second, contrary to major industrial powers, the three countries lack a strategy focusing on I4.0 per se. It is furthermore of paramount importance both to increase companies' awareness on the potential benefits of digitalisation (including industrial IoT) and to strengthen the workforce's digital skills. In general, many digital tools adopted by industrial companies do not pertain to the most advanced technologies that currently exist. Last, infrastructure, particularly the safe implementation of the 5G networks necessary to use industrial IoT, and cybersecurity represent a challenge for the years to come, as foreign industrialists wishing to invest in the three countries will expect efficiency and safety for the industrial data they might generate.

7.5 Digital Cooperation and the Future of Manufacturing in the Mediterranean

Digitalisation can help strengthen cooperation between Europe and North Africa and foster economic growth in both regions. In light of the recent debates taking place in Brussels around the implementation of EU-wide digital, innovation, and industrial policies, and given the series of recent strategies adopted or discussed by European institutions in these matters; the question of how North African countries can benefit from digitalisation and innovation demands attention. Synergies should be further built between existing European policies prioritising the transformation of the European industrial fabric through digitalisation on the one hand, and the European Neighbourhood Policy (ENP) on the other one.

The EU has often coupled the issue of digitalisation to that of industry, as emphasised by the 2016 communication "Digitising European Industry – Reaping the full benefits of a Digital Single Market", the renewed European Industrial Policy adopted in 2017 and some of the recent strategies released by the Von der Leyen Commission such as the 2020 new industrial strategy. The European data strategy is another noteworthy case, as it mentions "non-personal industrial data" as a "potential source of growth and innovation" and the objective to create a single European market for data. The market would notably aim at giving businesses "an almost-infinite amount of high-quality industrial data". The data strategy is presented as needing to be completed by a "broader industrial strategy for the data-agile economy" (EC, 2020b).

The package that the EU has built in terms of industrial policy, and the focus on digital technologies that it contains, can constitute a potential base for future engagement with the Southern Neighbourhood, as some already existing instruments can be proposed and extended to North African nations. These tools could indeed boost the digital transformation of North African industrial companies. In terms of public strategies that could qualify as industrial policy, there are now a variety of EU-level actions that seek structural change of the European productive fabric. These include the European Structural and Investment Funds, R&I frameworks such as the Horizon Europe programme, the SME support programme COSME, and other support vehicles such as the European Observatory for Clusters and Industrial Change (Benner, 2019). One can also mention the principle of providing public financing for Important Projects of Common European Interest on key technologies and infrastructure with potential beneficial spill-over effects on the Union's society, which was enacted in 2014. Frequent mentions of AI, IoT, 5G and 6G networks, cloud and edge computing, data centres, and supercomputers by the EC's recent communications confirm this renewed interest in technological, digital, and industrial matters.

There are now real opportunities to further integrate the industry–digitalisation nexus into the ENP. Indeed, the February 2021 "New Agenda for the Mediterranean" is the EU's joint communication on the Southern dimension of the ENP that insists on the potential of synergies between the EU and its Southern Neighbourhood in digital and industrial matters, in line with the strategies recently adopted by the Commission. The European Green Deal, the Hydrogen Strategy, the Industrial Strategy, and the SME strategy are all mentioned in the communication. The shift is justified by the "growing interdependence" recognised by the communication, which was further stressed by the COVID-19 pandemic that the communication explicitly mentions. The document therefore insists on the opportunity presented by the pandemic to further integrate "industrial supply chains between the EU and its Southern Neighbours". The communication also states the aim to replicate the ecosystems approach adopted in the framework of the communication on the new European industrial strategy by favouring the development of "Industrial clusters within the Southern Neighbourhood", which "could help economic development by connecting businesses to global and regional value chains, reducing the isolation of SMEs, promoting innovation, and generating more trade and investment" (EC & HR/VP, 2021).

As the EU refocuses on industrial policy, this is an opportunity to build a stronger industrial partnership, including a strong focus on digital industries and the digitalisation of industry. Morocco and Tunisia, in particular, are well positioned to benefit from this opportunity, as they are considered to be important partners for the EU. Since 2008, Morocco has enjoyed an "advanced status" towards the EU, while Tunisia contracted a "privileged partnership" with the Union in 2012. Tunisia was also the object of a joint communication in 2016 titled "Strengthening EU support to Tunisia", which vowed to help "mainstream the digitalisation of SMEs" (EC & HR/VP, 2016). Nevertheless, the communication did not result in major achievements. Morocco and Tunisia are now among the 18 non-EU countries associated to the Horizon Europe programme, and recent calls have been made to include them in other programmes, including the "Next Generation EU" recovery plan (El Karoui, 2021). Accession of North African countries to EU programmes in R&I, support to SMEs, digitalisation, and training, together with the identification of key areas of industrial cooperation and increased investment in infrastructure and logistics, would help mobilise private investment in key sectors and upgrade the North African industrial fabric, notably through digitalisation. In turn, such actions would reassure firms and encourage them to invest in the EU's Southern Neighbourhood, which could benefit European industrial ecosystems through a densification of value chains.

7.6 Conclusion and Recommendations

The importance of digitalisation in industrialisation has been demonstrated by various actors from the government to the private sector in Egypt, Morocco, and Tunisia. The countries have built experience and knowledge in designing sectorial policies, and notably industrial and digital ones. Nevertheless, these strategies are often poorly evaluated (because of a lack of data) or fail because of over-optimism or poor implementation. The prioritisation of the manufacturing sector when tackling the digital transition remains low and should be encouraged. The EU could play a role to make sure this digitalisation is placed high on the official agendas of Egypt, Morocco, and Tunisia and that appropriate follow-up and execution ensue. It should consolidate cooperation with its Southern Neighbourhood in industrial matters and give access to its various tools in R&I, infrastructure, and industrial policy.

The first issue that needs to be tackled for digitalisation to play a stronger role in the North African manufacturing sectors is the necessity to ensure better funding in this matter. Two components should be distinguished: VC and industrial policies. VC instruments should be better promoted to provide new forms of funding (away from lending) for nascent start-ups and help them gain maturity. Public investment in VC could thus be funded by entities of the European development finance architecture, with investment being channelled by private VC funds (funds of funds models) providing funding at all stages of start-ups' development. Involving North African institutions in more EU programmes, initiatives, and instruments would also be a welcome move. Moroccan and Tunisian association to the Horizon Europe programme is a first step that should be followed by similar ones, with the ultimate goal to ensure better dialogue between North African and European institutions, notably in the private and academic spheres. Better funding could also be provided by the EU to support investment in digitalisation for manufacturing companies, for instance, through North African public funds dedicated to the upgrading of industrial production. This could be a way to promote the reinforcement of cross-Mediterranean value chains. Funding could also be intensified for rationalised and clearer skilling programmes and infrastructure relating to digitalisation. Targeted fiscal advantages could also be provided by the three countries for companies digitalising their operations or training their workforce to use digital tools.

The second recommendation we make is centred on digital strategies. Technical support for their formulation and implementation could be deepened, and synergies should be sought in that regard. One possible programme with which to seek synergies could be the Jobs and Growth Compacts, an instrument created by the EU in 2012. These compacts were created to identify the most promising value chains at national and regional levels. Their aim is to make sure FDI pours into value chains with the best possible impact on job creation, notably in manufacturing and processing. Synergies between both programmes could thus be an avenue to pursue. Mechanisms allowing for regular exchanges on digital strategies and industrial policies could also be supported to reinforce cross-Mediterranean value chains. Fora gathering SMEs in North Africa, at the Mediterranean level and at African regional economic communities' level should also be multiplied for private sector entities to identify, share, and implement good practices, notably relating to digitalisation. This would ensure better ownership and efficiency in the conduct of digital policies. Strategies specifically dedicated to I4.0 and the coupling of digital and industrial strategies could also be an area to work on for North African states, and the EU could help design them.

Third, we advocate a multi-stakeholder and multi-scalar cooperation in digitalisation involving different actors from the AU and EU. The private sector is the best suited actor to drive the digital transformation of the productive fabric, and should therefore be encouraged to act more freely, which implies that measures should be taken to improve the business climate. Academic institutions should be more actively engaged by reinforcing their role in promoting the digitalisation of industrial companies. Technology parks and clusters can be tools to integrate the efforts of various stakeholders. Different public agencies (in charge of the digital economy, of vocational training, of industry and exports promotion) and professional organisations should also be engaged and contribute to policymaking and to a better understanding of digital-related issues and challenges by lawmakers. Last, synergies should be mapped between the different existing instruments provided by the Union for the Mediterranean, the EU, and the AU.

References

African Union (2020). "The Digital Transformation Strategy for Africa (2020–2030)". https://au.int/en/documents/20200518/digital-transformation-strategy-africa-2020-2030 (Accessed 28 January 2022).

European Union-African Union Digital Economy Task Force Digital Economy Task Force (2019). "New Africa-Europe Digital Economy Partnership. Accelerating the Achievement of the Sustainable Development Goals". https://digital-strategy.ec.europa.eu/en/library/new-africa-europe-digital-economy-partnership-report-eu-au-digital-economy-task-force (Accessed 15 September 2022).

Aiginger, K., and Rodrik, D. (2020). "Rebirth of Industrial Policy and an Agenda for the Twenty-First Century", *Journal of Industry, Competition and Trade*. 20, pp. 189–207. https://doi.org/10.1007/s10842-019-00322-3

AUC/OECD (2019). *Africa's Development Dynamics 2019: Achieving Productive Transformation, Éditions OCDE*. Paris: CUA, Addis Ababa, https://doi.org/10.1787/c1cd7de0-en (Accessed 28 January 2022).

AUC/OECD (2021). *Africa's Development Dynamics 2021: Digital Transformation for Quality Jobs, AUC*. Addis Ababa: OECD Publishing, Paris. https://doi.org/10.1787/0a5c9314-en (Accessed 28 January 2022).

Ben Khalifa, A. (2020). "Programme de mise à niveau et digitalisation de l'industrie tunisienne: éléments d'évaluation", Notes et analyses de l'ITCEQ, n° 66 - Décembre 2020. http://www.itceq.tn/innovation.php (Accessed 15 September 2022).

Benner, M. (2019). *Industrial Policy in the EU and its neighbourhood: Learning from Policy Experimentation*, European Commission, Joint Research Centre (JRC). https://doi.org/10.3390/economies7020044 (Accessed 28 January 2022).

Bianchi, M., Colantoni, L., Guesmi, K., Moisseron, J.-Y., and Sartori, N. (2018). "Assessing European Energy and Industrial Policies and Investments in the Southern Mediterranean Region from a Bottom-up Perspective", MEDRESET Working Papers, N°34 Available at: https://www.iai.it/en/pubblicazioni/assessing-european-energy-and-industrial-policies-and-investments-southern (Accessed 28 January 2022).

Cour des Comptes du Royaume du Maroc (2014). "Rapport sur l'Evaluation Maroc Numeric 2013. Rapport particulier n°05/13/CH IV". http://www.courdescomptes.ma/fr/Page-27/publications/rapport-particulier/evaluation-de-la-strategie-maroc-numeric-2013/3-85/ (Accessed 28 January 2022).

Dworkin, A. (2020). "A Return to Africa: Why North African States Are Looking South." *European Council on Foreign Relations (ECFR)*. https://ecfr.eu/publication/a_return_to_africa_why_north_african_states_are_looking_south/ (Accessed 28 January 2022).

Economic Complexity Index (2019). Available at: https://atlas.cid.harvard.edu/rankings (Accessed 28 March 2022)

El Karoui, H. "La stabilité du Maghreb, un impératif pour l'Europe", Institut Montaigne. https://www.institutmontaigne.org/publications/la-stabilite-du-maghreb-un-imperatif-pour-leurope (Accessed 28 January 2022).

European Commission, and High Representative of the Union for Foreign Affairs and Security Policy (2016). "Joint Communication to the European Parliament and the Council. Strengthening EU support for Tunisia". https://op.europa.eu/en/publication-detail/-/publication/af317533-8623-11e6-b076-01aa75ed71a1/language-en (Accessed 28 January 2022).

European Commission, and High Representative of the Union for Foreign Affairs and Security Policy (2020). "Joint Communication to the European Parliament and the Council. Towards a comprehensive strategy with Africa". https://op.europa.eu/en/publication-detail/-/publication/55817dfb-61eb-11ea-b735-01aa75ed71a1/language-en (Accessed 28 January 2022).

European Commission, and High Representative of the Union for Foreign Affairs and Security Policy (2021). "Joint Communication to the European Parliament, the Council, the European Economic and Social Committee and the Committee of the Regions. Renewed Partnership with the Southern Neighbourhood. A New Agenda for the Mediterranean". https://eur-lex.europa.eu/legal-content/EN/TXT/?uri=JOIN:2021:2:FIN (Accessed 28 January 2022).

Görlich, D. (2021). "How Does the Digital Transformation Change Global Value Chains?", *Italian Institute for International Political Studies (ISPI)*. https://www.ispionline.it/it/pubblicazione/how-does-digital-transformation-change-global-value-chains

-29590#:~:text=Due%20to%20the%20digital%20transformation,country%20and
%20finalized%20in%20another, (Accessed 28 January 2022).

Lanz, R., Lundquist, K., Mansio, G., Maurer, A., and Teh, R. (2018). "E-Commerce
and Developing Country-SME Participation in Global Value Chains", *Staff Working
Paper ERSD-2018-13*, World Trade Organization, Economic Research and Statistics
Division. https://doi.org/10.30875/ec5f0f21-en. (Accessed 28 January 2022).

Schwab, K. (2016). *The Fourth Industrial Revolution*. Currency.

Tanchum, M. (2020). "Europe-Mediterranean-Africa Commercial Connectivity:
Geopolitical Opportunities and Challenges", *Konrad Adenauer Stiftung*. https://
www.kas.de/en/web/poldimed/single-title/-/content/europe-mediterranean-africa
-commercial-connectivity-geopolitical-opportunities-and-challenges (Accessed 28
January 2022).

United Nations Conference on Trade and Development (2019). "UNCTAD B2C
E-Commerce Index 2019", *UNCTAD Technical Notes on ICT for Development n°14*.
https://unctad.org/topic/ecommerce-and-digital-economy/measuring-ecommerce
-digital-economy (Accessed 28 January 2022).

Warwick, K. (2013). "Beyond Industrial Policy: Emerging Issues and New Trends",
OECD Science, Technology and Industry Policy Papers, n° 2, Éditions OCDE, Paris.
https://www.oecd-ilibrary.org/science-and-technology/beyond-industrial-policy
_5k4869clw0xp-en (Accessed 28 January 2022).

World Bank (2019). https://data.worldbank.org/indicator/NV.IND.MANF.ZS?end
=2019&locations=EG-MA-TN&start=2002 (Accessed 28 January 2022).

8

DIGITAL WATER

An Analysis of EU and US Digital Water Initiatives in Africa

Tamanna Ashraf

8.1 Introduction

Water is a vital resource for survival and human development. The United Nations' global Agenda 2030 identifies access to clean water and sanitation as one of the Sustainable Development Goals (SDG 6). Water scarcity is a major problem facing much of the African continent. Global population is expected to increase from 7.7 billion in 2017 to between 9.4 and 10.2 billion by 2050, with half of the growth occurring in Africa (WWAP 2018). The growing demand, compounded by African countries' generally low economic development, makes addressing water scarcity a seemingly impossible task that puts a heavy burden on the existing weak water infrastructure. For example, in January 2018, government officials in Cape Town, South Africa, announced that the city was just 90 days away from running out of municipal water, thus reaching "day zero". Cape Town's "day zero" was brought on by the result of three consecutive years of lower-than-average rainfall. Extreme water scarcity is already a reality in most parts of Africa.

Even before the adoption of the SDGs, the European Union (EU) was aware of Africa's water scarcity and development-related challenges. Inspired by the 2000 UN Millennium Summit, 2002 UN World Summit, and the May 2002 EU Council Resolution on water management in developing countries, the European Union Water Initiative (EUWI) was established in September 2002, aiming to coordinate the EU and member states' funding in the field of water development (EUWI 2012). The EUWI is a strategic partnership process that brings together EU institutions, member states, and non-state actors with the goal to coordinate their financial support to develop policies in the field of water in Africa. After the first 2000 EU–Africa summit among heads of state in Cairo, the second such meeting in 2007 established the Joint Africa–EU Strategy

DOI: 10.4324/9781003274322-8

(JAES). The EUWI and the JAES at that time signalled the intention to shift their relationship away from a donor-recipient level to a strategic level.

To increase the profile of the EUWI, the then president of the European Commission, Romano Prodi, and Danish prime minister (PM) Anders Fogh Rasmussen attended the launch ceremony. The Africa-EU Strategic Partnership on Water Affairs and Sanitation led to two Working Groups for Africa. One of the working groups focused on water and sanitation, chaired by Denmark. The other working group focused on integrated water resources management chaired by France. One of the key objectives of the EUWI was to establish a platform for effective partnerships at all levels and to develop regional and sub-regional cooperation (EUWI, 2012). One of the core objectives of the EUWI was public–private sector cooperation to promote transboundary cooperation in the implementation of integrated water resource management (IWRM) principles. The principle of partnership and cooperation was echoed in the JAES which aimed to elevate the EU–Africa relationship to a strategic level by cooperating in eight areas, including climate change, energy, regional economic integration, trade and infrastructure, science, information society, and space.

Along with water scarcity, water quality is another concern in Africa. Water quality consists of the physical, chemical, and biological properties of water. Water quality is heavily dependent on geography. Specifically, areas with higher population density and rapid economic growth, or conflict are affected by poor water quality. For example, household and industrial waste is a major source of pollution of Lake Tanganyika in Bujumbura, Burundi (Manishatse, 2017). The 2018 report by the United Nations Educational, Scientific, and Cultural Organisation (UNESCO) focused on nature-based solutions to meet both water scarcity and water quality–related issues. However, due to the rapid pace of growth in water demand that comes with economic development, nature-based solutions may not work in many parts of Africa (Muller 2018). Therefore, technology and digital solutions, with a deep understanding of the unique regional and local hydrological challenges in Africa, offer an alternative solution.

Since nature-based solutions may not be the most effective means to ameliorate Africa's water scarcity and quality concerns, the EU's efforts in Africa's water development must focus on establishing water infrastructure using digital water technologies. Based on that premise, the chapter addresses two questions. First, how can the European Union expand its efforts to develop Africa's water infrastructure and achieve the goals outlined in the JAES? This chapter asserts that by incorporating digital water in water infrastructure projects, the EU can achieve its goals of cooperating in areas such as climate change, infrastructure, and exchange of scientific information. More broadly speaking, close cooperation on digital water enhances the strategic importance of the Africa–EU relationship. The second question asks, what have been the contributions of other western development agents in Africa's water sector? To answer the second question, the chapter will compare the EU's past and existing projects with the projects funded by the United States. The utility of such comparison is for the

EU to identify best practices when it comes to undertaking water infrastructure projects in developing countries and to learn from the mistakes or successes of the United States.

Section 8.2 clarifies the concept of digital water and discusses Africa's water security–related challenges. Section 8.3 elaborates on the past and current EU projects in various African countries that aim to implement digitalisation of water at any stage of production or consumption. Projects were chosen based on their use of digital water technology. Section 8.4 discusses past and present developmental projects in the water sector by the United States. The objective is to compare the EU's efforts with that of another main development partner in the continent. Analysing the strengths and shortcomings of the projects funded by another major development partner in Africa's water sector would facilitate the EU in making a unique contribution to the development of Africa's water infrastructure sector. The chapter will argue that the EU can draw lessons on how to promote climate-friendly development projects in developing countries. Finally, Section 8.5 will compare the EU's efforts with the projects funded by the United States to highlight the opportunities for the EU to propose possible policy measures supporting the digitalisation of Africa's water infrastructure.

8.2 Africa's Water Security and Digital Water

In this chapter, I provide a brief conceptual discussion over water security. However, to do so, I begin by illustrating how the problems associated with Africa's water scarcity and the underdevelopment of water infrastructures are directly linked to the security and territorial integrity of the EU member states. Water security as a concept gained prominence in the post–Cold World era as traditional military-centric security studies became less relevant. According to UN Water, water security is the ability of a population to maintain sustainable access to an adequate amount of water to sustain livelihoods, and socio-economic development while ensuring protection against pollution and water-related disasters without endangering the ecosystem (UN Water 2013). Thus, water security is a multifaceted concept that also includes water quality where the human contribution is most conspicuous.

The understanding of water security in the social sciences is dependent on the specific framing and can vary with academic disciplines. In the study of international affairs, water security often becomes part of the overarching national security debate since it is intricately linked with environmental and energy security and even food security (Cook & Bakker 2012). The link between water scarcity and violence also has been thoroughly established (Homer-Dixon et al. 1993).

Water scarcity and quality are major obstacles to the social and economic development of African countries. In sub-Saharan Africa (SSA), drought is a constant natural risk that obstructs farmers' livelihoods and threatens both food and economic security at an individual, national, and international level (WWAP 2012). In addition, water scarcity has been a conspicuous factor in political and social instability in Africa. For instance, drought cycles in the Horn of Africa are getting shorter. In 2011 alone, around 184,000 Somalis fled to neighbouring countries due to water and food insecurity (WWAP 2012). War and droughts also continue to create food security problems in South Sudan (Krampe et al. 2020). Persistent drought in the Horn of Africa, particularly in Somalia, displaced around 599,000 people by 2016 (UNOCHA 2017).

Lack of food and resources can compel people to search for food, water, and income through alternative and illegal means like piracy. Beyond the Horn of Africa, water plays a crucial role in security-related concerns like terrorism. Recognising the strategic importance of water bodies and water infrastructures, terrorist groups like Boko Haram have overtaken the Lake Chad area, a sanctuary for displaced and desperate people, to boost recruitment by offering employment (Hugh 2019). Hence, in already fragile governance structures, water security concerns threaten to further destabilise countries in the region, as is the case with Nigeria, and Niger (Krampe et al. 2020).

In addition to terrorism, water scarcity and access can exacerbate existing ethnic tensions. For example, access to pasture lands and water has triggered conflicts in Darfur (Cumming 2015). The case of Darfur shows that water security issues can also impact the EU's general and security interests in the region given its role as an active partner and mediator. Ensuring that there is adequate and stable access to clean, affordable water without jeopardising the environment can also reduce violence. Therefore, the EU has a vested interest to invest in the development of water infrastructure in Africa. Thorny issues like Darfur, Boko Haram, and piracy require efforts beyond simple aid giving and call for measures to bolster governance and infrastructure, as envisioned in the JAES (Biondo, 2020). One way that the EU can achieve this is by developing Africa's water infrastructure sector through the utilisation of digital technology to address water scarcity and improve water security.

8.2.1 Digital Water

Digital water is the idea of using digital technologies to increase the efficiency, reliability, and resiliency of water supply and water infrastructure at all stages of production and consumption (IWA 2019). By exploiting the information collected through digital technologies and artificial intelligence, national and local municipalities (and even smaller communities) can extend their local water resources, reduce non-revenue-generating water use (ibid.), and improve water governance. By increasing efficiency and reliability, the consumers can have access to clean water at affordable prices, while the municipalities can increase revenue by lowering production costs and reducing non-paying customers. Furthermore, a digital approach to water infrastructure can create new business opportunities and improve transactions (UK Water Partnership 2020).

Digital water is useful at all three stages of production. At the source level, where water is extracted from the watershed, surface, groundwater, or even wastewater collection, digital technologies can aid in the remote monitoring of water flow, water levels, pH levels, and temperature. Once the water is collected at the treatment facility, digital sensors and algorithms can enhance the treatment process and even provide a solution for the maintenance of the facility. On the consumption end, digital meters and mobile applications can improve customer service, allowing the consumer to monitor consumption and reduce the bill. According to the International Water Association (IWA), digital meters can help municipalities to eliminate billing errors and non-paying customers (IWA 2019).

African countries have made great strides in the digitalisation of their economies. Innovation is apparent in the water development sector as well, which has attracted European companies to invest in the continent. For example, in a public–private partnership between the Nairobi Water and Sewerage Company, Safaricom, and Grundfos (a Danish water engineering firm), water vending machines were installed in Nairobi's slums to improve the poor's access to clean, affordable water and reduce the influence of water cartels. As a result, the weekly water expenditure in the slum reduced from USD 2.5 to 2.5 cents (Ndung'u 2018). Grundfos predicts that digitalisation is going to be a big part of the future of water infrastructure around the world including Africa (African Review 2020). Big Data collected from digital water technologies can be used to predict droughts. This allows African countries to better adapt to extreme weather events and mitigate the related socio-economic challenges.

The European Union can build on the existing involvement of private actors in the digitalisation of Africa's water sector to expand its presence. European companies are getting involved to promote innovations to address Africa's water scarcity problems. In 2018, when Cape Town was facing an imminent "day zero", Siemens hosted the inaugural #DigihackAfrica2018 to find technological solutions to South Africa's water and energy needs. The winning team presented a system of decentralised intelligent water management systems to ameliorate South Africa's water loss due to leakage. The country loses 37% of water due to leakage, which is about 4,500 billion litres annually (Letsebe 2018). The decentralised water management system will detect leaks, monitor water flow and pressure, and alert technicians of any change through a mobile app, allowing them to attend to the problem (ibid.). This is a prime example of digital water. European companies like Grundfos and Siemens recognise the importance of the digitalisation of Africa's water sector. Furthermore, events like #DigihackAfrica2018 demonstrate that the ideas already exist in the private sector to address Africa's water scarcity challenges digitally. The EU has traditionally relied on its soft power tools (Biondo, 2020). Collaboration with European and African private sector actors to improve Africa's water infrastructure can be another avenue to enhance its soft power capabilities and achieve the objectives of JAES.

8.3 Past and Current EU Water Projects and Digital Water

At the institutional level, the EU has taken the initiative to engage with African partners in the water sector. The European Commission established the EUWI to support the development of the water infrastructure sector in developing countries, including countries in sub-Saharan Africa. However, at the time of its conception, digitalisation of water was not a key objective, even though some of the projects have incorporated digital water technology marginally. One of the two African Working Groups (AWG), the African component of the EUWI, tackled integrated water resources management (IWRM) through Country Dialogues while the other dealt with water and sanitation. The AWG selected the Democratic Republic of Congo (DRC), Ghana, Ethiopia, Mozambique, Rwanda, and Zambia to hold dialogues. Initially, EUR 10 million was allocated across the Volta and Niger Rivers, Lake Chad, Lake Victoria, and the Orange-Senqu River.

The motivation behind the EUWI was to further the Commission's foreign policy ambitions (Fritsch et al. 2020) and by integrating the concept of IWRM to stress sustainable practices. The JAES further outlined these ambitions as it aimed to further cooperation in critical areas like security, climate change, and infrastructure. However, the Country Dialogues under the EUWI proved to be largely disappointing due to inadequate resources and time and involved less ownership of the process in some of the countries (Fritsch et al. 2017). For the African actors, the Country Dialogues were perceived as a way to raise funds, whereas the European Commission saw them as political tools (ibid.). Therefore, the overall efforts of the EU through the AWG were perceived by the African partners as largely ineffective and imposed by external actors. Similarly, during the meetings between the European Commission and African Union Commission under the JAES, the African delegates perceived certain issues like LGBTQ rights as an imposition in internal affairs (Biondo 2020). Meetings under the EUWI and JAES indicate that despite intentions for cooperation and partnership, interests can diverge.

8.3.1 Project 1: Lake Tanganyika Water Management Authority

Apart from the political dialogue on cooperation and development, there are field-level efforts by the EU. One tangible example of the EU's efforts to develop Africa's water infrastructure is the Lake Tanganyika Water Management Authority, or the LATAWAMA project, to preserve Lake Tanganyika. An analysis of this project is necessary to assess the EU's efforts in Africa's water sector and also its implementation of digital water. Although there are elements of digital water technology in this project, the concept remains underused. Lake Tanganyika is the second largest lake in Africa after Lake Victoria. It originates in the Democratic Republic of Congo and has four other riparians which are: Burundi, Tanzania, Zambia, and Rwanda. In 2019, the Lake Tanganyika

Authority (LTA) and the EU funded the LATAWAMA project to increase local awareness and sustainably improve the water quality and ecosystem of the Lake. Under the project, labs and wastewater facilities were built in cities along the Lake of the riparian states and were strengthened to improve water quality. The EU provided EUR 6.9 million to fund wastewater treatment and build labs. Additionally, the EU allotted EUR 20.2 million to build and update ports like the Bujumbura Port (Burundi) and the Mpulungu Port (Zambia). The goal was to create a database by collecting water samples and share across the facilities in different countries. Although the creation of the shared database is a help-ful measure to monitor the water quality, it is unclear whether the project will implement digital water technologies any further.

Another important component of the LATAWAMA project is to optimise the operation of the Bueterere Wastewater Plant to treat the wastewater sludge of Lake Tanganyika. This aspect of the project provides an opportunity for the EU to implement digital technology. Digital technology can be used to man-age sludge in an environmentally sustainable way. In EU countries, innovative technology uses wastewater to produce biogas. However, such technology uses incineration for energy production, which is an expensive method, that also comes with environmental consequences (Bizimana et al. 2021). Since countries like the Netherlands have incorporated cutting-edge membrane technology to separate the carbon dioxide and methane from wastewater to produce biogas (Dutch Water Sector 2020), there is an opportunity for technology transfer from the EU to the African countries. Furthermore, using digital technologies for wastewater management and energy production will go further to increase the appeal of digital water technologies in Africa and encourage scientific coopera-tion between the EU and Africa as envisioned by the JAES.

8.3.2 Project 2: MADFORWATER in North Africa

Aside from East Africa, the EU has also engaged the North African Countries to address water scarcity. The region (encompassing Morocco, Tunisia, Algeria, Libya, and Egypt) is projected to see a 47% increase in water demand between now and 2035 due to population and economic growth (MADFORWATER 2020). This region contains only 1% of the world's freshwater, and more than 80% of that goes towards agricultural production (ibid.). In 2015, under the EU's Horizon 2020 programme, the MADFORWATER project was launched to improve the quantity and quality of Egypt's, Morocco's, and Tunisia's water resources by treating wastewater for agricultural consumption.

The first phase of the project included a countrywide analysis of water vul-nerability and stress. The second phase emphasised the adaptation of innovative technologies for wastewater treatment. The MADFORWATER project imple-ments the concept of digital water by extending it to the agriculture sector in a dry climate. The Souss-Massa region of Morocco is characterised by a semi-arid to sub-desert climate. The agriculture sector employs 51% of the workforce, making it a strategic sector of the overall economy (Mansir et al. 2018). The project also included an open-source software to determine the proper amount of irrigation with different water types and even determine the required fertiliser input (since treated wastewater contains a level of nutrient) (Frascari et al. 2018). A computer programme is used to monitor the water against the plant demand and climatic demand and relay that information to the farmers (Egen Green 2021). This programme also allows for direct interaction between the farmers (consumers) and the water treatment facilities. Moreover, with instructions on how much water and fertiliser to use, the farmers can avoid excessive salt accumulation in the soil (ibid.). Thus, the digital water technology used in the MADFORWATER project can reduce soil pollution. In addition, the instructive nature of the software makes it user-friendly for farmers.

The Moroccan government is hopeful that wastewater treatment projects like this will reduce water pollution (Egen Green 2021). Thus, the MADFORWATER project demonstrates an effective use of the digital water concept and has generated hope for the adoption of similar technology by multiple other African governments. However, at this time, the project is limited to a narrow number of locations in Egypt, Morocco, and Tunisia. Steps should be taken to expand it to other areas of those countries and to other countries in Africa.

Based on the MADFORWATER and the LATAWAMA projects, it is apparent that the European Union is cognisant of water scarcity issues in Africa and its short-term and long-term repercussions in the continent and beyond. Improving African countries' access to safe potable water and sanitation facilities seems to be the EU's priority. At the current stage, the European Union's use of digital technologies to improve water infrastructures in both rural and urban areas seems to be limited. The locations of MADFORWATER (Souss-Massa) and the LATAWAMA (Bueterere) projects are limited to urban settings. The concept of digital water may look different in a rural setting. In a rural setting creative, digital solutions are needed to monitor water flow (such as the flotation devices), water quality, and transmit that to a field office. The data generated from these remote locations can then be transmitted to a central water facility, promoting the centralisation of water resources. Since rural areas may lack adequate power resources, digital water technologies will have to depend on solar power sources and be maintained and operated locally.

The LATAWAMA projects are operating in a handful of African countries and implement digital technologies in a limited manner in the collection, treatment, and distribution processes of water consumption. There are greater opportunities to implement digital water technology in the treatment of wastewater, for example, in the Buterere Wastewater Treatment Plant. The MADFORWATER is a pioneering project that offers a sustainable solution to reduce the region's water scarcity issues. However, the project is operational in urban settings. Africa's water scarcity and infrastructure problems exist in rural settings as well. Therefore, more creative, innovative, and sustainable solutions using digital technologies in a rural setting are essential.

8.4 Developing Africa's Water Sector: The United States

While the EU has instigated or funded multiple water infrastructure projects using digital technologies, other development partners are active in the continent's water sector. Analysing the strengths and shortcomings of those projects is essential for the EU to compare its efforts with that of other active partners in the region. This would facilitate the EU to make a unique contribution to the development of Africa's water infrastructure sector and achieve the goals of the JAES. The successes and shortcomings of U.S. agencies' cooperation with African public and private sector actors could provide lessons for the EU.

The U.S. Agency for International Development (USAID) is an active partner in Africa's water and sanitation sector. Under the water supply, sanitation, and hygiene (WASH) programme, the USAID has engaged with various African partners to improve the water and sanitation infrastructure. USAID's efforts in Africa aim to improve health outcomes through sustainable WASH provision and to manage water for agricultural sustainably to enhance food security (USAID 2018). The U.S. Department of State recognises natural disasters, environmental degradation, and water scarcity as problems that can exacerbate political and social instability (ibid.). The underlying objective of USAID's developmental efforts in Africa is to improve the region's resilience and self-reliance in areas like health, education, economic growth, energy security, food security, and water security. The various projects undertaken by USAID implement digital water technologies.

Therefore, WASH is part of the U.S. Global Water Strategy to increase global water security and decrease the risks of political and social unrest. The U.S. Global Water Strategy identifies a list of high-priority countries,[1] where engagement in the water sector can serve national security interests. In the U.S. Government Global Water Strategy Report for 2017, improving the WASH sector is identified as a key focus of the USAID's efforts.

8.4.1 Project 1: WARIDI and Digital Water in Rural Setting

USAID has utilised modern technologies to improve water access in Tanzania which adheres to the concept of digital water but applies it in a rural setting. Tanzania is a high-priority country as identified by the U.S. Global Water Strategy. Under the Water Resources Integration Development Initiative (WARIDI) of 2016, the USAID contributed USD 48.8 million to improve WASH services in 20 locations in the Rufiji and Wami-Ruvu River Basins. As of September 2020, the various schemes of the WARIDI project gave over 400,000 people access to safe drinking water and over 1.2 million people benefit from better sanitation facilities (USAID 2020). The efforts towards digitalisation under the project start at the initial stage. Flotation devices containing equipment allow field experts to monitor the water flow. Doing so reduces experts' risk of being attacked by dangerous animals in the river (USAID Tanzania 2020). They can remotely access data from the weather stations, allowing for faster communication and sharing of information. In addition, it reduces uncertainty about water availability, allowing for better water governance. Projects like WARIDI demonstrate that digitalisation of water can work in rural locations, thereby expanding the scope of digital water and its implementation. In addition, projects like WARIDI demonstrate that digitalisation of water can support the overarching goals of improving climate resilience, sustainability, and governance, as outlined by the U.S. Government Global Water Strategy Report 2017.

It is apparent from the USAID's strategies and objectives that the United States is focused on WASH projects and improving access to water (and energy) in Africa rather than solely promoting digital water. According to the 2017 Water for World Country Plan for Tanzania and Uganda, improving WASH services remain a high priority, implying that digital water is not yet a priority. However, as WARIDI demonstrates, digitalisation of water can be a useful path towards that goal. Innovative projects like WARIDI that implement the digital water concept are occurring in 20 locations in Tanzania.

8.4.2 The U.S. Engagement in Africa's Water Sector: Lessons for the EU

Both the United States and the EU are active development agents in Africa's water sector. However, collaboration between them in the water sector is limited. One such example is seen outside of Africa, where the USAID-led project Water Infrastructure Support and Enhancement for Lebanon (WISE-Lebanon) included minor involvement from the EU as a donor. The implementation of digital water is evident in the consumption stage. It is unclear whether the project uses digital technology during water extraction, processing, and distribution stages. Additionally, in projects like the WISE-Lebanon, the EU's role is limited as a donor. However, the WISE-Lebanon project could encourage future cooperation between the EU and the United States that demonstrates a more active role from the former that goes beyond contributing funds.

Apart from future collaboration, the EU can draw lessons from the past and current engagements by the United States in Africa's water sector. The WARIDI project demonstrates that digital water can be successfully implemented in a rural setting, providing the chance to expand the EU's engagement in Africa's water sector. USAID has also worked with countries to help create National Adaptation Plans (NAPs) under the UN Framework Conventions on Climate Change (UNFCCC) that emphasise development rather than climate change. The lesson from the development of the NAPs was that a development-first approach better integrates climate change considerations into national development policies (Kim et al. 2017). Understandably, changing development policies to account for climate change–related risk may not be feasible for developing countries. Therefore, the developing countries may be more willing to adjust policies when the rhetoric is focused on development first and climate change second. Thus, the USAID findings could help the EU to achieve its goals under the JAES. Lastly, as the meetings under the EUWI and the JAES demonstrated, interests can diverge between the EU and the African partners. By emphasising a development-first rhetoric, the EU can avoid such perceptions.

8.5 Conclusion: Opportunities for Cooperation in EU–Africa Digital Water

Thus far, the European Union has had some achievements in the digitalisation of Africa's water infrastructure. Additionally, European private technology companies are engaging with African partners and experts to foster growth in telecommunication and technological ingenuity. The European Union has to take measures to deepen its engagements with both African leaders and experts and European and African private sectors working in the region to improve Africa's water sector. As it is apparent from the directive reports of the EUWI (2012) and the U.S. Government Global Water Strategy (U.S. Government 2017), both actors aim to improve the sustainability, efficiency, and governance of African countries' water sectors and facilitate the achievement of SDGs. These shared objectives can be the motivator for greater collaboration. Digitalisation of water can be a path towards the realisation of these objectives and help the EU expand its role from an aid-giving partner to a stronger development partner.

Various European companies have implemented innovative projects across Africa and engaged with the African private sector. As the #DigihackAfrica2018 event indicates, European companies like Siemens can promote creative solutions to various problems in Africa, including the water sector. Others like Futurepump (a British pump manufacturer) are installing solar-powered pumps in certain rural areas of Kenya and Uganda. These pumps collect data to monitor water levels (Bhalla 2020). Moreover, solar-powered pumps allow the operation and collection of data in rural settings. European hydro-engineering companies like Grundfos and Futurepump realise that digitisation can ameliorate Africa's water security issues. Thus, the EU needs greater collaboration with the private sector (both European and African) to garner cutting-edge technology in digital water to achieve its goals under the JAES. Such public–private cooperation could be a boon for European companies as well.

Lastly, after the February 2022 Africa–EU Summit, the Joint Vision for 2030 stated that investment in digital infrastructure is a key component of building a sustainable and prosperous Africa and Europe (European Council 2022). Even though the 2022 Summit did not address important issues for African countries (such as finding a durable solution for asylum seekers from Africa, and the EU waiving patents on COVID-19 vaccines), promoting development and digital infrastructures were discussed (Sattar 2022). Therefore, the EU's promotion of digital water in Africa's water sector is even more pertinent.

Note

1 The list of countries include the DRC, Ethiopia, Ghana, Kenya, Liberia, Madagascar, Mali, Mozambique, Nigeria, Senegal, South Sudan, Tanzania, and Uganda.

References

African Review (2020). Digitalisation: The future of the water sector. Available at: https://www.africanreview.com/manufacturing/water-a-environment/digitalisation -the-future-of-the-water-sector (Accessed: 5 November 2021).

Bhalla, N. (2020). Water shortage in Africa is a deadly problem but this innovative solution could change that. World Economic Forum [online]. Available at: https://www.weforum.org/agenda/2020/02/solar-pumps-big-data-africa-water-energy/ (Accessed 4 February 2021).

Biondo, K. D. (2020). Moving beyond a donor-recipient relationship? Assessing the principle of partnership in the joint Africa-EU strategy. *Journal of contemporary African studies. [Online]* 38(2), pp. 310–329.

Bizimana, A., Wu, B. and Idriss, A. A. (2021). Analysis of adapted sewage sludge treatment and Disposal Routes in Bujumbura, Burundi. *Open Access Library Journal,* 8, p. e7319. https://doi.org/10.4236/oalib.1107319

Cook, C., and Bakker, K. (2012)., Water security: Debating an emerging paradigm. *Global Environmental Change [online].* 22, pp. 94–102. https://doiorg.ezproxy.fiu.edu /10.1016/j.gloenvcha.2011.10.011

Cumming, G. D. (2015). The European Union in Sudan: A missed opportunity? *Round Table (London). [Online]* 104(4), pp. 473–488.

Dutch Water Sector (2020). More biogas from sewage sludge in Amsterdam. Available at: https://www.dutchwatersector.com/news/more-biogas-from-sewage-sludge-for -amsterdam (Accessed 30 March 2022).

Egen Green (2021). *MADFORWATER: Pilot Plant P3 for Treatment and Reuse of Municipal Wastewater (Agadir, Morocco)* [Video]. Available from https://www.youtube.com/watch ?v=naYwuW8IEKc (Accessed 12 February 2022).

European Council (2022). Sixth European Union Africa Summit: A Joint Vision of 2030. Available at: https://www.consilium.europa.eu/en/press/press-releases/2022/02/18/ sixth-european-union-african-union-summit-a-joint-vision-for-2030/ (Accessed 12 February 2022).

European Union Water Initiative (2012). The first ten years of the European Union water initiative: 2001–2012. [PDF]. Available at: https://europa.eu/capacity4dev/file/23765 /download?token=xZwKcWsk (Accessed 30 March 2022).

Frascari, D., Zanaroli, G., Motaleb, M. A., Annen, G., and Belguith, K. (2018). Integrated technological and management solutions for wastewater treatment and efficient agricultural reuse in Egypt, Morocco, and Tunisia. *Integrated Environmental Assessment and Management [online].* 14(4), pp. 447–462. Available from https://www.madforwater .eu/scientific-publications/ (Accessed 30 March 2022).

Fritsch, O., Adelle, C., and Benson, D. (2017). The EU Water Initiative at 15: origins, processes and assessment. *Water International [online].* 42(4), pp. 425–442. Available from https://doi.org/10.1080/02508060.2017.1330816

Fritsch, O., Benson, D.; Adelle, C., and Massot, A. (2020). Three faces of the European Union water initiative: Promoting the water framework directive or sustainable development? *Water Alternatives [online].* 13(3), pp. 709–730. Available at: https://www

.water-alternatives.org/index.php/alldoc/articles/volume-13/issue-3-1/597-a13-3 -15 (Accessed 30 March 2022).

Homer-Dixon, T., Boutwell, J., and Rathjens, G. (1993). Environmental change and violent Conflict. *Scientific American* [online]. 268(2), pp. 38–45. [viewed January 24, 2020]. Available at: www.jstor.org/stable/24941373 (Accessed 30 March 2022).

International Water Association (2019). Digital water: Industry leaders chart the transformation journey [online]. [viewed May 2021]. Available from https://iwa -network.org/publications/digital-water/ (Accessed 30 March 2022).

Hugh, B. (April 2019). Unemployment, terrorism, water scarcity compounded in WANAME region by climate change [online]. Utah State University. [Viewed 5 July 2021]. Available at: https://www.usu.edu/cai/student-research/studentpaper-hugh (Accessed March 2022).

Kim, Y. et al. (2017) A perspective on climate-resilient development and national adaptation planning based on USAID's experience. *Climate and Development*. [Online] 9(2), pp. 141–151.

Krampe, F., Goor L. V. D., Barnhoorn, A., Smith, E., and Smith, D. (2020). Water security and governance in the Horn of Africa [PDF]. *Policy Paper 54*. Stockholm International Peace Research Institute. Available at: https://www.sipri.org/publications/2020/ sipri-policy-papers/water-security-and-governance-horn-africa (Accessed on July 5 2021).

Letsebe, K. (2018). Hacakthons seek drought-prevention solution. Available from https:// www.itweb.co.za/content/KWEBbvyakx2vmRjO

MADFORWATER (2020). *MADFORWATER*. Available at: https://www.madforwater .eu/ (Accessed May 15, 2021).

Mansir I., Bouchaou L., Choukr-allah R., Chebli B., and El Otmani M. (2018). Groundwater Resources Scarcity in Souss-Massa region and alternative solutions for sustainable agricultural development. In: Calvache M., Duque C., Pulido-Velazquez D. (eds). *Groundwater and global change in the Western Mediterranean Area.* Environmental Earth Sciences. Available at: https://doi.org/10.1007/978-3-319 -69356-9_22

Manishatse, L. J. (2017). Ake Tanganyika pollution poses major risk for Bujumbura residents. Available at: https://www.iwacu-burundi.org/englishnews/lake -tanganyika-pollution-poses-major-risk-for-bujumbura-residents/ (Accessed 30 March 2022).

Muller, M. (2018). Why UNESCO's 'natural solutions' to water problems won't work in Africa [online]. *Down To Earth*. Gale General OneFile. [Viewed 10 May 2021]. Available from link.gale.com/apps/doc/A531494766/ITOF?u=miam11506&sid =ITOF& xid=091e483d (Accessed 19 March 2021).

Ndung'u, N. (2018). Harnessing Africa's digital potential: New tools for new age. *Brookings Insitute [online]*. Available at: https://www.brookings.edu/research/harnessing-africas -digital-potential/ (Accessed 30 March 2022).

Sattar, A. (2022). Europe Africa summit disappoints: Limited progress on inequality. Available at: https://impakter.com/europe-africa-summit-disappoints-limited -progress-on-inequality/ (Accessed 30 March 2022).

U.K. Water Partnership (2020). Digital water: Capitalising on the commercial opportunities [PDF]. Available at: https://www.theukwaterpartnership.org/ publications/digital-water-a-global-opportunity-for-the-uk (Accessed 30 March 2022).

UNOCHA (UN Office for the Coordination of Humanitarian Affairs) (2017). Somalia: Drought response situation report no. 5 [PDF]. Available at: https://reliefweb.int/

report/somalia/somalia-drought-response-situation-report-no-5-23-april-2017 (Accessed 5 July 2021).

UN Water (2013). *Water security and the global water agenda: A UN-Water analytical brief.* Available at: http://www.unwater.org/publications/water-security-global-water-agenda/ (Accessed 30 March 2022).

U.S. Agency for International Development (2018). USAID: Water and development strategy 2013–2018 [PDF]. Available at: https://www.usaid.gov/documents/1865/usaid-water-and-development-strategy-2013-2018 (Accessed 30 March 2022).

U.S. Agency for International Development (2020). Tanzania: Water resources integration development initiative [PDF]. Available at: https://www.usaid.gov/sites/default/files/documents/WARIDI_Fact_Sheet_Q4_2020.pdf (Accessed 30 March 2022).

U.S. Agency for International Development Tanzania (2020). USAID water resources management in Tanzania [Video]. *YouTube*. Available at: https://www.youtube.com/watch?v=XT5i4uMXrSM (Accessed 30 March 2020).

U.S. Government (2017). U.S. Government global water strategy 2017 [online]. Available at: https://www.usaid.gov/what-we-do/water-and-sanitation/us-global-water-strategy (Accessed 30 March 2022).

WWAP (World Water Assessment Programme) (2012). *The UN World Water Development Report 4: Managing Water Under Uncertainty and Risk [PDF File]*. Paris. UNESCO. Available at: http://www.zaragoza.es/ciudad/medioambiente/onu/en/detallePer_Onu?id=71 (Accessed 30 March 2022).

WWAP (World Water Assessment Programme) (2018). *The United Nations World Water Development Report 2018: Nature-based solutions for water [PDF file]*. Paris. UNESCO. Available at: https://www.unwater.org/publications/world-water-development-report-2018/ (Accessed 30 March 2022).

9

DIGITALISATION AND REVENUE MOBILISATION IN GHANA

The Role of Evidence-Based Stakeholder Engagements

Andrew Agyei-Holmes, Bernardin Senadza, and Felix Ankomah Asante

9.1 Introduction

Since the mid–1980s, Ghana has reformed its tax institutions to reduce its dependence on aid (Osei and Quartey, 2005). Despite these reforms, Ghana's domestic resource mobilisation remains low. In 2018, Ghana was one of seven countries in sub–Saharan Africa (SSA) whose tax to GDP ratio stood below 15%. Legal and administrative reforms may be necessary to address aspects of the problem but will not be sufficient to address other aspects. In the last two decades, therefore, the Ghana Revenue Authority (GRA) has embarked on a new approach focused on the digitalisation of tax transactions. The objective is to reduce face-to-face human interactions in tax administration to save time and cost for both tax collectors and taxpayers.

As a result, domestic taxes are now largely managed via online solutions and international trade taxes have become paperless. That is, paper-based transactions are gradually being moved online. The GRA introduced the Total Revenue Integrated Processing System (TRIPS) in 2011 with the aim of moving domestic tax administration to computer-based applications. TRIPS is a computer application which seeks to improve the back-office activities of tax administration. In the past these back-office activities were slowed down by the sheer number of physical documents which tax collectors found difficult to manage manually.

To further foster this transition from manual operations to online systems, the Integrated Tax Application and Preparation System (ITAPS) was introduced by GRA in 2019 to support TRIPS by providing an interface for taxpayers to interact with tax collectors. ITAPS facilitates online payment and record keeping for domestic taxes by taxpayers. Additionally, international trade taxes were digitalised so that importers can submit trade documents and receive feedback from customs offices through online platforms. This digitalisation drive for

DOI: 10.4324/9781003274322-9

international trade taxes administration in Ghana culminated in a Paperless Port System in 2017.

Anecdotal evidence suggests that the movement of revenue mobilisation activities from manual processes to digital platforms is leading to some gains. These gains include widening of the tax base, increased quantity of taxes collected by GRA, and time and cost savings for both tax collectors and taxpayers. However, the digitalisation of tax revenue mobilisation in Ghana has its own challenges spanning from skill gaps to infrastructural deficits requiring attention by duty bearers. One way to encourage duty bearers in charge of the digitalisation of revenue mobilisation to address these challenges is through stakeholder dialogue. That is, a platform which allows relevant stakeholders to engage with duty bearers to provide feedback for continuous improvements is critical – a subject matter which this chapter seeks to address. Our chapter argues that a thought-out dialogue process, relying on best practices and lessons learnt, can help improve the digitalisation process. When supported by international stakeholders (like the former UK-DFID), stakeholder engagements have the potential to appeal to duty bearers to act on addressing challenges associated with digitalisation programmes in Ghana and in other contexts across Africa.

Using primary and secondary data obtained in 2019 from tax collectors, taxpayers (domestic and international trade) and systems managers, this chapter first demonstrates that digitalisation is driving progress in tax revenue mobilisation in Ghana through improved efficiency. Persisting challenges relate to staffing and technological infrastructure. Second, we argue that stakeholder engagement is key to addressing challenges that digital revenue mobilisation systems may face. This is because it does not only bring the challenges to the attention of duty bearers, but also allows stakeholders to discuss workable solutions. Finally, we conclude with lessons learnt and suggest some avenues where future African Union (AU) and European Union (EU) cooperation could focus in the area of digitalisation and revenue mobilisation. We note here that although the UK is no longer a member of the EU, the lessons learnt from their involvement in the Ghanaian case may still be useful in an AU–EU cooperation.

9.2 Tax Collection and Digitalisation in Ghana

Low levels of tax revenue mobilisation have characterised Ghana's national accounts for a long period. And in fact, in 2001 the country opted for the International Monetary Fund's (IMF) highly indebted poor country initiative (Bank of Ghana, 2003). Existing evidence suggests that reforming the way in which the tax collection institutions work could help address this issue (Appiah, 2013). In response, reforms in Ghana's tax collection system, spearheaded by the Government of Ghana and the GRA, have promoted reforms. Despite significant progress brought about by these reforms in the tax collection space, challenges remain. This section examines the various digitalisation initiatives implemented in Ghana. It argues that despite some of the desired outcomes being achieved, an institutional framework to promote continuous dialogue among stakeholders could promote additional benefits.

In the last four decades, tax revenue mobilisation reforms in Ghana have focused on two broad themes: administrative and technological improvements. Administrative reforms redefined responsibilities of institutions that collect taxes. In some cases, new institutions were introduced or existing ones merged to enhance efficiency (Osei and Quartey, 2005). On the other hand, technology-related reforms were pursued, driven by automating tax administration systems to save time and reduce cost through digitalisation (ISSER, 2019).

To support these cost- and time-saving objectives, GRA started generating unique Tax Identification Numbers (TIN) for taxpayers in 2002 (Bugbilla and Asamoah, 2016). It removed some manual international trade tax payment procedures, thus automating various processes. This simplified the procedures for import tax payment. Additional tools to further the technological innovations in tax administration were introduced. Two of these innovations concerned domestic taxes (TRIPS and ITAPS), and a third concerned international trade taxes (Paperless Port System). TRIPS was introduced in 2011 to support back-office activities undertaken by domestic tax collectors. ITAPS, a user interface, was introduced in 2019 as a front-office tool to augment TRIPS. The Paperless Port System introduced in 2017 allows importers to clear their goods using online tools to engage with customs officials.

Notwithstanding the fact that Ghana started much earlier than some of its neighbours like Nigeria (ICAEW, 2019), in comparison, many European countries had digitalised tax revenue mobilisation before Ghana began to do so. Whilst the use of online services for tax administration is ubiquitous in the EU, on the African continent these approaches are quite new. Therefore, Ghana's reforms could benefit from the experiences of EU member states and possibly serve as a model for AU member states planning to digitalise their revenue mobilisation platforms. As the Organisation for Economic Co-operation and Development (OECD) Tax Administration Series suggests, there has been a significant shift in OECD countries towards e-administration with increasing options for online filing of tax returns as well as online payments. On average, e-filing rates for personal income tax are now above 70% and those for corporate income tax are around 85% for OECD members (OECD, 2019). The statistics in Ghana may not come close to those in Europe, but digital tools can contribute to further improvements. As we shall see in the following subsections, the narrative is changing with the introduction of TRIPS/ITAPS and Paperless Port System, despite some setbacks.

9.2.1 TRIPS and ITAPS

As noted earlier, the TRIPS and ITAPS platforms serve domestic tax collection processes; the former at the back-end and the latter customer-facing. There is evidence to show that the domestic tax collection environment is improving gradually because of these technologies. For instance, an evaluation report by the World Bank on these tools highlighted significant successes in tax administration, business registration, and licensing following the implementation of the TRIPS (World Bank, 2016a). As of 2016, the tax base had widened considerably with an estimated 400,000 new taxpayers listed. Between January and July 2017, over 154,000 tax returns were processed using TRIPS, representing a 43% increase over the same period in 2016. By July 2017, about 890,000 Tax Identification Numbers had been issued using TRIPS. From 2010 to 2015, the amount collected in taxes tripled and by 2015, an estimated 62% of tax revenue was collected via TRIPS. This reflects an enhanced efficiency in tax collection (World Bank, 2016a).

Despite these positive developments, key informant interviews conducted with tax collectors in various tax offices across Ghana on TRIPS revealed several loopholes in its implementation. First, not all tax processes can be undertaken on the TRIPS platform and some features of the software are completely inaccessible. Second, the system experienced frequent slowdowns during peak periods creating delays. Third, users and other stakeholders reported issues about the system not being able to correct some errors, failures in tax credit inputs, wrong user specifications, inaccessibility of some features, inability to capture advance payments, and occasional loss of data. Reporting and receipts also fail to capture the different types of transactions, making auditing problematic (ISSER, 2019).

9.2.2 Paperless Port System

Similarly, the Paperless Port System, which was envisioned and implemented by the GRA to simplify the payment of trade (import and export) taxes through online solutions, has its ups and downs. An interim assessment of the Paperless Port System by several stakeholders during a forum organised by the Ghana Shippers Council in November 2018 suggests significant progress in the first year of the implementation of the paperless system. First, participants noted a reduction in the number of agencies involved in the inspection and examination of goods at the ports since the introduction of the paperless system – this has cut down on the time required for goods inspection. Second, since the system relies on a computer algorithm to randomly select containers for inspection, only 55% of all containers need to be opened, as opposed to 100% prior to the introduction of Paperless Port System.

Third, the custom's "long rooms" – where documents were physically submitted for examination by customs officials – have been transferred to an online portal on which importers can transact business. All trade documents are now submitted electronically, reducing the incidence of document falsification. Fourth, importers can submit their documents electronically without having to commute to GRA offices. Electronic submission has also enhanced error detection and improved the audit and investigation procedures. According to data presented by the Ghana Community Network (GCNet), the operator for the Paperless Port System in 2018, 43% of containers are cleared within 24 hours and about 70% of them cleared within 72 hours (ISSER, 2019). These improvements are buttressed by the World Bank's Doing Business Report. In 2016, the time taken to clear imported goods was significantly higher (282 hours for documentary compliance and 282 hours for border compliance) (World Bank, 2016b). In 2018, one year after the introduction of the Paperless Port System, the time to import improved significantly – importers spent 76 hours on average for documentary compliance and 89 hours for border compliance (World Bank, 2018).

Despite the improvements brought about by the Paperless Port System, key informant interviews conducted by the Institute of Statistical, Social and Economic Research (ISSER) with key stakeholders in 2019 suggest that significant challenges persist. These include occasional downtimes from servers of the service providers (GCNet) as reported by both tax collectors and taxpayers. During downtimes, procedures at the ports grind to a halt and impede the smooth flow of activities. In addition, some clearing agents submit trade documents which are full of mistakes – an issue which in the past was not so because GRA officials physically inspected the documents and helped agents to correct mistakes before submission. This increases queries generated by the system and impedes quicker and easier document verification.

On the basis of the challenges outlined in Section 9.2.1 and 9.2.2, Ghanaian civil society, in collaboration with the former UK-DFID, called for engagements amongst stakeholders and duty bearers to find answers to the challenges faced by TRIPS and Paperless Port System so as to optimise benefits. The Private Enterprise Federation (PEF), an umbrella body of Ghanaian businesses, was a key advocate for simplified tax payment procedures to reduce the cost of compliance. PEF suggested that these shortfalls were driven in part by a lack of structured strategy for communicating the processes to the business community and the public at large. This gap, according to PEF, resulted in a lack of awareness and appreciation of reform gains by stakeholders. Consequently, this results in their non-use by beneficiary stakeholders or in the inability of users to give feedback to duty bearers for continuous improvements. Section 9.3, therefore, examines how a collaboration between former UK-DFID and Ghanaian Civil Society, mainly represented by PEF and supported by academia and the media helped to bring some of these challenges to the attention of duty bearers for action to be taken.

9.3 Business Enabling Environment Project (BEEP) and Evidence Gathering for Engagement

As demonstrated in Section 9.2, digitalising Ghana's tax revenue mobilisation has been a key conduit for efficiency improvements. However, challenges remain, which need to be addressed. In this section, we argue that stakeholder recognition of challenges in any digitalisation drive in Ghana – and potentially in other

African countries – is a good first step to address challenges, but is not sufficient. A second important step is to create and promote an enabling environment for stakeholders to engage with duty bearers leading the reforms. To enhance the potential success of such engagements, this drive should be supported by reliable evidence put together through research which throws light on, and provides deeper insights into, the key issues at stake.

This process of guiding and promoting dialogue amongst stakeholders is yielding some results in Ghana. In future, if any AU and EU collaborations in other countries seek to digitise their tax revenue mobilisation, similar stakeholder engagements could be considered. In addition, a good ground to promote efficiency of such engagements can be nurtured if it involves collaboration amongst local NGOs, the media, government (agencies), research institutions, and relevant international donors.

To this end, PEF, which received financial support from the former UK-DFID to initiate Ghana's dialogue, provides interesting lessons for similar initiatives across Africa. PEF initiated and launched a consortium of collaborators under a project dubbed Business Enabling Environment Project (BEEP) in 2015. The aim was to encourage implementing agencies like GRA to take the necessary steps to address challenges catalogued by members of PEF or identified through formally commissioned research. To support the BEEP programme through research, ISSER undertook a study to understand the progress made by the digitalisation process, persisting challenges, and the ways through which these challenges could be addressed. The study found that despite the slow pace with which online facilities were rolled out, taxpayers benefitted from significant cost and time savings. Moreover, tax collection is becoming less tedious since the online platforms facilitate seamless workflows. There are, however, inherent challenges within TRIPS/ITAPs and the Paperless Systems.

9.3.1 The TRIPS and ITAPs Case

(i) From the taxpayers' perspective, there were frequent system slowdowns and breakdowns of the TRIPS application resulting in long queues at the tax offices. This in turn led to delays in accessing services at the office and loss of productive hours. In cases where there were frequent breakdowns and slowdowns of the system, taxpayers were either forced to wait until system recovery or had to resort to the manual mode of acquiring such services. Customers continue to complain about the manual processes, which they think should have been eliminated by the electronic system, TRIPS. In response to this challenge, GRA introduced the ITAPS in 2019 to help taxpayers to directly input their records online and make the necessary payments via the same portal, thus reducing the paper work further.

(ii) From the tax administrators' point of view, although TRIPS is a valuable tool, there are some drawbacks to it. Some GRA offices use obsolete computers with less computing power, which slow down the operation of TRIPS. Aside from obsolete computers, tax collectors note that downtime of the TRIPS system is quite common, corroborating the view of taxpayers. Most GRA offices surveyed in 2019 point to the breakdown of the TRIPS system when the deadline for any of the tax payments was due. The system experiences a lot of stress and, in some cases, fails this stress test and breaks down completely. Officers of GRA are forced to go back to the manual system and then catch up electronically when the system recovers. Some breakdowns of the system have also been linked to bad weather conditions by GRA staff.

(iii) There are also critical staff skill gaps for TRIPS as noted by some GRA branch managers. The rollout of TRIPS started with business registration and basic tax requirements. Thus, staff members working in the Tax Payer Services Unit, who were responsible for providing these services, became acquainted with most parts of the TRIPS platform quickly. This was not the case for the Audit and Compliance Units of GRA. The lack of adequate training for all staff renders some of them inefficient in the use of some aspects of the TRIPS platform. Hence, they sometimes resort to manual processes even when the TRIPS platform is working well.

(iv) Finally, the TRIPS software is designed to use intranet and prevents staff from working with it outside the GRA offices. This reduces flexibility as staff cannot do additional work outside the office on the TRIPS platform after working hours. Also, officers on the field undertaking monitoring of businesses cannot log in directly into the system. They have to come back to the office to gain access to TRIPS. A situation which some GRA staff suggested a virtual private network (VPN) could help address.

The potential for TRIPS to facilitate the work of the tax collector is promising. However, for rapid progress to be made, infrastructure issues such as up-to-date computers, adequate server capacities, and reliable intranet connectivity augmented with VPN need to be resolved. Furthermore, bridging the skill gaps of staff will also be key for any African country which intends to undertake a similar intervention. These are important issues to be considered if an AU–EU collaboration contemplates undertaking similar programmes in other African countries.

9.3.2 Paperless Port System

(i) Taxpayers suggest that the compliance stage of the goods clearing process poses the most difficult challenge. At the compliance stage, GRA officials crosscheck to ensure that all import documents submitted comply with customs requirements. Despite electronic submission of documents for compliance checks, the process can sometimes take a relatively long time. Respondents indicated that it sometimes takes three days to get feedback on compliance. It was purported that some compliance officers unnecessarily stall the process, causing the overall time used to clear imports to increase. As one respondent puts it,

[Compliance] is where the main challenge is. If you are lucky, within hours it's here, if you are not lucky, one week or two weeks [and] it's hanging in there. This is purely the human factor.

(ii) A second challenge faced by users of the Paperless Port System is internet reliability. The prevalence of internet network instability/unreliability has often stalled the process of clearing goods. Just like in the case of TRIPS, rainy seasons have been particularly daunting, as power outages and internet fluctuations are frequent. Thus, when the Paperless Port System goes down because of internet problems, it can even take a week for goods to be cleared.

(iii) Congestion, particularly at the point of exit, is one significant cause of delays in the clearance process. Given that at the time of this study in 2019 there was only one exit gate each at the two major sea ports in Ghana (Takoradi and Tema), an importer could be in a queue for several hours because of congestion at the final exit gate. Here, some stakeholders, including importers, suggested that additional gates at the point of exit could help address the problem. The gates could also be automated to read barcodes which allows trucks which have been cleared to leave the port without additional human interface to save time.

In sum, both TRIPS/ITAPS and Paperless Port System can promote time and cost efficiency. However, the roll-out of these platforms has faced setbacks related to supporting infrastructure, logistics, and staffs' skill gaps. As noted at the beginning of this section, knowing what the challenges are does not in itself address them. In Section 9.4, therefore, we present how stakeholder engagements underpinned by this research promoted dialogue to generate what industry players and government agencies agreed could be the way forward.

9.4 Stakeholder Engagements

Sections 9.2 and 9.3 demonstrate some progress, not least cost and time savings in revenue mobilisation as a result of digitalisation. For example, importers no longer need to go to GRA offices to submit compliance documents saving them time and transport cost. However, significant setbacks related to infrastructure reliability and staffing persist. To tackle these challenges, it was vital to bring stakeholders together to brainstorm and fashion out the way forward. In Ghana, the BEEP with financial support and guidance from UK-DFID organised stakeholder engagements, resulting in actionable points, which duty bearers took on board to improve the system. In this section we elaborate how duty bearer and stakeholder dialogues can generate knowledge to address digitalisation related challenges. Moving forward, we believe the lessons learnt in the Ghanaian case can play a key role in designing and implementing similar programmes in other African countries within the context of an AU–EU collaboration. We emphasise that using a mix of different stakeholder engagement methods or approaches yields greater results.

Tax collectors, taxpayers, and the media were brought together to discuss the findings of ISSER's study over a four-month period. During this period, progress, challenges, and a way forward for online tax administration were carefully examined to find out what can be done and who should do it. Three modes of engagement were used for these stakeholder dialogues: seminars/workshops, radio and TV shows, and private meetings with top tax collection officials.

First, during a seminar, ISSER presented its research proposal to taxpayers, tax collectors, and civil society to validate methodologies for a proposed survey. This was followed by a stakeholder workshop to discuss survey findings. Second, ISSER, PEF, and GRA officials made radio and TV appearances. Half of this air time was in English, and the other half was in *Twi*. The public was allowed to phone in and participate in the discussions, thus generating insights for GRA in terms of what can be done. Episodes organised in *Twi* (a Ghanaian language) were more popular and engaged a wider audience than those organised in English. Third, board room meetings with top officials of the tax administration system were undertaken by ISSER and PEF. During these meetings, specific questions were put to the duty bearers related to infrastructure, staffing, and quality of staff, and how these issues are militating against the progress of digitalisation of tax administration. The evidence from ISSER's study was shared with them, and they were given the opportunity to speak to what their outfits are doing to address the challenges.

The main threats to the successful organisation of such dialogues are threefold – cost, quality and reliability of research, and the buy-in of duty bearers. The cost of research, the cost of organising physical meetings, and the cost of procuring prime time on radio and television can be quite expensive. In this case, former UK-DFID bore all these costs and provided additional support for partners to demonstrate value for money on a regular basis. This ensured that the resources were spent on the intended purpose, and the funder was assured that potential wastage was avoided.

For stakeholders to confidently engage with evidence, they must be assured that the methods for data gathering and analyses are reliable. Finally, the willingness of duty bearers to attend and participate fully in the engagements can be nurtured through trust building by the leader of the consortium, which in Ghana's case was PEF. What the BEEP consortium found helpful was to get a very respected civil society individual to negotiate and convince top-ranking officials of GRA that these meetings were not meant to criticise their work, but to support them in making progressive changes. A further boost to this effort by the BEEP consortium was to identify a staff member of the GRA who was sympathetic to our course to encourage other colleagues of theirs to get on board.

With the cost, confidence, and trust issues out of the way, the three different stakeholder engagements discussed challenges and made suggestions for action. For some of the issues, duty bearers have acted on them, and for others assurances were given that attention will be paid to them in the near future. Below, we elaborate on some of the suggestions and actions taken:

(i) Inadequate staffing – Evidence from the ISSER's study shows that only a third of the staff required is available, especially in the Audit Unit of GRA. Therefore, files kept piling up, exacerbating delays in service delivery. Stakeholders recommended that GRA should modify TRIPS so that staff can access it remotely after work and complete assignments where necessary. In response, GRA did not only agree to consider the suggestion but also requested additional staff from the government of Ghana through the Ghana National Service Scheme to provide an interim staffing support to auditors. These new hands are helping bridge the staffing gaps.

(ii) Staff skill gaps – Although training on the use of TRIPS is organised every now and then for staff, ISSER's study found that their busy schedules preclude them from making time for it. Those who make the time cannot concentrate because they are consistently called back to the office to attend to some duties. Short video tutorials and online platforms (where staff can send questions and receive real time feedback) were recommended by stakeholders. Although these materials and online support were yet to be made available in 2019, in some of the tax offices, the systems administrators, per the directive of GRA and based on recommendations from the dialogues, deployed resident technical staff to support users who may need help in operating the TRIPS.

(iii) Technology – Network and connectivity issues persist. As a result, the TRIPS application slows down and is unable to resist the stress during peak periods. Rainy days also put the system under severe stress. Investment in bigger and faster server systems was recommended to GRA by representatives of PEF and the ISSER study. Based on this recommendation, GRA officials agreed to speed up the process of replacing all radio networks currently being used to manage TRIPS to faster and more reliable internet services so that information can be exchanged more easily.

(iv) Congestion at the exit gates at the ports was also raised by the ISSER study. GRA officials responded by saying that plans were advanced to increase the gates to 16 and also automate their operation. In 2019, after expansion and renovation of some parts of the Tema Port, the 16 gates promised were delivered.

(v) Corruption – incidences of bribery and favouritism are still prevalent in the view of some taxpayers. To get through the compliance stage quickly, some customers alleged that some officials demanded bribes from them. Effective supervision and monitoring of compliance officials were noted as the way forward. Duty bearers promised that they would improve the monitoring of personnel. They have also installed several CCTV cameras in the ports to deter potential acts of corruption.

Although these challenges and ways to address them derive from the Ghanaian case, some of these challenges and experiences may be encountered in other

African countries as well. As we have seen here, the stakeholder engagements did not only generate options for action but also encouraged duty bearers to act where they could.

9.5 Conclusion

This chapter examined the role of digitalisation in tax revenue mobilisation in Ghana. Specifically, it investigated how platforms created for stakeholder dialogues could promote the process. We find that digital technologies for collection of both domestic and international trade taxes like TRIPS/ITAPS and Paperless Port System have brought efficiency improvements through cost- and time-saving for both tax collectors and taxpayers. However, important infrastructure, such as the reliability of intranet/internet services associated with the operations of these platforms, is weak. This makes their use frustrating for stakeholders. Similarly, skills and competences of staff are sometimes inadequate. Additionally, the human factor continues to delay some aspects of the online services. Taken together, a stakeholder dialogue around these issues proved to be useful in prompting duty bearers to act in addressing challenges. For example, to address the skill gap, the GRA brought in additional staff to provide prompt support. Significant changes have also been made to port infrastructure, including an increase in the number of exit gates, to reduce the time spent to exit the port after an importer has received the necessary clearance.

If AU–EU collaboration were to consider similar digitalisation exercises on the African continent, there are three key lessons that need to be considered. In the first instance, internet reliability in African countries is not the same as in the EU. Given the primary importance of reliable internet and digital infrastructure in delivering efficient digitalised tax collection systems, attention should be given to establishing systems which can thrive on minimum network quality and also allow offline actions to be undertaken. These tools work best on updated computers. In budgeting, therefore, an eye should thus be kept on replacing or updating the relevant computers.

Second, a sufficient number of well-trained staff is key to efficiently digitalise tax collection. While technology is an important factor in all these activities, the human factor cannot be ignored. In Ghana and in other African countries, tax collectors are traditionally used to the manual processes. Thus, transitioning to the use of online services may be a steep learning curve. It is therefore paramount to incorporate training of staff into the planning process from the onset by agents driving any such initiative. At best, this should happen before the roll-out of the digitalisation procedure. One strategy which is working in the Ghanaian context is to get some resident IT personnel to provide day-to-day support to staff. Although this comes at an extra cost, it may eventually be crucial to enhance efficiency.

Finally, an elaborate stakeholder mapping at the onset of digitalisation is key. The view here is to bring these stakeholders together for dialogue on how systems should be rolled out to meet the needs of users. In the Ghanaian experience, such stakeholder engagements proved to be very helpful, although it required significant capital outlays by a donor (UK-DFID). For example, the dialogue encouraged duty bearers to employ more staff where they were lacking, encouraged them to make changes to port infrastructure where necessary and also commit to an enhanced monitoring of their staff to prevent corruption. Dialogue with the public was also found to work best when local languages were used.

References

Appiah, H. L. (2013). *Tax Reforms & Revenue Mobilization: A Case Study of the Mining Sector of Ghana*. MPhil Thesis, University of Ghana.

Bank of Ghana (2003). *Report on the Mining Sector. Research Department, 1, Issue 2*. Accra: Bank of Ghana.

Bugbilla, D. and Asamoah, E.O. (2016). An analysis of trade facilitation at the ports and borders of Ghana: Implications on the mobilization of government revenue. *International Journal of Business and Social Science*, 7(3), pp.65–71.

ICAEW (2019). *Digitlisation of Tax: International Perspectives*, 2019 Edition. ICAEW Thought Leadership.

ISSER (2019). *State of the Ghanaian Economy Report 2018*. Accra: Institute of Statistical Social and Economic Research.

OECD (2019). *Use of Digital Technologies Set to Increase Tax Compliance*. OECD's Tax Administration Series, 8th Edition. https://www.oecd.org/ctp/administration/use-of-digital-technologies-set-to-increase-tax-compliance.htm (accessed 10th February 2022).

Osei, R.D. and Quartey, P., (2005). *Tax reforms in Ghana* (No. 2005/66). WIDER Research Paper.

World Bank (2016a). *Doing Business 2016: Measuring Regulatory Quality and Efficiency*. Washington, DC: World Bank.

World Bank (2016b). *Project Performance Assessment Report: E-Ghana Project*. Report No. 108359. Washington, DC: World Bank.

World Bank (2018). *Doing Business 2018: Reforming to Create Jobs*. Washington, DC: World Bank.

10

WHERE PRIVACY MEETS POLITICS

EU–Kenya Cooperation in Data Protection

Benedikt Erforth and Charles Martin-Shields

10.1 Introduction

The global competition for digital leadership is in full swing. Between surveillance capitalism (Zuboff, 2019) and state-led digital surveillance (Andersen, 2020, Greitens, 2021, Wang, 2021, see Jili, 2022 this volume), the European Union (EU) seeks to promote its interests through what it calls a "human centric" model which it believes will achieve a "safe and open global Internet" (EU, 2020b, p. 13). Under the auspices of the European Commission under President Ursula von der Leyen, the EU has vowed to shake off the image of being a second-tier digital power and accelerate a structural transformation towards a green, sustainable, and digital economy – at home and abroad (Reiners, 2021). Accordingly, the EU budget for the next seven years, the so-called multiannual financial framework 2021–2027 (MFF 2021-2027), is geared to stimulate the European Union's digital transformation.[1] With regard to the external dimension, and cognisant of the fact that digitalisation is a global phenomenon, the EU seeks to "put forward a new approach to digital transformation that projects European values onto the international stage" (EU, 2020a, see also EU, 2021a, EU, 2021b). The European neighbourhood and Africa play an increasingly important role in the EU's efforts to shape the global digital order (EU, 2021, p. 2). The EU deems close cooperation with Africa in the realm of data protection essential to the New Africa-Europe Digital Economy Partnership and a crucial step towards an African Single Digital market (EU, 2020f, p. 5-6).

Among the list of proposed tools to realise the EU's digital strategy at the global scale, the EU's regulatory power stands out. Through its standard setting capacities paired with its market size, the "EU has the ability to promulgate regulations that shape the global business environment, leading to a notable 'Europeanization' of many important aspects of global commerce" (Bradford,

DOI: 10.4324/9781003274322-10

2020, p. xiv). In its Communication *Shaping Europe's Digital Future,* the European Commission affirms that the "European model has proved to be an inspiration for many other partners around the world" and that "the EU should leverage its regulatory power, reinforced industrial and technological capabilities, diplomatic strengths and external financial instruments to advance the European approach and shape global interactions" (EU, 2020b, p. 13). Home to the world's most advanced privacy and data protection regime, the Commission stresses the importance of partner countries' legislative alignment as a means to realise a human-centric digital future. Successful alignment is contingent on several factors. First, it requires buy-in from partner countries. Second, and deriving from the first point, a shared understanding of the issues at stake must emerge. Simply using an identical nomenclature is not a sufficient condition for creating common practice, as Hapraz and Shamis (2010) have shown in their work on Israeli perceptions of Europe's normative power. Third, in the specific case of data protection, a legal environment needs to exist or emerge that can translate political commitments into applicable law along with the necessary enforcement mechanisms. Fourth, public opinion needs to support and adopt newly introduced regulations to align norms and practices. These processes occur in parallel and at different levels.

In this chapter, we use the case of Kenya and its 2019 data protection legislation to retrace a specific alignment process and understand why there could be limits to the EU's regulatory externalisation strategy. Together with Uganda, Kenya is one of two East African governments to have enacted data protection legislation prior to the COVID-19 outbreak (Mwanzia, Kapiyo, and Ayazika, 2021, p. 5). Given its significant role as a regional digital hub and economic powerhouse, Kenya is positioned to become a regional standard setter in digital privacy. On the other hand, the Kenyan government has continued to de-anonymise digital channels, whether through rules requiring the registration of mobile phone SIM cards, updating national ID cards to include digital chips and biometric data, or expanding the surveillance environment against the backdrop of the coronavirus pandemic (Mwanzia, Kapiyo, and Ayazika, 2021). Although many other countries in Africa engage in similar practices, Kenya's dominant role in the region makes it a particularly salient case for our research. Knowledge about alignment processes and outcomes in Kenya can inform our understanding of similar processes in the wider region and provide lessons for a European externalisation strategy.

In order to explore the opportunities and challenges of EU–Kenyan regulatory cooperation and alignment in the digital field, the chapter proceeds as follows. First, we present a short conceptual discussion around the issue of regulatory externalisation and outline the EU's strategic approach to norm externalisation and various instruments in the field of data protection. Second, we explore the recent regulatory developments in Kenya focussing on the 2019 Data Protection Act, the EU's involvement in this process and the law's implementation against the backdrop of post-1990s Kenyan security politics. Whilst the adoption of the

2019 Data Protection Act constitutes a significant leap towards citizens' privacy rights – signifying a strong degree of partner country buy-in – challenges persist at the operational level. We draw on five expert long interviews with Kenyan lawyers and other stakeholders to better understand the legal and sociopolitical issues that could shape the future of digital privacy in Kenya (McCracken, 1988). Finally, we conclude by summarising the main findings, which point to the normative and practical limits the EU's regulatory externalisation strategy is confronted with.

10.2 The "Brussels Effect": Externalising Europe's Regulatory Framework

Different strands of literature argue that the EU's greatest source of power is rooted in its ability to shape the rules of the game and create acceptance for those rules. The idea of the EU being different (sui generis) from other actors in the international system, exercising a unique type of power, can be traced back to François Duchêne's (1972) notion of civilian power. Since its inception, the concept has fascinated observers of EU politics, notwithstanding its conceptual fuzziness (Orbie, 2006). Notably, Ian Manners, in his influential article 'Normative Power Europe' (2002), helped update and popularise the original idea of understanding the EU's power in different terms. In privileging norms and the power to "set world standards in normative terms" (Rosecrance, 1998, p. 22), Manners provides the theoretical framework that allows us to interpret the EU's discourse and actions on digital technologies as a means to exercise power abroad. He refers to three components constituting the civilian nature of the EU and allowing it to externalise its norms and regulations: its economic power, the primacy of diplomatic cooperation, and the willingness to resort to legally binding supranational institutions (Manners, 2002, p. 236-237).

Externalisation "occurs when the institutions and actors of the EU attempt to get other actors to adhere to a level of regulation similar to that in effect in the European single market or to behave in a way that generally satisfies or conforms to the EU's market-related policies and regulatory measures" (Damro, 2012, p. 690). Externalisation, which amounts to the wielding of soft power, occurs in two stages: (i) the (un)intended externalisation of policies, norms, and standards and (ii) the actual adoption of those by non-EU actors (success) (Damro, 2015, p. 1344, Harpaz and Shamis, 2010). By definition, the EU's ability to influence future outcomes is largely limited to the first of the two stages.

Over the years, the EU has emerged as the globe's most prominent standard setter on issues of consumer protection, competition, and trade. In the digital economy in particular, the EU's power to regulate global markets is significant. Examples of the EU's efforts to externalise norms in the digital realm include "the adoption of the Groupe Spécial Mobile (GSM) standard for mobile telephony [which] is cited as 'one of the best examples of the export of European regulatory approaches, European standards and European technology' (EU, 2007,

p. 6)," and the enactment of the General Data Protection Regulation (GDPR). Examining the reach of the EU's GDPR and the Commission's voluntary Code of Conduct Countering Illegal Hate Speech Online, Bradford (2020, p. 1; 131) describes the extraordinary impact of what she terms *Brussels Effect* – the "EU's unilateral ability to regulate the global marketplace". Bradford shows that the EU's regulatory pursuits were initially driven by internal motivations but today "are also shaped by external motivations" with the EU having recognised "the importance of promoting international standards for the protection of personal data". Mostly the EU's regulatory power is rooted in its ability to call on companies to "incorporate privacy considerations into the product development", be it out of economic or technological considerations (Bradford, 2020, p. 144). With multinational companies not only applying European privacy regulation but also advocating for GDPR-type laws in non-EU markets, governments across the world emulate EU regulations and demonstrate the de jure and de facto impact of the Brussels Effect (Bradford, 2020, p. 167-168).

The EU's policymaking in the digital field emanates from the triptych of normative, market, and regulatory power. This holistic approach to policymaking combines the EU's moral (and interest-driven) compass, with its institutional ability to translate policies into prevailing practice, and the necessary lever (the common market) to push for their acceptance.[2]

The European Commission's 2020 data strategy outlines the EU's "proactive international approach" and reveals the underlying rationale that motivates EU action in this field. Referring to the international dimension of data governance, the strategy reads as follows:

> Building upon the strength of the Single Market's regulatory environment, the EU has a strong interest in leading and supporting international cooperation with regard to data, shaping global standards and creating an environment in which economic and technological development can thrive, in full compliance with EU law. At the same time, European companies operating in some third countries are increasingly faced with unjustified barriers and digital restrictions. The EU will continue to address these unjustified obstacles to data flows in bilateral discussions and international fora – including the World Trade Organisation – while promoting and protecting European data processing rules and standards ... The Commission is convinced that international cooperation must be based on an approach that promotes the EU's fundamental values, including protection of privacy.
>
> *(EU, 2020e)*

The strategy relies on the connection of third parties to the European data space and the active promotion of European standards and values abroad. The EU seeks to facilitate the free flow of data whilst maintaining the protection of personal data as a fundamental right, and considers that the "best way to achieve these objectives is to work towards convergence of the data protection frameworks of third countries with that of the EU" (EU, 2020f, p. 2). Accordingly, the EU actively supported the legislative process of the Kenyan data protection bill in 2019 and later should cite Kenya as a positive example of a country where the adoption of rules modelled on the GDPR succeeded (Interview 1; EU, 2020e, p. 24).

The instruments and approaches the EU uses to achieve these objectives fall into the category of "intended externalization of policies, norms and standards" (Damro, 2015, p. 1344). Amongst other things, EU action in partner countries seeks to "increase awareness of the importance of personal data protection as a pre-requisite to data exchanges with the EU", to "enhance the knowledge of the EU data protection legal framework in partner countries", and to "develop common approaches to personal data protection" (EU, 2020f, p. 2). The list effectively shows the different dimensions of norm externalisation that involve aspects of knowledge sharing and the active diffusion and institutionalisation of EU norms and standards in partner countries.

So far, most of the literature examining EU externalisation strategies in the digital realm has largely dealt with the issue in relation to the digital superpowers of this world, neglecting other regions and partners (Bendiek and Römer, 2019; Bradford, 2020; for an exception see Schneider, 2020). What's more, norm externalisation can only be fully understood if both the first and the second stages of externalisation, that is the externalisation process itself and its adoption, are considered. The impact of the *Brussels Effect* on comparatively smaller markets, such as Kenya, remains largely unaddressed. To better understand both opportunities and challenges that occur during processes of regulatory externalisation, the next section examines the 2019 Data Protection Act, the EU's involvement in this process, and the law's implementation against the historical backdrop of post-1990s Kenyan security politics. We focus on the early implementation phase, as well as the sociopolitical aspects of state security and individual rights. All of these factors influence, and will influence over time, the implementation of digital privacy and data protection regulation in practical terms.

10.3 Regulatory Externalisation and Alignment in Kenya

Prior to 2019, data protection in Kenya was subsumed under the heading of the right to privacy in the 2010 Constitution (Government of the Republic of Kenya, 2010). Article 31 of the Constitution acknowledges every person's right to privacy and recognises data protection in two instances. First, every person has the right not to have "information relating to their family or private affairs unnecessarily required or revealed" (article 31(c)). Second, every person should be protected from having "the privacy of their communications infringed" (article 31(d)). These provisions, however, are not absolute but can be limited by law (Makulilo and Boshe, 2016, p. 325). In addition, various sector regulations contained privacy provisions (e.g. banking, national security, or health-related regulation), yet no "stand-alone comprehensive law governing data protection" existed (PWC, 2018).

Despite this absence of a central legal framework, Kenya's privacy reform did not start with a clean slate. Instead, the reform can be traced back to cyber law reforms in the East African Community in the early 2000s. These occurred against the backdrop of Kenya's considerable economic growth and the country's major developments in information and communication technology (Makulilo and Boshe, 2016, pp. 318-320). As a signatory to the Universal Declaration of Human Rights and a state party to the International Covenant on Civil and Political Rights, Kenya "is under the obligation to put in place privacy legislation" (Makulilo and Boshe, 2016, p. 325). Taken together, these factors led to a draft data privacy bill in 2013 that, through revision, turned into the 2019 Data Protection Act.

The 2019 Data Protection Act (Kenya Gazette Supplement, 2019) is derived directly from the original 2013 privacy draft bill. It acts as an omnibus data protection law that takes inspiration from the EU's GDPR and serves as stand-alone comprehensive law governing data protection and privacy. The law regulates the handling of data by the government and both national and international corporations. Since the adoption of the law in November 2019, the EU and its member states, notably Germany, have continued to support Kenyan efforts in the realm of data protection by providing financial and technical expertise to the newly established Office of the Data Protection Commissioner. The Commissioner starting from scratch, having to set up both staff and offices, offers a unique opportunity for the EU to co-constitute Kenyan privacy narratives and contribute to the promotion of European norms. This exercise, however, brings along challenges, ranging from technical difficulties on the computing and infrastructure side of data protection, to active resistance on the part of government or other stakeholders. In the concrete case of the Kenyan Data Protection Commissioner, an overly strong EU involvement would put into question the very legitimacy of the office, which is rooted in absolute independence (more on this point, below).

10.3.1 The Implementation Challenge

Both the Data Protection Act (DPA) 2019 and the regulatory body that handles its enforcement are quite new. Therefore, it is not yet possible to definitely assess its success. Based on current and historical conditions, we can try to understand how this legislation is likely to evolve over time. We examine this in two ways. First, from the legal procedural perspective. Second, from the historical political perspective.

We conducted five interviews involving Kenyan lawyers, civil society, and business representatives to understand the legal and technical issues related to implementing the DPA. The interviewees explained a set of core technical challenges for getting the legislation to work effectively in practice. One of the key starting points is public buy-in. Until recently, the centrality of digital privacy had not been of great interest to the general public. The interviewees referred to several events that eventually propelled a major change in public sentiment on the topic. One of those events was the Cambridge Analytica scandal, which involved political parties hiring the data firm Cambridge Analytica to send targeted social media posts to voters, further raising the profile of data privacy for the Kenyan public (Interview 2). More importantly, in preparation for the 2017 elections, political parties mined cash transfer account data to register voters without their knowledge (Interview 4). Another case in which the public became aware of data mismanagement was Radisson corporation losing control of customer data in 2020 (Interview 4). These events pushed data privacy into the mainstream of the Kenyan debate, and the government and private sector started to pay greater attention to data security. For companies maintaining economic ties with European partners, the newfound interest in secure data handling was also a reaction to the legal requirements stemming from the GDPR (Interview 3).

Still, the public continues to accord little attention to the right to privacy. This is particularly critical in the Kenyan context, where politicians have a strong tendency to act on public sentiment (Interview 4). A recent poll commissioned by Amnesty International (2021) found that only 54% of Kenyans know about their right to privacy, whereas 70% of Kenyans remain unaware of the existence of the Data Protection Act. Only 18% of Kenyans are aware of the Office of the Data Protection Commissioner. Unlike the GDPR, there was no period of public participation in the lead-up to the 2019 Act. In comparison, 69% of the EU population above the age of 16 have heard about the GDPR and 71% of people have heard about their respective national data protection authority (EU, 2020g). Aside from civil society organisations that focus on privacy, public sentiment tends to fade quickly after each scandal (Interview 2).

The 2019 Act does not foresee a transition period that would allow the legislator, private actors, and civil society to adapt to the new regulatory framework. A limiting factor to its successful implementation is that the current budget allocated to the data protection office is KES 15 million, approximately €150,000. This is far too little given the scope of what the Data Protection Commissioner (DPC) is tasked with and barely covers staff salaries (Interview 4). Some observers assume that the lack of funding is purposeful – there is a data protection office, yet it lacks the personnel that could effectively do the job (ibid.). Others do not see a deliberate agenda behind the underfunded office and the operational challenges that come along with it. Instead, they explain these with reference to a hasty finalisation of the legislative draft.

Thirty-five per cent of Kenyans view interference from government as the greatest threat to the Office of the DPC (Amnesty International, 2021). The DPC is officially under the auspices of the ICT ministry. A cabinet minister oversees the data privacy office (Interview 2). This presents obvious conflicts of interests since regulatory offices are meant to be independent. The situation is further complicated by the fact that the commissioner, who should be politically independent, is married to a leader of one of the national political parties (Interview 4). Given the politics in play, there are serious questions about the way the state can use private data for security and policing. As our interviewees pointed out, the 2019 Data Protection Act contains a small, but important, exception: in the case of a national security threat, the Act does not protect private data.

10.3.2 Privacy and the Political History of Violence

Part VII.51.2(c) of the Data Protection Act (Kenya Gazette Supplement, 2019) lays out an important exception to data security and privacy: "if it is necessary for national security or public interest" (p. 933). Kenya's history of political violence itself does not preclude a future where digital privacy regulation is effectively implemented. Yet, a precise definition of "security" is lacking (Interview 2). With the introduction of further amendments to the Official Secrets Act in December 2020, the government grants far-reaching powers to the Cabinet Secretary of Interior and Coordination of National Security and further undermines data protection as inscribed in the Kenyan Constitution (Andere, 2021). Against the backdrop of Kenya's history of political violence, this ambiguity should raise concerns about privacy in practice. Histories of political violence shape how citizens view the state, often long after the violence itself. This can be observed in countries as varied as Ecuador (Capelle, Jadhav, and Mocrieff, 2020), Spain (Iturriaga, 2019), and Germany (Dimmroth and Schünemann, 2017). Thus, the history of political violence is likely to shape how the wider public views the legitimacy of state regulation of privacy.

The relationship between citizens and the Kenyan police has been marked by violations of civil rights (Ombati, 2019), and credible reports of extra-judicial killings carried out by the police after the 2007 election and under the banner of counter-terrorism operations (Boazman, 2014). Moreover, security partners like the United States and the United Kingdom shape the preferences of the Kenyan security policy. The implementation of counter-terrorism policies that align with the interests of Western security partners has led to infringements on civil and human rights (Mogire and Agade, 2011), and driven a wedge specifically between the state and Kenya's Somali and Muslim populations (Lind, Mutahi, and Oosterom, 2017). Within this context, various telecommunications and ICT regulations, such as registering mobile phone SIM cards, were put in place. While registering SIM cards is not an unorthodox policy, it raises questions of surveillance and privacy in contexts where state security is a central aspect of politics (Donovan and Martin, 2014). In the Kenyan context, the role of the security services in surveillance, extra-judicial killings (e.g. Boazman, 2014), and abuses of police power cannot be ignored when assessing the effects of how a GDPR-style privacy regulation would work in practice.

Digital technology has created new openings for citizens to share their experiences of violence, thus working towards greater transparency and peace

(Maina, 2015). Meanwhile, the Kenyan government responded to the volume of hate speech propagated on mobile phone networks and social media by reducing privacy. This brings us back to the aforementioned SIM card registration rules that came into effect in 2013. According to Bowman and Bowman (2016), these rules were specifically intended to reduce hate speech and support a peaceful election. In fact, they led to a full spectrum of Kenyan citizens self-censoring what they said on digital channels. This kind of surveillance in combination with the ongoing counter-terrorism stance of the government has led to a uniquely intensive targeting of Muslim communities, preventing their political mobilisation, and limiting their agency in daily life (Badurdeen, 2018). Along with direct surveillance, the Kenyan government has extended their counter-terror and policing efforts into the mobile money transfer space, demanding a wider range of identity documentation to use these services (Wanjohi, 2017).

This history of abuse by the security services and a lack of privacy in the digital space was a key reason that the recent efforts by the Kenyan government to institute a digital, biometric ID for all Kenyans ran into pushback from civil society organisations and privacy advocates (Eken, 2019). The National Integrated Identification Management Systems and the personal *Huduma Namba* (service number) would have centralised sensitive data of all Kenyans, including GPS coordinates, DNA, and other biometrics, were it not for the intervention of the courts. The lack of clarity around how the data would be used, stored, secured, coupled with wider privacy issues, led to a court case that struck down mandatory registration and limited the usage and transfer of data.

The Kenyan case presents a political history and present where privacy and data protection may be encoded in regulation and law. While this would make commercial cooperation easier, privacy and data protection may not be extended in a practical way to all Kenyans. If the goal of regulatory externalisation includes both commercial and rights foci, understanding the political context in which regulations are implemented is critical.

10.4 Conclusion

The digital industry, ICTs, and the governance of the digital space rank high in the list of priorities of Kenyan policymakers and development cooperation partners. At the same time, these issues figure prominently among the EU's strategic priorities and present a suitable topic to test the limits of the EU's regulatory externalisation strategy. Therefore, we focused on data protection and the right to privacy as one specific dimension of EU–Kenya cooperation.

By supporting the setting up and implementation of a robust data protection framework the EU follows a policy-first approach, according to which international cooperation serves the purpose of the European strategic agenda. This agenda is composed of tangible commercial and geopolitical interests as well as strong normative leanings. Additionally, international cooperation and commercial relationships are expected to foster improvements in governance and strengthen human rights in partner countries.

Does the Data Protection Act, modelled on the GDPR, achieve that? It is too early to tell since Kenya is still setting up the administrative apparatus to enforce it. Still, we can observe considerable strides that have been made towards securing citizens' rights to privacy. At the same time, implementation challenges prevail, which are in parts linked to a lack of resources, an early stage of capacity development, and a legislative framing that foresees substantial exceptions allowing for state-led surveillance. There is no consensus among experts as to whether these exceptions can be ascribed to a deliberate agenda by the Kenyan government or are rather an expression of procedural neglect. In this context, the EU confronts the difficult task to support a process without undermining the independence and sovereignty of the very institutions it seeks to promote. In other words, the externalisation of European norms requires the EU to strike a careful balance between interference and indifference.

The second, more important, challenge – or consideration – relates to the importance of the historical and political context when it comes to norms externalisation. The GDPR-inspired data protection framework should not be mistaken for a European product simply copied and applied to a different context. Such interpretation would inevitably lead to the wrong conclusions being drawn about its effectiveness and impact on citizens. On the contrary, the Data Protection Act – despite the strong resemblance with its European predecessor on paper – must be understood as a Kenyan exercise, emerging from a Kenyan context and whose characteristic traits are influenced by the role of security politics, the reactive way politicians act in response to public sentiment, and the issue of how the regulator's independence unfolds and is (or is not) reinforced during the implementation phase.

Expanding data protection and privacy to all Kenyan citizens thus goes beyond the EU's efforts to promote the GDPR via legislative alignment abroad. The EU has to engage with the organs of the state, particularly the police and security agencies and the Office of the DPC, to support transparency and reform. Without a focus on the politics of privacy versus security and economic growth, the EU risks ending up with data protection and privacy regulations that create robust commercial partnerships while the digital rights of citizens ebb and flow with the politics and perceptions of state security.

Notes

1 Out of the proposed EUR 132.8 billion that are dedicated to the "Single Market, Innovation, and Digital", EUR 8.6 billion (or 6.4%) are reserved for the digital realm through the Digital Europe Programme and the Connecting Europe Facility. In addition, it is to be assumed that a considerable share of Horizon Europe (EUR 75.9 billion) and InvestEU (EUR 2.8 billion) will be allocated to foster digitalisation broadly speaking (EU 2020b). The European Council concluded on 2 October 2020 that "at least 20% of the funds under the Recovery and Resilience Facility will

be made available for the digital transition". Being provisioned with EUR 672.5 billion, this share equals EUR 134.5 billion in loans and grants for fostering Europe's
digital transition (EU 2020c, p. 4). More recently, the EU Commission has introduced a yet-to-be-implemented Global Gateway connectivity strategy, which also
aims to support EU digital projects abroad.
2 The distinction between the different concepts (civilian/normative power, market
power, and regulatory power) is less clear-cut than demonstrated here. In fact, each
of the concepts shares considerable overlap with the other two, making them rather
open-ended and complementary than mutually exclusive.

References

Amnesty International (2021). *Kenyans Still Unaware of Data Protection and Right to
Privacy.* Available at: https://www.amnestykenya.org/kenyans-still-unaware-of-data
-protection-and-right-to-privacy/ (Accessed 18 September 2021).
Andere, B. (2021). 'Kenya's sneak attack on privacy: Changes to the law allow government
access to phone and computer data.' *Access Now.* [Viewed on 18 September 2021].
Available at: https://www.accessnow.org/kenya-right-to-privacy/
Andersen, R. (2020). 'The panopticon is already here.' *The Atlantic* (September). [Viewed
on 9 July 2021]. Available at: https://www.theatlantic.com/magazine/archive/2020
/09/china-ai-surveillance/614197/
Bach, D. and Newmann, A. (2007). 'The European regulatory state and global public
policy.' *Journal of European Public Policy* 14(6), pp. 827–846.
Badurdeen, F.A. (2018). 'Surveillance of young Muslims and counterterrorism in Kenya.'
In M.T. Grasso and J. Bessant Eds. *Governing Youth Politics in the Age of Surveillance.*
London: Routledge. pp. 92–107.
Bendiek, A. and Römer, M. (2019). 'Externalizing Europe: The global effects of
European data protection.' *Digital Policy, Regulation and Governance.* 21(1), pp. 32–43.
Boazman, S. (2014). 'Inside Kenya's death squads.' *Al Jazeera.* Available from: https://
interactive.aljazeera.com/aje/kenyadeathsquads/#film (Accessed 10 June 2021).
Bowman, W. and Bowman, J.D. (2016). 'Censorship or self-control? Hate speech, the
state and the voter in the Kenyan election of 2013.' *The Journal of Modern African
Studies.* 54(3), pp. 495–531.
Bradford, A. (2020). *The Brussels Effect: How the European Union Rules the World.* Oxford:
Oxford University Press.
Buzan B., Waever, O. and de Wilde, J. (1998). *Security: A New Framework for Analysis.*
Boulder: Lynne Rienner Publishers.
Capella, M., Jadhav, S., and Moncrieff, J. (2020). 'History, violence and collective
memory: Implications for mental health in Ecuador. '*Transcultural Psychology.* 57(1),
pp. 32–43.
Damro, C. (2012). 'Market power Europe.' *Journal of European Public Policy.* 19(5), pp.
682–699.
Damro, C. (2015). Market power Europe: Exploring a dynamic conceptual framework.
Journal of European Public Policy. 22(9), pp. 1336–1354.
Dimmroth K., and Schünemann W.J. (2017). 'The ambiguous relation between privacy
and security in German cyber politics.' In: Schünemann W., Baumann MO., eds.
Privacy, Data Protection and Cybersecurity in Europe. Cham: Springer.
Donovan, K. and Martin, A. (2014). 'The rise of African SIM registration: The emerging
dynamics of regulatory change.' *First Monday.* 19(2). https://doi.org/10.5210/fm.v19i2
.4351

Duchêne, F. (1972). 'Europe's role in world peace.' In: R. Mayne, ed. *Europe Tomorrow: Sixteen Europeans Look Ahead.* London: Fontana. pp. 32–47.

Eken, M. (2019). 'Kenya's controversial digital ID scheme faces pushback.' *Open Society Justice Initiative.* December 19. Available at: https://www.justiceinitiative.org/voices /kenyas-controversial-digital-id-scheme-faces-push-back (Accessed 10 June 2021).

EU (2007). *Commission Staff Working Document – The External Dimension of the Single Market Review – Accompanying Document to the Communication from the Commission to the European Parliament, the Council, the European Economic and Social Committee and the Committee of the Regions: A Single Market for 21st Century Europe.* Available at: https://eur-lex.europa.eu/legal-content/nl/TXT/?uri=CELEX%3A52007SC1519 (Accessed 11 May 2021).

EU (2020a). *European Commission: Shaping Europe's Digital Future.* Available at: https:// ec.europa.eu/digital-single-market/en/policies/foreign-policy (Accessed 11 May 2021).

EU (2020b). *Communication from the Commission to the European Parliament, the Council, the European Economic and Social Committee and the Committee of the Regions: Shaping Europe's Digital Future.* Available at: https://eur-lex.europa.eu/legal-content/EN/TXT/PDF/ ?uri=CELEX:52020DC0067&from=en (Accessed 11 May 2021).

EU (2020c). *European Council.* Special meeting of the European Council (17, 18, 19, 20, and 21 July): Council Conclusions.

EU (2020d). *European Council.* Special meeting of the European Council (1 and 2 October 2020): Council Conclusions.

EU (2020e). *Communication form the Commission to the European Parliament, the Council, the European Economic and Social Committee and the Committee of the Regions: A European Strategy for Data (COM(2020) 66 Final).* Available at: https://eur-lex.europa.eu/ legal-content/EN/TXT/PDF/?uri=CELEX:52020DC0066&from=EN (Accessed 18 May 2021).

EU (2020f). *Annex 8 of the Commission Implementing Decision on the 2020 Annual Action Programme for the Partnership Instrument.* Available at: https://ec.europa.eu/fpi/content /partnership-instrument-annual-action-programme-2020_en (Accessed 21 May 2021).

EU (2020g). *Commission Report: EU Data Protection Rules Empower Citizens and Are Fit for the Digital Age.* Press Release June 24. Available at: https://ec.europa.eu/commission/ presscorner/detail/en/ip_20_1163 (Accessed 3 February 2022).

EU (2021a). *European Commission. Roadmap Initiative: Communication on a[sic] Europe's Digital Decade: 2030 Digital Targets (Ref. Ares(2021)1152850).*

EU (2021b). *European Commission. Communication from the Commission to the European Parliament, the Council, the European Economic and Social Committee and the Committee of the Regions: 2030 Digital Compass: The European Way for the Digital Decade ((COM(2021) 118 Final).*

Government of the Republic of Kenya (2018). *Third Medium-Term Plan (2018–2022): Transforming Lives: Advancing Socio-economic Development Through the "Big Four".* Available at: http://vision2030.go.ke/wp-content/uploads/2019/01/THIRD -MEDIUM-TERM-PLAN-2018-2022.pdf (Accessed 18 May 2021).

Government of the Republic of Kenya (2010). *The Constitution of Kenya, 2010.* Available at: http://www.kenyalaw.org:8181/exist/kenyalex/actview.xql?actid=Const2010 (Accessed 16 June 2021).

Greitens, S. (2021). The global impact of China's surveillance technology: Issues for U.S. Policy. In: *Essays on the Rise of China and Its Implications (2020–21 Wilson China Fellowship).* Available at: https://www.wilsoncenter.org/sites/default/files

/media/uploads/documents/ASIA-210304%20-%20The%20Wilson%20China
%20Fellowship%20report%20-%20web.pdf (Accessed 9 July 2021).

Harpaz, G. and Shamis A. (2010). 'Normative power Europe and the state of Israel: An illegitimate EUtopia?' *Journal of Common Market Studies*. 48(3), pp. 579–616.

Interview 1. (2021). Interview with EU official. June 11 (interview by authors).

Interview 2. (2021). Interview with Mugambi Laibuta. July 5 (interview by authors).

Interview 3. (2021). Interview with Joe Gaithaiga and Jeehan Kassam, PWC. August 16 (interview by authors).

Interview 4. (2021). Interview with Kenyan lawyer and columnist. August 17 (interview by authors).

Interview 5. (2021). Written exchange with representatives of Article 19. September 9.

Iturriaga, N. (2019). 'At the foot of the grave: Challenging collective memories of violence in post-Franco Spain.' *Socius*. https://doi.org/10.1177/2378023119832135

Jacobsen, K.L. (2019). 'Biometric voter registration: A new modality of democracy assistance?' *Cooperation and Conflict*. 55(1), pp. 127–148.

Kenya Gazette Supplement. (2019). *The Data Protection Act. No. 24 of 2019*. Available at: http://kenyalaw.org/kl/fileadmin/pdfdownloads/Acts/2019/TheDataProt ectionAct__No24of2019.pdf (Accessed 9 June 2021).

Krause, V. and Otenyo, E. (2005). 'Terrorism and the Kenyan Public.' *Studies in Conflict and Terrorism*. 28(2), pp. 99–112.

Lind, J., Mutahi, P., and Oosterom, M. (2017). '"Killing and mosquito with a hammer": Al-Shabaab violence and state security responses in Kenya.' *Peacebuilding*. 5(2), pp. 118–135.

Maina, G. (2015). *New Technology for Peace in Kenya. Report: Leveraging Local Knowledge for Peacebuilding and Statebuilding in Africa*. New York: International Peace Institute.

Makulilo, A. and Boshe, P. (2016). 'Data protection in Kenya.' In: A. Makulilo, ed. *African Data Privacy Laws* (Vol. 33): Cham: Springer. pp. 317–336.

Manners, I. (2002). 'Normative power Europe: A contradiction in terms?' *Journal of Common Market Studies*. 40(2), pp. 235–58.

McCracken, G. (1988). *The long interview*. Newbury Park: Sage Publications.

Mogire, E. and Agade, K.M. (2011). 'Counter-terrorism in Kenya.' *Journal of Contemporary African Studies*. 29(4), pp. 473–491.

Mwanzia, S.W., Kapiyo, V., and Ayazika, Ph. (2021). 'Unseen eyes, unheard stories: Surveillance, data protection, and freedom of expression in Kenya and Uganda during COVID-19.' Article 19 *Eastern Africa*.

Nyabola, N. (2017). 'Nyayo House: Unravelling the architecture and aesthetics of torture.' *The Elephant*. Available at: https://www.theelephant.info/ideas/2017/08/17 /nyayo-house-unravelling-the-architecture-and-aesthetics-of-torture/ (Accessed 6 September 2021).

Ombati, C. (2019). 'Flying squad unit disbanded, officer moved in restructuring plans.' *The Standard*. December 31.

Orbie, J. (2006). 'Civilian power Europe: Review of the original and current debates.' *Cooperation and Conflict*. 41(1), pp. 123–128.

PWC (2018). *Regulatory Alert: Implications of the GDPR on Kenyan Entities*. Available at: https://www.pwc.com/ke/en/pdf/regulatory-alert-Implications-of-gdpr.pdf (Accessed 19 May2021).

Reiners, W. (2021). 'Die Digitalisierungsstrategie der Europäischen Union – Meilensteine und Handlungsfelder zwischen digitaler Souveränität und grüner Transformation.' *Integration*. 44(4), pp. 266–286.

Rosecrance, R. (1998). 'The European Union: A new type of international actor.' In: J. Zielonka, ed. *Paradoxes of European foreign policy*. The Hague: KluwerLaw International, pp. 15–23.

Roth, M. (2020). 'Europa muss digitale Macht sein. Gastbeitrag von Michael Roth.' *Frankfurter Allgemeine Zeitung*. 4 October.

Schneider, I. (2020). 'Datenschutz, KI un digitale Rechte in Mexiko – Europa als Referenzmodell?' *Vorgänge - Zeitschrift für Bürgerrechte und Gesellschaftspolitik*. 231/232, pp. 131–145.

Wang, M. (2021). 'China's techno-authoritarianism has gone global: Washington needs to offer an alternative.' *Foreign Affairs* (April 8). Available at: https://www.foreignaffairs.com/articles/china/2021-04-08/chinas-techno-authoritarianism-has-gone-global (Accessed 9 July 2021).

Wanjohi, P.M. (2017). 'Curbing mobile phone terrorism and financial fraud: A Kenyan perspective.' *Journal of ICT Standardization*. 4(3), pp. 237–246.

Zuboff, S. (2019). *The Age of Surveillance Capitalism: The Fight for a Human Future at the New Frontier of Power*. New York: PublicAffairs.

11

DIGITALISATION IN SCIENCE AND TECHNOLOGY POLICY

Engagement, Alignment, and Misalignment Between the European Union and South African Data Protection and Privacy Frameworks[1]

Michael Gastrow and Rachel Adams

11.1 Introduction

Science policy and technology policy have historically been characterised by international collaboration. In the era of digitalisation, policies that regulate the use of data, and the innovation systems that underpin the generation and uptake of new digital technologies, have become critical instruments of national and international politics. In this chapter, we explore the ways in which a developing country, South Africa (SA), has engaged with a major bloc of developed countries, the European Union (EU), in its pursuit of strengthened local capabilities, and alignment with international changes in the regulation of data and digital technologies. In this context, we investigate and juxtapose the emergence of data privacy and data protection regulation in both jurisdictions. In contrast to the co-ordinated and collaborative framework for SA–EU science and technology partnerships, disjunctures in the development and direction of data privacy and protection regulation in the two jurisdictions present potential problems for South Africa's digital economy, as well as avenues for further research.

Our analysis distinguishes between the roles of science policy and technology policy, since these are each distinct (although interrelated) policy spheres. Within innovation systems, there are fundamental links between science policy and digitalisation – including funding for basic and applied research in digitalisation, building infrastructures and capabilities for such research, and setting framework conditions for science (for example, intellectual property regimes and regulatory systems). The scope also includes the social science of digitalisation. However, digitalisation policy has largely focussed on technology – particularly on governing the technologies of digitalisation. A broad understanding of digitalisation policy, including all of the above dimensions, is therefore appropriate, since digitalisation intersects with many other governance and policy domains.

DOI: 10.4324/9781003274322-11

South Africa's cooperation with the EU is arguably its most important international science and technology partnership (Pandor, 2012). Since the 1996 South Africa–EU Science and Technology Cooperation Agreement, a decades-long multifaceted strategic alliance has been created. This chapter reviews the scope of SA–EU science and technology partnerships in the digital space. Within this broad canvas, we focus specifically on data protection and privacy, and the manner in which the South African and European legislative and policy frameworks have co-evolved. We take this focus because the regulation of data flows is one of the critical framework conditions for digitalisation, as well as an important instrument in the domain of international science and technology diplomacy. Following a brief examination of the emergence of regulation in both jurisdictions, we analyse the implications of alignment and misalignment between the two sets of regulations – including the emergence of restrictions on international data flows that are critical for innovation and scientific development. In conclusion, we reflect on the potential to achieve greater alignment, close gaps between regulatory frameworks, and direct efforts towards mutual objectives.

11.2 Science and Technology Cooperation Mechanisms

International cooperation plays an important role in science policy. It helps to create the framework conditions for scientific collaboration, mobilises funding and capabilities for globalised research, and sets the research agenda. This international engagement in the realm of science policy is also referred to as "science diplomacy". According to the Royal Society and the American Association for the Advancement of Science, there are three dimensions to science diplomacy. Firstly, "science in diplomacy" refers to the ways in which scientific advice informs and supports foreign policy objectives. Secondly, "diplomacy for science" seeks to facilitate international scientific cooperation and the development of international relations to support the scientific enterprise. Thirdly, "science for diplomacy" focusses on scientific cooperation as a means of improving international relations (Royal Society, 2010). As the South African–EU relationship has been active in all three of these areas, this section sets out to provide a brief overview of the evolvement and function of the different SA–EU cooperation agreements currently in place, in order to provide a broader context for the evolution of SA and EU digital policy.

Science diplomacy between South Africa and the EU has a rich history. Following South Africa's emergence from international isolation in 1994, the newly elected democratic government recognised the importance of science and technology to South Africa's development and strategic objectives, and set about establishing the institutional mechanisms, policies, and partnerships to drive the national knowledge economy (Masters, 2016). A Science and Technology White Paper published in 1996 emphasised the role of science and technology as instruments for economic growth, social development, and poverty alleviation. The

Department of Science and Technology was created in 2002, and reconfigured as the Department of Science and Innovation (DSI) in 2018. Guided by the White Paper, one of the major priorities of the DSI has been to develop and implement a strategy for international scientific and technological cooperation (Pandor, 2012; Simelane, 2015, Department of Science and Innovation, 2021).

Due to South Africa's relatively small national system of innovation, international cooperation is essential for leveraging local capabilities. At the same time science content becomes increasingly important for critical foreign policy issues. The DSI's International Cooperation and Resources programme is responsible for facilitating bilateral and multilateral scientific cooperation, including a focused strategic partnership with the EU. The establishment of a South African Department of Science and Innovation representation in Brussels has taken forward digital policy engagement with EU institutions (that is, the Joint Research Centre and different branches of the European Commission) and encouraged new bilateral agreements between the South African government and individual EU member states. The DSI's diplomatic efforts are supported by its cooperation with other South African departments, including the Department of Trade and Industry, the Department of Environmental Affairs, and the Department of International Relations and Cooperation. Internally, many of South Africa's national public research institutes host dedicated teams focussed on international cooperation. These multiple channels and modalities of science diplomacy steer the implementation of a number of substantive science and technology cooperation mechanisms.

South Africa and the EU have a well-established diplomatic relationship that has facilitated the development of new knowledge and partnerships with a focus on digitalisation. At South Africa–EU Summits, the presidents of South Africa, the European Council, and the European Commission have consistently lauded the role played by science and technology in South Africa–EU relations. At the 2018 summit, the parties issued a joint statement in which they declared to intensify collaboration in key areas such as open science, big data platforms, digital and Information and Communications Technology, as well as sectors linked to Industry 4.0. At a sectoral level, cooperation has included South Africa's leadership in the Science, Information Society and Space Partnership of the Joint Africa–EU Strategy (African Union, 2021a), which encompasses a range of political and policy dialogues, including a Digital Economy Task Force (African Union, 2021b). South Africa's role as co-chair with the European Commission of the Group on Earth Observations (Department of Science and Innovation, 2018) is also significant, as it underpins cooperation towards the development of an integrated Earth observation system.

One of the most significant cooperation mechanisms is the Science Technology and Innovation (STI) co-operation programme, created within the framework of the European–South Africa Science and Technology Advancement Programme (ESASTAP). The SA–EU STI system enables researchers to set up their interdisciplinary research networks across Europe and South Africa. Another ESASTAP initiative, the Eureka STI networking programme, provides a platform for research and development (R&D) cooperation in the private sector. Eureka's Eurostars programme is dedicated to research-performing small and medium enterprises (SMEs), many of which are active in the digital space. Direct collaboration has frequently been supported by the EU's apex research programmes, including its Framework programmes and the Horizon 2020 programme. South Africa has become one of the most significant developing country partners in these research programmes, fostering deeper linkages and growing capacity in the South African innovation system. At the meso-level, the SA–EU Dialogue facility encourages policy dialogues on digitalisation (Gastrow, 2019). The South African Presidential Commission on the Fourth Industrial Revolution, which was active from 2019 to 2020, consulted widely with European stakeholders in shaping its recommendations for South African digital policy (Presidential Commission on The Fourth Industrial Revolution, 2019).

Another platform for engagement is the New Africa-Europe Digital Economy Partnership. Supported by the Digital Economy Task Force, which comprises public and private sector representatives from the EU and the African Union (AU), the Africa-Europe Digital Economy Partnership brings together different actors from both continents to discuss the digital transformation in Africa. The EU Commission's approach to digitalisation in Africa is based on the notion of "Digital4Development". The concept frames digitalisation as a global priority and emphasises the value of mainstreaming digital aspects to the entire range of development policies and actions:

> "Digital4Development" is a framework for mainstreaming digital technologies into development policy, contributing to the achievement of the Sustainable Development Goals and ensuring effective delivery based on existing policies, funding instruments and partnerships involving the public and private sectors. Digital4Development should be guided by a vision that maximises the uptake of digitalisation as a strong driver for economic growth in partner countries and reduces the digital divide by providing access for all, with particular emphasis on women, youth and vulnerable groups, and on their education.
>
> *(European Commission, 2017, p. 15)*

The main goals of the framework are to accelerate universal access to affordable broadband, develop digital skills and capabilities, improve the business environment, and facilitate access to finance and support services to boost digitally enabled entrepreneurship, and accelerating the adoption of e-Services and the development of the digital economy for achieving the Sustainable Development Goals.

A cognate engagement is that of the Policy and Regulation Initiative for Digital Africa (PRIDA). This is a joint initiative of the AU and the EU, together with the International Telecommunication Union (ITU), funded by the EU's Pan

African Programme. The initiative aims to support regulatory harmonisation in order to develop broadband supply in Africa – with the ultimate aim of universally accessible and affordable broadband across the continent. It also aims to develop the digital capabilities that underpin broadband demand, as well as build policy capabilities among AU member states in the domains of internet and data governance. The AU plays an important role in working to harmonise ICT and data policies and regulatory frameworks – a critical objective as data policies co-evolve globally.

In its broad sweep, then, there are multiple effective channels for diplomacy and mechanisms for engagement in the domain of digitalisation policy. The scope of digitalisation is so wide that the outcomes of these interactions differ significantly in different domains. We therefore take a specific focus on the question of data protection and data privacy – an issue at the heart of digitalisation policy in both the EU and South Africa.

11.3 Data Protection and Privacy

As digitalisation continues to unfold across the world, the regulation of data has emerged as a central policy issue with wide-ranging effects across many domains. Within this scope, the question of data privacy and data protection is critical. Digitalisation makes increasing demands for personal information, whether through ecommerce, social media, online health platforms, online financial platforms, or recruitment platforms. At the same time, particularly in countries with a strong tradition of human rights, there is growing demand for privacy. This dynamic causes a long-term and growing friction between individuals who require more privacy, and organisations that require more personal data. Accordingly, regulations like South Africa's Protection of Personal Information Act (POPIA) and the EU's General Data Protection Regulation (GDPR) are essential for working through this friction

Data protection and privacy regulations constitute a global response to this emerging regulatory need. A recent review by the United Nations Conference on Trade and Development (UNCTAD, 2021) found that 128 out of 194 countries have already put in place legislation to secure the protection of data and privacy, and that across the world such legislation is being developed and amended to keep up with technological change.

In this, a distinction must be made between data privacy and data protection – the former refers to policies, the latter to mechanisms. The principles of data privacy delineate who may have access to data. The tools of data protection provide the mechanisms required to appropriately restrict access to data. Compliance regulations provide guidelines so that the privacy requests of users are responsibly implemented in both public and private sectors.

The range of policy domains that are impacted by data protection and privacy regulation is vast. It includes the processing of personal health information and any other personally identifiable information such as social security or ID numbers, addresses, names, birthdates, contact information, IP address, cookie data, genetic data, biometric data, racial or ethnic data, surveillance data, or data related to sexual orientation. Technological mechanisms for conforming to data protection requirements include data loss prevention, protection, firewalls, encryption, and endpoint protection.

The evolution of data privacy and protection regulation in the EU and South Africa reveals both areas of alignment and misalignment. In our analysis, we briefly examine the history of regulation in both jurisdictions, and the implications of the ways in which the two sets of regulation have and have not reached alignment.

The process of drafting the POPIA began in 2003, and was principally based on the EU Data Protection Directive 95/46/EC, a predecessor of the European GDPR (although the POPIA includes some stricter provisions). In this sense, there were early efforts to align South Africa's data regulation with international conventions and best practices. However, the extended timeframes for the promulgation, adoption, and implementation of the POPIA led to subsequent misalignments. The act was signed into law in 2013 and partially enforced in 2014, allowing for the establishment of the Information Regulator in 2016. However, it was not until 2020 that the POPIA came into effect. An extra 12-month grace period was granted to allow institutions to become compliant with the Act. Hence, after the law was finalised and signed by the then president of South Africa, it took another eight years until it finally entered into force. At the time of writing, South African firms are finalising their adjustments to conform to the POPIA – while those that have already established data protection guidelines to conform to the GDPR will have a head start.

In the interim, the EU moved onto the more comprehensive GDPR. In 2016, the GDPR replaced the bloc's Data Protection Directive, which was brought into effect in1995, and was therefore outdated in its regulation of data in the context of contemporary digitalisation. The GDPR provides an overarching framework for regulating data within the EU's jurisdiction and stands as the most comprehensive piece of data protection legislation in the world. It requires that firms protect the personal data and privacy of EU citizens for transactions that occur within EU member states and regulates the sharing of personal data of EU citizens outside the EU.

The GDPR applies to all data processing activity undertaken by a controller in the EU, as well as any processing of personal data of EU citizens even if the processing does not take place in the EU. This expands the impact of the GDPR to other jurisdictions, in which any entity that processes EU citizen data in the course of providing goods and services must comply with the GDPR.

There are many similarities between the POPIA and the GDPR. Both set high-level principles (such as transparency and accountability) for how personal information should be processed. Under the principle of accountability, both regulations require that the parties processing personal information demonstrate compliance with a range of conditions. However, the GDPR offers a much stronger framework for regulating data flows of personal information. This comparable strength of the GDPR to the POPIA may place undue restrictions on South Africa's participation in international data flows that are critical for innovation and scientific development.

GDPR and POPIA are fairly similar overall, albeit with some differences in terminology, organisation of the respective articles, and greater specificity on the part of GDPR. Significantly, the POPIA protects both individuals and legal entities, while the GDPR does not protect legal entities; therefore, firms and other legal entities face different requirements in the EU and South African jurisdictions: some EU firms and organisations are exempt from having to keep records or have a data protection officer, while this is not the case in South Africa. The POPIA requires all organisations to have a data protection officer, while the GDPR only requires some organisations to do so. There are differences between the functions of the Information Regulator (under the POPIA) and the Supervisory Authority (under the GDPR). Under the POPIA, responsible parties are required to obtain authorisation from the Regulator to process personal information. On the other hand, the GDPR Supervisory Authority monitors compliance, but does not require authorisation. The requirement for authorisation creates additional protection in South Africa, but also an additional regulatory hurdle.

Both the GDPR and the POPIA are guided by a cognate set of rights with respect to personal information, although the terminology used to describe these rights differs somewhat. Both provide for the right to be notified that personal data is being used, the right to access one's personal data, the right to request the correction or deletion of personal information, the right to not have personal information processed for the purpose of direct marketing by means of unsolicited electronic communications, the right to complain to the regulator, and the right to effective judicial remedy.

The POPIA's aim is to regulate the processing of personal information in South Africa, whether by public or private bodies. In this way, it stands against violations to the right to privacy of persons living in South Africa and against the exploitative use of personal information in the growing information society. Decisively, in the Act's opening Preamble the drafters of the POPIA emphasised that the law bore in mind that "consonant with the constitutional values of democracy and openness, the need for economic and social progress, within the framework of the information society, requires the removal of unnecessary impediments to the free flow of information, including personal information" (POPIA Preamble). The POPIA seeks, therefore, to regulate – but not impede – the flow of data that has become the central (and centralising) infrastructure of the contemporary world, to ensure that human rights, most pertinently the right to privacy, are not violated in the process.

The POPIA creates an obligation to report data breaches, closing a regulatory loophole that had previously allowed data breaches to go unreported due to a lack of formal obligations to do so. The POPIA requires that organisations report suspicions of unauthorised access to personal data to the Information Regulator, and in some cases, to the data subjects. The POPIA also regulates the offshoring of data, and the cross-border provisions of the POPIA must be met when sending data out of the country.

The GDPR restricts the sharing of personal data outside of Europe. In fact, the GDPR provides that European personal data can only be shared with countries outside of Europe that have a data protection regime that provides a similar level of protection to the GDPR. Together with an opinion from the European Data Protection Board, the European Commission has the power to make decisions on the level of adequacy of data protection regimes. To date, it has thus far deemed the following countries as offering an adequate level of data protection: Andorra, Argentina, Canada (commercial organisations), Faroe Islands, Guernsey, Israel, Isle of Man, Japan, Jersey, New Zealand, Switzerland, and Uruguay (European Commission, 2021). These decisions take some time to reach, and notably, the European Commission has not yet declared any African country as being safe for European personal data to be shared with. Given that the POPIA was promulgated in 2013, long before the final version of the GDPR was issued, it is likely that South Africa will not be granted adequacy by the European Commission. In a broader sense, the same is true for any other African country that does not have a data protection law or a data protection law deemed to offer as high a level of data protection as the GDPR.

This has important implications for open science and the participation of countries like South Africa in international science and innovation enterprises. While data sharing with a European country is possible if there are other adequate written legal agreements in place on a case-by-case basis,[2] the GDPR may well act as a barrier to international data sharing, even for scientific purposes.

One area where this is particularly important for the progress of science in general, and for Africa in particular, concerns genetic research. Following the success of the human genome project in assembling full human genomes, and the importance of this work for genomic research and researchers globally, standards were developed to try and ensure that such research is made open access (Gaffney et al., 2020). However, with the advent of the GDPR, sharing such data may be more difficult (Powell, 2021). This is partly because genetic data cannot be completely de-identified, one of the key conditions required by data protection laws for data sharing. Although this is the case, it requires significant technical know-how, expertise, and resources to identify an individual from their genetic data. For African science to benefit from genetic research, more African genetic data is required to ensure its representativeness (Adams et al., 2021). In this sense, it is critical that data protection law does not hinder scientific progress, and exemptions for research from the more burdensome conditions for lawful processing that data protection laws set out must be sought. Research has already shown that the POPIA has disrupted health research (Thaldar and Townsend, 2021), although the more recently published POPIA code of conduct for research aims to ease restrictions within the provisions of the law (Adams et al., 2021).

The areas of alignment and misalignment in data protection and privacy law across the GDPR and the POPIA have significant implications for South Africa. While the initial development of the POPIA made progress in aligning South African regulation with international standards, the nearly two decades of elapsed time have subsequently created a disjuncture between European and South African regulatory frameworks. Considerable economic activity depends on whether South Africa is deemed to have an acceptable framework for data sharing with the EU. If this is not achieved, it will create major constraints on the potential for partnerships, trade, investment, science, and innovation across the two jurisdictions. It would entrench limitations to economic activity that entails the use of personal data originating in the EU jurisdiction. This would have widespread cross-sectoral impact, since many sectors require the processing of personal information. Given that business process outsourcing, and call centres are a major growth sector in South Africa, the impacts on economic growth and human development will be wide-ranging. Other areas of potential negative impact include the medical, retail, marketing, education, logistics, media, and tourism sectors.

11.4 Conclusion

South Africa has a well-developed relationship with the EU with regard to science and technology, characterised by established diplomatic channels for engagement, and a wide range of institutional mechanisms to foster scientific and technological partnerships. This science diplomacy framework has been purposively built by the post-Apartheid government as part of its efforts to open and expand the South African national system of innovation. In the era of digitalisation, these partnerships and mechanisms have been leveraged to support R&D, innovation, investment, capability-building, and the development of networks. Moreover, South Africa participates in valuable EU–African platforms for engagement in the area of digitalisation policy and development.

However, in the domain of data regulation, specifically the regulation of data privacy and data protection, there are significant areas of misalignment. Institutional misalignment emerged from the process of developing legislation in the EU and South Africa. When South Africa enacted the POPIA, the GDPR had not yet been developed. During the 18 years that passed between the initial drafting of the POPIA in 2003, and its coming into effect in 2021, the goalposts moved at the EU level. As a consequence, South Africa may be facing widespread detrimental effects to its digital economy. A clear lesson from this course of events is that the regulation of the digital environment needs to be rapid and responsive, or risks falling behind.

Political factors also come into play. The GDPR makes demands of countries outside the EU to conform to its standards or face a degree of exclusion from its digital economy. The power dynamic inherent in this requirement is, to some degree, colonial in its expectation. In South African debates about emerging data policy, geopolitical powers, including China and Russia, may exploit this evident dynamic to turn the direction of policy towards their own interests. Exclusion from European markets may strengthen ties between South African and other jurisdictions. Data sharing, and the economic activities underpinned by data sharing, may have greater potential to develop and grow between jurisdictions that do not face the exclusionary criteria of the GDPR. Combined with a geopolitical agenda in which global powers are contesting to gain traction on the African continent, the result may prove to the detriment of both SA–EU relations and SA–EU economic ties. If powers such as Russia and China also face exclusion from European data markets, they may find common cause with South Africa, which may harm/weaken the country's human rights agenda and positions on global data protection agreements.

Therefore, it is critical that data regulation is developed in a manner that is congruent with other aspects of science, technology policy, and diplomacy. If South African data regulation creates barriers to science and innovation, then it is working against other efforts to expand South Africa's cooperation with the EU. There exists a strong argument for South Africa to bring the POPIA more closely in line with the GDPR – the political overtones of such a move notwithstanding. The EU is one of South Africa's major trading partners, and it would be a net loss to South Africa to distance itself from the EU's digital economy. Parliament could potentially amend the POPIA accordingly. Another option could be for the information regulator to interpreting the POPIA in a manner that is aligned with the GDPR. However, no political or policy signals have been made that either of these outcomes is likely.

Overall, these dynamics, sometimes those of integration and sometimes those of divergence, highlight the need for an integrated approach to digitalisation policy and diplomacy in South Africa. The enormous scope of digitalisation policy makes this difficult, since it has markedly different characteristics, technologies, politics, and challenges in different sectors and applications. However, as the world becomes increasingly digital, it also becomes increasingly important for all actors in the policy space to become aware of the overall policy landscape.

There is a juxtaposition between the generally strong digital science and technology engagement between the EU and South Africa, and the degree of misalignment with respect to data protection. Broadly, there is productive science and technology engagement in terms of capacity-building, network development, business development, innovation, and science – but misalignments in core data policies could undermine some of this. These outcomes show how science and technology policy are formed in an international context. Politically, an expectation that South Africa aligns with Europe has political overtones of a centre-periphery relationship. At the same time, such alignment would be a practical way to boost digital connections between the EU and South Africa. All this points towards a need for greater co-ordination in South African–EU relations to encompass not only a wide range of disparate platforms and partnerships, but to integrate the development of the core data policies that cut across the digital world and have the potential to have major impacts on innovation systems and digital economies.

Looking beyond the SA–EU relationship, the question of international cooperation in the area of data regulation has relevance within broader geopolitical conversations. The EU is pursuing continent-to-continent engagements, with the aim of building broader data-sharing possibilities. The analysis of SA–EU alignment raises questions for further research: How realistic are these ambitions is if adequate data sharing arrangements with a close partner such as South Africa present such a challenge? And what changes in the approaches of the EU, and its partner countries, might facilitate more effective data sharing? The South African case illustrates that closer and more timeous engagement and alignment throughout the policy cycle would be a first step.

Notes

1 Thanks to the DSI/NRF/Newton Fund Trilateral Chair in Transformative Innovation, the 4IR, and Sustainable Development for its support – this work has been partially supported by the National Research Foundation of South Africa (Grant Number: 118873).
2 As was determined in the recent Schrems II judgement which found that the United States does not offer adequate levels of data protection for European personal data: Data Protection Commissioner v Facebook Ireland Ltd and Maximillian Schrems. Available at: https://www.epic.org/privacy/intl/dpc-v-facebook/ireland/ (last accessed 21 May 2021).

References

Adams, R. et al. (2021). 'POPIA code of conduct for research.' *South African Journal of Science*. 117(5/6), Art. No. 10933. https://doi.org/10.17159/sajs.2021/10933.

African Union (2021a). *Africa-EU Partnership. 4*. Available at: https://africa-eu-partnership .org/en/categories/science-information-society-and-space?page=20 (Accessed 21 December 2021).

African Union (2021b). *Digital Economy Task Force*. Available at: https://africa-eu -partnership.org/en/digital-economy-task-force-detf (Accessed 7 December 2021).

Department of Science and Innovation (2018). *South African to chair group on earth observations*. Available at: https://www.dst.gov.za/index.php/media-room/latest -news/2664-south-africa-to-chair-group-on-earth-observations-geo (Accessed 7 December 2021).

Department of Science and Innovation (2021). International cooperation and resources. Available at: https://www.dst.gov.za/index.php/about-us/programmes/international -cooperation-and-resources (Accessed 7 December 2021).

European Commission (2017). *Digital4Development: Mainstreaming Digital Technologies and Services into EU Development Policy*. Commission staff working document. Available at: https://europa.eu/capacity4dev/public-ict/documents?sort=views&order=desc (Accessed 7 December 2021).

European Commission (2021). *Adequacy Decisions: How the EU Determines if a non-EU Country Has an Adequate Level of Data Protection*. Available at: https://ec.europa.eu/info /law/law-topic/data-protection/international-dimension-data-protection/adequacy -decisions_en (Accessed 7 December 2021).

Gaffney, J. et al. (2020). 'Open access to genetic sequence data maximizes value to scientists, farmers, and society.' *Global Food Security*. 26. https://doi.org/10.1016/j.gfs .2020.100411.

Gastrow, M. (2019). 'Policy options framework for the fourth industrial revolution in South Africa.' An Output of the SA-EU Strategic Partnership Dialogue Conference on Disruptive Technologies and Public Policy in the Age of the Fourth Industrial Revolution.

Masters, L. (2016). 'South Africa's two track approach to science diplomacy.' *Journal for Contemporary History*. 41(1), 169–186. https://doi.org/10.18820/24150509/jch.v41i1.9

Pandor, N. (2012). 'South African Science Diplomacy: Fostering global partnerships and advancing the African agenda.' *Science and Diplomacy*. 1(1). Available at: http://www .sciencediplomacy.org/perspective/2012/south-african-science-diplomacy.

Powell, K. (2021). 'The broken promise that undermines human genome research.' *Nature*. 590, pp. 198–201. https://doi.org/10.1038/d41586-021-00331-5.

Presidential Commission on The Fourth Industrial Revolution. (2019). 'Summary report and recommendations.' *Government Gazette No. 42388*.

Royal Society. (2010). *New Frontiers in Science Diplomacy: Navigating the Changing Balance of Power*. Available at: https://royalsociety.org//media/Royal_Society_Content/policy/ publications/2010/4294969468.pdf

Simelane, T. (2015). 'Science and technology diplomacy and South Africa's foreign policy.' *South African Foreign Policy Review*. 2, p 41–58. Africa Institute of South Africa.

Thaldar, D.W. and Townsend, B.A. (2021). 'Exempting health research from the consent provisions of POPIA.' *Potchefstroom Electronic Law Journal*. 24. https://doi.org/10.17159 /1727-3781/2021/v24i0a10420

United National Conference on Trade and Development. (2021). *Data Protection and Privacy Legislation Worldwide*. Available at: https://unctad.org/page/data-protection -and-privacy-legislation-worldwide (Accessed 7 December 2021).

12

PUTTING PEOPLE AT THE CENTRE OF DIGITAL POLICY

Mechanisms for Citizen Engagement in Nigeria

Joe Abah, Krista Baptista, Connor MacKenzie, and Anand Varghese

12.1 Introduction

Digital technologies offer countries economic, social, and political opportunities. But without robust national policies and regulations, technology's trade-offs can worsen the very issues they seek to improve.

As of September 2021, a majority of African countries have written or passed some degree of national policy, regulation, or law that addresses an issue in the technology sector (Abimbola, 2021). This chapter focuses on the process by which national-level digital policies, regulations, and bills are developed, with a specific focus on how policymakers engage diverse stakeholders in this process, particularly citizens. When stakeholders ranging from consumers (both current and future), businesses, industry associations, civil society organisations (CSOs), to other community representatives, have mechanisms to provide their opinions regarding a proposed legislative procedure, the final outcome will better represent all public interests and is more likely to achieve its intended goals (Hutahaean, 2016). Furthermore, when stakeholders participate in the policymaking process the practice becomes more transparent, which leads to higher levels of trust regarding divisive topics (OECD, 2017). Finally, when stakeholders are equal partners in the policymaking process, this provides an opportunity for collaboration and co-creation between various interest groups.

Despite the general benefits of stakeholder engagement in the policymaking process, there is rarely a level playing field between the various stakeholders. Citizens face knowledge, organisational, and time constraints that limit their ability to engage in policymaking themselves. They often rely on newly formed CSOs that specialise in digital technologies to serve as their agent in the digital policymaking processes. Likewise, consumer groups represent subscribers' specific interests and industry associations represent corporate interests in the

DOI: 10.4324/9781003274322-12

technology sector. These two stakeholder groups dispose of superior resources, political access, and knowledge, leading to power asymmetries amongst stakeholder groups.

Like many other African countries, Nigeria aspires to diversify its economy by further developing its nascent technology sector. As Africa's largest democratic country and host to the continent's largest mobile phone market, Nigerians are eager to enjoy technology's benefits and mitigate against any potential negative consequences from digital transformation (The World Bank, 2019). As a result, Nigerian policymakers in the National Assembly and related federal agencies are developing technology policies, regulations, and bills to mitigate trade-offs without stifling national development. Nevertheless, this chapter argues that citizen-centric engagement in recent national-level digital policymaking is still insufficient in Nigeria. Despite the existence of guidelines for public consultation, citizen-centric engagement is minimal and tends to occur after national policies and regulations have already been introduced. This chapter also uses Nigeria as a case study to examine the extent that external institutions, such as the European Union (EU), can support these efforts. The EU's commitment to multi-stakeholder participation in the development of a digital society has positioned the institution well for supporting other countries during their own digital transformation. With the African Union-European Union (AU-EU) Digital for Development (D4D) Hub's recent formation, there is a fresh opportunity for these two institutions to work together in prioritising inclusive and people-centric digital transformation throughout African countries.

Section 12.2 provides an overview of Nigeria's policymaking processes in the technology sector. It describes how national policymakers engage with different stakeholders and explores power asymmetries between them. Section 12.3 and Section 12.4 analyses stakeholder engagement in four technology policy and regulatory areas: expanding internet access, data protection in the digital economy, free speech on social media, and digital identification. Section 12.5 concludes by outlining possibilities for more advanced citizen-centric policymaking that donors and institutions, among them the AU-EU D4D Hub, can support.

12.2 Nigeria's Policymaking and Stakeholder Engagement Processes

12.2.1 The Policymaking Process

Policymaking is the process through which state and non-state actors – that is, non-governmental and private stakeholders – influence the inception and development of policies, regulations, and bills addressing a specific problem. In Nigeria, state actors include the presidency, federal ministries and agencies, the judiciary, and the legislature (Popoola, 2016). Through executive orders, the president can develop and issue policies that federal ministries or agencies implement. The judiciary involves itself in the policymaking process via judicial reviews of existing policies, regulations, and laws. However, since the legislature and federal agencies are state actors who most frequently interact and consult with civil society stakeholders, this chapter focuses on the policymaking process carried out by these two institutions.

In Nigeria, publicly elected policymakers in the National Assembly, composed of the Senate and House of Representatives, possess the legal authority to design policies, regulations, and bills, whilst public officials at federal agencies are responsible for implementing adopted legislations (Popoola, 2016). Concerning the technology sector, public officials include those at the Federal Ministry of Communications and Digital Economy (FMoCDE), which contains the National Information Technology Development Agency (NITDA) and the Nigerian Communications Commission (NCC).

There are multiple mechanisms for legislators and federal agencies to consult with stakeholders during the policy formulation phase. The consultation process can involve a National Assembly committee developing a draft policy, regulation, or bill internally and inviting specific stakeholders to join working groups and provide comments (Philip, 2013). Stakeholders who do not receive such an invitation may submit written memoranda on the draft. Additionally, federal agencies such as NITDA have published processes for "ensuring stakeholder inclusiveness in the rule making process" (NITDA, 2017). This process outlines detailed steps on how to request public comments, provide stakeholders with notice, and includes a web portal for them to submit comments on draft-regulation for review.

A bill before the legislature must go through three readings. The first reading essentially tables the bill. The second reading is the first opportunity for a debate by members, after which the bill is approved to be considered by the relevant committee of the legislature. Consideration by the relevant committee will often involve a public hearing where stakeholders can attend and comment on the draft. A bill is passed only after it has been read a third time, following a debate. Government agencies will also often hold public hearings on topical policy issues. The NCC has hosted 17 such hearings between 2009 and 2020 (Public Inquiries). Since 2015, however, the attendance by stakeholder groups at these hearings has been low, with only one instance featuring a technology-focused CSO (Public Inquiries 1-5). Low attendance by stakeholder groups indicates that these groups themselves can improve participation in policymaking and might be a reflection of the general sense of powerlessness amongst citizens – a sentiment that has grown in the last decades (Aibieyi, 2014).

Finally, policymakers typically engage stakeholder groups after a first draft of a policy, regulation, or bill has been proposed. However, by not engaging stakeholders during the inception phase, the consultation process may not address specific problems stakeholders hope to resolve and further discourages participation. In addition, these mechanisms for engagement are not outlined in a national-level policymaking guide. Rather, each federal ministry or agency is responsible for its own engagement processes. Without national standardisation, stakeholder engagement for technology policymaking varies between respective ministries and agencies.

12.2.2 Stakeholders Involved in Policymaking

When stakeholder groups do engage with policymakers, they fall into three categories: industry associations, consumer groups, and technology-focused CSOs. The first two groups represent specific business interests as well as digital consumers. Technology-focused CSOs attempt to represent a broader public view. However, power asymmetries between stakeholders often preclude technology-focused CSOs' perspectives from having a substantial impact on the policymaking process.

The first stakeholder group, industry associations, encompasses actors like the Association of Telecommunications Companies of Nigeria (ATCON) and the Association of Licensed Telecoms Operators of Nigeria (ALTON). This stakeholder group represents Nigeria's large telecommunications companies. ATCON and ALTON work to advance the sector's growth and development. Whilst these industry associations do not typically engage directly with the Nigerian public, they work to influence policies that can indirectly affect citizens through areas such as expanded internet access or a more competitive digital economy. Since industry groups are major contributors to Nigeria's development and are critical to laying the foundation for national-level digital transformation, national policymakers often seek these stakeholders' input on relevant draft policies and regulations that will affect the telecommunications sector. Furthermore, industry associations benefit from significant financial support and organisational strength, which improves their ability to dedicate resources to influence the policymaking process.

The second stakeholder group that policymakers engage with are consumer groups such as the Association of Telephone, Cable, TV, and Internet Subscribers of Nigeria (ATCIS) and the National Association of Telecommunications Subscribers of Nigeria (NATCOM). These two consumer groups collaborate with National Assembly policymakers and other agencies such as the NCC to promote the interests of Nigeria's telecom subscribers. Consumer groups focus on ensuring that current digital consumers benefit from low prices and reliable access to telecommunications. They are less focused on representing the broader public interest and the needs of the unconnected, or potential future consumers. For example, ATCIS has called on the NCC to oppose mobile data price increases and ensure that current telecommunication subscribers have reliable internet services (ICT Monitor Worldwide, 2020). ATCIS's focus is on existing subscribers' concerns, not the issues unconnected individuals face. Furthermore, like industry associations, consumer groups are well resourced, which improves their ability to work alongside national policymakers during stakeholder engagement and secure a seat at the policymaking table.

The third stakeholder group responsible for representing the public interest in policymaking consultations are technology-focused CSOs such as the Paradigm Initiative and the Centre for Information and Technology and Development (CITAD). Nigeria's technology-focused CSOs promote and represent a diverse portfolio of the public's concerns regarding technology and advocate for digital rights. Unlike industry associations and consumer groups, technology-focused CSOs directly liaise with the broader public, including those who currently use technology and those who do not. Technology-focused CSOs engage with many Nigerians to better understand "on-the-ground" perspectives on national technology policy and regulations and provide the public with technical information about issues in technology. For example, in June 2021, the Paradigm Initiative and CITAD organised a stakeholder engagement session with the public to educate people about digital rights issues concerning the Nigerian government's digital identification programme (Njiaba, 2021).

Although technology-focused CSOs are important to stakeholder engagement in policymaking and represent the public's position on technology issues, they are new organisations and remain disadvantaged compared to the other two more established stakeholders. Technology-focused CSOs face financial constraints that the other two stakeholders do not. Their relationship with the government can often be antagonistic. They are expected to hold the government accountable, which is often uncomfortable for policymakers. Following the recent Twitter ban in Nigeria, for example, Paradigm Initiative along with 55 CSO co-signers published an open letter demanding the immediate reinstatement of the platform and accused the Federal government of digital human rights abuses (Communications, 2021). Public confrontations often lead to a situation in which the government and technology-focused CSOs struggle to find common ground, potentially hampering National Assembly working groups' ability to include those stakeholders as participants in the policymaking process. Lastly, although technology-focused CSOs are the public's direct line to the policymaking process, public awareness of such groups is limited. This is due to the general public's unfamiliarity with technology policy and regulation as well as a low level of public outreach by the CSOs themselves. As more Nigerians use digital technologies and services, their understanding of these issues may increase, a potential lever for more frequent public engagement.

All three stakeholder groups play an important role in assisting national policymakers in developing legislation for the technology sector. But they differ in the interests each group represents and the capabilities they have to carry out public engagement. Similarly, the degree to which ordinary Nigerians show interest in technology policy-related issues varies significantly. This discrepancy in the public interest can affect the levels of public engagement in the policymaking process. To demonstrate these dynamics and Nigeria's current levels of citizen and CSO engagement in digital policymaking, the next section examines four priority areas that have drawn attention from policymakers in recent years: expanding internet access and affordability, data protection in the digital economy, free speech on social media, and digital identification.

12.3 Assessing Citizen and CSO Engagement in National-Level Digital Policymaking

12.3.1 Expanding Internet Access and Affordability

Nigeria's national policymakers wish to provide reliable internet access and more affordable mobile internet through national policies. In 2020, 2G covered 89%, 3G covered 74%, and 4G covered 37% of the country, with significant usage disparities between the north and the south (Nigeria Federal Ministry of Communications and Digital Economy, 2020). Mobile data prices still need to fall 97% to reach the 2% of monthly net income standard the Alliance for Affordable Internet recommends (Adeleke, 2020). To prevent high prices and a lack of connectivity from worsening Nigeria's digital divide and to increase marginalisation, national policymakers launched the Nigerian National Broadband Plan (NNBP) 2020–2025 in March 2020. The NNBP provides a national policy for improving internet access and affordability through improved infrastructure and cost-sharing initiatives with the telecommunications sector.

In October 2020 and March 2021, the FMoCDE and Broadband Implementation Steering Committee (BISC) engaged in consultations with 29 publicly listed external stakeholders (ITedgenews, 2020) to collect input (Imah, 2021; Nigeria FMoCDE, 2020). However, of those 29, only 2 were technology-focused CSOs despite broadband access and affordability affecting the public and contributing to the digital divide (Nigeria FMoCDE, 2020). Rather, national policymakers engaged directly with industry association stakeholders such as ATCON to solicit ideas about how the telecommunications industry could help achieve the NNBP's objectives and expand broadband (Onwuaso, 2020). By not engaging with stakeholders equally, it becomes more likely that the NNBP fails to reflect a diversity of stakeholders' perspectives, particularly those with less influence. For example, although the NNBP makes mention of lowering mobile internet prices to 2% of net monthly income and advance last-mile connections to rural and underserved areas, there are no clear steps for how to achieve such outcomes. Had the consultative process involved more citizen–centric stakeholders, especially those who represent individuals living in last-mile areas, there might have been a more defined strategy on how to achieve these objectives.

Whilst the stakeholder consultation process did engage with stakeholder groups at varying levels, most consultations were conducted ex post. Once national policymakers had written the NNBP, the FMoCDE and BISC engaged with stakeholders. As a result, the consultation process did not intend to change the main policy points but rather to brief stakeholders, brainstorm ideas about meeting objectives, and build support for the NNBP. The limited engagement with technology-focused CSOs and ex post consultations meant that the poli-cymaking process left important gaps in terms of consumer inputs into the NNBP. Instead, policymakers wrote the policy and then consulted with indus-try associations to generate ideas for implementation and achieve shared goals. Although industry associations are committed to increasing broadband access and bring people online, the methods to obtain such a goal diverge between the public and business. Businesses focus on expanding mobile broadband net-works to bring more people online. Certain members of the public, however, prefer publicly available Wi-Fi hotspots, as they are more affordable. Without policymakers hearing citizens' concerns from the start, the NNBP does not go far enough in fully engaging a broad range of Nigerian citizens to resolve the digital divide.

12.3.2 Data Protection in the Digital Economy

Since Nigeria's 1999 Constitution, data protection has been a constitutionally protected right that guarantees citizens will not have their data or personal infor-mation collected by a third party without explicit consent (Stears Data, 2021). However, over the last several years, technology companies have found ways to use their digital platforms or services to track and collect digital data of individu-als without acquiring such consent. To address this problem and continue to defend data protection, the National Assembly passed a digital data protection regulation known as the Nigeria Data Protection Regulation (NDPR) in 2019 (OneTrust DataGuidance, 2020).

The policy development and stakeholder engagement process for NDPR highlights a long-standing policymaking trend in developing countries, adopting Western countries' regulations as their own. In developing the NDPR, national policymakers adopted many of the features of the EU's General Data Protection Regulation (GDPR), one of the most comprehensive data protection laws that provide EU citizens with control over their digital data and how businesses can access it. The GDPR and NDPR use the same definition for a data controller and processor; they identically categorise personal data, and apply the same regula-tions to their citizens at home or abroad (OneTrust Data Guidance, 2020).

Whilst the NDPR may have mirrored the GDPR in *substance*, Nigeria did not mirror the *process* that the European Commission (EC) followed to develop the GDPR. The EC undertook extensive stakeholder engagement processes when drafting the GDPR (EC. Expert Groups, 2021). The EC held consultations in a multi-stakeholder working group consisting of civil society, businesses, and industry associations to incorporate public comments about the GDPR (EC. Expert Groups, 2021). This working group still regularly meets to assist the EC in overcoming regulatory challenges and provides members with first-hand knowledge about the GDPR's implementation. (EC. Expert Group, 2021). The continuous stakeholder engagement process means the regulation maintains stakeholder inputs and can adapt more readily to changes.

Although the NDPR did not involve stakeholder engagement in the policy-making process, official supplementary policymakers at NITDA did host information sessions for stakeholders about becoming NDPR compliant (OneTrust DataGuidance, 2020). This process demonstrates opportunities for stakeholders to engage with national policymakers, but only once the data regulation was already in place. As such, this engagement process is an opportunity for stakeholders to learn more about a technical regulation and how to comply with it rather than influence processes for regulation development.

Since Nigerian stakeholders did not have many opportunities to comment or engage during the policy development process, NDPR received criticism from several stakeholders after its introduction (This Day, 2019). ALTON publicly expressed concerns about NITDA acting as the lead agency for implementing the data protection regulation rather than the primary telecommunications regulatory body, the NCC (ITedgenews, 2019). ALTON feared that too many agencies involved themselves in data regulation, resulting in over-regulation, which stifles innovation in the digital economy. Because the NDPR did not include a consultative process, ALTON raised its concerns through public memoranda (ITedgenews, 2019). Additionally, technology-focused CSOs such as the Paradigm Initiative criticised the NDPR's development process and its shortfalls (This Day, 2019). Paradigm critiqued the NDPR for not going far enough in data protection and publicly urged national policymakers and the president to pass the more comprehensive Data Protection Bill that has been stuck in the National Assembly since 2019 (Okeowo, 2021).

12.3.3 Free Speech on Social Media

Social media platforms are an effective tool for citizens to engage in public discourse and information sharing. Social media provides civic advocates a decentralised platform to freely express critical political views, even when governments attempt to restrict critical speech in other non-digital mediums. Although Nigeria guarantees freedom of speech, national policymakers have a history of limiting critical speech in print journalism under the guise of national security (Ewang, 2019b). To maintain this control, national policymakers have attempted to exert similar power on social media platforms.

The Protection from Internet Falsehood and Manipulation Bill 2019, also known as the 2019 Social Media Bill, prohibits statements on social media that are "likely to be prejudicial to national security" and "those which may diminish public confidence" in Nigeria's government (Ewang, 2019a). The 2019 Social Media Bill was national policymakers' second attempt to restrict online speech after introducing a similar, albeit unsuccessful, bill in 2015 (Ayeni, 2020). National policymakers wrote the 2019 Social Media Bill as a response to public protests and online anti-government organising, such as the #EndSARS hashtag, first used in 2017 by social organisers and then extensively during the movements second wave in 2020 (Ayeni, 2020).

The policymaking process and level of stakeholder engagement for the 2019 Social Media Bill were unique. Nigerian social media users were vocal about their dissatisfaction with the Social Media Bill and felt it did not correctly reflect citizens' views and perspectives. Therefore, technology-focused CSOs advocated for the public perspective in the policymaking process to stop the bill's development and passage in the National Assembly. The Paradigm Initiative played a prominent role by engaging the public and national policymakers through email campaigns, opinion publications, speeches, and hashtags (Administrative, 2019). Additionally, Paradigm ran a sophisticated social media strategy to educate the public about the bill's restrictions on their online freedoms. Ahead of public hearings by the Senate Committee on Judiciary, Human Rights, and Legal Matters, Paradigm identified and published specific clauses in the bill that would threaten fundamental rights (Administrative, 2019). CSOs' participation in the policymaking process and public opposition to the Social Media Bill led to the National Assembly indefinitely tabling the legislation (Onukwue, 2020).

Technology-focused CSOs' efforts in opposition to the 2019 Social Media Bill show that direct citizen engagement in policymaking is possible when the policy problem being addressed has significant implications on public life. Since the Social Media Bill would affect a digital platform and service with high everyday usage, the public dissatisfaction was amplified. Additionally, this instance showed that campaigning and advocacy were effective tools for raising awareness of a technology-related policy issue. CSOs were able to capitalise on their advocacy efforts and channelled the public's displeasure through the stakeholder engagement processes by attending multiple public hearings and writing official memorandums. As a result, the process was inclusive of many citizen voices and reflected diverse perspectives back to policymakers, leading to a technology policy that protected free speech on social media.

12.3.4 Digital Identification

The 2007 National Identity Management Commission (NIMC) Act requires all eligible Nigerians to register onto a digital database to receive a digital identity or National Identity Number. Digital identification programmes provide governments with accurate citizen-level data and grew in popularity across sub-Saharan Africa in recent years, with Kenya and Zimbabwe implementing similar programmes (Toesland, 2021). However, digital identification programmes can result in individuals being more easily monitored and suffering privacy violations through data breaches. Furthermore, registering the entire Nigerian population onto a digital identification platform requires a high degree of trust between the public and the government. Stakeholder engagement could help build that trust and ensure vulnerable groups can influence the project's design to reflect their concerns accurately.

For example, a common practice by the World Bank is to use its influence and require borrowers to engage in extensive stakeholder consultations, particularly with civil society, when undertaking a new programme. Since the World Bank is involved in Nigeria's digital identification programme through the Nigeria Digital Identification for Development (ID4D) project, there are clear World Bank–issued guidelines that require formal consultations with diverse stakeholders to ensure the program is inclusive and maintains stakeholder buy-in (Nigeria Digital Identification for Development Project, 2020). As such, in Nigeria, the legal and regulatory reform working groups were established to liaise between relevant government ministries, National Assembly committees, and stakeholders in the digital identification ecosystem, such as civil society (Nigeria Digital Identification for Development Project, 2020) (Njiaba, 2021). The working group's responsibility was to ensure their inclusion in the decision-making process and to ensure close consultations take place on sensitive matters including privacy and data protection (Nigeria Digital Identification for Development Project, 2020). Furthermore, this approach is self-reinforcing, as it provides the government with access to the public to dispel any rumours or misinformation surrounding digital identification. For example, during a stakeholder meeting held in June 2021, the government was able to interact with the public in a collaborative setting to clarify issues and solicit feedback on challenges (Njiaba, 2021). Technology-focused CSOs are also involved in this working group, with Paradigm Initiative and CITAD leading a coalition of smaller civil society actors that participate in the public dialogue regarding digital identification. The coalition pools resources' which improve the organisational capacity for smaller CSOs. One successful engagement the coalition led in the policy development process was the request that the NIMC adheres to the Abuja Federal High Court's 2019 ruling about the National Assembly passing regulatory safeguards before moving forward with the digital ID programme (Anderson, 2020). The coalition led by Paradigm and CITAD engaged with various grassroots organisations, social media activists, and other branches of civil society to draw attention to these issues and held a virtual webinar on how to do so (Anderson, 2020). By building a like-minded coalition, technology-focused CSOs raised the public's awareness about the risks associated with digital identification and channelled those concerns back to the working group.

The policymaking process for Nigeria's digital identification system highlights how there are ways for the public, civil society, and the government to work together and collaborate on technology policy. When outside pressure – for example from donors – supports the establishment of an inclusive multi-stakeholder working group, it can result in greater civil society participation that allows for a better representation of the public perspective.

12.4 Considerations for Advancement in Stakeholder-driven Policymaking

This chapter has argued that the benefits from stakeholder engagement, particularly with the public, are essential to design policies and regulations for the technology sector that effectively address technology's problems. As demonstrated in the development process for policies on internet expansion and data protection, civil society are often unable to adequately influence the process and provide the public viewpoint, leading to suboptimal outcomes. While there are some mechanisms for civil society engagement, which were utilised in reforms related to the 2019 Social Media Bill and digital identification system, there is room for more concerted efforts to increase citizen and stakeholder engagement, including micro, small, and medium enterprises who are not typically represented by industry associations. Section 12.5 proposes ways for regional, international, and multilateral institutions, to assist African countries in citizen-centric policymaking.

12.4.1 Support for Civil Society Organisations

In Nigeria, policymakers do engage with stakeholders during the policy development process. Yet, the uneven playing field amongst these groups tends to crowd the less powerful stakeholders out of the process. Whilst technology-focused CSOs already participate and achieve some results in policymaking, more consistent donor support could help them to enhance those efforts and overcome power asymmetries. The EU's long history of supporting civil society and stakeholder-led policymaking positions, as shown in the GDPR's policy development process, positions the institution well to support African CSOs through technical assistance on this topic. In addition, EU projects can support technology-focused CSOs through grants or capacity-building workshops to increase their organisational skills and ability to interact with national policymakers. By supporting technology-focused CSOs' efforts in evidence collection and original research on technology policy, these organisations can present policymakers with evidence-based comments during the consultation process, improving credibility with national policymakers. If sufficiently funded, technology-focused CSOs and general civil society can host more information sessions with the public to increase awareness about technology, digital rights, and the policymaking process itself. CSOs can also distribute short publications, online or through non-digital mediums, to highlight technology issues and explain involvement in policymaking – thus, potentially improving the public's desire to participate in hearings and overcome political apathy.

The EU–AU Digital for Development (D4D) Hub is an existing EU-supported initiative that is well placed to support technology-focused CSOs, general civil society, and private sector actors to engage in the technology policymaking process. The EU–AU D4D Hub's guiding principles include promoting sustainable digital transformations through multi-stakeholder involvement and placing citizens at the centre of the digital transformation (D4D Launch, 2021). It therefore consults with civil society but also with other relevant actors such as industry representatives, interested EU member states, international organisations, and institutional representatives from partner countries. Hosting regional workshops for technology-focused CSOs and cross-cutting CSOs can improve African countries' outcomes in citizen-centric technology policy development. Regional workshops also provide an opportunity for leaders at various CSOs to share how they address engaging with policymakers regarding technology policy. Such regional workshops are already planned as part of the Hub's activities; for example in March 2022, the EU–AU D4D Hub held the first "Africa-Europe D4D Hub Multi-Stakeholder Forum" and brought together the private sector, governments, academia, and civil society to build an inclusive digital society (D4D Hub, 2022).

12.4.2 Support for National Policymakers

National policymakers are vocal about their desire to include citizens and other stakeholder groups in policymaking. However, persuading citizens to participate in policymaking is a challenge, and therefore advancing national policymakers' knowledge on how to engage citizens in policymaking can be beneficial. The EU–AU D4D Hub can leverage the EU's comparative advantage in technology policy, especially data protection, and train national policymakers on citizen engagement. Trainings can demonstrate how the EU undertakes a multi-stakeholder approach, and it may share lessons about how such a process can be replicated in the African context. By learning from the EU's development process for technology policy, African national policymakers can better understand how to design ex ante stakeholder engagement, as well as the ongoing benefits associated with continuous stakeholder engagement via expert groups.

Trainings for national policymakers on best practices for stakeholder engagement can also lead to better outcomes in policy areas besides technology. By improving stakeholder-led governance, policymakers can develop better relationships with the public, which could help decrease apathy amongst the public.

12.4.3 National Stakeholder Engagement
Processes and Guidelines

Many of Nigeria's federal agencies already have published guidelines on the rule-making process and on how to engage with stakeholders. Whilst agencies do follow these guidelines and host public consultation, attendance by stakeholders, particularly citizen-centric stakeholders, is low. Often, Nigeria's federal agencies have different engagement methods and ways to publicise information regarding draft rules or hearings, leading to information overload and public confusion. For example, there is no clear mechanism for submitting public comments on the NCC website, whilst the NITDA website has a prominent portal for public comment submission.

In contrast, other African countries such as Uganda have developed universal stakeholder engagement manuals that all agencies follow (Uganda: Regulatory Reform, 2013). The Uganda policy clearly outlines when, how, and why policymakers must engage in stakeholder-led policymaking, which results in all agencies following standard practice. This standardised process can potentially increase stakeholder participation and reduce confusion across different Nigerian agencies that engage in technology policymaking.

12.4.4 Outside Actors' Leveraging Influence

The influence that international and multilateral actors have in requiring donor-funded projects to include multi-stakeholder initiatives is not uncommon, as demonstrated by the World Bank's decision to include a diverse working group in designing Nigeria's digital identification project. International and multilateral actors can influence a country's approach to multi-stakeholder engagement, especially by requiring that donor-funded projects include these kinds of processes. The incentive for financial support will encourage national policymakers to take seriously multi-stakeholder-led policymaking. However, such behaviour does risk producing a situation where stakeholder engagement simply becomes a box to check.

12.5 Conclusion

Technology's rapid rise on the African continent presents multiple problems and risks that national policymakers must address to achieve successful and inclusive digital transformations. The creation process for policies, regulations, and bills to protect against these risks lead to successful outcomes when all stakeholders – especially citizens and their representatives – are consulted in the policymaking process. By including the public's input through civil society actors, policymakers can gain a better sense of long-term issues related to technology, not only those issues that are important to more established stakeholders and their business interests. However, as the case study on Nigeria shows, stakeholder-led policymaking requires intentional reforms and support to reduce power asymmetries between stakeholder groups, create national-level stakeholder guidelines, encourage the public to participate in policymaking, and expand policymakers' resources to learn both from each other and from global best practices. International institutions, including the EU–AU Digital for Development Hub, can support these reforms through trainings that promote citizen engagement in policymaking and capacity development for civil society. These steps will provide a critical foundation for policies that increase citizens' trust in digital platforms and meet the policy demands that fast-changing digital technologies will continue to create in the future.

Acknowledgements

We thank Seun Adesina, Flora Hamilton, Monica Peiro, Alex Sekhniashvili, and Miriam Stankovich for their contributions to this research, as well as the various technical experts and representatives of local organisations who took the time to speak with us.

References

Abimbola, O., Aggad, F. and Ndzendze, B. (2021) 'What is Africa's digital agenda?', Berlin: Africa Policy Research Institute. Available at: https://afripoli.org/what-is-africas-digital-agenda (Accessed: 30 March 2022).

Adeleke, R. (2020) 'Digital divide in Nigeria: the role of regional differentials', *Africa Journal of Science, Technology, Innovation and Development*, 13(3), pp. 333–346. https://doi.org/10.1080/20421338.2020.1748335

Administrative (2019) 'Say no to the protection from the internet falsehood and manipulation bill, 2019', *Paradigm Initiative*, November. Available at: https://paradigmhq.org/say-no-to-the-protection-from-internet-falsehood-and-manipulation-bill-2019-sb-132/ (Accessed: 30 March 2022).

Aibieyi, S. and Obamwonyi, S. (2014) 'Public policy failures in Nigeria: pathway to underdevelopment', *Public Policy and Administration Research*, 4(9). Available at: https://citeseerx.ist.psu.edu/viewdoc/download?doi=10.1.1.838.3099&rep=rep1&type=pdf (Accessed: 30 March 2022).

Anderson, T. and Odhiambo, F. (2020) 'Partner spotlight: paradigm initiative's vision for ensuring good id and data protection in Nigeria', *Omidyar Network*, October. Available at: https://omidyar.com/partner-spotlight-paradigm-initiatives-vision-for-ensuring-good-id-and-data-protection-in-nigeria/ (Accessed: 30 March 2022).

Ayeni, T. (2020) 'Nigeria #EndSARS: Why social media bill threatens death penalty "for hate speech"', *The Africa Report*, November. Available at: https://www.theafricareport.com/51915/nigeria-social-media-bill-threatens-death-penalty-for-hate-speech/ (Accessed 30 March 2022).

Communications (2021) *Call on the Nigerian Government to Rescind Its Indefinite Suspension of Twitter's Operations in Nigeria. Paradigm Initiative*. Available at: https://paradigmhq.org/call-on-the-nigerian-government-to-rescind-its-indefinite-suspension-of-twitters-operations-in-nigeria/ (Accessed 30 March 2022).

Data & Digital Rights in Nigeria: Assessing the Activities, Issues and Opportunities (2021) *Stears data*. Available at: https://luminategroup.com/posts/report/data-digital-rights-in-nigeria-assessing-the-activities-issues-and-opportunities (Accessed 30 March 2022).

D4D Hub EU International Partnerships Digital for Development Hub (2021) *D4D Launch*. Available at: https://d4dlaunch.eu/ (Accessed 30 March 2022).

European Commission Expert Groups. (2021) *Multistakeholder Expert Group to Support the Application of Regulation (EU) 2016/679 (E03537)* [online]. Brussels. [Viewed 19 May 2022]. Available from: https://ec.europa.eu/transparency/expert-groups-register/screen/expert-groups/consult?do=groupDetail.groupDetail&groupID=3537

Ewang, A. (2019a) 'Nigerians should say no to social media bill', *Human Rights Watch*, 26 November. Available at: https://www.hrw.org/news/2019/11/26/nigerians-should-say-no-social-media-bill (Accessed 30 March 2022).

Ewang, A. (2019b) 'Nigeria's wavering commitment to freedom of expression broad claims of national security threaten rights', *Human Rights Watch*, 28 June. Available at: https://www.hrw.org/news/2019/06/28/nigerias-wavering-commitment-freedom-expression#

Hutahaean, M. (2016) 'The importance of stakeholders approach in public policy making', *Advances in Social Science, Education and Humanities Research*, 84. Available at: http://creativecommons.org/licenses/by-nc/4.0/ (Accessed 30 March 2022).

ICT Monitor Worldwide (2020) *ATCIS Seeks Improved Service Delivery for Telecom Subscribers*, 12 March. Available at: http://proxy.library.jhu.edu/login?url=https://www.proquest.com/wire-feeds/atcis-seeks-improved-service-delivery-telecom/docview/2376113024/se-2?accountid=11752 (Accessed 30 March 2022).

Imah, R. (2021) 'Nnamani, ATCON President highlights role of broadband in the development of a solid digital economy', *digitaltimesng*, 26 March. Available at: https://digitaltimesng.com/nnamani-atcon-president-highlights-role-of-broadband-in-the-development-of-a-solid-digital-economy/ (Accessed 30 March 2022).

ITEdgeNews (2019) *NITDA Tackles ALTON, Assures Stakeholders on Cooperation Among Sector Regulators*, 14 August. Available at: https://itedgenews.ng/2019/08/14/nitda-tackles-alton-assures-stakeholders-on-cooperation-among-sector-regulators/ (Accessed 30 March 2022).

ITEdgeNews (2020) *Telecom Regulator Harps on 'Stakeholder Engagements' as Key to Broadband Implementation*, 5 November. Available at: https://itedgenews.ng/2020/11/05/telecom-regulator-harps-on-stakeholder-engagements-as-key-to-broadband-implementation/ (Accessed 30 March 2022).

Nigeria Digital Identification for Development Project (2020). *Project Appraisal Document on a Proposed Credit pad3089*. Federal Republic of Nigeria: The World Bank. Available at: https://documents1.worldbank.org/curated/en/250181582340455479/pdf/Nigeria-Digital-Identification-for-Development-Project.pdf (Accessed 30 March 2022).

Nigerian Federal Ministry of Communications and Digital Economy (2020) *The Nigerian National Broadband Plan 2020 –2025* [online] Available from: https://www.ncc.gov.ng/documents/880-nigerian-national-broadband-plan-2020-2025/file (Accessed 30 March 2022).

Njiaba, V. (2021) 'Paradigm Initiative and CITAD Lead Stakeholder Engagement on Digital Identity', *Paradigm Initiative*, 7 June. Available at: https://paradigmhq.org/paradigm-initiative-and-citad-lead-a-stakeholder-engagement-on-digital-identity/

OECD (2017) 'Citizen participation in policy making', in *Government at a Glance 2017*. Paris: OECD Publishing. Available at: https://doi.org/10.1787/gov_glance-2017-67-en (Accessed 30 March 2022).

Okeowo, Y. (2021) 'Stakeholders seek passage of Data Protection Bill to strengthen NDPR', *TechEconomy.ng*, 18 June. Available at: https://techeconomy.ng/2021/06/stakeholders-seek-passage-of-data-protection-bill-to-strengthen-ndpr/

OneTrust DataGuidance (2020) *Key Takeaways: Comparing the NDPR and the GDPR*. Available at: https://www.dataguidance.com/opinion/key-takeaways-comparing-ndpr-and-gdpr (Accessed 30 March 2022).

Onukwue, A. (2020) 'Nigeria's social media bill suffers its biggest defeat yet', *Techcabal*, 9 March. Available at: https://techcabal.com/2020/03/09/social-media-bill-public-hearing/ (Accessed 30 March 2022).

Onwuaso, U. (2020) 'Pantami rallies stakeholders on broadband implementation', *Nigeria Communications Week*, 21 October. Available at: https://www.nigeriacommunicationsweek.com.ng/pantami-engages-stakeholders-on-broadband-implementation/ (Accessed 30 March 2022).

Philip, D. D. (2013) 'Public policy making and implementation in Nigeria: Connecting the Nexus', *Public Policy and Administration Research*, 3(6), pp. 56–64. Available at:

http://citeseerx.ist.psu.edu/viewdoc/download?doi=10.1.1.865.7254&rep=rep1 &type=pdf (Accessed 30 March 2022).

Popoola, O. (2016) 'Actors in decision making and policy process', *Global Institute for Research & Education*, 5(1), pp. 47–51. Available at: https://www.longdom.org/articles/ actors-in-decision-making-and-policy-process.pdf (Accessed 30 March 2022).

Public Inquiries (n.d.) *NCC Nigeria Communications Commission*. Available at: https://ncc .gov.ng/licensing-regulation/legal/public-inquiries (Accessed 30 March 2022).

The Republic of Uganda- A guide to policy development & management in Uganda (2013). Uganda: Regulatory Reform. Available at: http://regulatoryreform.com/wp -content/uploads/2016/09/Uganda-Revised-Guide-to-Policy-Development-Mgt -2013.pdf (Accessed 30 March 2022).

The Rule Making Process Regulation of NITDA (2017). *National Information Technology Development Agency (NITDA)*. Available at: https://rmp.nitda.gov.ng/download/The %20Rule%20Making%20Process%20Regulation%20of%20NITDA.pdf   (Accessed 30 March 2022).

The World Bank (2019) 'Nigeria's first digital economy diagnostic reveals a vibrant entrepreneurial ecosystem but rural areas are still without internet Access', 28 November. Available at: https://www.worldbank.org/en/news/press-release/2019 /11/28/nigerias-first-digital-economy-diagnostic-reveals-a-vibrant-entrepreneurial -ecosystem-but-rural-areas-are-still-without-internet-access (Accessed 30 March 2022).

This Day (2019) 'Divergent views trail NITDA's data protection regulation', August. Available   at: http://proxy.library.jhu.edu/login?url=https://www.proquest.com/ newspapers/divergent-views-trail-nitda-s-data-protection/docview/2277188183/se -2?accountid=11752 (Accessed 30 March 2022).

Toesland, F. (2021) 'African countries embracing biometrics, digital IDs', *Africa Renewal*, February. Available at: https://www.un.org/africarenewal/magazine/february-2021/ african-countries-embracing-biometrics-digital-ids (Accessed 30 March 2022).

13

DIGITAL SKILLS IN AFRICA

Prospects for AU–EU Collaboration

Sajitha Bashir and Chux Daniels

13.1 Introduction

The current global political climate seems the most appropriate to foster coop-eration between the European Union (EU) and the African Union (AU) with regard to digital skills. The EU's Comprehensive Strategy with Africa adopted in 2020[1] prioritises digital skills in three of the five thematic areas: the partner-ship for digital transformation, in which digital skills are emphasised as one of the four core priorities; the partnership for sustainable growth and jobs, and the partnership for migration and mobility. In particular, the partnership for digital transformation proposes several policy recommendations and actions that seek to mainstream digital skills, promote digital and transversal skills[2] in education cur-ricula, and facilitate digital skills development across all sectors (AU–EU Digital Economy Task Force, 2020). Similarly, the AU–EU task force recommendations, which broadly correspond with those in the Digital Transformation Strategy of the AU, privilege "digital skills and human capacity" as one of the five founda-tional pillars (African Union, 2020).

Besides the AU and EU, other global actors like the OECD and the World Bank have proposed new approaches to digital skills with implications for Africa's economic development and transformation (IMF, 2018; Bashir and Miyamoto, 2020; AUC/OECD, 2021; OECD, 2021; IFC, 2021; Bashir et al., 2021).[3] While the OECD focuses more on digital skills for employment and jobs, the World Bank's perspective adopts a broader approach that includes education and lit-eracy. The World Bank's Digital Economy for Africa initiative includes digital skills as one of the five foundational pillars, which are broadly similar to, but not identical with, those of the AU strategy. Addressing the digital divide is also cen-tral to realising Africa's Agenda 2063 and realising the Sustainable Development Goals (SDGs) both in Africa and globally (Mare, 2021). Other organisations,

DOI: 10.4324/9781003274322-13

such as the United Nations Broadband Commission, also identify digital skills as one of the enablers to overcome the digital divide in developing countries, including countries in Africa. According to a large-scale consumer survey conducted by the Global System for Mobile Communication Association (GSMA), the lack of digital literacy and skills is one of the greatest obstacles to increasing mobile internet usage in Africa (GSMA, 2019).

The conclusions, policies, and strategies from the above institutions suggest an apparent consensus that the lack of digital skills poses serious obstacles to the digitalisation of African economies and societies. This constraint impedes not only the use of digital technologies and tools in the production and consumption of goods and services, but also the creation of new types of jobs in the digital economy. The apparent consensus would also lead to the conclusion that digital skills could be an arena for cooperation not only between the EU and Africa (Daniels et al, 2020), but also with other actors such as the World Bank. However, despite statements of declarative intent, policies, frameworks, and strategies, we argue in the remainder of this chapter that the appropriate conditions do not yet exist for meaningful cooperation in the area of digital skills.

13.2 Barriers to Cooperation in Digital Skills

Digital skills are fundamental to the digital transformation of societies. They are crucial to the appropriation of digital technologies; even when physical and material access to these technologies increases, lack of digital skills determines the extent and type of usage of digital media (van Dijk and van Deursen, 2014). Nevertheless, lack of conceptual clarity about the precise meaning of "digital skills" undermines the validity and feasibility of the various recommendations and actions suggested to remedy the current situation in Africa.

13.2.1 Conceptualisation of Digital Skills: Current Discourse

Conceptual ambiguities around digital skills permeate recent high-profile policy reports of the EU and AU, two of which we highlight as examples. The first is the report of the Digital Economy Task Force (DETF), set up by the EU and AU, which proposes three "layers" of digital skills, each spanning a spectrum from basic to advanced: "digital skills for all"; "21st century skills in education" and "skills for ICT professionals, digital entrepreneurs and public institutions". The second is the AU's Digital Transformation Strategy (DTS) (AU, 2020). The strategy highlights two sets of skills, taken from the *Pathways to Prosperity Commission* report (Pathways for Prosperity Commission, 2019). The first set, "digital skills", comprises advanced digital skills and engineering knowledge, as well as "digital literacy" for general workforce. The second set, "digital complementary skills", appears to be a list of many skills, including socio-emotional skills, communication, language, creativity and adaptability; somewhat akin to the "21st century skills" referenced by the AU–EU DETF.

This lack of conceptual clarity, as explained in the preceding paragraph, is not unique to the examples and reports discussed above. A recent report by the International Telecommunication Unit (ITU) on Digital Skills includes "algorithmic literacy", three levels of digital skills (relating to the use and creation of digital tools), and "human-based computation skills", involving the combination of machine computing with human thought (ITU, 2020).

The different approaches and frameworks illustrated above reflect the problems relating to defining a new set of skills that, just a few years ago, were not recognised as core competences of the workforce or an essential part of literacy for the population. Understandably, concepts regarding digital skills have evolved with the increasing penetration of digital technologies and digital information in the economy and society, the variety of digital devices and the development of the internet. Martin and Gudziecki (2006) traced the evolution of the conceptions of computer or ICT literacy, information literacy, media literacy, and communication literacy, among other literacies in the "pre-digital" era, which have influenced the emergence of concepts relating to digital literacy and skills. Over the years, the conception of digital skills has evolved from "ICT skills", which focused on technical competences related to the use of computers and software application, to include multiple literacies as well as reflective competences. The use of ICT for creative purposes has also been increasingly stressed. In this regard, Ito et al. (2008) contend that children's participation in society does not only require the ability to access "serious" online information and culture, but also the ability to creatively participate in recreational and social activities online. Reflecting this trend, a recent review compares 13 digital literacy frameworks, drawn mainly from Europe across five areas: operational and technical; information and cognition; digital communication; digital content creation; and strategic (Iordache et al., 2017).

Meanwhile, technical competences themselves have been widened to encompass a variety of devices, software, applications, and, more generally, the use of digitally available information. The emergence of new general-purpose data-driven technologies and Artificial Intelligence (AI) that are finding applications in multiple sectors has raised the demand for both user (general consumer/workers) and developer skills in these areas. Finally, threats to safety and privacy caused by the interconnectedness of infrastructure, devices, and data flows require a basic level of citizen and workforce competences that need to be incorporated into a definition of digital skills.

A further distinction arises between the digital literacy competences for the general population (as citizens in a digital society) or workforce and the specialist competences for ICT professionals and technicians. The latter are normally developed through formal education and training programmes at the post-secondary level (in technical-vocational institutions or engineering programmes).

Conceptual clarity about the types and definitions of digital skills would help to identify practical areas of collaboration between the EU and Africa in developing these skills. Recent work by the EU and the World Bank provides a roadmap for African countries to adopt a meaningful framework on which to develop digital skills programmes. The EU's Digital Competence Framework for Citizens (DigComp)[4] is a milestone in the development of a general digital literacy competences framework targeted to citizens, building on the earlier DigEULit project and careful review of several frameworks. It focuses on five domains, twenty-one competences, and four levels of proficiency (ranging from foundational to highly specialised). Several versions of DigComp have been updated, with the latest revision, DigComp 2.2, starting in January 2021 and possibly ending in early 2022. As of 2020, the DigComp framework was being used in 16 EU countries, guiding the development of curricula in education and training, student assessment and by employers to assess the competences of students. Additionally, the framework provides "the conceptual basis for the calculation of the digital skills part of the European Digital Economy and Society Index",[5] which tracks the evolution of EU member states in digital competitiveness (European Commission, 2020a, b). The DigComp framework was subsequently adapted by UNESCO as the Digital Literacy Global Framework (DLGF), incorporating two additional domains that were considered relevant for developing countries (UNESCO, 2018).

The World Bank, through its work on the Digital Economy, has further developed this framework to distinguish explicitly between digital skills for digitally literate citizens (to access services and participate in a digital society) and digital skills for the workforce. The latter are broken up further into digital skills for the ICT and ICT-enabled sectors, and the general workforce in all sectors (Bashir et al., 2021; World Bank, 2021). For digital literacy and digital skills for the general workforce, the World Bank adopts the UNESCO/DigComp 2.1 framework, while for the workforce in the ICT sectors, it recommends adopting specialised frameworks for engineers and technicians, such as the EU e-competence framework as a benchmark. In most countries, however, there are specific national frameworks for engineering- and technician-level programmes; the EU e-competence framework, with the required adaptations to local contexts, can be used to benchmark these programmes.[6]

Another line of evolution has been the development of digital skills frameworks for specific occupations within the general workforce (that is, excluding the information technology sector). With respect to the EU DigComp framework, two groups of occupations have attracted the most attention due to their importance for the digital economy and for digital society: civil servants and teachers. For example, Spain has launched a training programme targeting public employees. The programme's content and assessment are aligned with the DigComp competences and proficiency levels. Relatedly, the EU has developed DigCompEdu, a digital skills framework specifically designed for the teaching profession, which informs the professional training and continuous upgrading of teachers (Redecker, 2017). These frameworks have in turn been adapted by other countries in the EU.

13.2.2 The Digital Skills Ecosystem

The rapid evolution of concepts and definitions highlights two other aspects which differentiate digital skills from other types of skills or competences. The first is that digital skills cannot be acquired without access to digital technologies, considered in a broad sense. Relatedly, it is vital that relevant concepts and frameworks are regularly updated as technologies evolve. The second is that digital skills are closely intertwined with other key skills, without which meaningful digital skills cannot be acquired. These aspects have important policy and programmatic implications in the African context.

The acquisition of digital competences requires access to devices, applications, digital content, and a certain level of connectivity. In advanced economies, this broader ecosystem has developed rapidly, making the instruments for acquiring digital competences accessible to the majority of the population, even if there are still significant inequalities between population groups in levels of access. This is especially true in educational institutions, thereby ensuring that the younger generation and new entrants into the labour market have the foundational digital skills required of all citizens. However, this is not the case in Africa, especially sub-Saharan Africa, where the most common device may be a simple mobile phone with low speed and unreliable connectivity, and limited access to the internet. Acquiring anything but the most rudimentary digital skills in such a context is challenging.

Many primary and secondary schools have no computers and limited or no connectivity. Teachers often lack basic digital skills and tools while local digital content is not readily available in most countries (Owusu-Ansah et al., 2018; Quaicoe and Pata, 2020). The programmatic implication is that the development of the digital skills ecosystem and digital skills programmes in the African context requires urgent attention. As an example, whether Massive Open Online Courses (MOOCs) can be used to impart digital skills to 300 million Africans by 2025 – an objective of the AU Digital Transformation Strategy – depends not only on the availability of the course content, but also on access to devices and affordable internet.

A practical challenge arising from the close link between digital technologies and digital skills is that digital skills frameworks will need to be regularly updated in order to retain their practical relevance for education and training providers. The slow response time of education and training systems in Africa to changes in industry practices, with respect to digital skills, has been a long-standing problem, which is likely to be aggravated by the digital transformations underway. Addressing this challenge requires capacity building in relevant ministries and regulatory agencies, but also more nimble processes for approving education and training programmes.

13.2.3 Digital Skills Competences

Digital skills are related to other core skills. And the fact that related core skills are not adequately imparted in the education and training systems in Africa also poses a challenge. The World Development Report (World Bank, 2019) distinguishes between three types of skills – cognitive skills, socio-emotional skills and technical skills – which are interrelated and reinforce each other (especially cognitive and socio-emotional skills). Digital skills are related to these types of skills, and indeed depend on certain cognitive skills such as foundational literacy and numeracy, as well as socio-emotional skills. In the African context, where children and young people sometimes lack foundational literacy and numeracy even after completing primary education, and a large section of youth are outside the formal education system, digital skills cannot be imparted on their own (IFC, 2019, 2020, 2021). In European countries, on the other hand, a young person or working adults who have not acquired "digital skills" in school can be taught these skills through short-term programmes.[7]

It follows that foundational digital skills programmes for young people in Africa, delivered outside school, would need to include foundational literacy, numeracy and socio-emotional skills. In such context, digital skills programmes delivered within schools will be successful only to the extent that foundational skills are also strengthened. The programmatic implications are that imparting digital skills within schools requires careful integration with upgrading of curricula and teaching within schools and training institutions. Meanwhile, delivering digital skills to young people outside the school system requires innovating the content of the programme and the delivery models involving the private sector.

13.3 The State of Digital Literacy Programmes in Africa

Digital skills programmes can be delivered through formal education and training systems, as an integral part of the curriculum, and through informal means outside the education system, through short-duration courses. This section presents data on the current status of both types of programmes, which should form the basis of future EU–Africa collaboration. The review focuses on sub-Saharan Africa (SSA).

As discussed in the previous section, the delivery of digital skills programmes requires an ecosystem. The lack of basic infrastructure, connectivity, devices, and trained staff limits the delivery of meaningful programmes (Bashir et al., 2021; Daniels et al., 2021; Dosso et al., 2021). However, paucity of precise data on these parameters for most African countries, especially in primary education, continues to pose a major challenge both in deepening understanding of the issues and in designing and implementing appropriate policy and programme interventions. As a result, school education systems provide limited training in digital skills, even at the secondary level (Quaicoe and Pata, 2020). Most primary and secondary school leavers will have no formal training even in foundational digital skills. Extensive levels of investment are thus required to enable even basic levels of internet connectivity and digital devices in school education.

Even South Africa, which has a relatively well-developed school infrastructure and high level of internet penetration, has struggled with providing broadband to schools. South Africa's official policy for providing broadband access in the country, known as South Africa Connect, published in 2013,[8] set a target of having all schools connected at 10 Mbps and 80% at 100 Mbps by 2020. In 2018, less than 20% of schools had connectivity for teaching and learning (University of Chicago Law School, 2020). Even those which had some level of connectivity often lacked the required high-speed and reliable connection and an adequate number of devices; the latter was often due to the lack of secure building infrastructure. The roll-out of the policy was hampered by difficulties in procurement, delays in decisions regarding the technology, and lack of technical expertise at the school level. Further, the adoption of ICT in education does not depend on infrastructure alone. Other factors such as governance models, the capabilities and skills of teachers and learners, the e-culture in place in the relevant institutions, and the levels of implementation matter (Ramoroka, 2021).

There is limited publicly available information on digital skills programmes in Africa outside the education system. The World Bank's Digital Economy country diagnostic reports completed between 2019 and 2021, each of which has a chapter on digital skills, have been the most comprehensive survey to date of the supply of digital skills programmes (World Bank, 2020). These reports provide information on digital skills programmes being inside and outside the formal education system by private providers and NGOs (World Bank, 2020).[9] Although somewhat uneven in their coverage, mainly due to the lack of the availability of systematic data, these studies highlight important findings. The reports confirm that digital skills programmes within school education are limited, for the same reasons cited above.

Outside the formal education system, there are several digital skills programmes delivered by private providers, but they operate on a small scale and are limited in their coverage. The World Bank reports (World Bank, 2019; 2020) provide information on digital skills programmes from 21 countries, and are currently the most exhaustive survey of privately provided digital skills programmes. Analysis of the programmes undertaken for this study shows that just 37 programmes could be identified in the assessed countries; no programmes were identified in three countries. Most of these programmes are linked to entrepreneurship programmes or other projects. The programmes offered by the private sector are often not clearly related to any digital skills competency framework, making it hard to assess what level of digital skills is provided. Additionally, there is no information about the quality, effectiveness, or costs of these programmes. There is no systematic assessment of digital skills. The most common form of assessment is the International Computer Driving License (ICDL). While this is available in a few countries, it has several limitations since the assessment is at a computer centre and tests skills related to use of desktops/laptops.

A recent GSMA report, which researched digital skills needs, indicated that Ghana has a large number of informal training programmes, often linked to entrepreneurship initiatives. However, in line with the World Bank assessments discussed above, the report found that the programmes are concentrated in a few large urban centres, have relatively small coverage (of several hundred people), focus on intermediate to advanced level digital skills, and use a classroom and computer-based delivery mode (GSMA, 2021).

There are several national and regional initiatives led by large technology companies, such as Google's Digital Skills for Africa programme.[10] Despite its name, the programme focuses on a narrow range of foundational-level digital marketing competences and is delivered online. The lack of publicly available information on the coverage, effectiveness, and impact of such programmes and others implemented by smaller, local organisations renders it difficult to develop evidence-based public policy to scale up approaches that have been successful.

In SSA, there are no specific large-scale initiatives to build the digital competences of important occupation groups identified earlier, such as teachers and civil servants. Training of teachers is impeded by the same factors as that of students: the lack of a functioning digital ecosystem in education. The training of civil servants is an important precondition for building digital leadership capabilities in organisations (or institutional) levels, which are essential to bring about the broader digital transformation agenda of the government (Daniels, 2015; AU, 2020; Daniels et al, 2021). The lack of systematic digital skills training of civil servants and staff in the ministries, agencies, and relevant bodies concerned with education and skills training is of special concern, as it impedes the design, management, and implementation of policies, regulations, programmes, and projects related to digital skills training of the population and workforce.

The gaps in the digital skills capabilities of civil servants and government staff in ministries and agencies are reflected in the absence of national digital transformation policies in many SSA countries, and specifically policies related to digital skills. Many SSA countries still have to either formulate their digital strategies or articulate a framework for digital literacy and skills into their policies. In general, education sector policies follow the traditional approach of providing "ICT in education" – that is, the use of technology in education, rather than a focus on key digital skills that young people should acquire for current and future jobs (Blignaut et al., 2010). A few countries have emphasised the role of digital skills in their digital transformation strategies, among them Ethiopia, Kenya, and Nigeria.[11] Even so, these strategies do not clarify the types of digital skills to be developed. For instance, Kenya's "Digital Economy Blueprint" states that the focus area of the digital skills pillar is "to develop the digital skills training framework from primary to university" but lists the objective "to increase the number of graduates having been trained in Advanced Digital skills" (GoK, 2019, p. 62). These include areas such as AI, machine learning, robotics, the Internet of Things, and so on. The skills to be developed for school children, out-of-school youth, the workforce, and citizens as a whole are not mentioned.

13.4 The Demand for Digital Skills in Sub-Saharan Africa: A Potential Enabler to Drive EU–Africa Collaboration

A strong market demand could influence private training providers and African governments (in their capacity as policymakers as well as providers of public education and training) to adjust and upgrade their digital skills programmes. Indirectly, this also generates an interest for greater cooperation with external actors. As digitisation spreads across sectors, the demand for digital skills is likely to increase due to two factors: (1) an increase in the total number of jobs requiring diverse levels of digital skills and (2) a shift to jobs requiring digital skills, combined with a reduction in jobs not requiring these skills. A recent study of the arrival of fast internet in 12 SSA countries, between 2006 and 2014, finds that employment increased, primarily in higher-skilled occupations (although there was also an increase in the employment of less-educated workers) (Hjort and Poulsen, 2019). This increase in employment is due to a growing number of firms in sectors using ICT, as well as due to greater use of the internet to improve productivity in existing firms. Although the study does not explicitly examine digital skills, it suggests that the increase in higher skill occupations may increase the demand for digital skills essential in the use of digital applications.

The introduction of the mobile payment system M-PESA in Kenya indicates how job losses and job creation may affect different sectors (Choi et al., 2020). Direct job losses in the banking sector were estimated to be about 6,000 between 2014 and 2017. However, the total number of jobs increased in the same period through an additional 70,000 mobile payment agents, and indirect job creation in other sectors through access to credit and cost reductions enabled by digital financial services. The study suggests that the adoption of digital technologies "has the potential to have a better impact on lower-skilled and lower educated workers in SSA than it does in higher-income regions" (Choi et al., 2020, pp 2-4). This is because the relatively small size of the manufacturing sector reduces the risk of large-scale job losses through automation of tasks in manufacturing. Another factor is that adoption of certain digital technologies (such as use of the internet and social media for communications and marketing, digital financial services, and digital platforms for e-commerce and hiring) requires relatively low levels of education and skills but could still lead to productivity improvements and expansion of small enterprises.

A likely scenario is, therefore, that digital technologies may impact sectors such as retail through e-commerce and the "gig economy" through digital labour platforms, rather than manufacturing through robotics and 3D printing. A corollary of this is that the level of digital skills required in most new jobs is likely to be at the basic/foundational level. Information on e-commerce platforms and the jobs they generate is not readily available. The role of digital labour platforms in Africa is still relatively small. Out of the global investment in digital labour platforms between 1998 and 2020, Africa, Latin America, and the Arab states together received only 4% (ILO, 2021). Further, digital labour platform workers in Africa tend to be employed on location-based platforms (for example, taxi and delivery services) rather than web-based platforms (through which workers perform specific jobs such as graphic design, website design, and programming tasks). The former tends to employ lower-skilled workers who require basic digital skills.

An example of a location-based platform is Uber, which has an estimated 150,000 active drivers in Africa as a whole. Local ridesharing platforms have also emerged, but job numbers are not known. A case study of Uber workers in Tanzania found that the digital skills required by drivers included the ability to use the smartphone features, especially using maps for navigation, online safety, e-payment, and online communications, while other skills such as problem-solving and critical thinking were also important (ITU, 2020). Uber itself offers just six hours of training, usually in one day, focused on the essential job-specific skills. The majority of drivers acquire skills on the job or through peer learning, but many lack the ability to read maps or communicate online.

Web-based online work is yet to take off in a significant way in Africa, except in a few countries such as Kenya and Nigeria. Digital infrastructure (that is to say, reliable, fast, and cheap broadband access – supported by physical infrastructure, especially reliable electricity in the case of Nigeria) is the main limiting factor. As countries invest in these infrastructures, the digital skills requirements of platform workers are likely to rise.

While most of the demand for digital skills is likely to be at the foundational level, higher-level digital skills are required to build and maintain the digital infrastructure, as well as the nascent modern manufacturing sector. There is evidence that the manufacturing sector is growing in parts of SSA and several countries, such as Ethiopia, Kenya, Ghana, Nigeria, Rwanda, and Senegal (UNIDO, 2021).[12] And that countries in this group are making efforts to attract FDI in manufacturing, setting up industrial parks, and so on.

A more systematic study on the demand for digital skills in the region was undertaken by the IFC in 2021. Using the methodology outlined in an earlier study for Ghana (IFC, 2020), but with revisions that incorporate the digital skills frameworks suggested in the World Bank work on digital skills mentioned above, the study covered Cote d'Ivoire, Kenya, Mozambique, Kenya, Nigeria, and Rwanda (IFC, 2021). Thus, it could estimate the demand for digital literacy skills at different proficiency levels as well as the demand for specialised skills for the ICT-enabled sectors. About 57 million jobs are expected to require digital skills in these five countries by 2030: about half the jobs in Kenya, between 35% and 45% jobs in Cote d'Ivoire, Nigeria, and Rwanda, and about 20% in Mozambique. About 2 million of these jobs will be in the ICT and e-commerce sectors. The demand for skills is therefore primarily for general digital literacy skills, and especially at the foundational level (70%) and at the intermediate level (23%) (IFC, 2021).

Hence, the demand for digital skills is not mainly from narrowly defined ICT professions. Instead, it stems from more generic occupations and for basic-level digital literacy skills. This is not to underplay the importance of the skills for the ICT professions: although this represents a relatively small proportion of the digital skills demand, in absolute numbers. Nevertheless, we note that the requirement for advanced digital skills is substantial (two million jobs). Therefore, an upgrade in the capacity of higher education and technical training institutions is essential to deliver job-relevant training.

13.5 Conclusion: In Search for a Meaningful AU–EU Cooperation on Digital Skills

This chapter set out to show why the appropriate conditions for a meaningful AU–EU cooperation in digital skills do not yet exist. Three impeding factors were identified: first, there is a lack of conceptual clarity regarding the precise meaning of digital skills, as reflected in the digital transformation strategies of the AU and various African countries; second, provision of digital skills training depends on creation of an appropriate ecosystem, including connectivity, devices and content, which are lacking; and, third, there are significant gaps in the coverage and quality of education and training programmes resulting in lack of foundational literacy, numeracy, and other cognitive skills that are essential for imparting digital skills. The current supply of digital skills programmes in the formal education system and through private providers in informal settings is relatively small, especially in sub-Saharan Africa, and covers only a small range of digital skills. Scaling up digital skills programmes both within the education system and outside will require addressing these constraints.

There is no doubt that the demand for digital skills will increase. The likely evolution of African economies will require generic basic digital literacy skills for workers in the informal sector and small enterprises, supplemented with literacy and numeracy skills where required, as well as some higher-level digital skills for the ICT professions. The focus of public policy should be to implement mass digital skills training at various levels – basic/foundational and advanced – in the interest of encouraging broad-based productivity improvements through adoption of digital technologies to drive the overall digital transformation of the economy.

A meaningful basis for AU–EU cooperation in digital skills can draw upon the EU's strengths and experience in developing digital skills frameworks that identify the competences and proficiency levels required for the workforce and citizens. These need to be adapted to African contexts and occupations; work done by the World Bank and others in this direction can also provide the basis for this cooperation. Another pillar of AU–EU cooperation could focus on developing the ecosystem for digital skills development, including infrastructure; access to connectivity, devices, and digital content; as well as an enabling policy environment. Even foundational-level digital skills training, in the African context, has to be linked to other basic educational competences, such as literacy and numeracy.

Notes

1 See, also for example, Africa-EU Partnership for current priority topics, available at https://ec.europa.eu/international-partnerships/topics/africa-eu-partnership_en. Referenced 21 October 2021.
2 https://www.oecd.org/coronavirus/en/data-insights/digital-skills-are-needed-across-a-wide-variety-of-jobs
3 See also, for example, WEF (2020), Africa needs digital skills across the economy - not just the tech sector, https://www.weforum.org/agenda/2020/10/africa-needs-digital-skills-across-the-economy-not-just-tech-sector/
4 https://ec.europa.eu/jrc/en/digcomp/digital-competence-framework
5 "The Digital Economy and Society Index (DESI) is a composite index that summarises relevant indicators on Europe's digital performance and tracks the evolution of EU Member States in digital competitiveness". "The DESI Index addresses five main areas, Connectivity, Human capital, Use of internet, Integration of digital technology, and Digital public service" - https://eufordigital.eu/library/digital-economy-and-society-index-desi-2020/
6 The lead author has been involved in developing the DE4A. See Digital Economy for Africa (DE4A) - https://www.worldbank.org/en/programmes/all-africa-digital-transformation.
7 See for example: Digital Europe Programme: https://digital-skills-jobs.europa.eu/en/about/digital-europe-programmeme
8 Department of Communications, Republic of South, South Africa Connect: Creating Opportunities, ensuring inclusion. South Africa's Broadband Policy, 20 November 2013, https://www.dtps.gov.za/dcdt/images/documents/Broadband/gazette_version_1__bb_policy__4_dec_2.pdf
9 See also for example World Bank DE4A reports available at https://www.worldbank.org/en/programmes/all-africa-digital-transformation/country-diagnostics; downloaded in April 2021.
10 https://learndigital.withgoogle.com/digitalskills
11 See for example: Digital Ethiopia 2025: A Digital Strategy for Ethiopia Inclusive Prosperity, https://tapethiopia.com/wp-content/uploads/Ethiopia-Digital-Strategy-2020.pdf; Digital Economy Blueprint: Powering Kenya's Transformation, https://www.ict.go.ke/wp-content/uploads/2019/05/Kenya-Digital-Economy-2019.pdf; National Digital Economy Policy and Strategy (2020-2030), Nigeria, https://www.ncc.gov.ng/docman-main/industry-statistics/policies-reports/883-national-digital-economy-policy-and-strategy/file
12 In the second quarter of 2021, "an expansion of manufacturing output was recorded in many African countries, such as South Africa (39.3%), Rwanda (30.2%), Senegal (22.6%) and Nigeria (4.6%)". Source: See also: https://www.un.org/en/observances/africa-industrialization-day

References

African Union (2020). *The Digital Transformation Strategy for Africa (2020–2030)*. Available at: https://au.int/en/documents/20200518/digital-transformation-strategy-africa-2020-2030 (Accessed: 30 March 2022).

AUC/OECD (2021). *Africa's Development Dynamics 2021: Digital Transformation for Quality Jobs*, AUC, Addis Ababa/OECD Publishing, Paris. Available at: https://doi.org/10.1787/0a5c9314-en (Accessed: 30 March 2022).

AU-EU Digital Economy Task Force (AU-EU DETF). (2020). *New Africa-Europe Digital Economy Partnership: Accelerating Achievement of the Sustainable Development Goals*, Available at: https://ec.europa.eu/international-partnerships/system/files/new-africa-eu-digital-economy_en_0.pdf (Accessed: 30 March 2022).

Bashir, S. and Miyamoto, K. (2020). Digital skills: Frameworks and programmes. World Bank, Washington, DC, World Bank. https://openknowledge.worldbank.org/handle /10986/35080 License: CC BY 3.0 IGO.

Bashir, S., Arney, L., Khan, J. and Lim, V. (2021). Digital skills: The why, the what and the how. *Methodological Guidebook*, Available at: https://thedocs.worldbank.org /en/doc/0a4174d70030f27cc66099e862b3ba79-0200022021/original/DSCAP -MethodGuidebook-Part1.pdf (Accessed: 30 March 2022).

Blignaut, AS, Hinostroza, EJ, Els, CJ and Brun, M. (2010). ICT in Education Policy and Practice in Developing Countries: South Africa and Chile Compared through SITES 2006, *Computers & Education*, 55 (4): 1552–1563.

Choi, J., Dutz, M. A. and Usman, Z. (eds.). (2020). *The Future of Work in Africa: Harnessing the Potential of Digital Technologies for All. Africa Development Forum Series.* Washington, DC.: World Bank.

Daniels, C. U. (2015). Organisational Capabilities for Science, Technology and Innovation Policy Formulation in Developing Countries: The case of Nigeria's Federal Ministry of Science and Technology. PhD, University of Sussex.

Daniels, C. U., Ustyuzhantseva, O. and Yao, W. (2017). Innovation for inclusive development, public policy support and triple helix: Perspectives from BRICS, *African Journal of Science, Technology, Innovation and Development* 9(5), 513–527.

Daniels C.U., Erforth B., Floyd R. and Teevan C. (2020). Strengthening the digital partnership between Africa and Europe European think tanks group (ETTG), Available at: https://ettg.eu/wp-content/uploads/2020/10/ETTG-Publication-Strengthening -the-digital-partnership-between-Africa-and-Europe.pdf (Accessed: 30 March 2022).

Daniels, C. U., Dosso, M., and Amadi-Echendu J. (eds.) (2021). *Entrepreneurship, Technology Commercialisation, and Innovation Policy in Africa.* Cham: Springer Nature.

Dosso M., Nwankwo C.I., and Travaly Y. (2021) The Readiness of Innovation Systems for the Fourth Industrial Revolution (4IR) in Sub-Saharan Africa. In: Daniels C., Dosso M., Amadi-Echendu J. (eds) *Entrepreneurship, Technology Commercialisation, and Innovation Policy in Africa.* Cham: Springer. https://doi.org/10.1007/978-3-030-58240-1_2

European Commission. (2020a). *Digital Economy and Society Index (DESI) 2020 Thematic Chapters,* Available at: https://eufordigital.eu/library/digital-economy-and-society -index-desi-2020/; https://eufordigital.eu/wp-content/uploads/2020/06/DESI202 0Thematicchapters-FullEuropeanAnalysis.pdf (Accessed: 30 March 2022).

European Commission. (2020b). *Digital Education action Plan 2021–2027 Resetting Education and Training for the Digital Age.* Commission Staff Working Document.

GoK (Government of Kenya). (2019). *Digital Economy Blueprint: Powering Kenya's Transformation,* Republic of Kenya, Available at: https://www.ict.go.ke/wp-content/ uploads/2019/05/Kenya-Digital-Economy-2019.pdf (Accessed: 30 March 2022).

GSMA (2019). Connected society: The state of mobile internet connectivity 2019, GSMA, Available at: https://www.gsma.com/mobilefordevelopment/wp-content/ uploads/2019/07/GSMA-State-of-Mobile-Internet-Connectivity-Report-2019.pdf (Accessed: 30 March 2022).

GSMA (2021). Understanding people's mobile digital skills needs Insights from India and Ghana. Available at: https://www.gsma.com/mobilefordevelopment/wp-content/ uploads/2021/05/Understanding-peoples-mobile-digital-skills-needs.pdf (Accessed: 30 March 2022).

Hjort, J. and Poulsen, J. (2019). The arrival of fast internet and employment in Africa, *American Economic Review*, 109(3), 1032–1079.

IFC (International Financial Cooperation) (2019). *Digital Skills in Sub-Saharan Africa Spotlight on Ghana,* Available at: https://www.ifc.org/wps/wcm/connect/ed6362b3

-aa34-42ac-ae9f-c739904951b1/Digital+Skills_Final_WEB_5-7-19.pdf?MOD
=AJPERES&CVID=mGkaj-s (Accessed: 30 March 2022).

IFC (2020). *Digital Skills in Sub-Saharan Africa: Spotlight on Ghana*, Available at:
https://www.ifc.org/wps/wcm/connect/ed6362b3-aa34-42ac-ae9f-c739904951b1
/Digital+Skills_Final_WEB_5-7-19.pdf?MOD=AJPERES (Accessed: 30 March
2022).

IFC (2021). *Demand for Digital Skills in Sub-Saharan Africa Key Findings from a Five-Country
Study: Côte d'Ivoire, Kenya, Mozambique, Nigeria, and Rwanda. International Financial
Cooperation*, Available at https://www.datocms-assets.com/37703/1623797656
-demand-for-digital-skills-in-sub-saharan-africa.pdf (Accessed: 30 March 2022).

ILO (2021). The role of digital labour platforms in transforming the world of
work. *World Employment and Social Outlook 2021.* Geneva: International Labour
Organization.

IMF (2018). "The Future of Work in sub-Saharan Africa". Washington, DC: International
Monetary Fund, Available at: https://www.imf.org/en/Publications/Departmental
-Papers-Policy-Papers/Issues/2018/12/14/The-Future-of-Work-in-Sub-Saharan
-Africa-46333 (Accessed: 30 March 2022).

Iordache, C., Mariën, I., and Baelden, D. (2017). Developing digital skills and
competences: A quickscan analysis of 13 digital literacy models. *Italian Journal of
Sociology of Education*, 9(1), 6–30.

Ito et al. (2008). "Living and Learning with New Media: Summary of Findings from the
Digital Youth Project". *The John D. and Catherine T. MacArthur Foundation Reports on
Digital Media and Learning*, Available at: https://files.eric.ed.gov/fulltext/ED536072
.pdf (Accessed: 30 March 2022).

ITU (International Telecommunication Union) (2020). Digital Skills Insights 2020,
ITU, Available at: https://academy.itu.int/sites/default/files/media2/file/Digital
%20Skills%20Insights%202020.pdf (Accessed: 30 March 2022).

Mare A. (2021) Addressing Digital and Innovation Gender Divide: Perspectives from
Zimbabwe. In: Daniels C., Dosso M., Amadi-Echendu J. (eds) *Entrepreneurship,
Technology Commercialisation, and Innovation Policy in Africa*. Cham: Springer. https://
doi.org/10.1007/978-3-030-58240-1_3

Martin, A and Grudziecki, J. (2006). DigEuLit: Concepts and tools for digital literacy
development, *ITALICS. Innovations in Teaching and Learning in Information and Computer
Sciences* 5(4), 249–267.

OECD (2021). *The OECD Framework for Digital Talent and Skills in the Public Sector, OECD
Working Papers on Public Governance*, No. 45, Paris: OECD Publishing. https://doi.org
/10.1787/4e7c3f58-en.

Owusu-Ansah, C.M., Rodrigues, A. and Van Der Walt, T. (2018). Factors influencing
the use of digital libraries in distance education in Ghana, *International Journal of
Libraries and Information Studies* 68(2), 125–135.

Pathways for Prosperity Commission (2019). The digital roadmap: How developing
countries can get ahead. *Final Report of the Pathways for Prosperity Commission.* Oxford,
UK, Available at: https://pathwayscommission.bsg.ox.ac.uk/sites/default/files/2019
-11/the_digital_roadmap.pdf (Accessed 20 January 2022).

Quaicoe, JS and Pata, K, 2020. Teachers' digital literacy and digital activity as digital
divide components among basic schools in Ghana, *Education and Information Technologies*
25(5), 4077–4095.

Ramoroka, T.M. (2021) Prospects of successful blended pedagogies in South Africa:
Planning, governance and infrastructure considerations, *Development Southern Africa*
38(5), 799–815.

Redecker, C. (2017). European framework for the digital competence of educators: DigCompEdu. In: Punie, Y. (ed). *EUR 28775 EN*. Luxembourg: Publications Office of the European Union.

UNESCO (2018). *A Global Framework of Reference on Digital Literacy Skills for Indicator 4.4.2*, UNESCO, Available at http://uis.unesco.org/sites/default/files/documents/ip51-global-framework-reference-digital-literacy-skills-2018-en.pdf (Accessed: 30 March 2022).

UNIDO (United Nations Industrial Development Organisations). (2021). *World Manufacturing Production Statistics for Quarter II 2021*, Available at: https://www.unido.org/resources-statistics/quarterly-report-manufacturing (Accessed: 30 March 2022).

University of Chicago Law School - Global Human Rights Clinic. (2020) Access denied: internet access and the right to education in South Africa. *Global Human Rights Clinic*. 1. https://chicagounbound.uchicago.edu/ghrc/1

Van Dijk, J. and van Deursen, A. (2014) *Digital Skills: Unlocking the Information Society*. New York: Palgrave Macmillan.

World Bank (2019). *World Development Report 2019: The Changing Nature of Work*. Washington, DC: World Bank.

World Bank (2020). *Digital Economy for Africa Country Diagnostic Tool and Guidelines for Task Teams*, Available at: https://thedocs.worldbank.org/en/doc/694441594319396632-0090022020/original/DE4ADiagnosticToolV2FINALJUNE24.pdf (Accessed: 30 March 2022).

WB (World Bank) (2021). Digital skills: The Why, the What and the How, https://thedocs.worldbank.org/en/doc/0a4174d70030f27cc66099e862b3ba79-0200022021/original/DSCAP-MethodGuidebook-Part1.pdf

WEF (World Economic Forum) (2020). Africa needs digital skills across the economy - not just the tech sector, https://www.weforum.org/agenda/2020/10/africa-needs-digital-skills-across-the-economy-not-just-tech-sector/

14

DIGITALISATION AND TRANSFORMATIVE LEARNING FOR SUSTAINABLE FUTURES IN RURAL AFRICA

Leaving No One Behind

Niyanta Shetye, Heila Lotz-Sisitka, Eike Albrecht, Sarah Durr, Dirk Marx, Dumisani Chirambo, Luke Metelerkamp, and Verena van Zyl-Bulitta

14.1 Introduction

The COVID-19 pandemic has highlighted the interdependent nature of a globalised world. It has also shown the significance of digitalisation for global connectivity trade, and cooperation. Unequal access to digital tools, technologies, and connectivity – the so-called digital divide – affects both Europe and Africa at different levels. This divide exists not only between continents, but also between urban and rural areas. The latter are particularly at risk of being left behind during the next stage of technological development (Cowie et al., 2020). This digital divide hinders growth and trade and reduces learning opportunities for those with little to no access to internet and digital tools. Hence, this chapter shows that digital learning can support informal education, provided practical issues faced by communities are accounted for, discussed, and platforms are customised for continued uptake.

Increased access to digital technologies will have a positive effect on gross domestic product (GDP) growth on both continents, especially in Africa. It is estimated that for Africa, a 10% increase in mobile internet penetration will result in a 2% increase in GDP per year and improved youth employment (Google and IFC, 2020; Abdulkadir and Asongu, 2022). Scores of publications by United Nations (UN) entities, academic journals, and other sources engage with the question as to how to improve access and quality of connectivity, infrastructure, data governance, and technology transfer (ITU, 2020a; ITU 2021; Ndubuisi et al., 2021; Al-Ruithe et al., 2019). However, the literature rarely looks at the social context in which these initiatives and projects are implemented and which also governs the uptake and continued use of such solutions. Hence, understanding the social context of rural agricultural communities is crucial as it either catalyses or hinders transformative learning and the uptake of digital solutions.

DOI: 10.4324/9781003274322-14

Agriculture will play a role in facilitating green transitions and sustainable futures in both the AU and EU. Approximately 54% of all workers in sub-Saharan Africa (SSA) are employed in agriculture while in some countries the number is as high as 70% (Gwagwa et al., 2021). Also, in the EU the role agriculture plays in green transitioning and sustainable futures cannot be ignored. About 4.3% of the EU's population works in the agricultural sector, ranging from below 5% in Germany and France to 17.5% in Bulgaria and approximately 23% in Romania (Eurostats, 2018). This is due to mechanisation and increasingly also digitalisation or "smart farming" (Wolfert et al., 2017), leading to fewer people being employed in the sector. This differs considerably from agro-based economies especially in sub-Saharan Africa (Bruzzone, 2021). Agriculture is also a major contributor to climate change, biodiversity loss, and land degradation in both Africa and Europe. For example, greenhouse gas (GHG)-emissions coming from the agricultural sector in Europe account for 12.74% of total EU GHG-emissions (EEA, 2021), while in Africa, the agricultural sector accounts for 18% of total GHG-emissions (AfDB, 2020).

In both Africa and Europe, land is a factor in addressing environmental and development challenges by combating desertification, adapting to climate change, land degradation, and mitigation of the effects of droughts. Addressing these issues will not just require policy interventions but also resilience building through transformative learning approaches in small-scale agricultural communities, which depend on land for their source of income. This requires a combination of innovation, ambition and pragmatism among youth, the private sector, and international organisations who are deploying new tools and technologies such as agri-innovation applications to assist small-scale farmers. These tools can effectively facilitate learning for small-scale farm holders on sustainable agricultural practices and methods of reducing food waste in communities while building resilience to climate change. With this view in mind, the authors focus on new and emerging trends along AU–EU cooperation, namely two areas: (1) green transition (2) digital transformation from a vantage point of inclusiveness.

Our argument is that AU–EU cooperation in digitalisation should include dialogues on low-cost and effective digital solutions which can be deployed in rural agricultural communities. These dialogues should be tailored to benefit both continents by facilitating mutual learning of experiences and practices. Mutual learning is needed as rural communities in both SSA and the EU are in dire need of low-cost and effective solutions. Furthermore, we highlight that these solutions, which have the potential to address global challenges, such as climate change, land degradation, and biodiversity loss, should be adapted to the social context of rural communities for their continued uptake.

14.2 The Nexus of Education, Sustainability, and Digital Innovation for Small-Scale Agriculture

An emerging body of research focuses on the nexus of education, sustainability studies, and digital innovation (Albrecht et al., 2014; Leal Filho et al., 2021; Cerone and Persico, 2014; Selwyn, 2012; Nickerson and Zodhiates, 1989).

Having said this, there is still a significant knowledge gap on the deployment, uptake, and continued use of digital applications and platforms aimed at small-scale agricultural communities. These communities face practical day-to-day challenges related to old mobile equipment, high data costs, or little memory storage capacities. Hence, this chapter navigates such practical challenges faced by small-scale agricultural communities, which are usually the target audience of such platforms, yet often cannot access them.

One of the most comprehensive reports on digital transformation, *Towards our Common Digital Future*, by the German Council on Global Change (WGBU, 2019), takes a holistic approach to digitalisation, learning, and education, which it also applies to the agricultural sector. The authors of the WGBU report advocate the use of digital platforms while also giving a range of applications for citizen-science and lifelong learning initiatives. The WGBU 2019 report (pp. 225) also underscores that, "the promotion of digital skills is a necessary but insufficient prerequisite for transformation education". It argues for a shift from education for digitalisation and sustainability to "future proofing" education (WGBU, 2019). Accordingly, it emphasises the need to systematically incorporate digital learning tools into educational and lifelong learning programmes within a wider paradigm of "placing digitalisation in the service of global sustainability" with investment in common good-oriented technology and infrastructure being crucial (WGBU, 2019). However, the report takes a holistic view and does not incorporate low-cost and effective digital solutions for rural agricultural communities.

Academic literature (Pick and Nishida, 2015) and the recent UNESCO policy on education for sustainable development – 2030 corroborate the WGBU report and stress the need to give attention to the implications of digitalisation for the education sector. The UNESCO report emphasises cooperation and partnerships between the education sector, sustainability science communities and ICT communities, and equal sharing of the benefits of technological progress (UNESCO, 2020; 2021b). However, as outlined below, rural communities in both Africa and Europe are currently grappling with digital learning and teaching while addressing digital divides (Fuchs and Horak, 2008; Oyedemi, 2012). Hence, the deployment of low-cost and effective digital solutions is a key area where AU–EU cooperation could benefit rural communities through policy and practice knowledge exchanges.

In relation to our chapter and unlike the WGBU, the literature review conducted by Rolandi et al. (2021) on existing impacts of digitalisation on agriculture in rural areas in Italy does not provide a holistic picture of the potential impacts in rural areas. For Germany, a study exists on the unintended side effects of digitalisation in agriculture (Scholz et al., 2021), but it does not consider the special situation of smallholder farmers. At the same time, a study conducted in France states that little has been done so far to address the relation between digitalisation and agriculture, while also concluding the need to include diversity in Agricultural Innovation Systems (AIS) and the need for further research (Schnebelin et al., 2021). In contrast to the above, studies conducted in Benin, Mali, Nigeria, and

Kenya within local stakeholder groups by Daum et al. (2021) state that megatrends, such as mechanisation of agriculture, digital agriculture, and youth engagement in agriculture, are favoured. However, there are serious concerns in terms of digital divides, failure of state-led digital agriculture programmes, and regarding the quality of digital services as well as the exclusion of smallholder farmers in rural Africa. Having said that, Daum et al. (2021) call for policy dialogues on digitalisation and inclusive agricultural transformation in Africa.

Building upon these insights, this chapter seeks to establish pathways forward for AU–EU cooperation for low-cost mobile digital solutions meant for learning and education for rural agricultural communities to address digital divides. However, it should be noted that African rural small-scale agricultural communities are more impacted by the digital divide than their European counterparts, owing to even less digital access and mobile internet penetration, high data costs, and poverty.

14.2.1 How Low-Cost Digitalisation Can Benefit Africa

Vulnerable communities still struggle to access basic goods (water and food) and services (education and learning opportunities) while simultaneously facing new challenges such as climate change (UNDP, 2019; 2020). Addressing these basic needs is central to achieving the SDGs (UN, 2015). Participation in key economic sectors, information sharing, and formal as well as informal education are factors that influence the well-being of current and future generations (UNESCO 2020; 2021b). The COVID-19 pandemic has shown how important digital technologies are in education. While COVID-19 was a driver for innovation, it also resulted in the exclusion of communities on the margins of digitalisation. For example, post-COVID-19 statistics show that 85% of children did not have learning opportunities due to lockdowns (UNESCO Institute for Statistics, 2020; Angrist et al., 2021). At the same time, research conducted in Ethiopia, Kenya, Liberia, Tanzania, and Uganda confirmed a significant loss of learning due to COVID-19. The insights shared by Angrist et al. (2021) demonstrate a half-year of learning loss in school children. Hence, this proves the need to introduce low-cost and effective solutions which facilitate learning at all levels.

The influence of disruptive technologies, especially mobile phone technology, is producing entry points for wider populations including rural communities in SSA to participate in education, learning opportunities, employment, and information sharing (GSMA, 2019; 2020; Breuer and Groshek, 2017). Since the pandemic created disruptions in formal education systems all over the world, it also proved to be a driver for informal learning and online participation and exchanges (Li and Lalani, 2020; ITU, 2020b; Albrecht and Zschiegner, 2020). Recent technological advances have shown a growing demand for new digital skills to participate in learning, employment, and digital markets, with this need emerging also amongst rural agricultural communities in Africa (OECD, 2019; Myovella et al., 2020).

14.2.2 Education and Learning for Implementing the SDGs

To achieve the SDGs, there is a need to focus on learning that complements formal education. Low-cost digital learning tools have the potential to deliver on SDG 4 and its indicators, especially Target 4.7 which emphasises ESD as a lifelong process.

This space for learning under new conditions offers interesting possibilities for establishing cooperation between the AU and EU in the areas of the green transition and digitalisation (UNESCO, 2016; 2021b; AUC/OECD, 2021). This is particularly pertinent now as the COVID-19 pandemic has increased capacities of learners and tutors for using e-learning platforms, internationally and in Africa (AUC/OECD, 2021; UNESCO, 2021a). These platforms are rapidly transforming how we acquire skills and knowledge (Abugre et al., 2021). However, exclusions and inequalities remain a reality, especially for learners in low-income countries and rural areas, since even the best digital solutions do not work if there is no access to internet (Affouneh et al., 2020; Abugere et al., 2021; UNESCO, 2021a).

14.2.3 Digital Divides and the Need to Focus on Low-Cost and Effective Technologies

Regardless of the recent increase in digital and internet use referred to above, there is still a prominent digital divide both within and between AU and EU countries, including urban and rural areas (Fuchs and Horak, 2008; Brown and Czerniewicz, 2010; ITU, 2020c). Rural areas in both continents generally have much slower internet at their disposal. Data from the International Telecommunication Union (ITU) in 2020 shows that only 22% of rural population in Africa has access to 4G internet services in contrast to 77% of the urban population. In Europe, 86% of the rural population have 4G internet services in contrast to 100% of the urban population. The digital gender divide is also apparent, as women in least developed countries are 33% less likely to have internet access than men (ITU, 2020c). This means that access to internet and digital learning opportunities remains vastly uneven in both continents, posing a challenge for small-scale farmers, learners, and agricultural businesses.

Even where the digital divide seems less severe, such as in South Africa (one of the countries in Africa with the highest level of smartphone penetration), in-field observations reveal that one must avoid equating access to a smartphone with meaningful participation in digital education and learning systems (Durr, 2020; Lotz-Sisitka et al., 2021). Some of the major barriers facing smartphone users include:

Old mobile phones being incompatible with recent operating system updates;
Low-cost mobile phones with limited storage space and processing power;
Data costs associated with operating system upgrades, downloading and running
new apps;

Data bundles that provide affordable access exclusively to key social media apps,
     such as WhatsApp and Facebook;
Difficulties in learning how to use new apps, particularly for older users; and
Lack of electricity leading to high costs for recharging batteries.

14.3 Illustrative Case Studies of Low-Cost Green Transitioning, Digital Learning, and Agricultural Practices in Rural Africa

The literature review points to the need for research into low-cost and effective solutions, which can be deployed for learning around the green transition in rural areas for small-scale farmers. Our two case studies focus on the use of low-cost and low-data social messaging services as these have emerged as a powerful transformative force, even in the face of unequal data access, distribution, and beneficiation (GSMA, 2020). In Africa, with 46% mobile device infiltration, mobile phones are the primary and often only point of entry to gaining access to necessary information and digital learning resources. There is also recognition that an increase in access to internet as well as digital tools with suitable training and education will enable small scale farmers to benefit from digitalisation, and that this can contribute to food security, sustainable development, and economic well-being (Ordu et al., 2021).

We see interesting, often youth-led, digital innovations emerging in Africa, especially around low-cost mobile technology innovations coupled with electricity infrastructure, e-commerce, e-health, and online education and learning solutions (PWC, 2016; Duarte, 2021). With the demographic dividend of a young population in Africa, there is already a surge in use of disruptive technologies such as ICTs, mobile applications, and big data analysis that is unconstrained by legacy, and much potential for further innovations. According to the "We are Social" 2017 Digital Yearbook, seven of the ten highest growing mobile adoption countries in the world were in Africa (We are Social, 2017). In many developing nations, where the installation of earlier technology was too expensive, mobile phones were the first pieces of digital communication technology to infiltrate rural areas (Aker and Mbiti, 2010).

Digital technologies have also provided ICT-based solutions for Sustainable Development as co-learning and information sharing platforms and mobile phone applications are an increasingly popular mechanism for supporting learning in rural areas. For example, in Malawi, some of the ICT-based agri-innovation apps that have recently emerged include the Regreening Africa App (European Commission, 2021), Kilimo Salama (Safaricom and UAP insurance, 2010), E-mlimi, and Mlimi hotline (World Vision, 2019) which connect agricultural communities and facilitate co-learning among farmers. Other examples include Kurima Mari, which is an integrated agricultural learning app launched in Zimbabwe and now expanding into Malawi and Uganda (FAO, 2017). These examples of applications for mobile phone–supported green transition and digitalisation seek to catalyse learning in rural areas at grassroots level. Many have been made possible through partnership with European organisations, showing that there is already AU–EU cooperation emerging in this field. These are interesting examples because they facilitate wider social learning in communities, and they have a reach beyond the formal educational institution (Metelerkamp and Ferguson, 2021); a process also illustrated by the two case studies below, which offer further insight into these developments.

14.3.1 Case Study 1: Food for Us (FFU), South Africa

The FFU project focused on design, development, introduction, and use of a new mobile application in a rural agricultural community to address on-farm food waste and market transformation to a local green economy. The main goals of the project were to reduce food waste, to address the disconnect in local supply chains, and to facilitate sustainable production and consumption opportunities in local communities by connecting producers and consumers of fresh produce within a given geographical radius. The 18-month FFU pilot project was initiated in 2017 by partners supported by the UNEP, with funding from the EU and Japan. The project also supported community learning to enable increased employment opportunities using a mobile technology solution. Several social infrastructures, networking, and social learning support activities were applied in the project, including an introductory workshop, an application training, a local supply chain "Match-Making" event, a project debriefing event, and an active open communication channel (WhatsApp group) between the application trial users and the app developers and researchers (Durr, 2020).

The uptake of the application was not as successful and far reaching as intended due to the common problem of "short-term investment" in innovations by international funding agencies. There was little natural expansion of its adoption within the community and the developers stopped working on the initiative when the funding ran out. This resulted in the traditional "failed development project" situation, a common problem when cooperation interventions fail to integrate well into local economies and value chain systems. One can ascribe this to the donor environment, but what also became clear was that there were other factors shaping the outcome. These included challenges, such as a lack of trust in new forms of technology, inadequate digital literacy, poor signal, and high data costs, which point to a complex range of issues influencing the digitalisation context. The investment into the social relationships between stakeholders was one of the more positive features of the FFU app project, as this led to an interesting co-engagement between the new digital technology and those leading its development. This led to the adoption of a more common and culturally familiar digital technology to support FFU's aims – namely WhatsApp (Lotz-Sisitka and Durr, 2019). This engagement on both the FFU application and WhatsApp supported farmers to achieve their goals, that is, increasing revenue through finding new customers. However, it was ultimately the social learning across the two digital platforms (FFU and WhatsApp), together with the on-site engagements, that helped to achieve the intended purpose of the specifically designed FFU app. Over time, relationships between buyers and sellers of produce developed and fresh produce was marketed to a larger audience. Transactions were increasingly made through the active WhatsApp group as the FFU app was unsuccessful in sustaining its initial "high flying" promise as being the "new technology" of preference. While the process of attempting to develop and introduce the FFU app led to the development of a new set of valuable social relationships, WhatsApp ultimately outperformed the FFU app as the platform capable of sustaining and operationalising these relationships.

Interestingly, this led to a process of merging the existing low-cost, culturally accepted, and widely used digital platforms that speak to the local context (local supply chain and market demands) with introducing and developing new digital technologies. It is also important to couple technological innovation with adequate investment (including short-term investment) alongside a robust understanding of the social context to assist in facilitating learning around the innovation, and develop a sustained use culture around the new technology to encourage effective use thereof. In such contexts, it is therefore necessary to adopt a combination of digital and other social learning practices for effective outcomes to emerge, instead of only relying on one digital mechanism or tool only. Substantive sustainability planning for cooperation and investment in such initiatives is necessary (Lotz-Sisitka and Durr, 2019; Durr, 2020). These reflect some of the contextual dynamics necessary when selecting digital tools in learning and development initiatives.

14.3.2 Case Study 2: Imvotho Bubomi Learning Network (IBLN), South Africa

The IBLN is a community-based agricultural learning network that emerged out of the Amanzi [Water] for Food Training of Trainers Course that started in 2014, growing exponentially over time in a rural farming context in South Africa. A WhatsApp group served as the learning network's primary means of communication since its inception in 2016, providing a space to share ideas and organise meetings. The learning network includes farmers, agricultural officers, agricultural students, NGO workers, and teachers, amongst others. Over a four-year period (2017–2020 included), the WhatsApp group chat volume calculated in words per year increased dramatically from 25,000 in 2017 to an estimated 125,000 in 2020, providing an expanding virtual space to facilitate knowledge sharing and discussion between the diverse participants. The WhatsApp group grew to include more than 100 participants, including farmers (50%), NGOs and academics (38.4%), government extension officers (5.8%), and agri-training institution personnel (5.8%). The virtual exchanges did not replace face-to-face meetings organised by the learning network, but instead extended them, offering evidence of the learning value of these long-term relationships. Often these engagements centred around a specific problem a network member had come across, and its resolution (Lotz-Sisitka et al., 2016; 2021).

Like the FFU case above, this uptake and sustained use of WhatsApp as a multimedia tool for seeking and sharing knowledge illuminates the power of using simple applications in digitalising learning in rural farming education processes. The cases also show that there are diverse factors affecting the sustainability of such initiatives. These include the way in which investments in the technologies are conceptualised, and ways in which social infrastructure operates within a digital and social ecology to facilitate sustained engagement with digitalisation in marginal rural areas. Issues related to the relevance and experienced value by digital users are another factor to consider (Lotz-Sisitka et al., 2021).

14.3.3 Key Insights from the Cases

Experiences in supporting digitalisation and sustainability-oriented learning processes suggest that the process of digital innovation is far more akin to weaving a fine quilt than viral dissemination (Metelerkamp and Ferguson, 2021). The process of learning is deeply connected, respectful of the individual, and relational. Relationships exist between learners in the group, each learner and the facilitator, and between each learner and the technology platform. In both the IBLN and FFU, each user was carefully introduced to the apps by another user who referred them to the community project. Achieving scale in low-tech rural environments was a result of active human agents working as advocates, nodes, and multipliers for digital technologies. Thus, our work with digitalisation and learning for sustainable development demonstrates that the often "invisible work" of developing stakeholders' understanding for digital innovation is as important as the digital innovation itself (Cruz-Jesus et al., 2014; Durr, 2020; Lotz-Sisitka et al., 2021; Metelerkamp and Ferguson, 2021).

Table 14.1 shows a summary of the two cases, which offers a framework that considers both digitalisation and learning in a context of sustainability.

14.4 Implications for AU–EU Cooperation

Learning in the areas of green transition and digitalisation can occur along the lines of:

Developing transformative literacies and capabilities for reaching into communities that would otherwise have been difficult to engage due to their remoteness and smaller scales of their practices (that is, they fall outside of the mainstream "Smart Agric" and AIS digitalisation movements).

Developing anticipatory literacies, especially sharing expertise and knowledge on market transformation approaches and the use of ICTs, as well as value chain development within localised green economy systems.

Developing ICT literacies, with emphasis, as we have indicated above, on understanding localised ICT cultures, preferred tools, and developing ICT innovations from this vantage point in ways that remain accessible to those who

TABLE 14.1 Summary of Key Insights from the Case Studies

	Transformative literacy		Sustainability literacy		Anticipatory literacy		ICT skills	
	FFU	IBLN	FFU	IBLN	FFU	IBLN	FFU	IBLN
Similarities	Networks and relationships/ ecological sensibility.		Organic farming.		Consideration of local green economies and value chain thinking improved.		Posting produce on a platform.	Posting questions about practice on a platform.
Differences	Market transformation.	Food sovereignty dialogues.	Organic farming with focus on food surplus management.	Organic farming with focus on rainwater harvesting and conservation.	Improved attention to quality of food production (unexpected outcome from posting produce on ICT platform).	More extensive and systematic uptake of sustainable agricultural practice esp. water harvesting and organic production.	Younger community members had to mediate with other members of the community.	All community members were able to easily use the platform, unless they did not have phones.
Implementation challenges and key lessons	Market transformations need to be supported by wider structural changes in local economies.	Multipronged approaches are needed for supporting smallholder farmers who are victim of droughts and severe weather impacts.	Challenges connecting buyers and sellers around food surplus issues – needs simultaneous communication and co-learning.	Droughts and severe weather conditions affect farmers' practices, despite communications gains from ICTs.	Stronger relations between consumers and producers in local food value chains need to be pro-actively established for the ICT tools to work.	More attention to market creation for smallholder farmers, thus stronger focus on local food value chains to be pro-actively developed to support farmers learning with ICTs.	Platform too elaborate, data too expensive, required smartphones. Application updates produced instability and required many data for regular updates.	Need for face-to-face communications to include those without phones.
Potential for AU–EU cooperation	ICT platforms can create spaces for transformative relations and literacies to develop. They also create access to communities that would otherwise not be included in sustainable development praxis.		There is need for cooperation to develop ICT-supported approaches that also support organic/more sustainable forms of agriculture – sharing of knowledge resources is a high area of potential.		There is need for tools to support market transformations and developing localised green economies that are supported by suitable ICT tools that are locally relevant and widely used.		Keep ICT platforms simple and aligned with current ICT use practices, avoid overelaborate technology solutions; check assumptions before designing digital solutions.	

do not have easy access to data or internet platforms, smartphones and other technology tools.

As argued above, all of this requires investment in both the digital software and hardware, and the less obvious social context and understanding necessary for uptake and use of the digital tools around core practices of sustainability innovation.

Digital transformation is a part of the AU's and EU's COVID-19 recovery plans and climate neutrality plans (Anderson et al., 2020; Agwanda et al., 2021). Digital technologies are perceived as a way to monitor and reduce greenhouse gases while safeguarding livelihoods during disasters. In addition, digital solutions need electricity, but the worldwide trend of electricity production is shifting towards renewable sources (IEA, 2021). In the EU, member states and cities have started taking a much more proactive role in leveraging digital technologies for education (including adults) and reducing their carbon footprint (WGBU, 2019; Shetye, 2021). Furthermore, the EU's green deal intends to leverage digitalisation in urban mobility, industry, energy markets, energy efficiency, sustainable supply chains, and food systems, and views digitalisation as a key enabler for achieving the objectives of the green deal. However, even in the EU, there is a growing need to include rural communities in these plans.

The EU is an integral partner to Africa's development ambitions, particularly through the provision of finance, technology, and capacity building in the ICT domain. The EU is approaching digital partnerships with developing and emerging economies through Digital4Development Hubs (D4D) in some countries and through mainstreaming in other countries. These digital partnerships will include regulatory cooperation, addressing capacity building and skills, investment in international cooperation and research partnerships. However, it should be noted that most of the initiatives under the EU's external digital policy for Africa are surprisingly constructed as a one-way road, in the sense that the initiatives do not give scope for EU policymakers to learn, gain knowledge, and incorporate solutions in the European context. In terms of digitalisation for sustainable development, there are a couple of initiatives which stand out for incorporating low-cost and effective digital solutions for small-scale farmers that can offer insights into co-benefits and mutual learning around enabling a green transition (which benefit all societies) and digitalisation. The initiatives in which such mutual learning is possible include the African European Digital Innovation Bridge (AEDIB) and the Innovation Dialogue Europe Africa (IDEA).

14.5 Conclusion

As indicated in the introduction to this chapter, connectivity through digital means has increased substantively in the past few years. The EU's Africa Strategy (EP, 2021) recognises potential for cooperation in the areas of green transitions and digitalisation within the SDG framework. The AU–EU cooperation is also effective in terms of learning and agriculture for small-scale farmers in rural areas. We have offered a perspective on such cooperation with a view to placing the most marginalised at the centre of such cooperation potential, namely rural small-scale agricultural communities. While this is not the only possible focus for such cooperation, we have foregrounded smallholder farmers and agriculture in these settings in Africa. We have indicated that digitalisation – using low-cost mobile technologies introduced in social and technological ecosystems, building on adequate sustainability planning and careful engagements in communities of practice – is an important dimension of such cooperation potentials. This requires an ESD and learning as people need to learn how to use technologies in supportive learning-centred processes if they are to successfully shape sustainable development actions in ways that leave no one behind. We have also sketched a positive picture of existing and emerging AU–EU cooperation in this area, highlighting the trend towards expansion of digital competencies, skills, and technology, partly also because the majority of the population in Africa is much younger than in Europe. We have pointed to the possibilities of AU–EU cooperation to develop transformation, sustainability, anticipatory, and digital literacies around key areas of local green economies, food system value chains, and knowledge sharing. Mobile learning is among the fastest growing digital applications in Africa, and leapfrogging has already taken place. Mobile learning therefore offers a centrepoint for future innovation diffusion and expansion for green transitions and digital cooperation.

References

Adbulqadir, I. and Asongu, S. (2022) 'The asymmetric effect of internet access on economic growth in sub-Saharan Africa', *Economic Analysis and Policy*, 73, pp. 44–61. https://doi.org/10.1016/j.eap.2021.10.014

Abugre, J., Osabutey, E. and Sigue, S. (eds) (2021) 'Business in Africa in the Era of Digital Technology' In *Advances in Theory and Practice of Emerging Markets*. Cham: Springer. Swansea, UK. https://link.springer.com/book/10.1007/978-3-030-70538-1 (Accessed 5 April 2022).

AfDB (2020) *Drivers of Greenhouse Gas emissions in Africa: Focus on agriculture, forestry and other land use*. Available at: https://blogs.afdb.org/climate-change-africa/drivers-greenhouse-gas-emissions-africa-focus-agriculture-forestry-and-other (Accessed: 7 March 2022).

Affouneh S., Salha S. and Khlaif, Z. (2020) 'Designing Quality E-Learning Environments for Emergency Remote Teaching in Coronavirus Crisis', *Interdisciplinary Journal of Virtual Learning in Medical Sciences*, 11(2), pp. 135–137.

Agwanda, B., Dagba, G., Amankwa, P. and Nyadera, I. (2021) 'Sub-Sahara Africa and the COVID-19 Pandemic: Reflecting on Challenges and Recovery Opportunities', *Journal of Developing Societies*, 37(4), pp. 502–524. https://doi.org/10.1177/0169796X211032567

Aker, J. and Mbiti, I. (2010) 'Mobile Phones and Economic Development in Africa', *Journal of Economic Perspectives*, 24(3), pp. 207–232.

Albrecht, E. and Zschiegner, A. (2020) 'Das Gesetz zur Sicherstellung ordnungsgemäßer Planungs- und Genehmigungsverfahren während der COVID-19-Pandemie vom 20.5.2020' (The law of 20.05.2020 for securing regular planning and licensing procedures during COVID-19-pandemic), *UPR*, 2020, pp. 252–256.

Albrecht, E., Schmidt, M., Mißler-Behr, M. and Spyra, S. (eds.) (2014) *Implementing Adaptation Strategies by Legal, Economic and Planning Instruments on Climate Change*. Cham: Springer.

Al-Ruithe, M., Benkhelifa, E. and Hameed, K. (2019) 'A systematic literature review of data governance and cloud data governance', *Personal and Ubiquitous Computing* 23, pp. 839–859. https://doi.org/10.1007/s00779-017-1104-3

Anderson, J., Tagliapietra, S. and Wolff., G. (2020) *Rebooting Europe: A Framework for a Post COVID-19 Economic Recovery*. Available at: https://www.bruegel.org/wp-content /uploads/2020/05/PB-2020-01.pdf (Accessed: 7 March 2022).

Angrist, N. et al. (2021) 'Building back better to avert a learning catastrophe: Estimating learning loss from COVID-19 school shutdowns in Africa and facilitating short-term and long-term learning recovery', *International Journal of Educational Development*, 84, pp. 1–14. https://doi.org/10.1016/j.ijedudev.2021.102397

AUC/OECD (2021) *Africa's Development Dynamics 2021: Digital Transformation for Quality Jobs*, Available at: https://doi.org/10.1787/0a5c9314-en

Breuer, A. and Groshek, J. (2017) 'Assessing the potential of ICTs for participatory development in Sub-Saharan Africa with evidence from urban togo', *International Journal of Politics, Culture, and Society*, 20, pp. 349–368.

Brown, C. and Czerniewicz, L. (2010) 'Debunking the 'digital native': Beyond digital apartheid, towards digital democracy', *Journal of Computer Assisted Learning*, 26(5), pp. 357–369. https://doi.org/10.1111/j.1365-2729.2010.00369.x.

Bruzzone, B. (2021) *Agriculture in Africa 2021: Focus Report*. Oxford Business Group. Available at: https://oxfordbusinessgroup.com/blog/bernardo-bruzzone/focus -reports/agriculture-africa-2021-focus-report (Accessed: 7 March 2022).

Cerone, A. and Persico, D. (2014) 'Innovation and sustainability in education', *Satellite Events on Information Technology and Open Source*, 7991, pp. 3–16.

Cowie P., Townsend L. and Salemink, K. (2020) 'Smart rural futures: Will rural areas be left behind in the 4th industrial revolution?', *Journal of Rural Studies*, 79, pp. 169–176. https://doi.org/10.1016/j.jrurstud.2020.08.042

Cruz-Jesus F., Oliveira T. and Bacao F. (2014) 'Exploring the Pattern between Education Attendance and Digital Development of Countries', *Procedia Technology* 16, pp. 452–458. https://doi.org/10.1016/j.protcy.2014.10.112.

Daum, T. et al. (2021) 'Mechanisation, digitalisation, rural youth: Stakeholder perceptions on mega-topics for African agricultural transformation', *Social and Institutional Change in Agricultural Development*. Available at: https://papers.ssrn.com/sol3/papers.cfm ?abstract_id=3986086 (Accessed: 7 March 2022).

Duarte, C. (2021) 'Post-COVID-19: A chance to leapfrog Africa's development through digitalisation', *Africa Renewal*. Available at: https://www.un.org/africarenewal /magazine/march-2021/post-covid-19-chance-leapfrog-africas-development -through-digitalization (Accessed: 7 March 2022).

Durr, S. (2020) *Enabling social learning to stimulate value creation towards a circular economy: The case of the Food for Us food redistribution mobile application development process*. M. Ed Dissertation. Rhodes University.

European Commission (2021) *A mobile application helps African farmers manage and restore their land*. Available at: https://ec.europa.eu/international-partnerships/stories/mobile -application-helps-african-farmers-manage-and-restore-their-land_en (Accessed: 7 March 2022).

EEA (2021) *EEA Greenhouse Gases: Data Viewer*. Availale at: https://www.eea.europa.eu /publications/data-and-maps/data/data-viewers/greenhouse-gases-viewer (Accessed: 7 March 2022).

European Parliament (EP) (2021) *A New EU-Africa Strategy – A Partnership for Sustainable and Inclusive Development. At a Glance, Plenary March II 2021.* Available at: https://www.europarl.europa.eu/RegData/etudes/ATAG/2021/690516/EPRS _ATA(2021)690516_EN.pdf (Accessed: 7 March 2022).

Eurostats (2018) 'Farmers and the agricultural labour force – statistics. Eurostats, Statistics Explained.' Available at: https://ec.europa.eu/eurostat/statistics-explained/index .php?title=Farmers_and_the_agricultural_labour_force_-_statistics#Agriculture_ remains_a_big_employer_within_the_EU.3B_about_9.7_million_people_work_in _agriculture (Accessed: 7 March 2022).

FAO (2017) *Kurima Mari Version 2 Mobile Farming App Explainer.* Available at: https:// www.fao.org/family-farming/detail/en/c/1039815/ (Accessed: 7 March 2022).

Filho, W. *et al.* (2021) 'COVID19: the impact of a global crisis on sustainable development teaching', *Environment, Development and Sustainability*, 23, pp. 11257–11278. https://doi .org/10.1007/s10668-020-01107-z.

Fuchs, C. and Horak, E. (2008) 'Africa and the digital divide', *Telematics and Informatics*, 25(2), pp. 99–116 https://doi.org/10.1016/j.tele.2006.06.004.

Google and IFC (2020) *e-Conomy Africa 2020: Africa's $180 billion Internet economy future.* Available at: https://www.ifc.org/wps/wcm/connect/e358c23f-afe3-49c5-a509 -034257688580/e-Conomy-Africa-2020.pdf?MOD=AJPERES&CVID=nmuGYF2 (Accessed: 7 March 2022).

GSMA (2019) *The Mobile Economy 2019.* GSMA. Available at: https://data.gsmaintelligence .com/api-web/v2/research-file-download?id=39256194&file=2712-250219-ME -Global.pdf (Accessed: 7 March 2022).

GSMA (2020) *The Mobile Economy Sub-Saharan Africa 2020.* GSMA. Available at: https://www.gsma.com/mobileeconomy/wp-content/uploads/2020/09/GSMA _MobileEconomy2020_SSA_Eng.pdf (Accessed: 7 March 2022).

Gwagwa, A. et al. (2021) 'Road map for research on responsible artificial intelligence for development (AI4D) in African countries: The case study of agriculture', *Patterns* 2(12), 100381. https://doi.org/10.1016/j.patter.2021.100381

IEA (2021) *Global Energy Review 2021: Assessing the Effects of Economic Recoveries on Global Energy Demand and CO2 Emissions in 2021.* Available at: https://iea.blob.core.windows .net/assets/d0031107-401d-4a2f-a48b-9eed19457335/GlobalEnergyReview2021.pdf (Accessed: 7 March 2022).

ITU (2020a) *Connecting Humanity: Assessing Investment Needs of Connecting Humanity to the Internet by 2030.* Available at: https://www.itu.int/hub/publication/d-gen-invest-con -2020/ (Accessed: 7 March 2022).

ITU (2020b) *COVID-19: How Digital Learning Solutions Are Taking Shape.* Available at: https://www.itu.int/en/myitu/News/2020/05/06/09/00/COVID-19-How-digital -learning-solutions-are-taking-shape (Accessed: 7 March 2022).

ITU (2020c) *Measuring Digital Development. Facts and Figures 2020.* International Telecommunications Union. Available at: https://www.itu.int/en/ITU-D/Statistics /Documents/facts/FactsFigures2020.pdf (Accessed: 7 March 2022).

ITU (2021) *Connectivity in the Least Developed Countries Status Report 2021.* International Telecommunications Union. Available at: https://www.itu.int/hub/publication/d -ldc-ictldc-2021-2021/ (Accessed: 7 March 2022).

Li, C. and Lalani, F. (2020) *The COVID-19 Pandemic Has Changed Education Forever. This Is How.* World Economic Forum. Available at: https://www.weforum.org/ agenda/2020/04/coronavirus-education-global-covid19-online-digital-learning/ (Accessed: 7 March 2022).

Lotz-Sistika, H. and Durr, S. (eds.) (2019) *Exploring the Social Learning Value Enabled by Affordances of the Food for Us Mobile Application: The Story of a South African Food Redistribution App.* Grahamstown: Rhodes University.

Lotz-Sistika, H., Pesanayi, T., Weaver, K. and Lupele, C. (2016) *Water use and food security: Knowledge dissemination and use in agricultural colleges and local learning networks for home food gardening and smallholder agriculture.* Research report. Pretoria: Water Research Commission.

Lotz-Sistika, H. et al. (2021) *"Amanzi for Food": A social learning approach to agricultural water knowledge mediation, uptake and use in smallholder farming learning networks.* Research and Development Report. Pretoria: Water Research Commission.

Metelerkamp, L. and Ferguson, R. (2021) 'Transforming Education for Sustainable Futures Working Paper', in *Technological Transformations.* Grahamstown: Rhodes University Environmental Learning Research Centre.

Myovella, G., Karacuka, M. and Haucap, J. (2020) 'Digitalisation and economic growth: A comparative analysis of Sub-Saharan Africa and OECD economies' *Telecommunications Policy*, 44(2), pp. 1–12. https://doi.org/10.1016/j.telpol.2019.101856

Ndubuisi, G., Otioma, C. and Tetteh, G. (2021) 'Digital infrastructure and employment in services: Evidence from Sub-Saharan African Countries', *Telecommunications Policy*, 45(8), pp. 1–9. https://doi.org/10.1016/j.telpol.2021.102153

Nickerson, R. and Zodhiates, P. (eds.) (1989) *Technology in Education: Looking towards 2020, Technology in Education Series.* Hillsdale, N.J.: L. Erlbaum Associates.

OECD (2019) *Digital Opportunities for Better Agricultural Policies.* Available at: https://doi.org/10.1787/571a0812-en

Ordu, A., Cooley, L. and Goh., L. (2021) *Digital Technology and African Smallholder Agriculture: Implications for Public Policy. Africa in Focus.* Brookings Institute. Available at: https://www.brookings.edu/blog/africa-in-focus/2021/08/16/digital-technology-and-african-smallholder-agriculture-implications-for-public-policy (Accessed: 7 March 2022).

Oyedemi, T. (2012) 'Digital inequalities and implications for social inequalities: A study of internet penetration amongst university students in South Africa', *Telematics and Informatics*, 29(2), pp. 302–303. https://doi.org/10.1016/j.tele.2011.12.001

Pick, J. and Nishida, T. (2015) 'Digital divides in the world and its regions: A spatial and multivariate analysis of technological utilization', *Technological Forecasting and Social Change*, 91, pp. 1–17. https://doi.org/10.1016/j.techfore.2013.12.026

PWC (2016) *Disrupting Africa: Riding the Wave of the Digital Revolution.* Available at: https://www.pwc.com/gx/en/issues/high-growth-markets/assets/disrupting-africa-riding-the-wave-of-the-digital-revolution.pdf (Accessed: 7 March 2022).

Rolandi, S., Brunori, G. and Bacco, M. (2021) 'The digitalisation of agriculture and rural areas: Towards a taxonomy of the impacts', *Sustainability*, 13(9), pp. 1–16. https://doi.org/10.3390/su13095172

Salama, K. (2010) *About Kilimo Salama.* Available at: https://kilimosalama.wordpress.com/about/ (Accessed: 7 March 2022).

Schnebelin, E., Labarthe, P. and Touzard, J. (2021) 'How digitalisation interacts with ecologisation? Perspectives from actors of the French Agricultural Innovation System', *Journal of Rural Studies*, 86, pp. 599–610. https://doi.org/10.1016/j.jrurstud.2021.07.023

Scholz, R. W. et al. (2021) 'Vulnerabilität und Stützung der globalen Ernährungssicherheit durch digitale Daten' (Vulnerability and supporting global food security through digital data), in Scholz, R.W. et al. (eds.) *Supplementarische Informationen zum DiDaT-Weißbuch*

(Supplementary Information to the DiDaT-Whitepaper, pp. 1–195). Baden-Baden: Nomos Verlagsgesellschaft mbH & Co. KG.

Selwyn, N. (ed.) (2012) *Education in a Digital World. Global Perspectives on Technology and Education*. London: Institute for Education.

Shetye, N. (2021) 'Digitalisation for climate action in cities', in Albrecht, E., Palekhov, D., Kramm, S. and Mileski, T. (Eds.), *Transposition of the Acquis Communautaire: Environment and Migration*, 77 pp. 95–102. Hamburg: Dr. Kovac.

UN (2015) *Transforming Our World: The 2030 Agenda for Sustainable Development. Resolution adopted by the General Assembly on 25 September 2015*. A/RES/70/1. Available at: https://www.un.org/ga/search/view_doc.asp?symbol=A/RES/70/1&Lang=E. (Accessed: 7 March 2022).

UNDP (2019) *Human Development Report. 2019. Beyond Income, Beyond Averages, Beyond Today. Inequalities in Human Development in the 21st Century*. United Nations Development Programme. http://hdr.undp.org/sites/default/files/hdr2019.pdf (Accessed: 7th March 2022).

UNDP (2020) *Human Development Report. 2020. The Next Frontier. Human Development and the Anthropocene*. Available at: http://hdr.undp.org/sites/default/files/hdr2020.pdf (Accessed: 7 March 2022).

UNESCO (2020) *Education for Sustainable Development: A Roadmap. #ESDfor2030*. Available at: https://unesdoc.unesco.org/ark:/48223/pf0000374802.locale=en (Accessed: 7th March 2022).

UNESCO (2021a) *Supporting Learning Recovery One Year into COVID-19. The Global Education Coalition in Action*. Available at: https://unesdoc.unesco.org/ark:/48223/pf0000376061 (Accessed: 7 March 2022).

UNESCO (2021b) *Berlin Declaration on Education for Sustainable Development*. Available at: https://en.unesco.org/sites/default/files/esdfor2030-berlin-declaration-en.pdf (Accessed: 7th March 2022).

UNESCO, UNFCCC (2016) *Action for Climate Empowerment – Guidelines for accelerating solutions through Education, Training, and Public Awareness*. Available at: https://unfccc.int/files/cooperation_and_support/education_and_outreach/application/pdf/action_for_climate_empowerment_guidelines.pdf (Accessed: 7 March 2022).

UNESCO Institute for Statistics (2020) *UIS COVID-19 Response: Data to Inform Policies that Mitigate Setbacks in Education Gains*. Available at: http://uis.unesco.org/en/news/uis-covid-19-response-data-inform-policies-mitigate-setbacks-education-gains. (Accessed: 7th March 2022).

We are Social (2017) *2017 Digital Yearbook: Digital Data for Every Country in the World*. Available at: https://wearesocial.com/uk/special-reports/2017-digital-yearbook (Accessed: 7 March 2022).

WGBU (2019) *Towards Our Common Digital Future (Flagship Report)*. Available at: https://www.wbgu.de/en/publications/publication/towards-our-common-digital-future. (Accessed: 7 March 2022).

Wolfert, S., Ge, L., Verdouw, C. and Bogaardt, M. (2017) 'Big Data in Smart Farming – A review', *Agricultural Systems*, 153, pp. 69–80. https://doi.org/10.1016/j.agsy.2017.01.023

World Vision (2019) *e-mlimi: Transforming Farmer's Lives through Technology*. Available at: https://www.wvi.org/stories/malawi/e-mlimi-transforming-farmers-lives-through-technology (Accessed: 7 March 2022).

15

FEMINIST DIGITAL DEVELOPMENT

The Missing Jigsaw Piece in the European Union's Strategic Partnership with Africa

Zuzana Sladkova and Sumbal Bashir

15.1 Introduction

The future of development cooperation is digital. This chapter is an attempt to understand if it is also inclusive, that is, if it provides equal opportunities for women and girls to participate in the digital economy. The Africa–Europe digital partnership is ambitious, but it is important to keep a broader perspective of how digital transformation intersects with gender inequalities. The digital transformation brings great opportunities for progress in Africa's economy and society, but it also presents new vulnerabilities for meaningful participation by women and girls in the digital economy. Women and girls (not only) in Africa lag behind in their access to information and communication technologies, connectivity, digital skills, participation in digital careers, and leadership (Mare, 2021). This gender digital divide has been exacerbated by the COVID-19 pandemic (ITU, 2021). A feminist vision that centres the needs of women and girls will be necessary to ensure that digital transformation does not leave them behind.

The gender digital divide cannot be overlooked as it can worsen the inequality between not only women and men, but also the Global South and the Global North. In sub-Saharan Africa (SSA), women are 13% less likely than men to own mobile phones and 37% less likely to use mobile internet, making it the region with the second highest mobile gender gap in the world (GSMA, 2020). This is corroborated by the fact that Africa is also the region with the lowest internet penetration in the world (28.2% as compared to 82.5% in Europe). While the gender gap in access to the internet has been shrinking in Europe from 9.4% in 2013 to 5.3% in 2019, it has increased in Africa from 20.7% in 2013 to 33% in 2019 (ITU, 2019).

The gender digital divide in Africa closely correlates with the gender equality ranking of the continent (African Union, 2020; Mare, 2021). In the Global

DOI: 10.4324/9781003274322-15

Gender Gap Report 2020, sub-Saharan Africa (SSA) was ranked the third last region in terms of achievements in gender equality, while the Middle East and North Africa (MENA) was ranked last, with an estimated 95.1 years and 139.9 years, respectively, required to close the gender gap when proceeding at current pace (WEF, 2020). Taking action would have a significant economic impact: if 600 million more women across developing countries were connected to the internet, this could contribute up to USD 18 billion to global GDP (Intel, 2013). Against this backdrop, we ask about the change that is needed for the gender dimension to be fully addressed by digital transformation agendas across the world. More specifically, we ask what (policy) measures could the European Union (EU) take to prioritise and address the gender gaps in its strategic partnership with Africa, especially in its digital cooperation.

A stronger focus on gender equality becomes an opportunity for the EU to demonstrate its genuine interest to ensure a fair and sustainable world where no one is left behind. This would help create a future where digital transformation reduces gender gaps instead of worsening them, and in turn ensures a fairer society. The integration of gender aspects in digital policies also presents an opportunity to both the EU and the African Union (AU) to accelerate their progress towards achieving the SDGs. Against this backdrop this contribution makes a case for a strengthened political commitment to bring the needs of women and girls into the discussion about opportunities for Africa–Europe digital cooperation. We refer to this approach as Feminist Digital Development (FDD).

The study is based on a qualitative analysis of selected EU policy documents and communications released during the period 2014–2020. Section 15.2 delves into the intersection between digital and gender priorities in the EU's development cooperation and specifically within the financing instrument known as the Neighbourhood, Development and International Cooperation Instrument–Global Europe (NDICI–GE). Section 15.3 explores if and how the AU and the EU align on their shared vision for an inclusive digital transformation. Section 15.4 proposes guidelines for FDD grounded in the principles of feminist foreign policy (FFP) for integrating a feminist lens into the AU–EU partnership on digital transformation.

15.2 Europe's Global Ambition for a Values-Based Digital Leadership

In her inaugural address, President of the European Commission Ursula von der Leyen outlined the EU's vision for leadership in the digital transformation, stating, "we want to lead the way, the European way, to the Digital Age: based on our values, our strength, our global ambitions" (European Commission, 2020a). The Commission presented digitalisation as one of the top priorities for the next five years (2021–2027), taking the EU's ambition to become a global leader in the digital transformation to a new level (European Commission, 2020a). This priority is reflected in the new European Digital Strategy (2020-25), which puts forward the plan to position Europe on the global stage by exporting its model of digital transformation based on European values (European Commission, 2020b). Digital transformation is a relatively recent domain for the EU's foreign policy. It is also an urgent priority for the EU in its race for strategic autonomy and digital sovereignty[1] against the backdrop of geopolitical power struggles and competition in the digital arena (Hobbs, 2020; Liaropoulos, 2021). As the EU seeks to assert its leadership on the global digital stage, particularly in Africa, it remains to be seen how and to what extent "European values" – and specifically gender equality – will shape, inform, and guide this transition.

The growing emphasis on gender equality in the EU's External Action presents an interesting opportunity to analyse this question. Gender equality is one of the core values of the EU and is enshrined in its constitution and international treaties (European Commission, 2020c). The EU's commitment to gender equality dates to the 1997 Treaty of Amsterdam, which made it obligatory for European institutions to mainstream gender in all policy areas, including external action (EU, 1997). However, in the past, many feminist scholars have observed the limitation of the EU's *normative power* as a global gender actor,[2] pointing towards the failure of the EU to effectively mainstream gender equality in its external policies (Woodward and van der Vleuten, 2014; Guerrina and Wright, 2016; Muehlenhoff *et al.*, 2020). Guerrina and Wright (2016, p. 295) observe this as a "dissonance between the way the EU *sees itself* as a normative actor and *how it goes about* incorporating these fundamental values in the development and implementation of external policies".

An examination of the intersection between gender and digitalisation as joint priorities in the EU's External Action can help understand the EU's aspiration to have a normative influence on gender equality in its digital partnerships (Table 15.1).

The Juncker Commission (2014–2019) had taken some steps in the direction of mainstreaming digital transformation and gender equality in development cooperation (European Commission, 2017c). However, the Commission introduced digitalisation as a stand-alone priority only through an independent investment window of the European Fund for Sustainable Development (EFSD)[3] without further guidelines on how to mainstream gender for public and private investors (European Commission, 2017d). The initial proposal for the single external financing instrument NDICI-GE within the Multiannual Financial Framework (MFF) 2021–2027, with a budget of €79.5 billion for the years 2021–2027, mentioned digitalisation only once and gender seven times (European Commission, 2018). Major change happened with the appointment of the von der Leyen Commission and introduction of its new priorities such as the "European green deal" and "Europe fit for the digital age" (EU, 2019). This is reflected in the final text of the NDICI-GE regulation, which refers to digitalisation 18 and gender 47 times (Table 15.2).

Another milestone in this regard is the EU's Action Plan on Gender Equality and Women's Empowerment in External Action 2021–2025 (GAP III) for the period 2021–2025, which makes gender equality a cross-cutting priority of EU

TABLE 15.1 Key Milestones of the EU's Digital Agenda in External Action

Year	Milestones	Significance
2016	Council Conclusions on Mainstreaming digital solutions and technologies in EU development (European Council, 2016).	Digital technologies recognised as a tool to promote gender equality and women empowerment.
2017	New European Consensus on Development "Our World, Our Dignity, Our Future" (European Commission, 2017a).	Recognition of digitalisation as an enabler for "good governance, democracy, the rule of law, and human rights".
2017	The EU External Investment Plan (European Commission, 2017b).	Digital4Development introduced as an investment window of the External Investment Plan.
2017	Staff Working Document on Digital4Development: mainstreaming digital technologies and services into EU Development Policy (European Commission, 2017c).	Proposal for a "Digital 4 Equality Framework" to bridge digital gender divide through development cooperation.
2020	New European Digital Strategy 2020-25 (European Commission, 2020b).	The vision to reposition Europe on the global digital stage.
2020	Gender Action Plan III (European Commission, 2020c).	Targets for 85% of all new external action to contribute to gender equality, digital transformation as a thematic priority.
2020	Launch of the D4D Hub (European Commission, 2020d).	Multi-stakeholder platform for investments in the digital transformation of partner countries based on human-centric principles.
2021	Approval of NDICI-GE (Council of the EU, 2021).	€79.5 billion funding approved to support EU's development cooperation for 2021–2027.

TABLE 15.2 Prioritisation of Gender and Digital in NDICI Negotiations

Document (Keywords)	References to digital	References to gender equality		
		gender	women	girls
NDICI Proposal (European Commission, 2018)	1	7	6	0
NDICI 2021.(Council of the EU, 2021)	18	47	62	21

external action and has set the target for mainstreaming gender in 85% of all new external action. This is the first time that digital transformation has been introduced as a thematic priority area for GAP so that "women, men, girls and boys, in all their diversity, can equally participate in shaping the digital world of tomorrow" (European Commission, 2020e, see also Table 15.3).

TABLE 15.3 Prioritisation of Digital Transformation in Gender Action Plan

Document	Digital as a thematic priority	References to Digital
Gender Action Plan II 2016-20 (European Commission, 2015)	No	1
Gender Action Plan III 2021-25 (European Commission, 2020c)	Yes	27

Linking gender and digitalisation is quite new for the EU's development cooperation; having the right policies is only a start, and the real question is how efficiently the EU will be able to take the agenda forward to achieve the desired transformative change in the framework of its partnership with the AU and African countries (see Conseil Santé, 2020). Achieving this would require clear objectives, targets, and indicators to measure progress. The GAP III is a positive starting point as it makes accountability one of its five key pillars and provides a set of strategic objectives and indicators for measuring the gender impact of digitalisation (European Commission, 2020e); however, its success hinges on the actual adoption by the relevant digital projects and programmes.

15.3 Negotiating a Common Vision for a Values-Based Digital Transformation

EU leaders have committed to working with the AU and African countries towards inclusive digital cooperation. First, the EU's planning documents for development cooperation with African partner countries on digitalisation convey a promising outlook for promoting shared values and human-centric digital transformation (Table 15.1). Second, the EU–AU Digital Economy Task Force (EU–AU DETF), established in 2018, shares the vision of "an inclusive digital economy and society in which every citizen—notably women and young people—has the opportunity to participate in the digital world" (European Commission, 2019). Third, the EU's framework "Towards a Comprehensive Strategy with Africa" reiterates the commitment to partner with Africa on digital transformation and to integrate "good governance, democracy, human rights, the rule of law and gender equality in action and cooperation" (European Commission, 2020f).

However, gender comes up as a fragmented priority when it comes towards translating these commitments into practice (Jones et al., 2020; Vleuten and van Eerdewijk, 2020). At launch of the D4D Hub – a new EU-led multi-stakeholder platform – Jutta Urpilainen, Commissioner for International Partnerships, emphasised the need to address the gender divide, noting that "The digital economy will be a key driver of inclusive sustainable development in Africa only if we bridge the digital divide, including the gender divide" (European Commission, 2020d). And yet, gender does not seem to play a major role in the AU–EU

Flagship projects, which emphasise "human-centric", "fair", and "inclusive" digital development (Table 15.4).

Moreover, a close study of the EU's development cooperation suggests that values are one of the most complicated areas in the EU's relations with partner countries. In the past, the EU has relied on unidirectional approaches and conditional bilateral aid to advance its normative agenda, which has been met with criticism and resistance by African counterparts (Bodomo, 2019; Medinilla and Teevan, 2020; Marks, 2020). The EU already risks losing its influence on the continent given geopolitical shifts towards South–South cooperation and the engagement of China and other partners in the region. By emphasising a values-based approach to digital transformation, the EU positions itself in contrast to China, which does not tie its cooperation to conditionalities or a specific values agenda (Olivier, 2011; Bodomo, 2019; Medinilla and Teevan, 2020).

These developments suggest that the EU may think more strategically about its economic and market interests rather than upholding gender equality when moving forward with digital partnerships. However, now more than ever, the EU needs to recognise that values and interests do not have to be mutually exclusive and a more sophisticated strategy can align the EU and AU on shared values for development cooperation (Laporte, 2017; Teevan and Sheriff, 2019; Medinilla and Teevan, 2020). This would entail strengthening the political and strategic engagement with African counterparts to realise the vision of equality and shared ownership, which was also central to the Joint Africa-EU Strategy (Council of the EU, 2007). As many scholars note, the AU–EU partnership remains fragmented and governed by hierarchies and power-imbalances. For most of the key issues "the EU has continued to set or initiate the agenda and often fails to regularly consult its African partner" (Kell and Vines, 2020, p. 117). Similarly, the EU's approach to gender equality has also been criticised for a unidirectional approach and for its limited engagement of voices from African civil society and women's organisations (Debusscher and van der Vleuten, 2012; Debusscher, 2014; Knoll and Mucchi, 2020; Muehlenhoff et al., 2020). The

TABLE 15.4 Africa: EU D4D Hub Flagship Projects

Flagship	Significance
AU–EU D4D Hub	Multi-stakeholder platform for a "human-centric" digital transformation "to ensure the full protection of human rights in the digital age".
EU–AU Data Flagship	To promote "a fair and sovereign data economy based on shared values and policies that assure strong data protection and inclusive economic growth".
African-European Digital Innovation Bridge	To "strengthen digital innovation networks in Africa and promote intercontinental dialogue" between AU and EU. Digital and Entrepreneurial Skills Academy initiative to support youth and women.

Source: Adopted from D4D Hub (2020)

inequalities and asymmetries of AU–EU relations have often been the "stumbling block and a source for African hesitation, even reluctance, to engage in partnership" (Masters and Landsberg, 2021, p. 77). The EU would need to walk the talk on "the partnership of equals" (Herszenhorn, 2019) to work together with the AU to overcome the past trust deficit and realise the shared vision of inclusive digital transformation.

15.4 From Digital 4 Development (D4D) to Feminist Digital Development (FDD)

Feminist foreign policy (Aggestam and Bergman-Rosamond, 2016) can offer a normative framework for the EU to strive for a gender-inclusive digital transformation in its development cooperation with the AU. As Aggestam and Bergman-Rosamond (2016, p. 323) note, "the 'f-word' signals a strong political commitment to gender equality that is distinct from the one expressed in the more consensus-oriented international policy discourse on gender mainstreaming", and seeks to "renegotiate and challenge power hierarchies and gendered institutions that hitherto defined global institutions and foreign and security policies". Feminist foreign policy provides an opportunity to address the challenges in EU–AU relations as identified in previous section with its attentiveness towards "the stories and lived experiences of women and other marginalised groups at the receiving end of foreign policy conduct" and the linkages between the "political elites and civil grass root movements" and (Aggestam *et al.*, 2019, p. 23 and p. 27).

Several EU Member states, including Sweden, France, Spain, Luxembourg, and, most recently, Germany, have already adopted a feminist foreign policy (FFP). Based on the theoretical grounding of a FFP, we propose guidelines for integrating a feminist lens into the AU–EU partnership on digital transformation, which we hitherto define as "Feminist Digital Development" (FDD). These guidelines can be developed by the AU and EU into a framework to be implemented in the EU–AU D4D partnership. More particularly, we draw from the Government of Sweden's framework for a FPP based on the 3R approach (Rights, Representation, and Resources) to propose guidelines as a starting point to build this shared framework (Government Offices of Sweden, 2020).

A focus on rights encompasses "combating all forms of violence and discrimination" that restrict the freedom of action for women and girls" (Government Offices of Sweden, 2020). In the context of a FDD, it would mean working in collaboration with the African governments and civil society and grassroots organisations to identify and address the structural barriers that prevent women and girls from participating equally as "users, economic agents, and drivers of the data-driven society in the digital economy" (Bashir and Sladkova, 2020). The GAP III already commits to a "gender transformative,[4] rights-based, and intersectional[5] approach" for promoting gender equality. However, this needs to be expanded for digital partnerships, which includes examining one's own foreign policy for power relations that could contribute to marginalisation of women/girls. This also means that all digital projects and initiatives need to adopt a gender-sensitive analysis to cater to the needs of girls and women, as identified by the local partners. For instance, the AU–EU Digital Innovation Bridge flagship mentions that gender will be a focus area. A proper gender-sensitive analysis should be done to ensure that this digital bridge caters to the needs of women entrepreneurs. At the same time, the EU and African partner countries need to work together to put in place policies and frameworks to protect the digital rights of women.

Second, an emphasis on representation means that women and girls are an integral part of the policy and decision-making process in the design and implementation of the digital future. As mentioned earlier, scholars (especially those focused on feminism) have long called for the EU to engage more voices from women's organisations and civil society into the policy, programming, and decision-making process. The EU needs to move beyond lip service to "equal partnership" to taking concrete actions to ensure that African partners, and particularly women, are represented equally, both as decision-makers and as a part of civil society, including in design, implementation, and reporting on D4D projects.

Third, sufficient resources need to be dedicated to realise the need for mainstreaming gender and digital transformation in development partnerships. While having the 85% gender mainstreaming target for EU's External Action is laudable, it needs to be paired with concrete aid allocations to deliver on the promises. Furthermore, the EU must ensure that all investments, including those under the EFSD+, are gender sensitive, and try to ensure that some investments focus specifically on the needs of women, as identified by the local partners, particularly women.

The feminist digital development would provide the EU leadership with a shared vision to bridge the disconnect between the two agendas, which would need to be complemented with capacity building and/or training for the teams in Brussels, member state capitals, and EU delegations in partner countries to align them on the shared vision. Moreover, for a genuine digital partnership, the principles of development effectiveness (OECD, 2011), particularly country ownership and shared responsibility, need to be adopted and respected, to build trust and shared vision with African partners for an inclusive digital partnership.

15.5 Conclusion: Feminist Digital Future as the Way Forward

The EU has made a good start with its ambitious agenda for digital transformation and the gender targets for NDICI-GE. So far, the two priorities have been politically closely aligned, but they are still far from being intertwined together in the D4D agenda. As this chapter shows, it is yet to be seen if the EU will be able to translate its political drive for gender equality into tangible results and outcomes within the framework of the AU–EU digital partnership and the programming of the NDICI-GE.

The new era of EU development cooperation with Africa calls for a stronger mandate and commitment to gender equality and women and girls' empowerment to ensure that the digital transformation is fair and inclusive and bridges gender inequalities and digital divides instead of exasperating them. For this to happen, a feminist vision needs to be integrated into the agenda for digital transformation. The proposed guiding principles for Feminist Digital Development put forward this vision to improve the lives of women and girls (and also men and boys, people with disabilities, LGBTI and minorities) in the context of digital transformation. As the analysis in the prior sections shows, both the EU and AU would need to be ready to work together in a "partnership of equals" to take the steps towards the vision for feminist digital future.

Acknowledgements

This chapter developed out of the joint research of the authors during Policy Leader Fellowship (September 2020 to June 2021) at the School of Transnational Governance at the European University Institute.

Notes

1 Though these terms may have varying definitions, strategic autonomy broadly refers to the EU's ambition for "more resilience, more influence, and less dependence" (European Council, 2021), while digital sovereignty refers to "European leadership and strategic autonomy in the digital field" (EPRS, 2020).
2 The normative power framework explains the EU's power in international relations as its ability to influence and reshape norms "in its own image" (Manners, 2002, p.252; see also Debusscher and Manners, 2020).
3 ESFD is one of the EU's financial instruments to support investments, primarily in the EU neighbourhood and Africa (European Parliament, 2019).
4 A gender transformative approach is one which "aims to shift gender-power relations, for a positive change of the paradigm(s) that produce discriminations and inequalities" (European Commission, 2020c).
5 An intersectional approach is one that is "based on an acknowledgement of the multiple characteristics and identities of an individual, to analyse and respond to the ways in which sex and gender intersect with other personal characteristics" (European Commission, 2020c).

References

African Union (2020) *The Digital Transformation Strategy for Africa (2020–2030)*. Available at: https://au.int/sites/default/files/documents/38507-doc-dts-english.pdf/ (Accessed: 20 May 2021).

Aggestam, K. and Bergman-Rosamond, A. (2016) 'Swedish feminist foreign policy in the making: Ethics, politics, and gender', *Ethics & International Affairs*, 30(3), pp. 323–334.

Aggestam, K., Bergman Rosamond, A. and Kronsell, A. (2019) 'Theorising feminist foreign policy', *International Relations*, 33(1), pp. 23–39.

Bashir, S. and Sladkova, Z. (2020) Gender action for an inclusive post-pandemic digital transformation. *EUIdeas*. Available at: https://euideas.eui.eu/2021/01/08/gender

-action-for-an-inclusive-post-pandemic-digital-transformation/ (Accessed: 10 March 2021).

Bodomo, A. (2019) 'Africa-China-Europe relations: Conditions and conditionalities', *Journal of International Studies*, 12(4), 115–129.

Council of the EU (2007) *The Africa-EU Strategic Partnership. A Joint Africa-EU Strategy.* Press. Available at: https://www.consilium.europa.eu/uedocs/cms_data/docs/pressdata/en/er/97496.pdf/ (Accessed: 20 May 2021).

Council of the EU (2021) *Position of the Council at first reading with a view to the adoption of a Regulation of the European Parliament and of the Council establishing the Neighbourhood, Development and International Cooperation Instrument – Global Europe – Adopted by the Council on 26 May 2021.* Available at: https://data.consilium.europa.eu/doc/document/ST-6879-2021-REV-1/en/pdf/ (Accessed: 12 June 2021).

Conseil Santé (2020) *Digital4Women: how to enable women's empowerment in Africa through mainstreaming digital technologies and services in EU development programmes. Conseil Santé. Commissioned by DEVCO.* Available at: https://europa.eu/capacity4dev/public-gender/documents/digital4women-how-enable-women-empowerment-africa-through-mainstreaming-digital-4/ (Accessed: 12 June 2021).

Debusscher P. (2014) Gender mainstreaming on the ground? The case of EU development aid towards Rwanda, in: Weiner, Elaine and Heather MacRae (eds) *The Persistent Invisibility of Gender in EU Policy' European Integration online Papers (EIoP), Special issue 1,* Vol. 18, Article 4. https://doi.org/10.1695/2014004.

Debusscher, P. and van der Vleuten, A. (2012) 'Mainstreaming gender in European Union development cooperation with Sub-Saharan Africa: Promising numbers, narrow contents, telling silences', *International Development Planning Review*, 34(3), pp. 319–338.

Debusscher, P. and Manners, I (2020) 'Understanding the European Union as a global gender actor: The holistic intersectional and inclusive study of gender+ in external actions', *Political Studies Review*, 18(3), pp. 410–425.

D4D Hub (2020). Web. Available at: https://d4dlaunch.eu/#about/ (Accessed: 01 March 2021).

European Council (2016) *Council Conclusions on Mainstreaming Digital Solutions and Technologies in EU Development Policy.* Available at: https://www.consilium.europa.eu/en/press/press-releases/2016/11/28/conclusions-digital-solutions-and-technologies-in-eu-development-policy/ (Accessed: 12 June 2021).

European Commission (2015) *Joint Staff Working Document on "Gender Equality and Women's Empowerment: Transforming the Lives of Girls and Women through EU External Relations 2016–2020".* Available at: https://international-partnerships.ec.europa.eu/policies/gender-equality/gender-equality-and-empowering-women-and-girls_en#background-gap-i-and-ii/ (Accessed: 12 June 2021).

European Commission (2017a). *The New European Consensus On Development 'Our World, Our Dignity, Our Future'. Joint Statement By The Council And The Representatives Of The Governments Of The Member States Meeting Within The Council, The European Parliament And The European Commission.* Available at: https://ec.europa.eu/international-partnerships/system/files/european-consensus-on-development-final-20170626_en.pdf/ (Accessed: 12 June 2021).

European Commission (2017b) *European Fund for Sustainable Development (EFSD) Guarantee. Title: Investment window - Digital for Development.* Available at: https://ec.europa.eu/eu-external-investment-plan/sites/default/files/efsd-guarantee-windows-digital-for-development_.pdf/ (Accessed: 12 June 2021).

European Commission (2017c) *Staff Working Document Digital4Development: Mainstreaming Digital Technologies and Services into EU Development Policy.* Available at: https://digital

-strategy.ec.europa.eu/en/library/digital4development-mainstreaming-digital
-technologies-and-services-eu-development-policy (Accessed: 12 June 2021).

European Commission (2017d). *Your Guide to the External Investment Plan. Release No 1.* November 2017. Available at: http://higherlogicdownload.s3.amazonaws.com/ EVAL/3ca96412-dd14-40b5-a5e8-86f0bea1a4ff/UploadedImages/EC_External _Investment_Plan_Nov17_Newsletter.pdf/ (Accessed: 12 June 2021).

European Commission (2018) *NDICI Regulation. Proposal for a Regulation of the European Parliament and of the Council establishing the Neighbourhood, Development and International Cooperation Instrument.* Available at: https://eur-lex.europa.eu/legal-content/EN/ TXT/?uri=COM%3A2018%3A460%3AFIN/ (Accessed: 12 June 2021).

European Commission (2019) *New Africa-Europe Digital Economy Partnership – report of the EU-AU Digital Economy Task Force.* Available at: https://digital-strategy.ec.europa.eu/en/ library/new-africa-europe-digital-economy-partnership-report-eu-au-digital-economy -task-force#:~:text=The%20European%20Union%2DAfrican%20Union,African %20digital%20transformation%20can%20achieve/ (Accessed: 12 June 2021).

European Commission (2020a) *State of the Union address by President von der Leyen at the European Parliament Plenary.* Available at: https://ec.europa.eu/commission/presscorner /detail/en/SPEECH_20_1655/ (Accessed: 12 June 2021).

European Commission (2020b) *The European Digital Strategy.* Available at: https://ec .europa.eu/digital-single-market/en/content/european-digital-strategy   (Accessed: 25 April 2021).

European Commission (2020c) *Gender Action Plan: Putting Women and Girls' Rights at the Heart of the Global Recovery for a Gender-equal World.* European Commission. Available at: https://ec.europa.eu/commission/presscorner/detail/en/IP_20_2184/ (Accessed: 12 June 2021).

European Commission (2020d) *Team Europe: Digital4Development Hub Launched to Help Shape a Fair Digital Future Across the Globe.* European Commission. Available at: https:// ec.europa.eu/international-partnerships/news/team-europe-digital4development -hub-launched-help-shape-fair-digital-future-across-globe_en/ (Accessed: 12 June 2021).

European Commission (2020e) *Joint Staff Working Document – Objectives and Indicators to Frame the Implementation of the Gender Action Plan III (2021–25).* Available at: https:// eur-lex.europa.eu/legal-content/EN/TXT/PDF/?uri=CELEX:52020SC0284 &from=EN/ (Accessed: 12 June 2021).

European Commission (2020f) *Joint Communication to the European Parliament and the Council. Towards a Comprehensive Strategy with Africa.* Available at: https://ec.europa .eu/international-partnerships/system/files/communication-eu-africa-strategy-join -2020-4-final_en.pdf/ (Accessed: 12 June 2021).

EU (1997). *The Treaty of Amsterdam.* ISBN 92-828-1652-4. Available at: https://europa .eu/european-union/sites/default/files/docs/body/treaty_of_amsterdam_en.pdf/ (Accessed: 12 June 2021).

EU (2019). *European Union Priorities for 2019–2024.* Web. Available at: https://europa.eu/ european-union/about-eu/priorities_en (Accessed: 04 June 2021).

EU (2021). *Working Better Together as Team Europe. Through Joint Programming and Joint Implementation.* Web. Available at: https://europa.eu/capacity4dev/working-better -together (Accessed: 01 August 2021).

European Parliament (2019). *European Fund for Sustainable Development. Briefing, How the EU Budget Is Spent.* Available at: https://www.europarl.europa.eu/RegData/etudes /BRIE/2019/637893/EPRS_BRI(2019)637893_EN.pdf/ (Accessed: 01 August 2021).

EU4Digital. Web. Available at: https://eufordigital.eu/ (Accessed: 02 June 2021).

EPRS (2020) 'Digital sovereignty for Europe', *EPRS Ideas Paper*, Available at: https://www.europarl.europa.eu/RegData/etudes/BRIE/2020/651992/EPRS_BRI(2020)651992_EN.pdf (Accessed: 02 June 2021).

Government Offices of Sweden (2020) 'The Swedish foreign service action plan for feminist foreign policy 2019–2022', Available at: https://www.government.se/49700e/contentassets/9992f701ab40423bb7b37b2c455aed9a/utrikesforvaltningens-handlingsplan-for-feministisk-utrikespolitik-2021_eng.pdf/ (Accessed: 02 August 2021).

GSMA (2020) Mobile Gender Gap Report, Available at: https://www.gsma.com/mobilefordevelopment/wp-content/uploads/2020/05/GSMA-The-Mobile-Gender-Gap-Report-2020.pdf/ (Accessed: 02 August 2021).

Guerrina, R. and Wright, K.A.M. (2016) 'Gendering normative power Europe: lessons of the women, peace and security agenda', *International Affairs*, 92 (2), pp. 293–312.

Herszenhorn, D (2019) 'Von der Leyen ventures to the heart of Africa. In Ethiopia, Commission president says she seeks a 'partnership of equals' with African Union', *POLITICO*, Available at: https://www.politico.eu/article/european-commission-president-ursula-von-der-leyen-ventures-to-the-heart-of-africa-ethiopia-african-union/ (Accessed: 02 August 2021).

Hobbs, C. (ed.) (2020) *Europe's Digital Sovereignty: From Rulemaker to Superpower in the Age of US-China Rivalry, Essay Collection – European Council on Foreign Relations*, Available at: https://ecfr.eu/wp-content/uploads/europe_digital_sovereignty_rulemaker_superpower_age_us_china_rivalry.pdf/ (Accessed: 02 August 2021).

ITU (2019). Measuring digital development Facts and figures 2019. ITU Publications. Available at: https://www.itu.int/en/ITU-D/Statistics/Documents/facts/FactsFigures2019.pdf/ (Accessed: 02 August 2021).

ITU (2021). Gendered digital divide "Digitally empowered generation equality in the wake of Covid-19". Available at: https://www.itu.int/en/ITU-D/Regional-Presence/Europe/Documents/Events/2021/Gendered%20Digital%20Divide/Outcome_Report_GenderedDigitalDivide.pdf?csf=1&e=5yYFkK/ (Accessed: 02 August 2021).

Intel Corporation (2013). Intel announces groundbreaking 'Women and the web' report with UN Women and State Department, Available at: https://newsroom.intel.com/news-releases/intel-announces-groundbreaking-women-and-the-web-report-with-un-women-and-state-department/#gs.1vhdme/ (Accessed: 02 August 2021).

Jones, A. et al (2020) 'EU development cooperation with Sub-Saharan Africa 2013–201', ECDPM. Available at: https://ecdpm.org/wp-content/uploads/ECDPM-DIE_EU_development_cooperation_with_Sub-Saharan_Africa_202005.pdf/ (Accessed: 02 August 2021).

Kell,F. and Vines, A. (2020), 'The evolution of the Joint Africa-EU Strategy (2007–2020)', in Haastrup T. et al. (eds.) *The Routledge Handbook of EU-Africa Relations*. London: Routledge. https://doi.org/9781315170916

Knoll, A. and Mucchi, V. (2020) 'Africa-Europe relations beyond 2020: looking through a gender lens', *ECDPM Paper*, Available at: https://ecdpm.org/wp-content/uploads/Africa-Europe-Relations-Beyond-2020-Gender-Lens-ECDPM-Discussion-Paper-285-2020.pdf/ (Accessed: 02 August 2021).

Laporte, G. (2017) Do values still matter in the Europe-Africa partnership?, *ECDPM Talking Points Blog*, Available at: https://ecdpm.org/talking-points/values-matter-europe-africa-partnership/ (Accessed: 02 August 2021).

Liaropoulos, A. (2021) 'EU digital sovereignty: A regulatory power searching for its strategic autonomy in the digital domain" in Proceedings of the 20th European Conference on Cyber Warfare and Security.

Manners, I. (2002), 'Normative power Europe: a contradiction in terms?', *Journal of Common Market Studies*, 40 (2), pp. 235–58.

Mare A. (2021) Addressing digital and innovation gender divide: Perspectives from Zimbabwe, in: Daniels C., Dosso M., Amadi-Echendu J. (eds), *Entrepreneurship, technology commercialisation, and innovation policy in Africa*. Springer, Cham. https://doi.org/10.1007/978-3-030-58240-1_3.

Masters, L. and Landsberg, C. (2021) 'Foreign policy and EU-Africa relations from the European Security Strategy to the EU Global Strategy', Haastrup T. et al. (eds.) *The Routledge Handbook of EU-Africa Relations*. London: Routledge. https://doi.org/9781315170916

Marks, S. (2020) 'African Union to EU: We've got our own strategy, thanks. African Union says it doesn't need to be lectured on European values', *POLITICO,* Available at: https://www.politico.eu/article/commission-in-africa-ursula-von-der-leyen-frans-timmermans-moussa-faki/ (Accessed: 02 August 2021).

Medinilla, A. and Teevan, C. (2020), 'Beyond good intentions: the new EU-Africa partnership', ECDPM Discussion Paper, Available at: https://ecdpm.org/wp-content/uploads/Beyond-Good-Intentions-The-New-EU-Africa-Partnership-ECDPM-Discussion-Paper-267-2020.pdf (Accessed: 02 August 2021).

Muehlenhoff H.L., van der Vleuten A. and Welfens N. (2020) 'Slipping off or turning the tide? Gender equality in European Union's external relations in times of crisis', *Political Studies Review* 18(3), pp. 322–328.

OECD (2011). Busan Partnership for effective development co-operation: Fourth high level forum on aid effectiveness, Busan, Republic of Korea, 29 November – 1 December 2011, OECD Publishing, Paris, https://doi.org/10.1787/54de7baa-en.

Olivier, G. (2011) 'From colonialism to partnership in Africa–Europe relations?, *The International Spectator*, 46 (1), pp. 53–67.

Teevan, C. and Sherriff, A. (2019) 'Mission possible? The geopolitical commission and the partnership with Africa', Available at: https://ecdpm.org/wp-content/uploads/Mission-Possible-Geopolitical-Commission-Partnership-Africa-ECDPM-Briefing-Note-113.pdf/ (Accessed: 02 August 2021).

van der Vleuten, A. and van Eerdewijk, A. (2020), 'The fragmented inclusion of gender equality in AU-EU relations in times of crises', *Political Studies Review*, 18(3), pp. 444–459.

WEF (2020), 'Global gender gap report 2020', World Economic Forum, Available at: http://www3.weforum.org/docs/frican WEF_GGGR_2020.pdf/ (Accessed: 02 August 2021).

Woodward A.E. and van der Vleuten A. (2014), 'EU and the export of gender equality norms: Myth and facts', in: van der Vleuten A., van Eerdewijk A., Roggeband C. (eds.) *Gender Equality Norms in Regional Governance*. Palgrave Macmillan, London.

16

FOSTERING PROSPERITY FOR AFRICAN FEMALE ENTREPRENEURS

Opportunities for AU–EU Cooperation in Digital Entrepreneurship Networks

Francine Beleyi

16.1 Introduction

Evidence shows that when women earn a good living, they are more likely to transmit the benefits and skills acquired to their families and communities, reinvesting up to 90% of their incomes compared to 40% for men. In Africa, as elsewhere, more and more women are launching businesses. In fact, Africa has the highest number of women entrepreneurs per capita in the world, with a female entrepreneurship rate of 25.9% in sub-Saharan Africa. Nonetheless, female entrepreneurs in Africa are confronted with substantial challenges related to access to financial and non-financial services. They face an estimated USD 42 billion financing gap. Even when they own a business, the size and growth of their businesses remain constrained by lack of finance, barriers resulting from legal and regulatory frameworks and skills constraints (AfDB, n.d.). The potential benefits of the digital economy – including the impact of using digital tools in non-digital businesses – will only be fully realised if women have access to the necessary skills and opportunities.

Digital entrepreneurship networks that make use of simple tools such as Zoom, WhatsApp, Facebook, and other digital tools to connect entrepreneurs, can allow female entrepreneurs to share experiences and learn from communities of entrepreneurs online. They provide training and networking opportunities that can be essential to providing them with the skills and opportunities they need to grow their businesses. Digital entrepreneurship networks come in all shapes – from local and national networks to a growing number of continental and diaspora networks spanning multiple countries. Some networks began primarily as in-person networks, gradually developing a growing online presence, whilst others exist primarily online. There are digital entrepreneurship networks focused exclusively on female entrepreneurs, while others make an effort to have

DOI: 10.4324/9781003274322-16

strong female representation or even parity. Furthermore, some digital networks' principal role lies in the very act of creating a network, whilst others have grown out of other activities.

Digital entrepreneurship networks offer opportunities in terms of training and mentoring, marketing of products, and access to funding opportunities, thereby providing the essential resources entrepreneurs need in order to develop and grow their businesses. They can also help to develop members' entrepreneurial social capital by widening their networks and building their access to information and resources (Greve and Salaff, 2003). While digital networks were widely used before COVID-19, their uptake has been propelled forward by the pandemic and the consequent lockdowns and restrictions across the world. This has been equally true in Africa and in Europe, where an increasing number of networking and related training opportunities moved online. This move to online networks is likely to be a permanent phenomenon for many organisations delivering training and networking opportunities as it is efficient and allows for a growing number of transnational contacts, both within and across continents.

The chapter argues that the growth of digital networks can allow African female entrepreneurs to access formal and peer support, mentorship, and opportunities to market and pitch their products better. This can help them in many ways, including by enabling access to training opportunities and wider entrepreneurial social capital they need to develop their businesses, access new markets, and raise funds. Yet, women also face specific difficulties in accessing networks and associated opportunities, and thus specific attention needs to be paid to how to ensure equitable access.

Supporting women's economic empowerment and women's digital inclusion are key goals of European Union (EU) cooperation with Africa, and thus supporting and growing digital networks – including those that link Africa and Europe – should be integrated into the EU's digital strategy. However, as discussed in the remainder of this chapter, there are still many challenges to the roll-out and equal uptake of digital networks. More needs to be done to ensure that such opportunities are widely available and accessible by female entrepreneurs in Africa.

This chapter is based on a mixed methods approach, comprising a literature review on female entrepreneurship, digital networks, and role of the diaspora, the professional experience of the author and five interviews that provided additional insights to support the data from the literature. The interviews, conducted between April and May 2021, include the CEO of an African entrepreneurship hub, the first CEO of the largest entrepreneur programme in Africa, diaspora organisations, and experts (see Annex 1 for list of interviewees). All interviews were conducted remotely by video call with the aim of gathering practitioner knowledge on the challenges that female entrepreneurs in Africa face, how the diaspora may help advance entrepreneurship on the continent through the use of digital networks, and opportunities for African Union (AU)–EU cooperation in fostering prosperity for female entrepreneurs in Africa.

16.2 Women and Access to Entrepreneurship Networks

Networks play an important role for entrepreneurs as they provide links to start-up incubators and accelerators, as well as to investors, connecting entrepreneurs with resources, opportunities, information, labour, skills, and other contacts that help build entrepreneurial social capital (Greve and Salaff, 2003). This entrepreneurial social capital is vital to allowing entrepreneurs to build their businesses, particularly in the technology sector where access to the right contacts can be vital to access the resources to grow one's business (Maurer and Ebers, 2006).

Digital technologies allow users to access a number of networks and training opportunities online, something that has been speeded up by the advent of COVID-19. As a result, a growing number of networking opportunities have migrated online. For African female entrepreneurs, these include a variety of networks and training programmes such as networks that facilitate connections with African diasporas in Europe and beyond. Conversely, these networks allow diaspora entrepreneurs to connect and identify opportunities in Africa, offering the potential for win–win outcomes.

Yet women can face difficulties in accessing entrepreneurship networks and the associated opportunities. Light and Dana (2013) note that female entrepreneurs often lack the social networks to connect them with key "external networks that control essential business resources" (p. 606). External networks are those external to one's own company that can include contacts with incubators and investors vital to growing a business. However, feminist scholars take issue with this type of argument, which they argue tends to focus on deficiencies in women and how to "fix" those, rather than looking at deficiencies in the gender sensitivity of existing structures (Ahl, 2006). Such analysis also misses the potential strengths of women entrepreneurs and how these can be leveraged.

Ozkazanc-Pan and Clark Muntean (2018) emphasise that trust seems to play a big role in female entrepreneurship and that women are more relational than transactional in the way they approach networks. Existing male-dominated entrepreneurship networks, and the incubators and accelerators that these networks give access to, are often based on a more transactional approach that suits male entrepreneurs. Such male-dominated networks can be difficult for female entrepreneurs to adapt to as women's approach tends to be built on fewer, yet stronger, relationships. The choice of words to advertise and the channels that are chosen can be important to ensuring women see opportunities (Ozkazanc-Pan and Clark Muntean, 2018). In the online space, for example, women face additional obstacles, as they are more worried about online abuse by sexist trolls or psychological violence. Women tend to feel more comfortable in smaller groups, where they feel they can voice their opinion, share the challenges they face, and speak openly (Chair et al., 2020).

Opinion is divided on whether women-only networks or mixed networks are more effective. McAdam et al.'s (2018) study of the use of women-only networks by development agencies to promote women's entrepreneurship finds that the promotion of women-only networks, particularly in international cooperation, fails to generate "gender-capital". This they argue means that women-only networks segregate women and impede their credibility as entrepreneurs "due to an inability to access sufficient economic, social, cultural and symbolic capital" (p. 2). Other scholars, however, highlight the potential of women-only networks to foster supportive relationships between more senior and junior women, including mentoring. Additionally, they can increase the visibility of relevant issues and foster advocacy (Villesèche & Josserand, 2017).

This chapter explores how both women-only and mixed networks can play a role in building women's entrepreneurial social capital, stressing the importance of adapting networks to female entrepreneurs' needs.

16.3 Opportunities for Female Entrepreneurship

Context is also vital and will play an important role in creating further opportunities for African female entrepreneurs. At present, perhaps the most important economic development-influencing context is the African Continental Free Trade Area (AfCFTA), which came into effect in January 2021. Negotiations for the e-commerce protocol of the AfCFTA were fast-tracked to begin in 2021, with the aim to facilitate electronic transactions, boost investments in the digital infrastructure, and develop e-commerce (Banga et al., 2021). Realising the importance of context and the vital roles of women in entrepreneurship and Africa's socioeconomic development, Wamkele Mene, Secretary-General of the AfCFTA Secretariat, vowed to put women and young people at the heart of the AfCFTA agreement, including by improving access to trade and support to small and medium-sized businesses (Ighobor 2020). Yet, further research needs to be done to understand to what extent and in what ways the AfCFTA can in fact support the economic development of women in general, but, more specifically, female entrepreneurs in Africa.

The AU Digital Transformation Strategy (DTS), which emphasises the importance of creating an enabling environment for digital transformation in Africa, also points to the importance of gender in digital transformation. It indicates that special attention must be paid to the specific needs of women, and lays out the importance of gender-inclusive education frameworks and policies, the need to boost digital skills for women and girls, the specific role that digital tools can play in improving the life of women in agriculture, and the need to encourage women in research and innovation (AU 2020).

As this edited volume traces, digital cooperation has become an increasingly important component of the EU–AU partnership. The EU–AU Digital Economy Task Force (DETF) report mentions that the digital gender divide has increased in Africa despite decreasing globally and states that "there is a need to lower usage barriers related to costs and literacy, as well as to address stereotypes and gender inequalities hindering individual access to technology" (EC 2019, p. 30). It also specifically mentions the role of digital entrepreneurship in "promoting gender equality, bridging the digital divide and improving the inclusion of women for economic and social growth" (EC 2019, p. 38, also pp. 42–3).

At the same time, the EU–AU partnership is also building an important focus on networks as part of the digital partnership. One of the major flagships of the EU Digital for Development (D4D) Hub is the African European Digital Innovation Bridge (AEDIB) Initiative, which aims to connect the innovation ecosystems in Europe and in Africa. This initiative includes a strong focus on building networks, notably by looking to help build a Pan-African Network of Digital Innovation Hubs (DIHs) and to provide knowledge, expertise, and technology so as to allow companies to develop and grow (AEDIB, n.d.).

Meanwhile, the EU has committed to ambitious goals with regard to gender in its external action (Teevan et al., 2021) and in its recently published Gender Action Plan III, which includes digital cooperation as a new area to be highlighted in its external action (EC 2020). The EU still has some way to go to achieve its digital ambitions. As Sladkova and Bashir (2022) argue in this volume, it will be vital that digital and gender are both mainstreamed across EU programming.

In the next section, we discuss four of the key challenges that female entrepreneurs face in Africa.

16.4 How Digital Networks Can Support Female Entrepreneurs

As already mentioned, female entrepreneurs face a host of challenges related to access to financial and non-financial services. These include access to training, mentoring, and support, as well as access to finance, markets, and information. They also include social norms and issues around lack of confidence. This section traces some of the ways that digital entrepreneurship networks can meet these challenges and help women to develop their entrepreneurial social capital and to build thriving businesses.

16.4.1 Addressing the Lack of Business Training, Mentoring, and Support

There is a persistent gap in education and skills between male and female entrepreneurs in Africa. Self-employed women have completed fewer years of education than self-employed men. In addition, secondary school completion rates are 30% for female entrepreneurs as opposed to 40% for male entrepreneurs; while only 9% of female entrepreneurs have completed higher education, 12% of male entrepreneurs have (World Bank 2019).

Digital networks enable female entrepreneurs to access targeted business training and mentoring, as well as to form strong relationships with other entrepreneurs, and contribute to building entrepreneurial social capital. They also offer the possibility to connect African entrepreneurs with diaspora professionals in Europe and further afield.

An example of such an online network that provides training and mentoring opportunities is the African Women Entrepreneurship Cooperative (AWEC), allowing African female entrepreneurs to develop capacity, better run their businesses, generate more revenue, and create jobs in their communities (AWEC n.d.). Research carried out by AWEC found that African women desire: (1) equal access to long-term business management learning to fill gaps in terms of their business skills; (2) practical lessons that could be applied to their businesses immediately; (3) a strong network of their peers; and (4) business mentorship from senior professionals. AWEC utilised an innovative blended learning model that allowed female entrepreneurs from across Africa and its diaspora to join annual cohorts of 200 female entrepreneurs in a 12-month leadership and business management capacity building programme, regardless of geographic location, sector, or business size. The mentoring is delivered online by volunteers from the African diaspora, Europeans, Americans, and other nationalities. The mentee benefits from the knowledge and experience of a seasoned professional, improving their business acumen. Relatedly, mentees set goals during the programme and are held accountable for the realisation of the goals by the mentor.

Within three application cycles, AWEC had admitted female entrepreneurs from 52 African countries, creating a pan-African community of female entrepreneurs. Once they have completed the 12-month programme, the participants join a growing alumni network. In year two of the AWEC core programme, 72% of mentees increased their annual revenue following participation in the programme, 63% attracted new customers/clients, 43% hired new employees, 76% strengthened their business strategy, and 79% increased the quality of their network. This demonstrates how online networks can contribute to female entrepreneurs' social capital by providing training opportunities, mentoring, and access to wider support from a network or peers.

16.4.2 Access to Finance, Markets, and Information

One of the key barriers for African female entrepreneurs is the lack of access to financial and non-financial services. In sub-Saharan Africa alone, the financing gap for women is estimated at over USD 42 billion, according to the African Development Bank. The EU–AU partnership should work with financial institutions to offer targeted financial support to female entrepreneurs and create specific financial products to help them.

During the COVID-19 pandemic, women were also more adversely impacted. The pandemic resulted in an average drop in sales of 39% for female entrepreneurs versus a drop of 28% for male entrepreneurs in Africa. A combination of factors led to a greater impact on women, such as being overwhelmed in front-line jobs, loss of revenues due to poor digital skills, and increased responsibilities to care for children or older relatives. Only 13% of the female-led MSMEs reported receiving any kind of financing support despite efforts made by governments (IFC 2021b).

Digital networks enable increased access to finance and markets by increasing entrepreneurs' awareness of opportunities. Digital exchanges can increase knowledge of and ability to take advantage of such opportunities by helping female entrepreneurs to understand how things work, including market prospects across Africa and outside the continent. They also offer diaspora entrepreneurs the opportunity to learn about local markets and ways of doing business in Africa.

Similarly, digital networks can help African female entrepreneurs to access funding opportunities and grants – such as those offered by the Tony Elumelu Foundation (TEF) and the Afford Business Centre (ABC). Equally important, many of the initial small grants include training sessions on how to pitch a product to investors or create mechanisms for diasporas to fund SMEs in Africa. Thus, online networks and connectivity open a whole world of new opportunities regarding fundraising for start-ups and SMEs in Africa, particularly for female entrepreneurs.

With the launch of the AfCFTA, it is evident that there are a growing number of online initiatives aimed at connecting women across Africa to markets, and providing them with training and resources in order to do so. One key initiative is the International Trade Centre (ITC) SheTrades Initiative, launched to help women-owned businesses to access business opportunities that are created by the AfCFTA through capacity building, networking, and advocacy. The initiative is working with 50 women-led associations in Africa to realise this objective. The ITC SheTrades platform itself has reached its goal of connecting three million women by the end of 2021 (email correspondence, 20 December 2021). Initially, the ITC focused on building partnerships with governments, but ultimately it developed partnerships with Foundations like TEF that allowed it to connect with many more entrepreneurs (Interview, 21 April 2021). The platform works with stakeholders globally to create opportunities for female entrepreneurs. Supported by a web and mobile app, the platform allows female entrepreneurs to post offers on the platform to sell products and services. Buyers can browse these offers, order products and services, and post tenders to receive bids from sellers (ITC n.d.). Through projects and national chapters, ITC SheTrades is present in 25 countries.

Another relatively new initiative in this area is the 50 Million African Women Speak (50MAWS), which launched in 2020. It is an online business-networking platform that seeks to connect 50 million female entrepreneurs across Africa. It aims at providing African women with information and resources, allowing millions of women in Africa to start, grow, and scale-up businesses. The initiative was set up by three regional economic communities (COMESA, EAC, and ECOWAS) and funded by the African Development Bank (AfDB) after one of their studies showed that circa 70% of African women are financially excluded (AfDB 2019).

16.4.3 Social Norms and Confidence

Cultural barriers and social norms are factors that may prevent women from thriving as entrepreneurs and keep them in poverty. The findings from the Profiting for Parity report (World Bank 2019) highlight that when female entrepreneurs conform to social norms that confine them to household tasks and view men as the breadwinners, they are less likely to aspire to grow a large business. Digital entrepreneurship networks must integrate an understanding of how social norms can constrain women entrepreneurs in certain contexts, whilst also taking into account confidence issues.

Beyond formal training and mentoring opportunities, being part of entrepreneurship networks offers women knowledge, information, support, accountability, motivation, and encouragement to step up. They are no longer alone on their entrepreneurial journey but surrounded by other women who have had similar experiences, thus being able to offer advice to solve particular challenges. Women can tap into this network for support when they need it. Moreover, being part of a network increases accountability. By publicly committing to others, members are more likely to follow through with their commitments. Consequently, female entrepreneurs, who are supported by a network, are encouraged to try harder than if they were left on their own.

Even when women own a business, the size and growth of their businesses are often less than that of their male peers. The report *Women and E-commerce in Africa* by the International Finance Corporation (IFC 2021a) shows that historically women have traded in highly competitive markets such as fashion, or in markets with low margins. Thanks to e-commerce, some women are now entering lucrative fields with high margins such as electronics. If more women have the confidence to switch from sectors with low margins to sectors with higher margins, this could be a route for women to close earnings gaps and boost the performance of their businesses in the long run.

The same IFC research shows that if female entrepreneurs' sales reached parity with men's, the value of the African e-commerce market could increase by nearly USD 15 billion between 2025 and 2030. It will thus be vital to encourage women to enter high-value sectors in e-commerce traditionally occupied by men.

16.5 Ensuring Equal Access to Digital Networks and Associated Opportunities

As outlined in Section 16.2, women do not respond to opportunities in the same way as men (Ozkazanc-Pan and Clark Muntean, 2018), and therefore it is essential that their needs are built into the design and communication of networking and training opportunities.

Digital networks can be a great avenue to attract female entrepreneurs, but special attention is needed when advertising for training or business opportunities. For example, the choice of language in communications can be important. The African Foundation for Development (AFFORD) focuses on women and young people in their communication for the Afford Business Centre (ABC). Their emphasis on social enterprise, social impact, and sustainability was also seen as an important factor in attracting more women, who may be more interested in the social impact of their enterprise. In 2021, the launch of ABC Benin, a programme providing mentoring, business advisory, business development, and investment sessions, included about 50% female entrepreneurs (Interview, Stella Opoku Owusu – AFFORD, 21 April 2021).

The Tony Elumelu Foundation (TEF) entrepreneurship programme is another online training and mentoring programme, which is available to both women and men. TEF's vision is to create an ecosystem for everyone, both men and women, and provide equal opportunity to scale and thrive. They have empowered over 3,000 female entrepreneurs and TEF alumni have directly created an additional 35,000 jobs for women. CEO Ifeyinwa Ugochukwu has emphasised TEF's goal to achieve gender inclusivity and the "unique traditional and cultural barriers preventing women from fully engaging in entrepreneurship" (Tony Elumelu Foundation 2021b). Although the programme has not yet reached parity, TEF is working with the EU to launch a programme aiming to reach 2,500 female entrepreneurs (Tony Elumelu Foundation 2020). The partnership commits €20 million in financial and technical support for women-owned businesses, across all 54 African countries to provide increased access to market linkages, supply chains, and venture capital investments. They created another partnership with Google in June 2021 to empower 500 rural aspiring female entrepreneurs with USD 5,000 seed capital. Such programmes can help to bridge the gender opportunity gap and ensure parity for female entrepreneurs.

On the other hand, the Africa Technology Business Network (ATBN) focuses exclusively on supporting the acceleration of female entrepreneurs, working with digital innovation hubs and supporting ecosystems. Given their focus on female entrepreneurs, they adapted to the needs of the women they worked with, using a range of digital tools, like Facebook and WhatsApp groups, to connect entrepreneurs and mentors and creating their own app in Ghana to allow female entrepreneurs to download small courses (Interview, Eunice Baguma Ball – ATBN, 4 May 2021).

When digital networks are not exclusively focused on women, reaching parity between male and female participants – and responding to the specific needs of women – may require adopting innovative approaches. This includes notably adopting communication strategies and language that responds to the needs of female entrepreneurs. However, it may also be necessary to design initiatives exclusively for women so as to ensure that these initiatives respond to the specific needs of women.

16.6 Conclusion and Recommendations

This chapter has explored how female entrepreneurs in Africa make effective use of digital networks to facilitate access to peer support, mentorship, and business training, which can help to boost female entrepreneurs' confidence and capabilities to run more successful businesses, thereby increasing their entrepreneurial social capital. The business development facilitated by these opportunities is a crucial engine of economic growth and job creation and can be a key driver to African development. This in turn can help create thriving businesses and support job creation across the continent.

Facilitating female entrepreneurs to grow and create profitable businesses is vital to achieving SDG5 and to AU and EU goals around cooperation and job creation in Africa. Yet, it is vital to recognise the number of gender-specific constraints that female entrepreneurs face and the need for interventions to target these challenges. As the EU and AU embark on building a digital partnership, it will be essential that the needs of female entrepreneurs are integrated into all efforts to support entrepreneurship on the African continent. To achieve this goal, African female entrepreneurs need support to access capital, training, mentoring, and networks that open doors to new markets and finance, and allow them to grow their businesses. Digital entrepreneurship networks can allow female entrepreneurs to grow their businesses, to increase profitability and to move into high-growth and high-margin sectors in line with the recommendations of the IFC report (2021a). As outlined in the recommendations, the EU and AU can play an important role in supporting the development of these tools, and in turn in supporting female entrepreneurs.

In the aftermath of the outbreak of COVID-19, digital tools are a critical avenue to develop female entrepreneurs' capabilities and accelerate the growth of their businesses. Indeed, the COVID-19 pandemic has disproportionately impacted women. Reversing these trends will be key to ensuring women can compete in an increasingly digital economy following the pandemic.

- The growth of digital networks has the potential to offer African female entrepreneurs a host of different advantages, notably by improving their access to formal and peer support, mentorship and opportunities to market and pitch their products better. In the process, they can access invaluable training opportunities and build wider "entrepreneurial social capital". This, in turn, can play an important role in helping them to develop their businesses further, access new markets and financing opportunities.
- To be relevant and achieve greater participation, digital networks must offer value to women at all stages of their entrepreneurial journey, be focused on a clear purpose, and get the members to be proactive rather than being passive

consumers. A key to creating a thriving online community is to cultivate relationships, strong bonds, and create an environment where members add value by contributing as much as they receive.

- Both formal and informal networks can play an important role for the entrepreneur. Formal networks achieve the intended outcome, whilst informal networks may spring out of these formal networks to form richer and more organic connections.
- These networks are not just useful for new businesses but also to seasoned female entrepreneurs – the young entrepreneurs may bring more innovation, ideas, and digital savviness, while the more mature entrepreneurs bring their years of experience and hands on support.

There are still many challenges, and more needs to be done to ensure that African female entrepreneurs are able to access the digital networks and connectivity tools that allow them to grow and develop their businesses. Some recommendations on the way forward include:

16.6.1 Civil Society and the Diaspora

- Civil society organisations (CSOs) should play a greater role in bridging between African female entrepreneurs in Africa and their colleagues in Europe by developing digital networks. These can allow African entrepreneurs to learn from peers in international markets, while diaspora entrepreneurs could learn more about investing in African markets. This could open avenues for diaspora entrepreneurs to understand local political and economic policy dynamics, to build joint ventures and other forms of collaboration
- CSOs and diaspora entrepreneurs should engage with relevant policymakers, decision-makers and other institutions – at national, regional, and continental levels – to influence policy.
- Help create a diaspora engagement map with factsheets and information about opportunities for dialogue and cooperation with African diasporas, and notably about initiatives that target women or include a strong focus on gender equality. This could be done by strengthening the European Union Global Diaspora Facility.
- Support African diaspora in setting up networks and exchange platforms with other diasporas to see what worked and how to leverage different countries competitive advantages to best provide their support.

16.6.2 EU and AU Policymakers

There is a need for a greater effort to democratise digital technologies, including more investment in infrastructure, affordable connectivity, easier access to devices and greater digital literacy. This connects with the joint EU–AU joint priority to invest in infrastructure and skills in Africa.

- Establish a clear training agenda to help boost digital literacy for girls and women, including syllabi in local languages.
- Go beyond digital strategy developments and create a clear plan for gender parity when implementing digital projects to ensure that women's needs are analysed and met in project design and throughout implementation and reporting.
- Conduct training and campaigns to highlight the contribution of women to their country's development, including addressing exclusion towards women and change the way women's role in society is viewed and having full autonomy towards their future.
- Ensure that in implementing the planned Europe-Africa Digital Innovation Bridge, contacts are not just created between a privileged few, and that female entrepreneurs – less privileged women outside of major cities – are at the centre of this initiative.
- For the EU, adapt relevant programmes to local needs, notably when it comes to working with entrepreneurs, including female entrepreneurs. This requires a paradigm shift in how Europe deals with development in Africa, allowing young Africans – and especially female entrepreneurs – to set the pace and direction of travel.
- Focus on ensuring female entrepreneurs' access to the finance they need to ensure continuity of their business especially in crisis times.

With the new ways of working remotely following the outbreak of the COVID-19 pandemic, now is the right time to ramp up and accelerate the digital agenda in Africa and include women in a more inclusive growth agenda. Achieving this goal presents an important opportunity for AU–EU digital cooperation.

References

AEDIB (n.d.) *Vision*. Available at: https://aedibnet.eu/aedib/vision/ (Accessed: 2 March 2022).

AfDB (n.d.) *Why AFAWA?* Available at: https://www.afdb.org/en/topics-and-sectors/initiatives-partnerships/afawa-affirmative-finance-action-for-women-in-africa/why-afawa (Accessed: 15 June 2021).

AfDB (2019) 'Women are an excellent investment: finance leaders call for increased support for women in business.' 26 November 2019. Available at: https://www.afdb.org/en/news-and-events/press-releases/women-are-excellent-investment-finance-leaders-call-increased-support-women-business-32914 (Accessed: 20 December 2021).

Ahl, H. (2006) 'Why research on women entrepreneurs needs new direction.' *Entrepreneurship Theory & Practice*, 30 (5), pp. 595–621.

AWEC (n.d.) *Empowering African Women Entrepreneurs to Build Resilient Businesses*. Available at: https://www.weareawec.org/ (Accessed: 15 June 2021).

Banga, K., Macleod, J. and Mendez-Parra, M. (2021) 'Digital trade provisions in the AfCFTA: What can we learn from South–South trade agreements?' *ODI*, Available at: https://set.odi.org/wp-content/uploads/2021/04/Digital-trade-provisions-in-the-AfCFTA.pdf (Accessed: 15 June 2021)

Chair, C., Brudivg, I. and Cameron, C. (2020) 'Women's rights online. Closing the digital gender gap for a more equal world', *World Web Foundation*. Available at: https://webfoundation.org/research/womens-rights-online-2020/ (Accessed 15 June 2021).

EC (2019) 'Report of the EU-AU digital economy task force', 13 June 2019. Available at: https://digital-strategy.ec.europa.eu/en/library/new-africa-europe-digital-economy-partnership-report-eu-au-digital-economy-task-force (Accessed 30 May 2021).

EC (2020) 'EU Gender Action Plan III. An ambitious agenda for gender equality and women's empowerment in EU external action', 25 November 2020. Available at: https://international-partnerships.ec.europa.eu/system/files/2021-01/join-2020-17-final_en.pdf (Accessed 30 May 2021).

Greve, A., & Salaff, J. W. (2003) 'Social networks and entrepreneurship', *Entrepreneurship Theory & Practice*, 28 (1), pp. 1–22.

IFC (2021a) *Women and E-commerce in Africa*. Available at: https://www.ifc.org/wps/wcm/connect/topics_ext_content/ifc_external_corporate_site/gender+at+ifc/resources/women-and-ecommerce-africa (Accessed: 20 December 2021).

IFC (2021b) *COVID-19 and women-led MSMEs in Sub-Saharan Africa: Examining the Impact, Responses, and Solutions*. March 2021. Available at: https://www.ifc.org/wps/wcm/connect/industry_ext_content/ifc_external_corporate_site/financial+institutions/resources/covid19-and-women-led-firms-in-africa (Accessed: 20 December 2021)

Ighobor, K. (2020) 'Digital trade is the next big thing in Africa: Wamkele Mene, Secretary General, African Continental Free Trade Area Secretariat (AfCFTA),' *UN*. Available at: https://www.un.org/africarenewal/magazine/july-2020/digital-trade-next-big-thing-africa (Accessed 15 June 2021).

ITC (n.d.) *About SheTrades.com*, Available at: https://www.shetrades.com/en/about# (Accessed: 15 June 2021).

Light, I., & Dana, L. P. (2013) 'Boundaries of social capital in entrepreneurship', *Entrepreneurship Theory & Practice*, 37 (3), pp. 603–624.

Maurer, I., & Ebers, M. (2006) 'Dynamics of social capital and their performance implications: Lessons from biotechnology start-ups', *Administrative Science Quarterly*, 51 (2), pp. 262–292.

McAdam, M., Harrison, R.T. & Leitch, C.M. (2018) 'Stories from the field: women's networking as gender capital in entrepreneurial ecosystems', *Small Business Economics*, 53, pp 459–474. https://doi.org/10.1007/s11187-018-9995-6

Ozkazanc-Pan, B. & Clark Muntean, S. (2018) 'Networking towards (in)equality: Women entrepreneurs in technology', *Gender, Work and Organization*, 25 (4), pp. 379–400.

Sladkova, Z. and Bashir, S. (2022), 'Feminist digital development: the missing jigsaw piece in the European Union's strategic partnership with Africa', in: Daniels, C., Erforth, B. and Teevan, C. (eds.) *Africa–Europe Cooperation and Digital Transformation*. London: Routledge.

Teevan, C., Tadesse Shiferaw, L. and Di Ciommo, M. (2021) 'Taking the gender agenda forward in EU programming', *ECDPM*, 19 April 2021, Available at: https://ecdpm.org/publications/taking-gender-agenda-forward-eu-programming/ (Accessed: 30 May 2021).

Tony Elumelu Foundation (2020) *TRENDING: The Tony Elumelu Foundation and European Union Partner to Transform Economic Empowerment of African Women*. Available at: https://www.tonyelumelufoundation.org/news/eu-and-tef-partner-to-support-over-2500-african-women-entrepreneurs/ (Accessed: 15 June 2021).

Tony Elumelu Foundation (2021a) *Interview: TEF CEO, Ifeyinwa Ugochukwu Speaks on the 2021 TEF Entrepreneurship Programme with Africa24*. Available at: https://www.tonyelu

melufoundation.org/videos/interview-tef-ceo-ifeyinwa-ugochukwu-speaks-on-the
-2021-tef-entrepreneurship-programme-with-africa24/ (Accessed: 15 June 2021).

Tony Elumelu Foundation (2021b) *Ifeyinwa Ugochukwu Discusses Empowering Female African Entrepreneurs with GIZ*. Available at: https://www.tonyelumelufoundation.org
/news/ifeyinwa-ugochukwu-discusses-empowering-female-african-entrepreneurs
-with-giz/ (Accessed: 15 June 2021).

Villesèche, F. & Josserand, E. (2017) 'Formal women-only networks: literature review and propositions.' *Personnel Review*, 46 (5), pp. 1004–1018.

Annex 1: List of Interview Participants

1. Africa Technology Business Network (ATBN)
2. African Diaspora Youth Forum in Europe (ADYFE)
3. African Foundation for Development (AFFORD)
4. The Tony Elumelu Foundation (TEF) aka the biggest entrepreneur programme in Africa
5. Jacaranda Hub Zambia (woman-led hub)

INDEX

For Product Safety Concerns and Information please contact our EU
representative GPSR@taylorandfrancis.com
Taylor & Francis Verlag GmbH, Kaufingerstraße 24, 80331 München, Germany

www.ingramcontent.com/pod-product-compliance
Ingram Content Group UK Ltd.
Pitfield, Milton Keynes, MK11 3LW, UK
UKHW021824170925
462995UK00021B/908